GANDHI INDIA AND THE WORLD

An International Symposium

Gandhi India and the World

AN INTERNATIONAL SYMPOSIUM

Edited with an Introduction by

Sibnarayan Ray

PHILADELPHIA

TEMPLE UNIVERSITY PRESS

1970

First American edition 1970

© 1970 by S. N. Ray

Library of Congress Card No. 78-135343

SBN 87722-004-2

Set up in Australia by
The Hawthorn Press Pty Ltd
601 Little Bourke Street   Melbourne
Printed in the United States of America

CONTENTS

CONTRIBUTORS

S. P. AIYAR: Reader in Public Administration, University of Bombay. Publications: *Perspectives on the Welfare State* (ed.); *Gokhale and Modern India* (ed. with A. B. Shah); *The Politics of Mass Violence in India* (ed.); *Liberalism and the Modernization of India;* and *The Commonwealth in South Asia.*

AGEHANANDA BHARATI: Professor of Anthropology, Syracuse University, New York; born Vienna, studied Indology and Ethnology, migrated to India 1947 and obtained monastic ordination in the Sannyasi Order of Hindu monks; taught comparative religion and philosophy at Banaras Hindu University, the Royal Buddhist Academy at Bangkok and the Universities of Tokyo and Kyoto. Publications: *The Ochre Robe; A Functional Analysis of Indian Thought and Its Social Margins; The Tantric Tradition;* etc.

NIRMAL KUMAR BOSE: Commissioner for Scheduled Castes and Scheduled Tribes, Government of India; held several academic positions at the University of Calcutta 1938-59; was Director, Anthropological Survey of India; Gandhi's personal secretary 1946-47. Publications: *Cultural Anthropology; Studies in Gandhism; Modern Bengal; My Days with Gandhi; Selections from Gandhi* (ed.); *Gandhi in Indian Politics* (with P. H. Patwardhan); *Culture and Society in India;* etc.

AMIYA CHAKRAVARTY: Professor in the Department of Philosophy, State University College, New Paltz, New York; was Professor of Comparative Religions and Literature, Boston University 1953-66; taught at Visva-Bharati, Calcutta University, Yale, University of Kansas and the University of Michigan; distinguished modern poet in the Bengali language. Publications: *The Dynasts and Post-War Poetry; The Saint at Work; The Indian Testimony; A Tagore Reader* (ed.), besides several volumes of prose and poetry in Bengali.

DENNIS DALTON: Lecturer in Politics, School of Oriental and African Studies, University of London; pursued research in India on Gandhi and Roy. Publications: 'The Gandhian View of Caste, and Caste after Gandhi' in Philip Mason (ed.,) *India and Ceylon: Unity and Diversity;* 'M. N. Roy and Radical Humanism: The Ideology of an Indian Intel-

7

lectual Elite' in *Elites in India* (forthcoming); has recently completed a book entitled *Ideology in Modern India*.

AMLAN DATTA: Professor and Head of the Department of Economics, University of Calcutta. Publications: *A Century of Economic Development of Russia and Japan; Socialism, Democracy and Industrialization; Religion, Education and Development; Foreign Investment in Economically Underdeveloped Countries;* etc.

ADI H. DOCTOR: Lecturer in Politics, Marathwada University, Maharashtra, India. Publications: *A Probe into the Gandhian Concept of Ahimsa; Anarchist Thought in India;* and *Sarvodaya: A Political and Economic Study*.

MAURICE FRIEDMAN: Professor of Religion, Temple University, Philadelphia; member of the teaching faculty of Pendle Hill, the Quaker Center for Study, Contemplation and Dialogue at Wallingford, Pa.; member, Executive Committee of the Jewish Peace Fellowship. Publications: *Martin Buber: The Life of Dialogue; The Covenant of Peace: A Jewish Witness; Problematic Rebel: Melville, Dostoievsky, Kafka, Camus; The Worlds of Existentialism: A Critical Reader; To Deny our Nothingness: Contemporary Images of Man;* and *Martin Buber: Encounter on the Narrow Bridge* (forthcoming).

STEPHEN N. HAY: Associate Professor of History, University of California, Santa Barbara; taught at the University of Chicago 1956-64 and served as Research Associate at the East Asian Research Center, Harvard. Publications: *Dialogue between a Theist and an Idolator: An 1820 Tract Probably by Rammohun Roy* (ed.); *Southeast Asian History: A Bibliographic Guide* (ed. with Margaret H. Case); *Sources of Indian Tradition* (ed. with Wm. T. de Bary and others); and *Asian Ideas of East and West: Tagore and His Critics in Japan, China, and India*.

J. T. F. JORDENS: Senior Lecturer in Asian Civilization, Australian National University, Canberra; taught in the Department of Indian Studies, University of Melbourne, 1961-69; Myer Foundation Asian Fellow 1967-68 and visiting Lecturer at the University of Wisconsin 1968-69.

I. W. MABBETT: Lecturer in History, Monash University, Victoria, Australia; studied Sanskrit and Pali at Oxford and did research on ancient Indian political history. Publication: *A Short History of India*.

STANLEY MARON: Member of Kibbutz Maayan Zvi, Israel, where he 'divides his time between teaching and working in banana fields'; taught

8

at various universities in the United States, India and Pakistan; currently engaged in 'working at a theory of community capable of meeting the challenges of modernism, based on the successful achievements of the Kibbutz'. Publication: *Power and Purpose*.

J. C. MASSELOS: Lecturer in Indian History, University of Sydney; worked as a Research Fellow at the Heras Institute of Indian History and Culture, St Xavier's College, University of Bombay 1961-64; currently working on a study of the Muslims of Bombay, especially between 1906 and 1916.

ARNE NAESS: Professor of Philosophy, University of Oslo, Norway, since 1939; founding editor of *Inquiry*, a journal of philosophy and the social sciences. Publications: *Interpretation and Preciseness; Democracy, Ideology and Objectivity; Gandhi and the Nuclear Age; Communication and Argument; Four Modern Philosophers;* and *Skepticism*.

JAYAPRAKASH NARAYAN: Outstanding Gandhian and exponent of decentralised democracy; worked and studied in the United States 1922-29; founded the Congress Socialist Party 1934; took a leading part in the 'Quit India' campaign during the war and spent several years in prison; broke with the Congress and founded the Socialist Party 1948; joined the *Bhoodan* (land-gift) movement 1954 and withdrew from party politics to devote himself entirely to the Gandhian ideal of *sarvodaya*. Publications: *Why Socialism?; A Plea for the Reconstruction of Indian Polity; Towards a New Society; Three Basic Problems of Free India; Socialism, Sarvodaya and Democracy;* etc.

HUGH F. OWEN: Lecturer in History, and Director, Centre for Asian Studies, University of Western Australia; worked as a Research Scholar at the Australian National University 1961-65. Publication: 'Towards Nationwide Agitation and Organisation: The Home Rule League, 1915-18' in D. A. Low (ed.), *Soundings in Modern South Asian History*.

SIBNARAYAN RAY: Reader and Head of Indian Studies, University of Melbourne; taught at the Universities of Calcutta and Bombay; formerly Secretary, The Indian Renaissance Institute, Dehradun; member, Board of Directors, International Humanist and Ethical Union, Utrecht, Holland. Publications: *Radicalism; Explorations; In Man's Own Image* (with Ellen Roy); *M. N. Roy: Philosopher-Revolutionary* (ed.); *Vietnam: Seen from East and West* (ed.); *Bengali Intelligentsia and the West* (forthcoming); and six volumes of essays and one volume of poems in Bengali.

9

A. B. SHAH: Founder-President, Indian Secular Society, and Director of Programmes for India, International Association for Cultural Freedom; taught Mathematics and Statistics at the Universities of Bombay and Poona. Publications: *Scientific Method; Planning for Democracy and other Essays; Challenges to Secularism; Tradition and Modernity in India* (ed. with C. R. M. Rao); *India's Defence and Foreign Policies* (ed.); and *Higher Education in India* (ed.).

P. SPRATT: Author and journalist, member of the staff of *Swarajya*, Madras; joined Communist Party of Great Britain 1924, went to India 1926 to work in the communist movement, principal accused, Meerut Conspiracy Case 1929, sentenced 1932, released 1934, interned 1934-36; didn't resume membership of the Communist Party after release. Publications: *Gandhism, an Analysis; Blowing up India; Diamat as a Philosophy of Nature; A New Look on Marxism;* and *Hindu Culture and Personality.*

HUGH TINKER: Professor of Government and Politics, University of London; Director of Research, Institute of Race Relations, London. Publications: *The Foundations of Local Self-Government in India, Pakistan and Burma; India and Pakistan, A Political Analysis; Reorientations, Studies on Asia in Transition; South Asia, a Short History; Experiment with Freedom, India and Pakistan 1947; Political Forces in Asia* (ed., forthcoming), etc.

FOREWORD

Horace Alexander

A long-time friend of Gandhi's and interpreter of Gandhi to the western world, Horace Alexander is known also for his many humanitarian efforts in India and for his writings on Indian life and thought. Among Mr Alexander's books are Gandhi through Western Eyes *and* Consider India.

The Gandhi centenary year ended in October 1969; but it can hardly be doubted that, in the years to come, many more books or shorter writings about Gandhi will be published, for he remains a most unusual, and in some respects a highly controversial, figure. Apart from anything else, his claim to have found a way of action for nations and other sections of the human race that may enable them to fight for and to achieve freedom and justice without resort to the arbitrament of war gives him special significance in a world that is torn by violent conflict and that seems to be in some danger of total destruction. For American people especially, at a time when the issue of racial justice is inescapable, the fact that some leaders of the black community, especially Martin Luther King, have gone to Gandhi for their inspiration, may lead others to study his life and work.

Quite apart from that, in almost every aspect of life he had something to say that was unusual and original; and he attempted to put his convictions into practice far more radically than most men.

What sort of a human being was the Mahatma? I knew him for some twenty years, and watched him at work and play (if he did ever play—at least he certainly knew how to relax and laugh) over the years. First and foremost, he was a warm-hearted, friendly man, who loved to spend part of each day with children, and who seemed to them to be a light-hearted playmate, full of fun. He was always ready to find time to welcome any man or woman from any part of the world or from any walk of life, from kings to beggars, who wanted to meet him. Many of them found that he would show more interest in their domestic affairs than in their political notions. Although his public statements give the impression of an ascetic who encouraged young people to live austerely and to renounce marriage, he could chide a young bride who was still giving her time to public welfare for not getting on with the family. He could be the gentlest of men when dealing with humble,

11

simple people; but he could be sharp with those who seemed to suffer from an undue degree of self-importance.

In his later years Gandhi had a daily opportunity of making a public speech. Crowds came to his evening prayer meeting wherever he was; they expected to hear a speech from him and they were not disappointed, except on his one weekly day of total silence. These speeches were always delivered through a microphone in quiet, conversational manner, with no appeals to emotion and no oratorical devices. They were plain statements of his opinions, and they never descended to abuse of his critics, whether Indian or foreign. Indeed, I never heard him speak harshly of his political opponents, although he would say frankly what he thought of each public man, and whether he trusted him. He was always ready to meet and talk with opponents. I never saw him angry, though there were times, as during the Round Table Conference on the future government of India in London in 1931, when he said he was 'drinking the cup to the dregs'.

This book is what it claims to be: a symposium. Some of the writers knew Gandhi personally, and worked with him. Some never knew him. Some are his fellow Indians; others come from various other lands. Some are, so to speak, almost completely pro-Gandhi; others are anti-Gandhi in various degrees. (I believe he would have been happier among those who disagreed with him than among unthinking 'yes-men'.) Yet each has tackled a distinct aspect of Gandhi's life and thought, although there is a measure of overlap here and there. This is all to the good, as the same topic recurs with a different emphasis or slant.

Where did Gandhi get his main inspiration? The answer is not simple. Among modern authors the names of Tolstoy, John Ruskin, David Thoreau are recognized. He certainly found support for his growing convictions in the writings of these three men. But it would seem that he had gone some distance in the main directions of his inner life before he encountered any of these western authors. Gandhi himself speaks of the influence of some Indians, especially a Gujarati poet, Raychandbhai, whose fame has not reached the outside world—except through Gandhi.

Behind such secondary influences there must surely be some more fundamental sources in his own Hindu tradition. According to his own self-analysis his awakening came to him during his life as a young law student in London, partly at least from his contact with Christian missionaries both in London and later in South Africa, who tried to convert him to Christianity. He has recorded how, after conscientiously ploughing through most of the Bible, he came to the Gospel of Matthew, and to the Sermon on the Mount, which captured him completely. Even so, what stirred him was the discovery in the vivid form of that so-called sermon of truths that he had been striving after. The process had begun before that. It may not be easy to disentangle the many strands of religious inspiration and education that had been fermenting within him and which, indeed, continued to operate for many years. He himself would be the first to agree that he had absorbed much from the Christian scriptures and traditions; but also from Islam, from the teaching of the Buddha and indeed from the great scriptures of all the world. Yet, in the end, I think we must recognize that, if a single religious influence may be identified as paramount, we must call it Hindu. He was content to call himself a Hindu to the day of his death. In part this was because he held that a man should not, normally at any rate, try to change his religious affiliation. He should accept the fact of his birth into a given place and culture and should, if necessary, try to reform the tradition in which he has been nurtured, by bringing to it what he may have learnt from other sources. Gandhi himself, in his battle against untouchability and in other ways too, did his utmost to reform the Hinduism that he found prevalent in India during his lifetime.

When Gandhi began to work out his fundamental faith, it is clear that the example of his devout mother was one decisive influence. It was perhaps her example that led him to place so much value on regular times of prayer, on the taking of vows and on the discipline of fasting. It is true that his conception of prayer, of fasting, of religious exercises in general was his own, with a content of ethical commitment that seems alien to much religious exercise. So it may be said that he used the disciplines he had learnt from his mother for ends that may have been different from the things she lived for. Moreover, when he spoke of 'God', as he constantly did, the content of his idea of God was very different from the ideas that are current in most orthodox religious circles, whether Hindu, Christian or any other. His insistence that religion is meaningless unless it results in a lifetime of service for the needy does not seem like orthodox Hinduism. Yet when this and even more has been said, it remains true that the sources of Gandhi's first and main inspiration are Hindu. To be more precise, he insisted that the *Bhagavad Gita* was the scripture that gave him his nurture throughout his active life.

Many ordinary western readers may find it difficult to see the *Gita* as a textbook for a life of non-violence. Yet the fact must be recognized, as every Christian knows full well, that the texts of the world's great scriptures do mean very different things to different people; and we inevitably tend to attach meanings that are relevant to our own age, which may not have been the meanings intended by the original writers. Many of my fellow Christians would reject my interpretation of the

13

Gospels, and would perhaps even say that they are unchristian. On my side, I am tempted also to say that they seem to be leaving out of account whole aspects of the New Testament that do not suit them. Yet each of us may fairly claim, with complete honesty, that the New Testament as a whole has given us the main foundations for enabling us to face life's baffling problems. So varied is the mind of man. And so too Gandhi may have found in the *Gita* things that the scholar will say are not there; but they were there for him, just as great poetry opens up vistas of heavenly beauty which the poet himself may never have imagined.

One thing about Gandhi is very clear. For him a religious inspiration, or what he believed to be that, was a necessity of his being. All his political actions, all his moral decisions, were directly dependent on his fundamental conviction about the nature of the world and of man. These several aspects of his attempts to 'experiment' with the truths that he had striven to apprehend, are discussed in the chapters that follow.

Swarthmore, 1970

INTRODUCTION

Sibnarayan Ray

The first biography of Mohandas Karamchand Gandhi was published in London in October 1909 by Nasarwanji M. Cooper, editor of the *Indian Chronicle* (London), with an introduction by Lord Ampthill, Chairman of the South Africa British Indian Committee.[1] Gandhi, who was at that time on deputation in London, took an energetic interest in the publication of the book and even in its sales and distribution.[2] Its author, the Rev. Joseph J. Doke, was a Minister of the Johannesburg Baptist Church who met Gandhi for the first time in December 1907, became an ardent supporter of the struggle for justice for the Indians in South Africa and decided to 'write a short book—bright, graphic and reliable—' which would make the personality of the leader of the *satyāgraha* movement 'real to the people of England'.[3] He got the details of Gandhi's background and career mostly from Gandhi himself, but for the description of the personality and activities of his hero he relied on his own firsthand observations. Although he called Gandhi 'an Indian patriot in South Africa' the accent of his deeply-moving biographical essay was on Gandhi's saintliness and on the religious-ethical dimension of his politics.

While Doke's book was in the press Gandhi, in London, was trying to formulate clearly the larger implications of his campaign in South Africa. In the course of a speech at the Friends' Meeting House at Hampstead (13 October 1909) he indicated that his aim was to reconcile East and West, but that this would not be achieved by the Japanese method of assimilating Western civilization.[4] Next day in a letter to his friend and colleague, H. S. L. Polak, he amplified the point by categorically stating that 'East and West can only and really meet when the West has thrown overboard modern civilization, almost in its entirety'. The spirit of passive resistance, he affirmed, required rejection of 'almost every invention which has been claimed to be a triumph of civilization'—'railways, telegraphs, telephones', steamboats, 'machine-made clothing', cities which 'are the real plague spots', even medical science which 'is the concentrated essence of Black Magic', and hospitals which 'are the instruments that the Devil has been using for his own purpose'. True wisdom lay in so regulating society 'as to limit the material condition of the people'.[5] In another

15

letter, addressed presumably to Lord Ampthill, he stated that he dissented 'totally from the methods whether of the extremists or of the moderates' in India because 'either party relies ultimately on violence' which 'must mean acceptance of modern civilization . . . and consequent destruction of true morality'.[6]

The thesis linking non-violence with the rejection of modern civilization was explicated by Gandhi in his first major work, *Hind Swaraj*, written originally in Gujarati from 13 to 22 November 1909, during his return voyage to South Africa on board SS *Kildonan Castle*. It was published in two instalments in the *Indian Opinion* (11 and 18 December 1909); an English version made by the author under the title *Indian Home Rule* was issued by the International Printing Press, Phoenix, in March 1910.[7] On 4 April he sent a copy to Tolstoy with whom he had been in correspondence since the previous October and to whom he had already forwarded a copy of Doke's book.[8] Gandhi's thesis owed more to Tolstoy than to any other individual, and it is not surprising that Tolstoy in his acknowledgment pointed out that 'the question you treat in it—the passive resistance—is a question of the greatest importance not only for India but for the whole of humanity'.[9] In a subsequent and much longer letter, dated 7 September 1910, Tolstoy after analysing the 'absolute contradiction between the profession and the basis of the life of the Christian peoples' again mentioned the global significance of Gandhi's experiments in South Africa. 'Consequently, your work in Transvaal, which seems to be far away from the centre of our world, is yet the most fundamental and the most important to us, supplying the most weighty practical proof in which the world can now share and with which must participate not only the Christians but all the peoples of the world.'[10]

However, during the next ten years the world took scant notice of Gandhi or of his ideas and activities. He made his real political début with the nation-wide *hartāl* in India in April 1919, the year which also saw the first Indian editions of both *Hind Swaraj* and Doke's book. The non-co-operation movement of 1920-22 established him not only as the supreme leader of the Indian people but also as a person of world stature. Books now began to appear in India and abroad discussing the significance of his views and methods in the context of an era of wars, revolutions and mass movements. Among the early writers were Fenner Brockway, John Haynes Holmes, Kirby Page, Wilfred Wellock, Romain Rolland, Julietta Veillier, Rene Fullop-Miller, C. F. Andrews and Will Durant.[11] Miss Blanche Watson brought out in 1923 a compilation of American comments on non-violent non-co-operation.[12] In the thirties others joined in, among them, Richard Gregg,[13] Reinhold Niebuhr, Gilbert Murray,

16

Aldous Huxley, Bart de Light, and Martin Buber. In 1939 when on the occasion of Gandhi's seventieth birthday Sarvapalli Radhakrishnan brought out his volume of tributes the contributors, who were drawn from many parts of the world, were unanimous in recognizing the Mahatma as the greatest man of his age.[14] To Albert Einstein, he was 'unique in political history . . . a beacon to the generations to come'. Salvador de Madariaga saw in him a symbol of the emergence of politics 'from the cavern age'. 'Gandhi, at seventy', wrote Arnold Zweig, 'feels himself sustained by the best forces which the race of man has ever produced'.

In the 'forties, however, Gandhi's influence on Indian politics noticeably waned. The ambivalent attitude of the Congress to the war, the 'Quit India' movement launched in Gandhi's name but conducted mainly by people who had little faith in non-violence, the sharpening of communal conflict and the growth of extremist forces both of the Right and of the Left, the dramatic developments leading to Independence and Partition, gradually isolated the old man from the mainstream of public affairs. His last years were the loneliest and at the same time the most heroic in his long and extraordinary career.[15] When on 30 January 1948 it was brought to a violent close by the bullets of a Hindu fanatic, Vinayak Godse, the world in shock and grief joined momentarily in paying tribute to the great martyr. 'He was', said George Marshall, 'the spokesman for the conscience of all mankind'.[16] Nevertheless, in the following years India under Nehru's leadership moved step by step away from nearly everything that Gandhi stood for—first by adopting a political system based on western models, then by committing the country to industrialisation and modernization, and finally, after 1962, by deciding to step up rapidly its military and defence expenditure.[17] Only a few followers of Gandhi like Vinoba Bhave and Jayaprakash Narayan have continued to hold steadfastly to his ideals and methods, but the impact of their activities on the country has been altogether marginal.[18] It is true that in the United States the possibilities of *satyāgraha* were explored anew for a while by the great Negro leader, Martin Luther King,[19] but his tragic fate and subsequent developments as well as the obstreperous phenomenon of violence in every country today raise anguished doubts about the practical value of Gandhism in solving the problems of our times.

II

These doubts are unlikely to be silenced by the celebrations on an international scale of Gandhi's birth centenary in 1969 or the pious eulogies which go with the celebrations, but they should not obscure the fact that for two decades this physically frail individual did conduct a national movement involving millions which has hardly any parallel in history. The extraordinary nature of Gandhi's leadership with its consistent emphasis on non-violence in thought and action is clearly seen when contrasted with the major political upheavals of the inter-war years with their equally consistent record of violence, brutality and terror, to wit, Bolshevism in the Soviet Union, Fascism in Italy, Nazism in Germany, and developments in China and Japan, Portugal and Spain, and the countries of eastern Europe. In restrospect Gandhi's role in the decolonisation process which brought about India's independence may prove to be less decisive than is commonly assumed,[20] but no one is likely to dispute that for an understanding of the history of the twentieth century a careful scrutiny of Gandhi's personality and career and of the complex of ideas and methods known as Gandhism is of major importance. Such examination is all the more necessary since much of the proliferating literature on Gandhi so far has been unfortunately hagiographic in approach, written for the converted by the converted. It is also at least conceivable that the examination may help in providing some guide lines for dealing with the contemporary problems of social conflict, alienation and group dynamics.

There is general agreement that in the development of Gandhi's personality and his theory and practice of *satyāgraha* the years in South Africa were particularly crucial. He himself wrote at some length about this period at a later date in his *Autobiography* and *Satyāgraha in South Africa*, but the key primary documents are the two books published towards the end of 1909, his writings in *Indian Opinion* and other material compiled in the *Collected Works of Mahatma Gandhi*, vols. 1-12. It is evident from Doke's biographical sketch that not only did the evolution of *satyāgraha* go hand in hand with Gandhi's personal development but his charisma had a vital bearing on the effectiveness of his techniques of group action. This would suggest several lines of inquiry. To what extent was the basic structure of his personality already formed by the experiences of his childhood and early youth, in particular by his upbringing in a Gujarati *modh bānia vaishnava* family? How much did he owe to the influence of Jainism and the *bhakti* tradition? Was his study of the *Bhagavad-Gītā* as important as he subsequently claimed it to have been? How far was his personality altered by his experience of humiliation, *apartheid* and *bassekop* (bosshood) in the 'God-forsaken continent where I found my God'?[21] Gandhi later on claimed that the 'most creative experience' of his life was the bitter and lonely night at the Pietermaritzburg station in 1893.[22] This may well be so in that during that night he presumably took the momentous decision not to run away from ugly reality but to face it and try to change it by identifying himself with the suffering of its victims. But external evidence indicates that striking developments in his life style and ideas began about ten years later after he had read Ruskin's *Unto This Last*, which inspired him to organize the Phoenix Farm near Durban in 1904. Could it also be that apart from the problems raised by the first *satyāgraha* campaign of 1906 the very strain of his prolonged voluntary exile made him particularly receptive to the ideas of Tolstoy who was himself spiritually alienated from his society and civilization?[23]

Doke spoke of Gandhi's saintliness although this aspect became particularly pronounced after he took to the loin cloth during the *satyāgraha* movement of 1920-22.[24] However, in Gandhi's saintliness there is nothing in the nature of miracles or mystical experience, a feature which distinguishes him not only from traditional saints like Kabir or Chaitanya but also from modern saints like Ramakrishna or Sri Aurobindo. In fact, Gandhi's religion would seem to be much more occupied with personal and group morality than with any intuition of transcendence. It is reasonable to guess that there was some intimate connection between Gandhi's charisma and the vow of *bramacharya* (continence) which he took in 1906. But how much did this vow owe to the traditional ideal of *moksha* (liberation from rebirth), or the decision to dedicate himself completely to active social service, or an unconscious will to power? His ascetic ethic of voluntary suffering and self-abnegation was to him an unfailing source of inner strength and equipoise, but it did not always appear to preclude carefully planned advertisement of himself along with his cause, as we have already noted in the case of the publication of Doke's book. In the circumstances, it is not surprising that some of his critics and opponents, especially in India, insinuated that the Mahatma was really not all that saintly.

At least part of his success as a political leader Gandhi owed to qualities which are rarely associated with *mahātmās*—shrewdness, punctuality and organizational competence, scrupulous calculation of resources and their most profitable utilization, a flair for negotiation and drafting of documents, skill in subtly outmanoeuvring his rivals in public life, pragmatic flexibility which allowed him to retrace his steps when an enterprise proved to be overly hazardous, etc. It is hard not to suspect that elements of the *bānya* and lawyer survived in the man of truthfulness and love. In India his close friends and associates included some of the most wealthy and powerful business magnates, such as G. D. Birla, Ambalal Sarabhai and Jamnalal Bajaj.[25] However, it would be a gross oversimplification to conclude that he was at best a saint *manqué*. The record of his life bears ample witness to the genuineness of his faith and devotion, his profound and active compassion for the lowly and oppressed, his phenomenal gift for moving and inspiring them to great acts of courage, nobility and heroic sacrifice, his constant concern with the rightness of means and methods, and his unfailing readiness to accept suffering himself before calling upon others to do so in any effort. The complex nature and source of his charisma demand much more careful investigation than they appear to have received so far from his biographers.

The relationship between the personality of the leader and the movements organized by him raises another set of issues. The historic import of *satyāgraha* derives from its combination of non-violence with group-participation.[26] But how vitally does this rare combination depend on the physical presence of the charismatic leader? With Gandhi's departure from South Africa the movement there faded out into pathetic inconsequence. Gandhi himself, of course, put great stress on the training of *satyāgrahis*, but even with him as teacher very few of his disciples developed the inner resources to initiate, sustain and guide non-violent group action. Genuine charisma, as Max Weber has pointed out, can only be 'awakened' or 'tested', it cannot be 'learned' or 'taught'.[27] Routinization of charisma which is essential if it is not to remain a purely transitory phenomenon radically changes the character of charismatic authority. How fatally would this affect the dynamism of *satyāgraha?*

There is also the question of the size and character of the group which may be expected to act non-violently in a situation of crisis even when led by the most authentically charismatic personality. In South Africa the group which participated in *satyāgraha* was relatively small (according to Gandhi's report to Tolstoy, about 2500); it was also not very heterogeneous.[28] The early experiments in *satyāgraha* in India were also deliberately restricted to small homogeneous groups, but the non-co-operation campaigns which established Gandhi as a world figure involved vast masses of people. Although Gandhi strenuously worked at, and to an astonishing extent succeeded in, keeping these movements non-violent for a stretch of time, he was constantly confronted with problems which he found exceedingly hard, if not altogether impossible, to solve. The use of symbols, legends and rituals which had a strong appeal to certain classes and communities did not evoke equal response in others. What was much more serious, to sustain the enthusiasm of the masses promises of quick and spectacular results had to be held out (like '*swarāj* in one year') which, of course, did not materialize. There was always the danger that the participating masses, who were mostly not trained *satyāgrahis*, would resort to violence, or after a while relapse into sullen passivity when tangible gains were discovered to be disproportionately small in comparison with their needs and stirred-up expectations and the price in suffering and loss.[29] Gandhi's 'constructive programme' which, apart from its intrinsic importance, he expected would provide an answer to this problem, attracted few even among his close disciples. The movement of 1942 which exploited his authority without his being able to guide it. showed hardly any signs of the influence of his non-violent principles or techniques.

Can, then, a non-violent struggle maintain its unique character when undertaken on a mass scale, or does it, by its nature, require to be limited to small, highly disciplined and trained, and relatively homogeneous groups? Besides, how far did Gandhi's success, qualified as it was, depend on (a) the moral-political vulnerability of the British, and (b) the distinctive traditions of the Hindus? Would his methods have worked against a totalitarian tyranny of the Nazi type in Germany or the Stalinist type in east Europe? Do they have a chance, for example, in Czechoslovakia today? Would they evoke large-scale response in people with very different religious-cultural moorings, like the Muslims, or the Jews, or the Negroes in America?

Doke also indicated how Gandhi was at once a traditionalist and a revolutionary, how he imbued old beliefs and practices with new meanings and objectives, how, in particular, he adapted and transformed the well-known Hindu practice of *dharmā* into the novel praxiology of *satyāgraha*.[30] This is, of course, true although selective use of traditional elements in support of movements of social and political change is in no way peculiar to Gandhi. In India it had been tried, often with conflicting aims in view, by many predecessors and older contemporaries from Rammohun to Tilak.[31] Gandhi's remarkable success in the political use of tradition has generally tended to obscure the problems involved in his endeavour. Although his religious and social beliefs were in certain respects startlingly unorthodox and ecumenical, the traditions from which he drew primarily were those of the Hindu *bhakti* movements, especially of North and West India. A dispassionate inquiry has yet to be undertaken into the effect of his politicization of some of these traditions upon the alienation of the Muslims from the Congress, or of Bengal and parts of the South from the nationalist movement in the North. In a country historically as multi-cultural as India revival of traditions, especially by linking them with political mass movements, would appear to be fraught with the hazards of centrifugalism. It may secure emotional *rapproche-ment* between a particular community or the people of a particular region

21

and its leadership, but will it not also tend to activate dormant conflicts and rivalries between different communities and/or regional cultures? On the other hand, an unambiguous commitment on the part of the leaders to a rational and secular approach to the problems of the country would almost certainly take a much longer time to influence the tradition-oriented masses. But is it not also more likely to produce a more genuine sense of unity and common purpose, and in the long run a more stable basis of national reconstruction?

Gandhi's use of tradition reinforced the appeal of his charisma, but did it not also seriously weaken the rationalist movement that had been promoted in India during the 19th century by liberal reformers like Lokahitawadi, Vidyasagar, Akshaya Datta, Ranade, Agarkar, Sir Syed Ahmad Khan, Behram Malabari, and Viresalingam Pantulu? Again, while his concern for the 'untouchables' and his efforts to remove the prejudice of the caste Hindus were undoubtedly genuine, the criticism levelled against his approach by such leaders of the 'untouchables' as B. R. Ambedkar demands careful consideration.[32] It may also be necessary to consider whether his very personal, almost arbitrary, interpretation and utilization of the *Bhagavadgītā* did not help to strengthen the obscurantist style of thinking of the nationalist intelligentsia.

For an understanding and evaluation of Gandhism what appears to be particularly crucial is the *nexus* between non-violence and the social utopia which he described as *Rām Rāj*. Many followers of Gandhi while claiming to accept his ideal of *ahimsā* have been sceptical about his anarchist vision. It is, of course, possible to separate the two, but in Gandhi's thinking they were integral elements of a unified philosophy of life. The relation was explained fully for the first time in *Hind Swaraj*, and he never resiled from that position. In fact, *Hind Swaraj* occupies in Gandhism a place possibly even more important than does the *Communist Manifesto* in Marxism, or the *Discourse on Inequality* in Rousseau's political philosophy. To minimize its importance for the sake of making Gandhism respectable to non-Gandhians may be in tune with the contemporary spirit of revisionism; but it is certainly not fair to Gandhi.

The total rejection of modern civilization which is at the heart of the Gandhian utopia is the most obstinate element in his ideology. It may have some appeal to those young men and women in the west who from various motivations appear to have elected to 'drop out', but in the context of our times when every economically underdeveloped country is seeking to industrialize itself as quickly as possible it is unlikely to make much of an impact. Nevertheless, on this issue as on so many others, it would be, I believe, very much worth-while to consider carefully the

Gandhian position. Is it not at least possible that some of Gandhi's criticisms of modern civilization may on analysis prove to be as pertinent and fruitful as Marx's critique of nineteenth century capitalism? May not his stress on decentralization provide a valuable starting point for a reappraisal of some of the widely-held views on economic and political reconstruction which, in application, appear to have created more problems than they have been able to solve?

Finally, there is the claim that Gandhism provides an answer to international conflicts and war. On the face of it, the claim would seem to be rather tall, and in view of all the accumulating evidence of collective aggressiveness, it is hard to see what chance non-violent methods would have in dealing with the problem on a global scale. Gandhi, however, did try to formulate the primary principles of his methodology of non-violently resisting military aggression and of reducing armed conflicts between nations, although he had no occasion to experiment with these methods in the context of a war. Several writers in recent years have given their attention to the far-reaching implications of his methodology, and the pressure of our critical situation makes it virtually certain that the examination will continue.[33]

III

The project of an international symposium on Gandhi grew out of the recognition that not only was there ample scope for an exploration of some of the issues mentioned before but there was also a genuine need for it. Response from the experts whom I approached was prompt and enthusiastic, and so the project has now materialised in this volume.

The symposium opens with two papers which examine Gandhi's religious-moral development and its relation to Jainism and Hinduism. The following paper gives a critique of Gandhi's interpretation of the *Bhagavadgītā*, besides discussing the status of the *Gītā* in the Hindu tradition and its influence on modern Indian thought. The fourth paper makes a brief survey of the influence of Christianity and of some nineteenth century western thinkers on the shaping of Gandhi's mind.

They are followed by a group of five essays which discuss Gandhi in relation to some of his outstanding Indian contemporaries. What was the nature of the basic divergences between Tilak and his successor to the leadership of the nationalist movement? Gandhi and Gokhale deeply admired each other, but how close really were their political views? Was the prolonged controversy between Tagore and the Mahatma merely 'a case of misunderstanding and of a difference of emphasis'? What was it that drew Gandhi and Nehru into such close association even when their personalities and outlooks were basically so very different? Finally, there is the paradoxical case of M. N. Roy who throughout nearly his entire political career was the most consistently trenchant critic of Gandhi, but who during the last years of his life formulated a political philosophy which, at least on the face of it, shows striking similarities with some facets of Gandhism. Roy himself was never conscious of the similarities; in fact, to the end of his days he remained a materialist and a champion of modernization. This makes the argument regarding the interaction of ideologies all the more interesting. It is to be hoped that these essays may stimulate other scholars to undertake similar inquiries with reference to people like Aurobindo Ghosh, Annie Besant, Motilal Nehru, C. R. Das, Muhammad Iqbal, M. A. Jinnah, B. R. Ambedkar and Subhas Chandra Bose.

The next four papers respectively analyse the first non-co-operation movement of 1920-22, the reasons for Gandhi's failure to bring about Hindu-Muslim unity, the reaction of the Indian communists to the Mahatma and his leadership of the nationalist movement, and the record of the last years of Gandhi's life. The complex nature of Gandhi's personality and of his role in the history of modern India comes out sharply in these essays; they also underline the need for further research in this period by historians and social scientists.

The largest section, comprising seven papers, comes at the end of the volume and is devoted to expounding and assessing from various points of view some of the basic aspects of Gandhism. Two of the contributors in this section are internationally well-known Gandhians; they explain in their respective essays the principles of decentralization and the methodology of reducing conflicts both within a society and between nation states. An expert on the problems of economic growth discusses in his paper the positive significance of Gandhi's critique of industrialism and of his approach to economic re-construction. The remaining four papers examine the relevance of *satyāgraha* for our times, its pre-requisites, objectives, limitations and possibilities, its problems and achievements in the context of the race-conflict in the United States, and its bearing upon the endeavour for social justice and international co-operation. This section, I believe, contains some of the most valuable insights and criticisms on the subject of Gandhism.

The problems of editing a symposium of this nature are many, particularly since the contributors belong to four continents and most of them are separated from the editor by thousands of miles. It involved extensive correspondence particularly to ensure accuracy in quotations, biblio-graphical references and many small details, and to reduce the risk of one contributor unknowingly repeating some of the points made by another. (No editor may hope to eliminate this risk completely from a symposium of this type.) I am deeply grateful to the contributors not only for sending their valuable papers in time but also for responding promptly and generously to editorial enquiries, criticisms and suggestions. While each contributor is responsible for his own paper, I alone am to be blamed for all shortcomings in the plan, arrangement and editing of the volume.

Besides the contributors the book owes much to various persons and institutions:

The Australian National Advisory Committee of the UNESCO for a grant to cover contributors' fees and secretarial and research assistance expenses;

The Publication Fund Committee of the University of Melbourne for assistance towards cost of production of the Australian edition;

Prof. A. L. Basham, formerly Professor of the History of South Asia at the University of London, now Professor of Asian Civilization, Australian National University, Canberra, for his thoughtful Foreword;

Sir James Plimsoll for his unfailing support and encouragement in preparing this volume;

His Excellency Mr A. M. Thomas, the Indian High Commissioner at Canberra, for the gift of a set of reference books to the Department of Indian Studies;

The Librarian and staff of the Baillieu Library, University of Melbourne, for procuring many reference books on Gandhi from other libraries in Australia;

The Gandhi Centenary Committee of Victoria for its interest in the project;

Mr Paul Hofseth of Oslo for the first draft of his translation of Professor Arne Naess' paper from the original in Norwegian;

Miss Marian Maddern for her highly valuable assistance in checking bibliographical references and generally in editing the book;

Mr Newman Rosenthal, author of *Mahatma Gandhi: The Uncompromising Truth,* and Mr Richard Krygier for their friendly help and useful advice;

The Navajivan Trust, Ahmedabad, and Mr Shantilal H. Shah, M.P., its Managing Trustee, for permission to include extracts from the writings of Mahatma Gandhi;

Mr John Gartner of The Hawthorn Press Pty. Ltd., Melbourne, for his expert supervision of the Australian edition of this book;

Prof. A. B. Shah for assistance in arranging the Indian edition;

Miss Ingrid Oelschner, Mrs Christine Ali and Miss Susan Williams for typing and secretarial service;

and my colleagues and students at the University of Melbourne for many stimulating discussions and seminars on Gandhi and various aspects of Gandhism.

2 October 1969

Department of Indian Studies
University of Melbourne

NOTES

1 Joseph J. Doke, *M. K. Gandhi: An Indian Patriot in South Africa* (London, 1909); repr. G. A. Nateson & Co., Madras, 1919; repr. Publications Div., Govt. of India, Delhi, 1967.

2 See *The Collected Works of Mahatma Gandhi* (Publications Div., Govt. of India, Delhi, 1958), hereinafter *CWMG*, vol. 9 esp. pp. 343, 415, 464, 477, 492-93 and 503. Although Gandhi's correspondence during 1909 clearly shows that he personally arranged every detail of the publication including Lord Ampthill's introduction, the fact has been overlooked by his biographers.

3 Doke, op. cit. (Publications Div. reprint), p. 15.

4 *CWMG*, vol. 9, pp. 475-76.

5 *CWMG*, vol. 9, pp. 477-82. Letter to H. S. L. Polak, London, 14 Oct. 1909. For Gandhi's note on Polak in *Indian Opinion*, 3 July 1909, see in the same volume pp. 274-75.

6 *CWMG*, vol. 9, pp. 508-10. Letter to Lord Ampthill, London, 30 Oct. 1909. The photostat of the original in the Sabarmati Archives bears no date nor the addressee's name; the editors of *CWMG* deduced them from Lord Ampthill's reply to Gandhi of 1 November. D. G. Tendulkar, *Mahatma* (8 vols., Publications Div., Govt. of India, 1960-63), hereinafter *DGT*, vol. 1, p. 105, gave 9 October as the date of the letter, and claimed that it contained 'the first expression' of the ideas developed in *Hind Swaraj*. This is obviously incorrect, although Louis Fischer also gave the same date and made the same assertion.

7 *CWMG*, vol. 10, p. 6 gives the publication history of *Hind Swaraj;* also the full English text based on the 1939 revised new edition (pp. 8-68). The first Indian edition was brought out by Ganesh & Co., Madras, 1919.

8 See *CWMG*, vol. 9, pp. 444-46; 483, 528-29, 593, and vol. 10, pp. 1-5; 210 and 306.

9 *CWMG*, vol. 10, p. 505. Tolstoy's letter to Gandhi, Yasnaya Polyana, 8 May 1910.

10 *Ibid.*, p. 513.

11 See A. F. Brockway, *Non-Co-operation in Other Lands* (Madras, 1921); J. H. Holmes, *The Christ of Today* (Madras, 1922), and *Gandhi before Pilate* (New York, 1930); K. Page, *Is Mahatma Gandhi the Greatest Man of the Age?* (New York, 1922); W. Wellock, *Ahimsa and World Peace* (Madras, 1922); R. Rolland, *Mahatma Gandhi* (London, 1924); Julietta Veillier, *Mahatma Gandhi* (Madras,

1928; original in French, 1926); R. Fullop-Miller, *Lenin and Gandhi* (London and New Work, 1927); W. Durant, *The Case for India* (New York, 1930). For C. F. Andrews, see my essay on 'Tagore-Gandhi Controversy'.

[12] B. Watson (compiler), *Gandhi and Non-violent Resistance* (Madras, 1923).

[13] See R. B. Gregg, *Gandhi's Satyagraha* (Madras, 1930); *Gandhism vs. Socialism* (New York, 1932); *The Power of Non-Violence* (Philadelphia, 1934, Ahmedabad, 1938).

[14] S. Radhakrishnan (ed.), *Mahatma Gandhi Essays and Reflections on His Life and Work* (London, 1939).

[15] See in particular, N. K. Bose, *My Days with Gandhi* (Calcutta, 1953); Pyarelal, *Mahatma Gandhi: The Last Phase*, vols. 1 and II (Ahmedabad, 1956-58); also *DGT*, vol. 8.

[16] Louis Fischer, *The Life of Mahatma Gandhi* (Bombay, 1965; originally, London 1951), part 1, p. 8.

[17] Nehru clearly declared in the Lok Sabha (House of the People): 'I am not aware of our government having ever said that they adopted the doctrine of Ahimsa to our activities. They may respect it, they may honour that doctrine, but as a government it is patent that we do not consider ourselves capable of adopting the doctrine of Ahimsa'. *Lok Sabha Debates*, 15 February 1956. For an informative study of India's defence policy since independence, see L. J. Kavic, *India's Quest for Security: Defence Policies 1947-1965* (Berkeley and Los Angeles, 1967).

[18] See Del Vasto Lanza, *Gandhi to Vinoba* (London, 1956); Hallam Tennyson, *Saint on the March* (London, 1955); Suresh Ram, *Vinoba and His Mission* (ABSSS, Kashi, India, 1962); and J. P. Narayan, *Socialism, Sarvodaya and Democracy* (Bombay, 1964); and for a critical appraisal, A. H. Doctor, *Sarvodaya: A Political and Economic Study* (Bombay, 1967).

[19] See Martin Luther King, *Stride Toward Freedom* (New York, 1964); also Adam Roberts, 'Martin Luther King and Non-Violent Resistance', in *World Today*, June 1968, pp. 26-36; and C. Seshachari, *Gandhi and the American Scene* (Bombay, 1969).

[20] See R. C. Majumdar, *History of the Freedom Movement in India* (Calcutta, 1962-63), vol. 3. While Majumdar is very critical of Gandhi, his unconcealed admiration for Subhas Chandra Bose tends to influence adversely his discipline and detachment as a historian.

[21] Pyarelal, *Mahatma Gandhi*, vol. 1, *The Early Phase* (Ahmedabad, 1965), p. 292.

[22] *Ibid.*, p. 298; also *Harijan*, 10 December 1938.

[23] In a recent book, *The Revolutionary Personality* (Princeton, 1967), E. Victor Wolfenstein has attempted a comparative study of the personalities of Lenin, Trotsky and Gandhi by applying the methods of psycho-analysis to the world of politics. Some of his observations on Gandhi's adolescence and young manhood are quite shrewd, although his study is somewhat poor in details.

[24] Gandhi adopted the loincloth in September 1921. See 'Message on Loin-cloth, Madura', 22 September 1921, in *CWMG*, vol. 21, pp. 180-81. Also *DGT*, vol. 2, pp. 59-60. For its far-reaching significance see Gandhi, *Sermons from the Loin Cloth*, ed. T. K. Dutt (Lahore, 1942).

[25] See G. D. Birla's interesting book of reminiscences *In the Shadow of the Mahatma* (Calcutta, 1953). Also *To a Gandhian Capitalist* (Bombay, 1951).

[26] See Joan V. Bondurant, *Conquest of Violence* (Princeton, 1958); also Richard B. Gregg, *The Power of Non-Violence* (rev. Ind. edition, Ahmedabad, 1960).

[27] Max Weber, *The Theory of Social and Economic Organization*, ed. with an intro.

by Talcott Parsons (Free Press, New York, 1965), p. 367. Weber died in 1920, before Gandhi's rise to political eminence, but there is much in his analysis of charisma (see pp. 358-92) which may further a better understanding of Gandhi and his leadership problems.

[28] *CWMG*, vol. 9, Gandhi's letter to Tolstoy, 10 October 1909, p. 445.

[29] Some of these fears were expressed at the time by Besant, Tagore and others. See Annie Besant, *Coercion and Resistance in India* (London, 1919); also S. P. Aiyar (ed.), *The Politics of Mass Violence in India* (Bombay, 1967), esp. pp. 44-52. J. H. Broomfield in a recent study of Bengal politics in the twentieth century, *Elite Conflict in a Plural Society* (Berkeley and Los Angeles, 1968), has, I think somewhat glibly, dismissed Tagore's criticism of Gandhi as being the expression of a *bhadralok* (educated urban *élite*) view of politics (p. 150). While there is much that is valuable in his study, he shows little understanding of the peculiar problems of a non-violent mass movement.

[30] See Doke, op. cit., p. 99. Doke quoted Bishop Heber's account of the practice of *dharna*. For a penetrating study of Gandhi's harnessing of traditional elements to the requirements and purposes of a modern mass movement see Lloyd I. Rudolph and Susanne H. Rudolph, *The Modernity of Tradition* (Chicago and London, 1967).

[31] See Charles H. Heimsath, *Indian Nationalism and Hindu Social Reform* (Princeton, 1964); also, S. Natarajan, *A Century of Social Reform in India* (Bombay, 1962).

[32] See B. R. Ambedkar, *What Congress and Gandhi Have Done to the Untouchables* (Bombay, 1945). Also Dananjay Keer, *Dr Ambedkar, Life and Mission* (Bombay, 1962). Harold R. Isaacs, *India's Ex-Untouchables* (Bombay, 1965) gives a brief but thoughtful account of the Gandhi-Ambedkar controversy, and a survey of the position of the untouchables in India since independence.

[33] For a compilation of his writings on this theme, see M. K. Gandhi, *Non-Violence in Peace and War*, Parts 1 and 2 (Ahmedabad, 1945 and 1949). Richard Gregg's *The Power of Non-Violence*, esp. chapter 7, 'An effective substitute for war', is of seminal importance, but among recent studies the following may be consulted: *Civilian Defence*, a Peace News publication containing articles by G. Sharp, Arne Naess, J. D. Frank, etc. (London, 1964); Arne Naess, *Gandhi and the Nuclear Age* (The Bedminster Press, Totowa, New Jersey, 1965); G. Ramachandran and T. K. Mahadevan (ed.), *Gandhi: His Relevance for Our Times* (Rev. and enlarged 2nd edition, Delhi, 1967), esp. sections 3 and 5; and H. J. N. Horsburgh, *Non-Violence and Aggression, A Study of Gandhi's Moral Equivalent of War* (London, 1968).

28

JAIN INFLUENCES ON GANDHI'S EARLY THOUGHT

Stephen N. Hay

'It has been my experience,' wrote Gandhi in 1926, 'that I am always true [correct] from my point of view, and am often wrong from the point of view of my honest critics. I know that we are both right from our respective points of view.'[1] Gandhi's statement provides a fitting introduction to the subject of Jain influences on his early thought, for in this same article he explained his religious philosophy in terms of his own version of the Jain doctrine of the many-sidedness of reality, *anekāntavāda*. Simply put, this doctrine holds that reality is too complex to be apprehended from one standpoint only, and that one should therefore see each problem from all possible viewpoints. And so Gandhi continued:

> I very much like this doctrine of the manyness of reality. It is this doctrine that has taught me to judge a Mussulman from his standpoint and a Christian from his. . . . From the platform of the Jains I prove the non-creative aspect of God, and from that of Ramanuja the creative aspect. As a matter of fact we are all thinking of the Unthinkable, describing the Undescribable, seeking to know the Unknown, and that is why our speech falters, is inadequate and even often contradictory.[2]

Mohandas Karamchand Gandhi, seen from the viewpoint of his hereditary position in society, was a Kathiawadi Hindu of the *modh bānia* sub-caste. Seen from the viewpoint of sectarian traditions, he was a *vaishnava*, raised in the Vallabhacharya tradition dominant among Hindu *bānias* in nineteenth century Gujarat.[3] But non-Hindu influences also shaped his mental and spiritual development. For instance, Gandhi's mother, who exercised the greatest influence on his religious development, was herself raised in the *pranāmī* sect, noted for its latitudinarianism toward Islamic ideas and social contacts with Muslims.[4] In high school Gandhi's strict headmaster was a Zoroastrian, and his closest school friend was a Muslim. As a student in London and then as a young barrister in

South Africa, he was much impressed with Christian friends and their ideas. More influential than is generally known, however, were the ideas and the living examples of the members of the Jain faith whom Gandhi came to know as a boy and young man.

'Jainism was strong in Gujarat, and its influence was felt everywhere and on all occasions,' Gandhi recollected in his remarkable *Autobiography*. 'Jain monks would pay frequent visits to my father,' he related, 'and would even go out of their way to accept food from us—non-Jains. They would have talks with my father on subjects religious and mundane.'[5] Gandhi's own liking for the Jain *anekāntavāda* philosophy may have first been kindled by these discussions, which he was allowed to overhear. The possibility that his father came to admire the Jain practice of the confession of sins is suggested by the surprising calm and affection with which the usually stern father reacted when Gandhi confessed he had sold a chip of gold from his brother's armlet. After Gandhi's father died, his very religious mother relied at times on the advice of a Jain monk. When the eighteen-year-old Gandhi resolved to qualify himself to become a prime minister like his late father by studying law in London, she withheld her consent to the voyage until he had taken three solemn vows suggested by this monk—vows not to touch meat, wine, or women.[6]

Gandhi mentions without comment the fact that this Jain monk, Becharji Swami, belonged to the same sub-caste as the Gandhi family. Relations between Hindu *bānias* and Jain *bānias* had long been very close in his native Kathiawad peninsula of Gujarat. Jainism from the time of its organization under Mahavira in the sixth century B.C. had appealed most strongly to members of the *bānia* merchant community. By the twelfth century A.D. Jainism had become the dominant faith in the commercially-oriented region of Gujarat. From the sixteenth century onward, the *bhakti* movement of Vallabhacharya won many converts in Gujarat, but Jainism remained the predominant faith in the *bānia* community. Thus the very detailed *Bombay Gazetteer* of 1884 showed Jain *bānias* outnumbering *vaishnava* ones by a ratio of three to two, both in Gujarat as a whole (334,000 to 213,000) and in Kathiawad (96,150 to 63,400). As of the 1880's, the gazetteer tells us, these two 'sections of the Vānia community are knit together by social ties and in north Gujarat, Kachh, and Kāthiavāda they generally eat together and sometimes intermarry.'[7] This social intermixing both reflected and produced a continual cross-fertilization of religious ideas, which naturally affected Gandhi's parents and young Gandhi himself.

Except for his steadfast observance of his triple vow, Gandhi's stay in London from 1888 to 1891 removed him from Hindu and Jain influences and introduced him to Christian ones. He was also introduced by Theosophists to the *Gītā* and the life of the Buddha in Edwin Arnold's versions and began groping for a way to harmonize their teachings with those of Jesus. He was to return to this problem during his next stay abroad, in South Africa from 1893 to 1896.

On his return from England to India in 1891, however, he found more pressing problems confronting him. His fellow *modh bānias* in Bombay City had declared him an outcaste for breaking the traditional ban on travel to Europe and refused to re-admit him even after his performance of the *prāyaschitta* penance at Nasik. His outcaste status, shyness, and inexperience thwarted his hopes of earning a living in Bombay. Most painful of all was the news, conveyed to him the day he landed, that his dearly-loved mother had died shortly before. That same night, the friend who met him at the dock took him to his own house in Bombay and introduced him to a Jain relative, whose guidance was to solve for him his increasingly difficult problem of which religious ideas to accept and which to reject.[8]

Of this friend and guide, Raychand (or Rajchandra) Mehta, Gandhi later remarked: 'The more I consider his life and writings, the more I consider him to have been the best Indian of his times. Indeed, I put him much higher than Tolstoy in religious perception.'[9] At first Gandhi felt superior to Raychand because he had not gone to college or studied abroad.[10] Then, just as in Calcutta a few years earlier Narendranath Dutt (later Swami Vivekananda), a student of Western philosophy at Scottish Church College succumbed to the superior wisdom and spiritual magnetism of the self-educated mystic Sri Ramakrishna, so the anglicized young Gandhi felt himself irresistibly attracted to the saintly Raychand. The two had much in common. Raychand was only a year older than Gandhi. They conversed of course in their mother tongue, Gujarati. Both had come from the Kathiawad peninsula to work in Bombay: they were up-country boys in the big city. Raychand was, like Gandhi, the son of a *vaishnava* father, but his mother was a Jain. When Raychand was seven, the death and cremation of his closest friend, a Jain boy, had set him thinking deeply about the nature of life and soul.[11] When Gandhi met him he was a convinced Jain, a trusted partner in his Jain father-in-law's jeweller's shop, and an accomplished religious poet. Gandhi, then a 'briefless barrister', was equally impressed by Raychand's efficiency as a businessman and by his spiritual insight: 'I found his talk of absorbing interest. . . . His words went straight home to me. His intellect compelled as great a regard from me as his moral earnestness. . . . In my moments of spiritual crisis, therefore, he was my refuge.'[12]

31

Gandhi's outcaste status, by cutting him off from the orthoprax Hindu community, seems to have impelled him to seek out Jain friends during 1892 as he struggled unsuccessfully to establish a law practice in Bombay City. A second Jain friend in this period, less important than Raychand as a religious influence, but more important as a guide in Gandhi's chosen profession, was Virchand Gandhi (not related), described by an Indian admirer as 'a saint possessing the great qualities of goodness, kindness, purity and calmness'.[13] Both of Virchand's parents were Jain *bānias* from Kathiawad. One of the few Jains of his generation to receive a Western-style education, he had graduated in 1884 from Bombay's front-ranking Elphinstone College. Soon afterward he was made the secretary of the newly-founded Jain Association of India and took up the study of law. By the time M. K. Gandhi met him Virchand had successfully represented the Jain community in legal disputes in Kathiawad and Bengal. Gandhi invited Virchand to share his experimental vegetarian meals, and Virchand reciprocated by telling Gandhi unnerving stories about the difficulties of making a go of the law in Bombay, and by teaching him the principles of truth-finding embedded in the British Indian law of evidence.[14]

Within a year Gandhi failed to make ends meet in Bombay, had returned to Kathiawad, then left to take a position in South Africa. By 1893 Virchand found himself the official representative of the Jain faith at the first World's Parliament of Religions in Chicago. The Bengalis Vivekananda and Mozoomdar and the Ceylonese Buddhist Dharmapala sat beside him on the platform and made a greater impression on the public; but Virchand, like Vivekananda, won enough admirers in the United States to stay on there nearly two years, even organizing his followers into the short-lived Gandhi Philosophical Association. The lectures which Virchand delivered in America, England, and Bombay expounded the ancient Jain teachings in modern form.[15] We do not know whether or not he discussed these teachings with Gandhi in Bombay the previous year, but we do know that Virchand was a persuasive speaker[16] well-versed in such doctrines as the *anekāntavāda* which Gandhi liked so well. On the personal level at least, Gandhi appears to have been impressed, if not somewhat awed, by this energetic and successful Jain friend, who was six years his senior. Virchand's 'stories of stalwarts' of the Bombay bar such as Sir Pherozeshah Mehta and Badruddin Tyabji 'would unnerve me', Gandhi reminisced.[17]

In Raychand's case, however, we do have evidence for his influence on Gandhi's thinking in the three letters which he wrote Gandhi in South Africa and in Gandhi's comments on them. Soon after his arrival in Pretoria in 1893, Gandhi was befriended by a group of English evangelical

Christians and urged to become one of them. Grateful for their friendship, and sincerely searching for religious truth, Gandhi read a whole shelf of their books on Christianity and even went with them to a three-day revival meeting. His inability to resolve the conflicting claims of Christian and Hindu doctrines produced in him a 'mental churning', a 'spiritual crisis' which he could not resolve. Finally he decided to consult a number of religious authorities in India. In his characteristically thorough fashion, he drew up and mailed off a list of twenty-seven questions. The only answers that satisfied him were those of his friend in Bombay, the Jain poet-jeweller Raychand.[18]

Raychand's long Gujarati letter of 20 October 1894 is obviously a document of central importance to the understanding of the religious beliefs which crystallized in Gandhi's mind at this turning-point in his development. An incomplete and inaccurate English translation has recently been published in Ahmedabad. Of all Gandhi's biographers, only his secretary Pyarelal seems to have made use of the Gujarati text published in 1935, but Pyarelal's summary and translated excerpts do not bring out the characteristically Jain core of Raychand's system of ideas.[19]

Gandhi's first question was '*Atmā shu chhe?*' (What is the soul?). In reply Raychand expounded the central concept of Jainism, that of the *jīva*, the self or soul as a discrete, indestructible, non-material living substance whose true nature is complete consciousness, perfect knowledge, passionlessness, bliss, and freedom. Perhaps because Gandhi had used the term *ātmā* for soul, Raychand did likewise in his answer. Other Jain philosophers before him had done the same, perhaps in the spirit of *anekāntavāda* and in order to present the *jīva* concept to non-Jains by using the analogous Hindu term *ātmā*. In the course of his letter, however, Raychand gradually dropped *ātmā* and generally used the unambiguous term *jīva* instead.[20]

In answering Gandhi's first question, Raychand laid great stress on the Jain distinction between souls and material things, the two primal kinds of substances of which the universe has always been composed. (Jainism, like the *Sānkhya* philosophy, posits an eternal and uncreated universe which requires no Creator or Supreme Being to create, sustain, or redeem it.) The *jīva*, having become interfused with matter as a result of inattention to its true, non-material nature, naturally tries to free itself of this heavier substance, the physical body. As it succeeds, in the course of numerous incarnations, it rises to the top of the universe, then floats there in complete independence and awareness—of itself and of all other *jīvas* and material forms. This individualistic and pluralistic picture of the liberation of souls contrasts markedly with the monistic conception held by most Hindu schools, in which both the material world and the souls inhabiting it are the transient creations of the one Supreme Soul (*brahman*), each *ātmā* being finally reabsorbed into its Creator in much the same way a falling raindrop merges completely with the vast ocean from which it earlier arose.

To Gandhi's next question, '*Ishvar shu chhe?*' (What is God?), Raychand gave the Jain reply: 'God is an alternative name for the soul'.[21] Or, as J. L. Jaini, a modern Jain scholar (and translator into English of one of Raychand's books) has written: '. . . God is only the highest, the noblest, and the fullest manifestation of all the powers which lie latent in the soul of man'.[22] To Gandhi's third question, '*Moksha shu chhe?*' (What is liberation?), Raychand answered succinctly: 'As the soul is tied by anger and other passions [when] in the state of ignorance— that is, in the body or in other [material forms], so its emergence from all these [fetters]—its becoming free—this the wise call the path of liberation'.[23] The key idea here has been well-phrased by A. L. Basham: whenever the soul succumbs to one of the passions its 'natural brightness and wisdom is clouded over by layers of matter . . . [called] karma. . . . Therefore Jain ascetics subject themselves to rigorous courses of penance and fasting in order to set their souls free of the karma already acquired, while all their actions are most carefully regulated to prevent the further influx of karma in serious quantities'.[24]

Unfortunately, Gandhi's subsequent letters to Raychand have not been preserved, for if we had them we would be able to say more definitely to what extent the future Mahatma accepted these fundamental Jain doctrines. We may, nevertheless, try to reconstruct his reactions from less direct evidence. The closest source we have in point of time is Raychand's second letter, written nine months later, in which he distills his first reply into six propositions.[25] It seems hardly a coincidence that Raychand made these same six propositions the basis of a long poem composed during 1895-96, his *Atma-siddhi*, in which 'the true teacher' answers all his pupil's doubts, to the latter's boundless delight.[26] From Raychand's viewpoint at least, it appeared that his gifted pupil Gandhi had fully accepted his teachings. Toward the close of the poem the unnamed pupil exclaims: 'Everything is less than the soul'; 'You have shown me the separateness of the self [from the body], like the sword in its sheath'.[27]

Gandhi made two later comments on Raychand's letter. In his *Autobiography*, first published in 1927, he remarks that the letter 'somewhat pacified me'. His 1935 essay on Raychand contains a more positive reaction: '*Hu sānti pāmyo*' ('I obtained peace'), he declared.[28] His 'mental churning' was over. What particularly satisfied him, it appears, was the way in which Raychand's teachings resolved the conflict between the competing doctrines of the world's major religions, especially Hinduism, Christianity, and Islam. Without mentioning the *anekāntavāda* doctrine as such, Gandhi summarized Raychand's application of it, and of the Jain teaching of the soul, in his closing remarks on Raychand's crucial letter:

> Religion [*dharma*] is not different sets of opinions. Religion is not just reading or memorizing books known as scriptures or just believing everything said in them.
>
> Religion is the quality [*guna*] of one's soul [*ātmā*] and exists among men in a visible or invisible form. Through religion we are able to know our duties as human beings. Through religion we can recognize our true relationship with other living beings [*jīvo*]. It is obvious that this is not possible at all as long as we do not know our own selves. [*āpne potāne na olkhie*]. Therefore, religion is that discipline of spiritual selfperfection [*sādhanā*] through which we are able to know our own selves.
>
> This means that we should take this discipline from wherever it may be found. It may be found in India or Europe or Arabia.[29]

On this assumption, Gandhi found there was no need to change from the religion in which he had been raised:

> I became convinced that those [religious ideas] we can accept are found in Hinduism. Raychandbhai was responsible for bringing me to this position. The reader can thus imagine how much my respect for him must have increased.[30]

Gandhi's definition of religion as the quality of the soul and the process by which the soul comes to know its own self is not, as he may have believed, the highest ideal in Christianity and Islam. Instead, this definition is distinctly Hindu and Jain, and is integrally related to the doctrine of reincarnation which they hold in common. In Gandhi's final remarks on Raychand's letter, he omits—and the omission is significant—any mention of God, whether as *Ishvara*, or *Allāh*, and re-emphasizes the concept of the perfection of the soul or self, to the extent that formalized religion itself falls away as an irrelevant category. It is at this summit of his religious thought that we may question whether the term *vaishnava* still applies to Gandhi. 'I myself believe,' he wrote, immediately after quoting Raychand to this same effect, 'that all religions appear complete to those who follow them, and that all religions appear incomplete to those following other religions. From an independent standpoint all religions are both complete and incomplete. After a certain stage, all scriptures appear as bonds. . . . All men, remaining in their own religions, can obtain their own complete self-sufficiency [*svatantratā*], that is, their salvation [*moksha*]. For to obtain salvation means to become completely free of attachment and revulsion.'[31]

To summarize: Gandhi appears to have been deeply influenced by the Jain teachings of the soul and its path to liberation. These influences began operating in his youth through the Jain monks who advised his father and his mother. They affected him most strongly through his intimate friendship, conversation, and correspondence with the Jain reformer and poet, Raychand Mehta. And they resulted, it appears, in Gandhi's acceptance of the Jain ideal of *moksha* as the complete self-sufficiency of the soul *(svatantratā)* through its detachment from all passion and ignorance.

The question may be put: How deeply did these Jain influences affect Gandhi's beliefs and practices as a Hindu? The evidence indicates that he only became a Hindu by conviction when his Jain friend persuaded him that the religious ideas he could accept were found within Hinduism. That these same ideas are also (and more consistently) found in the Jain system did not strike him as particularly significant. Gandhi notes unconcernedly that Raychand 'used to tell me that he preferred the Jain philosophy. He believed that the Jain scriptures represent the highest point in the knowledge of the soul. This was his opinion, I must simply state this fact. Personally I consider myself completely unqualified to give an opinion of this subject'.[32] For Gandhi the problem of Jainism as distinct from, or an alternative to, Hinduism simply did not exist. 'I do not regard Jainism or Buddhism as separate from Hinduism', he observed in 1927.[33]

It is beyond the scope of this paper to analyze Gandhi's later career as a social, religious, and political reformer from the standpoint of the Jain ideas he accepted from his friend, Raychand Mehta. Such an analysis would interpret within a Jain framework Gandhi's *satyāgraha* concept, his insistence on truthfulness and non-violence as paramount virtues, his fasts, dietary restrictions and use of naturopathic cures, his taking the vow of *brahmacharya,* or chastity, within the married state, his limiting his clothing and other possessions, and so on. Such an analysis would not replace the conventional interpretation of these ideas and practices within the framework of Hindu traditions. Rather it would supply a second complementary interpretation within the Jain system of ideas and spiritual disciplines, which overlaps at many points the Hindu one.

Viewing Gandhi from both angles of vision simultaneously should give three-dimensional depth to many aspects of his personality and ideas. At the least, such an analysis would be in the spirit of the *anekāntavāda* theory of knowledge which Gandhi himself found so congenial to his own way of thinking.

NOTES

[1] Editorial in *Young India* (Ahmedabad), 26 January 1926, reprinted in M. K. Gandhi, *Truth is God* (Ahmedabad, 1955), p. 11.

[2] *Anekantavada* is mistranslated 'scepticism' in both Apte's and Monier-Williams' Sanskrit-English dictionaries. Its technical aspects are well summarized in George Bosworth Burch, 'Seven-Valued Logic in Jain Philosophy', *International Philosophical Quarterly* (New York), vol. 4, no. 1 (Feb. 1964), pp. 68-93.

[3] Manilal C. Parekh, *Sri Vallabhacharya: Life, Teachings and Movement* (Rajkot, 1943), pp. 371, 450, and *passim*.

[4] Pyarelal, *Mahatma Gandhi, vol. I: The Early Phase* (Ahmedabad, 1965), pp. 213-14. Pyarelal's source appears to have been Gandhi himself in a personal conversation. The best English-language source on the *pranamis* is P. Krishnamurty Iyer, *The Divine Message of Lord Prannath* (Panna, M.P.: Lord Prannath Temple, 1965). I am most grateful to Arvind Desai of Ahmedabad for providing me with this and the two other pamphlets cited in notes 10 and 11 below.

[5] M. K. Gandhi, *An Autobiography, Or The Story of My Experiments with Truth*, tr. by Mahadev Desai, 2nd ed. (Ahmedabad, 1940), pp. 33-34, 49.

[6] *Ibid.*, pp. 41-42, 55-56.

[7] *Gazetteer of the Bombay Presidency, vol. 9, part 1: Gujarat Population* (Government Central Press, Bombay, 1884), p. 70; *Gazetteer of the Bombay Presidency, vol. 8: Kathiawar*, p. 147.

[8] Gandhi, *Autobiography*, pp. 111-12, 120, 115-16. Note that two other aspiring lawyers in Bombay City during the 1890's, Virchand Gandhi (mentioned below) and Muhammad Ali Jinnah, both on excellent terms with their religious communities, managed to succeed where Gandhi (obviously not inferior to them in ability or education) failed.

[9] Quoted, without indication of the original source, in R. M. Gray and Manilal C. Parekh, *Mahatma Gandhi. An Essay in Appreciation* (Calcutta), 1931), p. 9. Raychand is mentioned in J. N. Farquhar, *Modern Religious Movements in India* (New York, 1916), pp. 327-28 as the leading reformer among the Jains of his day. His photograph appears in that volume facing p. 376.

[10] *Mahatma Gandhiji ane Srimad Rajchandra* (Mahatma Gandhiji and Shrimad Rajchandra); Amadabad; Oza Ayurvedic Pharmasi, preface 1993 Samvat [1935 A.C.], p. 11. I am grateful to Nandini Joshi and to P. J. Mistry for their assistance in reading and translating from this important pamphlet.

[11] *Mahatma Gandhi and Kavi Rajchandraji: Questions—Answered*, tr. by Brahmachari Sri Goverdhandas (Ahmedabad, n.d.), pp. 1-2. This is a translation (with an eight-page introduction) based on the Gujarati pamphlet cited in the preceding note.

[12] Gandhi, *Autobiography*, p. 113.

13 Motilal M. Munshi, quoted in *Speeches and Writings of Virchand R. Gandhi: The Karma Philosophy*, comp. Bhagu F. Karbhari (Bombay, 1924), p. 17. A Unitarian minister with whom Virchand stayed for a week while lecturing in England recalled that 'he shrank from even the smallest thing that inclined towards self-indulgence'—also one of Gandhi's traits. See Moncure Daniel Conway, *My Pilgrimage to the Wise Men of the East* (London, 1906), p. 192.

14 *Speeches and Writings of Virchand R. Gandhi: The Jain Philosophy*, 2nd ed., comp. Bhagu F. Karbhari (Bombay, 1911), pp. vi-ix; Gandhi, *Autobiography*, p. 119.

15 See Virchand Gandhi, *The Jain Philosophy, passim*, and his lecture, 'The Ethics and History of the Jains,' *The World's Congress of Religions: The Addresses and Papers Delivered before the Parliament*, ed. J. W. Hanson (Boston, 1894), pp. 445-50.

16 An American woman who had heard both Vivekananda and Virchand is said to have remarked: 'There is no comparison: Vivekanand[a] is an adept at vituperation, but Mr Gandhi is sincere and true. I admire Mr Gandhi more than any man I ever heard of.' Quoted in *Speeches and Writings of Virchand R. Gandhi: The Yoga Philosophy*, 2nd ed., comp. Bhagu F. Karbhari (Bombay, 1924), p. 280.

17 Gandhi, *Autobiography*, p. 119.

18 *Ibid.*, pp. 171, 113. Gandhi's questions, but not Raychand's answers, are given in English translation in *The Collected Works of Mahatma Gandhi, vol. 1 (1884-1896)* (Government of India Publications Division, Delhi, 1958), pp. 90-91.

19 Pyarelal, *Mahatma Gandhi, vol. I: The Early Phase*, pp. 327-31.

20 *Mahatma Gandhiji ane Srimad Rajchandra*, pp. 27-29, and *passim*.

21 *Ibid.*, p. 30.

22 Jagmanderlal Jaini, *Outlines of Jainism*, ed. F. W. Thomas (Cambridge University Press, 1916), p. xi. This publication of the Jain Literature Society is often referred to as a standard treatise on Jainism. This is the same J. L. Jaini who translated Raychand's *Atma-siddhi* (see note 26 below). He was helped in compiling his *Outlines* by an English Jain, Herbert Warren, whose own *Jainism in Western Garb, As a Solution to Life's Problems* (Madras, 1912) bears the subtitle, *Chiefly from Notes of Talks and Lectures by Virchand R. Gandhi, B. A.* Raychand, Virchand, Jaini and Warren thus form an interesting constellation of Jain writers active in the period 1895-1915. Their work was carried on by Brahmachari Shital Prasadji, who assisted both Warren and Jaini and later wrote *Jainism, A Key to True Happiness* (Jaipur, 1951).

23 *Mahatma Gandhiji ane Srimad Rajchandra*, p. 31.

24 A. L. Basham, 'The Basic Doctrines of Jainism,' in *Sources of Indian Tradition*, ed. Wm. Theodore de Bary, paperback edition (New York and London, 1964), vol. 1, p. 47.

25 *Mahatma Gandhiji ane Srimad Rajchandra*, p. 45.

26 *The Atma-siddhi (or the Self-Realisation of Srimad Rajchandra)* trans. with an introduction by Rai Bahadur J. L. Jaini (Ahmedabad, 1st ed. 1923, 2nd ed. 1960).

27 *Ibid.*, pp. 96, 97.

28 Gandhi, *Autobiography*, p. 171; *Mahatma Gandhiji ane Srimad Rajchandra*, p. 9.

29 *Ibid.*, pp. 19-20.

30 *Ibid.*, p. 9.

31 *Ibid.*, p. 22.   32 *Ibid.*, p. 21.

33 M. K. Gandhi, 'Why I am a Hindu', *Young India*, 10 October 1927, reprinted in Gandhi, *Truth is God*, p. 74.

GANDHI'S RELIGION AND THE HINDU HERITAGE

J. T. F. Jordens

Gandhi's religion was broad and deep. Growing out of the triple Indian heritage of Hinduism, Buddhism and Jainism, influenced by modern reform movements and by ideas and personalities from the west, it penetrated the whole of his thought and action, social, political and economic. Here we are concerned only with his personal religion and its relation to the Hindu heritage, classical and medieval. First we will consider the formative period in Gujarat, England and South Africa. Then we will study the Indian period from three points of view: Gandhi as a '*sanātana* Hindu', his 'Religion of Truth', and his place in the Hindu ascetic tradition.

I

Gandhi was born in Kathiawad, Gujarat, as member of the *modh bānias*, a merchant sub-caste. In Gujarat, 'pre-eminently a land of castes', the traders formed about 5.5 per cent of the total Hindu and Jain population, and the *modh bānias* constituted one-sixteenth of them. Of the traders, sixty-one per cent were Jains, the rest were *vaishnavas*. The *bānias* are said to be strict vegetarians, shunning liquor, 'prudent, sober, quiet, forbearing and inoffensive'. The majority of them, and all the *modh bānias*, were followers of the *vaishnavite* Vallabhacharya sect.[1]

As the young Gandhi used to sit in on his father's discussions with representatives of various faiths, he may have heard something about the theology of his sect, but it seems to have gone in one ear and out the other. He would certainly have been more aware of practical aspects of his family's sectarian cult. Great importance is given to the *gurus* (spiritual directors), all descendants from Vallabha, the founder. 'Each Guru has a temple of his own . . . (which) the devotees should visit at stated intervals.' The worship revolves around the idol of Krishna. The sect allows four different ways of *bhakti*, or devotional love, but of these 'there is only one which contemplates non-attachment to worldly objects'. According to Bhandarkar, 'moral rigidity culminating in indifference to worldly enjoyments and self-abnegation does not appear to be a characteristic of the school'. There was, nevertheless, one type of *bhakti*, called *maryāda*, which required restraint of the passions.[2] The Gazetteer mentions it too. 'Though the sect has no sadhus or anchorites, some of the followers take the . . . dedicatory vow', which ascetically restricts diet and contact.[3] The practices of Gandhi's mother, especially her vows, make one wonder if she followed *maryāda*. According to Pyarelal she was brought up in another sect, that of the *pranāmis*. The main object of their worship was the book of Faith compiled by one of the founders. Their *gurus* observed celibacy, and gave readings and conducted *kirtans* (hymn-singing sessions) in the temples. Gandhi remembered going with his mother to their idol-less temple.[4]

How, then, did the young Gandhi react to the religion of his family and his milieu? What impressed him in his father, who had 'that kind of religious culture which frequent visits to temples and listening to religious discourses make available to many Hindus', was that he was 'truthful, brave and generous . . . and incorruptible'. 'The outstanding impression my mother has left on my memory is that of saintliness.' From his account it is clear that it was not the content of their faith, but the moral quality of their observance that impressed him. Mother 'would take the hardest vows and keep them without flinching'. Several incidents strengthen this impression. He stopped his meat-eating not because of a change of opinion, but because 'deceiving and lying to one's father and mother is worse'. He was not worried by his rejection of their beliefs, but he was agonized by his moral lapses. He suffered deeply when confessing his petty thieving to his father; and the experience of his 'double shame', when he missed being present at his father's death because he was with his wife 'in the grip of lust', was veritably traumatic.[5]

His parents, devout *vallabhāchāris*, were regular temple-goers; the family even had its own temples; but ritual left him cold, and when he heard about immorality in some temples, he 'lost all interest'. Moreover, he went directly against some aspects of Hinduism with a reformer's zeal. His secret meat-eating was without religious scruples, undertaken and kept up for a year to become as strong as 'the mighty Englishman', and when he read the *Laws of Manu*, its doctrinal part turned him 'somewhat towards atheism'.[6] He recalled later how his disbelief in untouchability started at the age of twelve through his contact with Uka, the scavenger who served in the house. 'If I accidentally touched Uka, I was asked to perform the ablutions, and though I naturally obeyed, it was not without smilingly protesting that untouchability was not sanctioned by religion, that it was impossible that it should be so.'[7] When the caste-council brought pressure on him to forego his planned journey to England, and made him outcaste when he insisted on going, he did not care. His conflicts with the home traditions affected him greatly, as is evidenced by his planned and half-executed suicide pact.[8]

Yet, other aspects of Hindu religion did leave a lasting impression. His childish fears were many, among them his 'fear for ghosts and spirits'. Rambha, his nurse, an old servant of the family, 'suggested as a remedy for this fear, the repetition of *Ramanama*' (the name of the god Rāma).[9] In the context this was obviously not a devotional, but rather a superstitious act. Yet one wonders if the low-caste Rambha belonged to the *Kabirpanthi* sect, with their stress on 'keeping his [Rāma's] holy names forever on the lips and in the heart', and their wide use of devotional songs.[10] It is Rāma again, and not the Krishna of his own sect, who is the hero and god of the book that 'enraptured' him when hearing it at the age of thirteen: the *Rāmcharitmānas* of Tulsidas. The reader used to repeat *Rāmanāma* continuously and attributed his cure from leprosy to it. The public reading of the *Bhāgavata Purāna*, whose subject is Krishna, on the other hand, made no impact on him. Among the plays he would have seen, many must have had considerable religious and mythological content. However, he recalls only two: the play of Shravana, example of heroic parental devotion, and that of Harishchandra, who sacrificed all to truth. Again it was the moral quality of the plays that gripped and even 'haunted' his impressionable mind.[11]

In his youth, Gandhi remained unimpressed by, and even revolted against, the ritual aspects of Hinduism, the Krishna who was the god of his sect, the socio-ritual rules of caste, and he showed no interest for theological speculation or mysticism. He was, at least temporarily, attracted by *Rāmanāma*, more as an act of magic than as one of devotion, although he may also have been influenced by the devotional side of Rambha's religion. He loved the *Rāmcharitmānas*, but we are not told what exactly attracted him. One suspects it was its high morality because it was their moral teaching that imprinted just two plays indelibly on his mind. We presume that he also responded to the devotional hymn-singing of the *pranamis* and the *Kabirpanthis*, as it was the only ritual he ever adopted. Looking at the Hinduism of contemporary Gujarat, with its two main currents, the sentimental, sometimes sensual, non-ascetic, rather ritualizing, caste-conscious tradition of the upper-class *vaishnavas* adoring Krishna, and the other current derived from Ramananda, Kabir and Tulsidas, adorers of Rāma, popular, anti-caste, less ritualistic, and more ascetic, it is clear that the *modh bānia* boy was more attracted by the second. Yet, perhaps even more important than all this, underlying both his religious aversions and attractions, there was an extreme moral sensitivity, a premature fascination for right action, for ethics: 'One thing took deep root in me—the conviction that morality is the basis of things, and that truth is the substance of morality.' There also runs through his youth a current of independence of thought remarkable for that tender age. Cowardly as he was, and submissive to authority, he had a mind of his own. He recalls how he read a lot of pamphlets, and adds, 'it was a habit with me to forget what I did not like, and to carry out in practice whatever I liked'.[12]

In England, Gandhi went immediately in search of a vegetarian restaurant, not because of conviction, but because, on the insistence of his mother, he had taken the vow before leaving India. At the restaurant he bought a copy of Salt's *Plea for Vegetarianism*: 'From the date of reading this book, I may claim to have become a vegetarian by choice'. It was an intellectual conversion with strictly ethical motives, and also concerned with economy and hygiene. His experiments in the simplification of life were similarly motivated. Cutting out transport fares by walking, reducing eating expenses to a minimum, were all done conscientiously but without specifically religious motives. It is ironical that it was England that made him thus move back to some fundamental values of his tradition, which he had rejected as a youth: vegetarianism and austerity.[13]

In this his 'England of vegetarian Evangelicals and Theosophical reformers'[14] he started to read about religion. He discovered the *Bhagavadgītā*, which made an indelible mark on his mind. He also read Arnold's *Light of Asia* on the Buddha, Madame Blavatsky's *Key to Theosophy*, the Old Testament, which sent him to sleep, the New Testament, of which the Sermon on the Mount went straight to his heart, Carlyle's chapter 'The Prophet' in his *Heroes and Hero-worship*, and 'some book' about Bradlaugh's 'so-called atheism', which had no effect on him. This is the start of Gandhi's explicit study of religion. He declined joining the Theosophical Society saying, 'with my meagre knowledge of my own religion I do not want to belong to any religious body. Madame Blavatsky's work stimulated me with the desire to read books on Hinduism'. The Sermon on the Mount put in his mind Shamal Bhatt's 'For a bowl of water, give me a goodly meal', a line of the poem that had impressed him in his youth.[15] These two reactions indicate how in his early study of religion, his spontaneous reaction was to go back to rediscover his own tradition. Another significant pointer is that what impressed him in the *Gītā*, in the Prophet, and in the New Testament, was each time renunciation and austerity. Obviously Gandhi's selective reading mechanism was at work again, as in all three texts other aspects are even more emphasized than renunciation. The religious development of Gandhi in the English period was unspectacular, only inchoative, but two strong trends appear right from the start: a bias toward asceticism and an urge to rediscover his own tradition. The South African experience will strengthen these trends and they will be part and parcel of the mental make-up of the mature Gandhi when starting his Indian career.

For the young barrister who landed in Bombay in 1891, bitter sorrow and disappointment were in store. His mother had died during his absence, and when he started on his career, it was only to meet total frustration on account of his almost pathological shyness. His stubborn honesty made it impossible to fit quietly into the system with a decent income. So, when he was offered a job in South Africa by a firm, he gladly accepted. He had been in India for less than two years. Within a couple of weeks of his arrival in 'that God-forsaken continent where I found my God',[16] one is amazed to see the ineffectual, shy Gandhi call a meeting in Pretoria, and speak persuasively suggesting the formation of an organization for the Indian community. The Gandhi who would twenty years later return to India and take up the leadership of a vast mass movement, was born. He tells us the circumstances of this new birth. Since his arrival he had been humiliated again and again, and finally he was thrown out of his first class railway carriage. He 'sat and shivered' through the cold winter night in the railway station of Maritzburg. Thinking about his humiliation, a new dimension entered his thought: 'The hardship to which I was subjected was superficial—only a symptom of the deep disease of colour prejudice. I should try, if possible, to root out the disease and suffer hardship in the process'.[17] Hiren Mukerjee has very properly interpreted this event as Gandhi's 'illumination'. 'Ejection from the train and assault by the coach driver may seem trivial incidents, for such indignity and pain was being inflicted on many as a matter of course. But a shrinking and sensitive young man endured it with a fortitude that came to him as he realized he must do it for the sake not only of himself but of other people. It was the dawn in his mind of the conviction, that grew as he toiled on in South Africa, that suffering can be used creatively for the emancipation of people other than oneself. Years later, Gandhi would say: 'I must involve in my own experiment the whole of my kind'. At Maritzburg, his discovery was not complete, but it was there that he was born again, so to speak, into a life that was to be lived at a different level.'[18] Gandhi himself called it 'the most creative experience' of his life.[19] The new dimension of service to all transported Gandhi from an ego-centric, timid individualism to a dedicated awareness of his surroundings. The 'illumination' was certainly moral, but no specifically religious Hindu element is discernible in it. As we will see, its

43

light will progressively brighten the most heterogeneous aspects of his religion.

His religious development continues steadily along the lines established in England. His vegetarianism acquires a religious motivation: *ahimsā*, non-violence. Fasting, practised for some time 'purely for health reasons', is now done with the new motive of 'supporting the brahmacharya (continence) vow', of 'helping in the striving to conquer the flesh'. He tells how he decided to take the vow of complete continence during his ambulance work in the Zulu rebellion. 'During the difficult marches . . . the idea flashed upon me that if I wanted to devote myself to the service of the community in this manner, I must relinguish the desire for children and wealth and live the life of a *vanaprastha*—of one retired from household cares.'[20] It was thus the means to lead a life of perfect service, and in the hard struggle his two main aids then were his diet and the irrevocability of the vow. The simple life was another ideal initiated in England. In 1904 he read Ruskin's *Unto This Last* and decided to put his ideas into practice by founding the Phoenix settlement. The basic principles were simplicity of life and the dignity of labour. The first was in line with his asceticism-for-service, the second seems to have had no roots in his own tradition.[21]

These actions were supported by a lot of reading and thought. Some Christians put pressure on him to become a Christian, and he read a lot of Christian literature. His initial reaction is best symbolized in the following incident. When Mr Coates noticed the *vaishnava* rosary round Gandhi's neck, he called it a superstition and asked to let him break it. Gandhi answered, 'No, you will not. It is a sacred gift from my mother. . . . I do not know its mysterious significance. . . . But I cannot, without sufficient reason, give up a necklace she put round my neck out of love and in the conviction that it would be conducive to my welfare.' He still clings to Hinduism more out of loyalty than out of conviction. In fact, the Christian contacts brought about 'a mental churning' which he could not resolve by himself. So he wrote to religious authorities in India for advice. Among these was Raychandbhai, a Jain. This correspondence and his reading 'enhanced my regard for Hinduism and its beauties began to grow upon me'. The turning to Hinduism, which in England had been rather instinctive, now becomes a deliberate study, culminating in the discovery of the *Gītā* in depth. 'The Gita became an infallible guide of conduct. It became my dictionary of daily reference.'[22]

By the end of the African period, Gandhi's religion had grown considerably, but was still incomplete and not quite articulate. His various experiments in asceticism had deepened by being grafted upon the new growing trunk of his 'illumination'. His close contact with Christianity, after leading to crisis, brought him to the enthusiastic study of the Hindu heritage, crystallized to perfection for him in the *Gītā*.[23]

II

We turn now to the study of the Indian period. First we ask the question what Gandhi meant when he called himself a traditional Hindu. Taking his long statement 'I call myself a Sanatana Hindu'[24] as a basic framework, the following paragraphs will describe in his religion the place and meaning of authority, dogma, religious practice, *varnāshrama dharma*, and cow-protection.

As for authority, Gandhi accepted not only the Veda, but 'all that goes by the name of Hindu Scriptures' as divinely inspired, adding the Bible, Koran, and Zend Avesta. However, any interpretation, to be acceptable, must be in agreement with reason and moral sense, and moreover, true knowledge of the scriptures belongs to him only who has attained perfection. 'For me the question of diet was not one to be determined by the Shastras. It was one interwoven with my course of life which is guided by principles no longer dependent on outside authority.' The outside authority of scripture is overruled by an inside one, which develops in the renouncer, who becomes perfect in knowledge. Such a man would be the perfect *guru*. 'I believe in the Hindu theory of Guru,' he said, but 'only a perfect *gnani* (seer) deserves to be enthroned as Guru', and such a one he never found. So, he became his own *guru;* 'the voice within' became his supreme authority. The decision to fast when the striking mill-hands were flagging, came to him at a meeting, as a sudden 'light'.[25] The decision to fast for the untouchables was dictated during his sleep: 'I saw no form. But what I did hear was like a voice from afar and yet quite near. It was as unmistakable as some human voice definitely speaking to me, and irresistible. I was not dreaming. . . . The hearing of the voice was preceded by a terrific struggle within me. Suddenly the voice came upon me. I listened, made certain that it was the voice, and the struggle ceased. It was calm.'[26] Of his controversial methods of *brahmacharya*, he said: 'My brahmacharya knew nothing of the orthodox laws governing its observance. I formed my own rules as occasion necessitated.'[27] Ultimate religious authority for Gandhi lay within himself, not within scripture. In this he is as thoroughly Hindu as all great Hindu reformers. Shankara's and Ramanuja's respective interpretation of the *Gītā*, Madhva's onslaught on the *Brahmasūtras*, and the treatment of the Vedas by modern reformers are but a few examples of how in the Hindu tradition the last authority has always been the experience and vision of saints and reformers.

45

As for essential dogmas, Gandhi mentions three in his article: there is one God, man is subject to rebirth, but he can achieve liberation. He mentions them without any further explanation: his interest in dogma and theology was never great. He was fiercely Hindu in his deep-seated belief in *karma* and retribution. He ends the tale of his 'double shame' at his father's death saying, 'I may mention that the poor mite that was born to my wife scarcely breathed for more than three or four days. Nothing else could be expected'. And later he stated, 'I regard the birth of a bad son to me as the result of my evil past, whether of this life or previous'. Gandhi refers to God in many different, even contradictory ways: 'God is not a person . . . but a force; the undefinable mysterious Power that pervades everything; a living Power that is Love; the Maker, the Law-Giver; a jealous Lord', oscillating between the personal and the impersonal. 'The contents of the richest word—God— . . . will vary with the experience of each.'[28] They evidently varied for Gandhi himself according to his experiences. However much he may sometimes seem to be a monist, the name that came spontaneously to his lips was Rāma, the name chosen by Ramananda and his followers to indicate the one personal God, and the scripture he enjoyed most was Tulsidās' eminently theistic *Rāmcharitmānas*. *Avatārs* he accepted in many religions, but they did not enter his own religion. In fact, the very vagueness and manysidedness of Gandhi's concept of God was profoundly Hindu. Yet, despite this fluidity, there is one conception that grew ever stronger, overshadowed the others and became the best expression of his personal ideology: God is Truth. This will be further analysed in the next section.

Coming to religious practice, one notes that Gandhi formulates his conviction in a negative way: 'I do not disbelieve in idol-worship'.[29] Idol and temple worship, and other ritual, were theoretically accepted as valid, but they never were part of his own life. What practices did he perform? Reading of sacred texts, especially the *Gītā* was foremost, a practice with roots in the Vedas, where it was one of the 'five daily sacrifices'. Next we have *Rāmanāma*, recitation of the name of Rāma, increasingly important to the mature and ageing Gandhi. He had learned it from his nurse Rambha and in his letters he often recommends it, stressing its power 'for checking impure thoughts', 'to drive away all ghosts and spirits', as 'an invaluable remedy for mental illness',[30] etc. He called it 'a matchless treasure—the secret and power of Ramanama. Its magic transforms not only body and mind; it penetrates the environment.' 'When Ramanama holds sway, all illness vanishes.'[31] From the many references it is clear that the practice was an exercise in mustering mental power, psychic force, and not one of devotional effusion. As such it is closely connected with the ancient Hindu concept of *mantra*. Like the *mantra* also, it is much more than a word, it is divine power incarnate: 'more potent than Rama is nama',[32] in fact the name *is* the very essence of ultimate reality.[33] Gandhi believed that divine power was stored up within man, the *mantra* Rāma was its total expression, its magic formula, and repeating it in faith activated this power. All these ideas have a long history in Hinduism. Gandhi also advocated prayer, which is 'the earnest desire to be filled with the spirit of truth'. Again, prayer is not primarily conceived as a devotional, theistic, contemplative exercise of union, but rather as a mustering of inner force: 'At prayer time our speech is addressed to ourselves and is intended to shake off our torpor'.[34] Lastly, Gandhi also practised in his prayer meetings the singing of hymns. His religious practices, therefore, have little in common with the traditional and sectarian Hindu cult, but they all have their roots in his youth, and, on the whole, were more closely connected with the popular Rāma-cult than with the upper-class Krishna-cult.

The traditional Hindu social teaching is expressed in the term *varnāshrama dharma*, the system of duties of the classes of society and of the stages of life. The stages of life were never much more than a theory, but the duties of classes, linked with the doctrines of *karma* and rebirth had taken solid shape in the caste system. Untouchability was part of it, and this Gandhi never accepted. He rebelled against it as a youth, from South Africa onward he lived with untouchables and even performed their scavenging work, and in his old age he conducted a prolonged campaign against it. To him it was the curse of Hinduism. As for the rest of the caste system, he always rebelled against its abuses, but his ideas about the system itself underwent a marked change. Up to 1922 he accepted the system. His reasons were many, but the specifically religious ones were that it promoted control and discipline by its dietary and marriage restrictions, and that it was the natural order of society sanctioned by religion and determined by birth.[35] Then his views changed: caste was now a degeneration, 'caste must go'.[36] The *varna*-system had to be retained: the division into four classes, the *brāhmans*, specialists in learning, the *kshatriyas*, rulers and warriors, the *vaishyas*, farmers and traders, the *shudras*, labourers and servants. Although they were allowed to acquire the learning of another class, their occupations and duties still were determined by birth and heredity.[37] Now he rejects the restrictions on interdining and inter-marriage.[38] Finally he even came to accept that man can lose his *varna* by not observing its duties,[39] and thus he loosened *varna* from its connection with birth.

Thus Gandhi set out from a rather conservative acceptance of the

47

caste system, giving it a new religious motive, and accepting its old link with *karma* and rebirth. When he finally rejected the two essentials of the system, its connection with birth and its ritual taboos, he ended up with a *varna*-system very unlike the Vedic system and severing the very roots of caste. Equality, duty towards others, service, love, the essence of this basic vision, had gradually eroded *varnāshrama dharma*, and replaced it. Although this ideal was strongly influenced by the West, it was already part and parcel of much modern Hindu reform, and it featured largely, admittedly more as an ideal than as a reality, in the popular medieval *bhakti* current so strong in Gujarat.

In the basic text being analysed, Gandhi declares that 'the central fact of Hinduism is Cow-Protection'. To him the cow is not 'a sacred animal', but she has been 'selected for apotheosis', as symbol of the 'entire sub-human world', and through his protection of the cow man realises 'his identity with all that lives'. Cow-protection thus becomes the central symbolic act of non-violence, the essential ritual, one could say, of the Gandhian religion, the core of which was non-violence. Thus we have a new Gandhian synthesis of two traditional elements: non-violence and the veneration of the cow.[40]

Notwithstanding Gandhi's broadmindedness towards other religions, and their influences on him, his attachment to Hinduism grew deeper with the years: it was 'an indissoluble bond' like the one that bound him to his wife.[41] This attachment was also part of his deep nationalism, part of the *svadeshi* spirit. 'Svadeshi is that spirit in us which restricts us to the use and service of our immediate surroundings to the exclusion of the more remote. Thus, as for religion . . . I must restrict myself to my ancestral religion. . . . If I find it defective, I should serve it by purifying it from its defects.'[42]

III

Although Gandhi was thus a '*sanatana* Hindu', yet time and again he speaks of his religion not as Hinduism, but as something deeper: the 'Religion of Truth'. 'Let me explain what I mean by religion. It is not the Hindu religion which I certainly prize above all other religions, but the religion which transcends Hinduism, which changes one's very nature, which binds one indissolubly to the truth within and which ever purifies.' Is Gandhi's religion, even at this level, essentially Hindu? The bare statement of this religion is stark in its simplicity, containing three essential propositions: (a) God is Truth; (b) the only way to the full realization of truth is non-violence; and (c) non-violence is impossible without self-purification.[43] These propositions will now be analysed one by one.

'God is Truth' has in Gandhi's writings two different connotations. Sometimes it is 'a mighty effulgence', which man aims to see 'face to face', and of which he himself has only seen 'faint glimpses'. But 'if we had attained the full vision of Truth, we would no longer be mere seekers, but have become one with God, for Truth is God'. Thus Gandhi occasionally speaks about truth like an *advaitin* might speak about *brahman*, even going to the extent of saying that it 'alone is real and all else is unreal'.[44] Truth seems to stand here for a monistic absolute, the only final reality with which one can mystically identify. As such it is a traditional concept, and the choice of *satya*, derived from *sat*, 'being', is also significantly Hindu, going back to the *Upanishads*.[45] However, it is only rarely that truth appears in that vein. Mostly truth is linked with moral action, and that was why he changed the formula 'God is Truth' to 'Truth is God'. 'The essence of religion is morality', he said, and called his autobiography *The Story of My Experiments with Truth*. 'Truth is what you believe to be true at this moment, and that is your God,'[46] is probably the strongest expression of his conviction. This is the deepest ground of Gandhi's personal religion. Theological and philosophical speculation, revelation, devotion and ritual are all relative; the core of religion lies in facing truth in all action. Truth is right action, and here Gandhi's term inherits the riches of those ancient Hindu terms *dharma* and *rita*. But with a difference: for him there is no set of rules laid down in the *shāstras* and easy to follow. Truth has to be sought assiduously, honestly, agonizingly, in every act. Religion *is* that perpetual 'quest of truth', a 'path straight and narrow and sharp as the razor's edge'. And 'the still small voice within must always be the final arbiter when there is a conflict of duty'.[47] Here lies the ultimate justification of Gandhi's attitude to religious authority.

The second proposition of the 'Religion of Truth' is that the only way to its full realization is non-violence. 'To see the universal and all-pervading spirit of Truth face to face one must be able to love the meanest creature as oneself.'[48] Adherence to truth in action means that in every action one must identify oneself with all that lives. This involves many things, but from our point of view three seem most important. First, non-violence brings into the Gandhian ethic a specific philosophy of life: the sacredness and essential unity of *all* life, including its sub-human forms. Gandhi may claim to have found non-violence in other religions too,[49] but in the inclusion of sub-human forms he is fundamentally Hindu. Second, though his *ahimsā* is traditional, he transforms it in many ways. In the classical tradition it was interpreted differently according to *varna* and *āshrama*.[50] Vegetarianism was part of the *brāhman's* ethos only, and war was part of the warrior's duty, justified even in the *Gītā*. The *sannyāsi* had to follow a strict vegetarian diet, and was directed to be a model of the non-violent way of life. The medieval popular devotional movements then brought a stress on non-violence and spread these ideals into the lower classes. Gandhi made the *sannyāsi* model a universal rule, and yet, on the other hand, he allowed for exceptions abhorrent to the orthodox: e.g., mercy-killing, not only of sub-human, but even of human individuals,[51] and active participation in the war-effort. More significant still was the manner in which he broadened the concept by conceiving it in a positive way: 'It is non-violence only when we love those that hate us'. No doubt there is Christian influence here, yet we should remember that as an ideal it was part of popular *bhakti,* as Gandhi himself indicates when he recalls a Gujarati verse heard in his youth, 'But the truly noble know all men as one, And return with gladness good for evil done'.[52] Another way in which Gandhi broadened *ahimsā* was 'by positively inviting injury in a non-violent spirit, as a form of resisting evil'.[53] Thus it became a political weapon: 'The doctrine came to mean the vindication of truth, not by inflicting suffering on the opponent, but on one's self'. Of this aspect of *ahimsā*, the roots seem not to have been in his own tradition. Gandhi said that, 'Jesus Christ, Daniel and Socrates represented the purest forms' of it, adding that 'in India the doctrine was understood and commonly practised long before it came into vogue in Europe'.[54] He does not give any examples, and would have been hard put to find them.[55] The third aspect to stress in Gandhi's *ahimsā* is that it is not just a vision leading to meekness, but in fact the very essence of that 'new courage', that Gandhi found himself and wanted to instil in the whole of India,[56] a courage which is a force, 'the greatest force at the disposal of all mankind,' and one that has to lead to action: 'No man could be actively non-violent and not rise against social injustice no matter where it occurred'. 'Non-violence in its dynamic condition means conscious suffering. It does not mean meek submission to the will of the evil-doer, but it means pitting one's whole soul against the will of the tyrant.'[57] Like the aspect of self-inflicted suffering, this aspect of dynamic action too seems not to have been part of the traditional *ahimsā*.

The third and last proposition of Gandhi's 'Religion of Truth' is that non-violence is impossible without self-purification. This means to become 'absolutely passion-free in thought, speech and action; to rise above the opposing currents of love and hatred, attachment and repulsion'.[58] Under this heading he ranges his experiments in the control of palate, tongue, sex, and possessiveness. This self-discipline in all its aspects is part of the Hindu ascetic tradition, and will be discussed in the next section.

Gandhi's 'Religion of Truth' is thus essentially an ethic, only occasionally visionary when it looks at truth as the absolute ocean of light, but mostly intensely practical and immediate. Within, it listens to the voice of conscience; without, it looks upon all as part of the great community of life. It drives man to ascetic self-discipline, and propels him into action for the good of others. Truth, non-violence, and self-discipline complement each other, inspiring both service and asceticism, remaining throughout eminently down-to-earth. All these concepts have their roots in the Hindu tradition, but they were melted in the fire of Gandhi's life and recast and hammered into new shape on the anvil of his action.

IV

In this last section Gandhi's religion will be looked at from the point of view of the Hindu ascetic tradition. The Indian people came to see him as a *mahātma*, a saint, even as *avatār*, however much Gandhi himself resisted and even ridiculed it. As a young follower said: 'Gandhi is now marching as Buddha marched through India. . . . When you walk with him a light seems to emanate from him and fills you with its deep radiance. It is a new phenomenon, the present incarnation of Gandhi'.[59] Most aspects of his asceticism have emerged in the previous pages; the questions asked here are how this asceticism was in continuity with the Hindu tradition, and how Gandhi innovated.

In the classical tradition full renunciation was reserved for the fourth stage of life. Gandhi knew this: 'I am familiar with the superstition that self-realization is possible only in the fourth stage of life, i.e., *sannyāsa* (renunciation). But it is a matter of common knowledge that those who defer preparation for this invaluable experience until the last stage of life attain not self-realization but old àge amounting to a second and pitiable childhood'.[60] This classical view, however, was not accepted by Buddhism, Jainism and the sectarian movements, which called for initiation into *sannyāsa* at any stage. The initiation did involve a break with household and society, whereas Gandhi followed *sannyāsa* as a householder in society. Yet even here Gandhi knew some prototypes. Familiar as he was with Jainism, he must have known that the Jain householder could, by taking up successively stricter vows, gradually approximate the ideal of the monk. His own and his mother's considerable practice of vows strengthen this assumption. Another example he may have found in the sect of his

51

family, which did not have a special branch of ascetics, but provided an ascetic vow open to all followers.

The vow of *brahmacharya* was taken up at first in order to be free for service, but as his thought developed it became 'indispensable for self-realization'.[61] However, this self-realization of the mature Gandhi is not achieved in isolation, but in total service. The idea of service was not lost, but integrated into the deeper framework of truth and non-violence. Speaking as a *sanātana* Hindu he looks at it from yet another angle: self-realization as self-purification. 'The aim of human life is deliverance. As a Hindu, I believe that Moksha, or deliverance, is freedom from birth by breaking the bonds of the flesh, by becoming one with God. Now marriage is a hindrance in the attainment of this supreme object, inasmuch as it only tightens the bonds of flesh.' The concept of *brahmacharya* widened out to mean 'the way of life which leads us to *Brahma*—God',[62] and it included full control of thought, words and action not only in matters of sex but also in matters of diet and even of speech. His very negative view of sex[63] is certainly not part of the general Hindu tradition, which, while praising *sannyāsa*, does not condemn sex itself or the state of the householder, and it ignores also the *tāntric* tradition. Gandhi's perspective was that of the renouncer. In fact, there are two related aspects of his *brahmacharya* that are specifically Hindu, and also specifically part of much of the ascetic tradition: sex-control is seen as an essential part of the purification of the spirit by the suppression of matter, and secondly, as an important exercise for the accumulation of power.

Self-control is of paramount importance, 'for the whole superstructure of religion rests upon the foundation of self-control'. Gandhi seems to have harboured the idea that the body as such is an obstruction to the full play of the soul, that self-purification by 'breaking the bonds of the flesh' meant elimination of the body to let the spirit shine through: 'If we could completely obliterate in us the consciousness of our physical body, we would see Him face to face'.[64] Underlying Gandhi's asceticism there was the conviction that by asceticism the spirit is cleansed from matter, implying belief in the essential dualism of matter and spirit. In this Gandhi was perhaps more influenced by Jain ideas than by Hindu ones.

Gandhi also believed strongly that sex-control means accumulation of power. 'All power comes from the preservation and the sublimation of the vitality that is responsible for the creation of life.' 'A man, who is unchaste loses stamina, becomes emasculated and cowardly,' while in the chaste man 'secretions . . . are sublimated into a vital force pervading his whole being'.[65] The Hindu tradition abounds with stories of ascetics losing their power through women, as when the gods, threatened by the power accumulated by the chaste ascetic, engineer his seduction. Vivekananda's works, which Gandhi read in South Africa, abound with the power theme. The 'arrest of the semen' of *tāntric* rites[66] is also concerned with the loss of power. This profoundly Hindu power theme was part of other aspects of Gandhian religion. It pervades the concept of *Rāmanāma*. 'Anger controlled can be transmitted into a power which can move the world.' Of pure *ahimsā* he says that 'there is no limit to its power', and fasting '. . . like some potent medicines can only be taken on rare occasions and under expert guidance'.[67]

Many aspects of Gandhi's way thus link up with the Hindu ascetic tradition. In general he is more an heir to that tradition that sees the ascetic as the self-centered loner who strives to transform himself into a kind of superman, a wielder of power, a pure spiritual nomad (closely allied to Jain asceticism), than to the other tradition where ascetical striving is but a necessary prelude to the mystical, transcendental experiences, which are its prime goal. He differs from the Hindu tradition in two important ways. His asceticism, though individualistically concerned with purification of spirit and accumulation of power, is totally subsumed under his larger idea of service: 'The Himalayas of my penance are where there is misery to be alleviated, oppression to be relieved'.[68] And, whereas the tradition tends to foster feelings of achievement, superiority, and even arrogance, Gandhi did remain all his life a seeker, an experimenter. Like the ascetic, he found supreme authority within himself, and yet he never felt that he had arrived at the summit; one step was enough for him, and humble striving characterized his life to the last. Although he said, 'I am not an ascetic',[69] it was perhaps in his very asceticism that lay the roots both of his triumphs and of his failures. In a tradition where the distinction between the 'renouncer' and the involved 'man-in-the-world' was a basic one,[70] he strove to be both.

Perhaps we have looked at Gandhi's religion too much through his own eyes, ignoring questions of psychology and sincerity. Yet his own eyes are still the most penetrating where his own soul is concerned, in this man with extraordinary power of self-analysis and biting honesty. Gandhi is in his religion fundamentally a Hindu. Most of his ideas have deep roots in the Hindu tradition, and he constantly traced them back himself. But he was a reformer at heart. A Hindu reformer, going about reformation according to a basic Hindu pattern: re-interpreting scripture, re-shaping concepts, cutting out dead wood, always aware of continuity in the process of transformation. Both his Hinduism and his reformist zeal were inspired by and subordinated to something so specifically Gandhian that it transcended his Hinduism and the influence from other religions: the

53

vision that dawned upon him in South Africa of total service to all that lives in the complete renunciation of self. That vision was the fire through which all his actions and ideas had to pass. It reshaped the old concepts of *tapasyā, ahimsā, brahmacharya, satya, brahman, dharma,* into new ones, all thoroughly and obstinately Gandhian, and moulded them together into a new Gandhian framework. This made them often equally unacceptable to the traditional Hindu, the modern Hindu, and the religionless Indian, but their admiration for the man few could deny. Gandhian Hinduism or Hindu Gandhism as a religion cannot survive, but Gandhi will.

NOTES

[1] *Gazetteer of the Bombay Presidency,* vol. 9, part I, *Gujarat Population* (Government Central Press, Bombay, 1901), pp. 70-80, 89.

[2] R. G. Bhandarkar, *Vaisnavism, Saivism, and Minor Religious Systems* (Varanasi, 1965), pp. 76-82.

[3] *Gazetteer,* op. cit., p. 536.

[4] Pyarelal, *Mahatma Gandhi, vol. I: The Early Phase* (Ahmedabad, 1965), pp. 212-14.

[5] M. K. Gandhi, *An Autobiography, Or the Story of My Experiments with Truth,* tr. by Mahadev Desai (2nd ed., Ahmedabad, 1940), pp. 3-4, 17, 23. Hereinafter *Auto.*

[6] *Ibid.,* pp. 16, 23, 15.

[7] *Young India,* 27 April 1921. Reprinted in Homer H. Jack (ed.), *The Gandhi Reader: A Source Book of his Life and Writings* (New York, 1961), p. 162.

[8] *Auto.,* pp. 30, 19.

[9] *Ibid.,* p. 23.

[10] *Gazetteer,* op. cit., p. 540.

[11] *Auto.,* pp. 23, 24, 6.

[12] *Ibid.,* pp. 25, 9.

[13] *Ibid.,* pp. 35, 40, 42.

[14] S. H. Rudolph, 'The New Courage, An Essay in Gandhi's Psychology', *World Politics,* XVI (October 1963), p. 110.

[15] *Auto.,* pp. 48, 49.

[16] Pyarelal, op. cit., p. 292.

[17] *Auto.,* p. 81.

[18] Hiren Mukerjee, *Gandhiji: A Study* (Calcutta, 1958), p. 18.

[19] Pyarelal, op. cit., p. 298.

[20] *Auto.,* pp. 262, 238, 243, 245, 150.

[21] Cf. A. L. Basham, 'Traditional Influences on the Thought of Mahatma Gandhi' (typescript of a lecture delivered at the Australian National University, Canberra, to be published in a volume of collected papers on the Civil Disobedience Movement, under the editorship of Ravinder Kumar), pp. 25-26.

[22] *Auto.,* pp. 89, 99, 115, 195.

[23] Pyarelal (op. cit., pp. 710-11) says Tolstoy also helped Gandhi to resolve his

difficulties about Christianity: 'It was a great joy to him to discover that one could practise Christianity in its true sense without renouncing one's own faith, and that both Christianity and the Hindu religion had an identical goal and laid down rules of conduct for their respective votaries that were identical, though expressed in different idioms.'

[24] *Young India*, 6 October 1921. Reprinted in H. H. Jack, op. cit., pp. 167-72.

[25] *Auto.*, pp. 239, 333, 64, 318.

[26] H. S. L. Polak, H. N. Brailsford, and Lord Pethick-Lawrence, *Mahatma Gandhi* (London, 1949), p. 201.

[27] *All Men are Brothers, Life and Thoughts of Mahatma Gandhi as told in his Own Words* (Unesco, Paris 1958), p. 48. (Hereinafter *All Men.*) On this cf. Pyarelal, *Mahatma Gandhi, The Last Phase*, vol. I, book 2 (second ed., Ahmedabad, 1966), ch. XI.

[28] *Auto.*, p. 23; *All Men*, p. 49, ch. 2 *passim*, p. 77.

[29] H. H. Jack, op. cit., p. 168.

[30] *The Collected Works of Mahatma Gandhi* (Government of India Publications Division, Delhi, 1968), vol. 29, pp. 268, 392, 434.

[31] Pyarelal, *M. G., The Last Phase*, vol. 2 (Ahmedabad, 1958), pp. 242, 455.

[33] Cf. A. L. Basham, loc. cit., p. 9.

[34] Pyarelal, *ibid.*, p. 66.

[35] Cf. Polak and others, op. cit., p. 203; and B. R. Ambedkar, 'What Congress and Gandhi Have Done to the Untouchables', in M. D. Lewis (ed.), *Gandhi, Maker of Modern India?* (Boston, 1965), p. 48.

[36] *Harijan*, 16 Nov. 1935.

[37] N. K. Bose, *Studies in Gandhism* (Calcutta, 1947), p. 205; *Young India*, 21 January 1926; B. R. Ambedkar, loc. cit., p. 49.

[38] D. G. Tendulkar, *Mahatma, Life of Mohandas Karamchand Gandhi* (Government of India Publications Division, Delhi, in eight vols., new ed.), vol. 4, p. 42.

[39] *Harijan*, 28 September 1934.

[40] H. H. Jack, op. cit., p. 170.

[41] *Ibid.*, p. 171.

[42] In an address to a missionary conference in Madras, quoted in J. V. Bondurant, *Conquest of Violence, The Gandhian Philosophy of Conflict* (Princeton, 1958), p. 106.

[43] *All Men*, p. 56; *Auto.*, pp. 370-71.

[44] *Auto.*, p. 370; *All Men*, pp. 58, 66, 67.

[45] Gandhi himself quoted some twenty-five texts on the meaning of truth in the Hindu tradition, ranging from the *Upanishads* to Kabir in his 'Oriental Ideal of Truth', published in *Indian Opinion*, 1 April 1905, reprinted in *The Collected Works*, op. cit., vol. 4, pp. 392-94.

[46] *All Men*, p. 70; *Auto.*, p. xiv; *All Men*, p. 72.

[47] *Auto.*, p. xv; *All Men*, p. 68.

[48] *Auto.*, p. 370.

[49] *Young India*, 9 February 1922, p. 166.

[50] Cf. *Manusmriti, passim.* Treated in detail by A. L. Basham, loc. cit., pp. 11-14.

[51] *All Men*, p. 92.

[52] *All Men*, p. 86; *Auto.*, p. 25.

[53] A. L. Basham, loc. cit., p. 15.

[54] *All Men*, pp. 88, 99.

[55] A. L. Basham, in the article quoted, gives examples of the practice of *satyagraha* in the course of Indian history, but shows that these were meant to inflict suffering on others and thus to exercise power.

[56] S. H. Rudolph, loc. cit., p. 116.

[57] *All Men*, pp. 85, 89; *Young India*, 9 July 1925, quoted by J. V. Bondurant, op. cit., p. 26.

[58] *Auto.*, p. 371.

[59] R. C. Majumdar, 'Gandhi's Place in the History of Indian Nationalism', in M. D. Lewis, op. cit., p. 65.

[60] *Auto.*, p. 249.

[61] *Ibid.*, p. 233.

[62] H. H. Jack, op. cit., p. 177; *All Men*, p. 115.

[63] 'Sex . . . is only meant for the act of creation. Any other use of it is a sin against God and humanity.' *All Men*, p. 112.

[64] *All Men*, p. 115; H. H. Jack, op. cit., p. 177; *All Men*, p. 65.

[65] *All Men*, p. 112; H. H. Jack, op. cit., p. 115; Pyarelal, *Last Phase*, vol. I, book 2, p. 211.

[66] In his *Gandhi, A Study in Revolution* (London, 1968), Geoffrey Ashe suggests (pp. 261-62, 368) a similarity between Gandhi and Ramakrishna in their tantric-type attitude to women. There is a similarity in as far as both were concerned with harnessing sex-power; but, whereas Ramakrishna endeavoured to be a woman in the mystical sense of being the bride of Krishna, this was not the case with Gandhi. More than anything he wanted to be a 'mother', and he also admired in womanhood the strength of non-violence.

[67] *All Men*, p. 109; *Auto.*, p. 20; *Harijan*, 11 March 1939, p. 46, quoted by N. K. Bose, op. cit., p. 159.

[68] Pyarelal, *M. G., The Last Phase*, vol. 2, p. 211.

[69] *All Men*, p. 116.

[70] Cf. L. Dumont, 'World Renunciation in Indian Religions', *Contributions to Indian Sociology*, no. 4, 1960, pp. 33-62.

GANDHI'S INTERPRETATION OF THE GITA
An Anthropological Analysis

Agehananda Bharati

Modern philosophers, the post-Wittgensteinian lot to be exact, and cultural anthropologists who are interested in ideology rather than in the more orthodox fields of kinship and social organization, have reached a tacit agreement: to state their axioms somewhere at the beginning of their report. This is what I must do first, both as an an anthropologist and as a philosopher.

I am not an admirer of Gandhi, and I have made that quite clear in all my writings and in numerous lectures on several continents. I believe Gandhi was quite wrong in many matters relating to facts about religion, Hindu and other; and I believe that he dissimulated knowledge which he must have had, for political, or other situationally justifiable, purposes. Perhaps the crassest of such dissimulations was his statement about Buddhism, made to Buddhists, in which he insisted that the Buddha believed in God, and implied that he had preached theism. I have dealt with this statement elsewhere.[1] I do not believe in a politician's prerogative to slant factual information for reasons of policy, and I insist that such procedure, however exigent from the politician's or the social reformer's angle it may seem, is intellectually dishonest. I am also aware that 'intellectual honesty', in the somewhat pedantic sense in which I understand it, may be of no concern to people whose commitment is to social reform rather than academic elucidation.

Secondly, I reject Gandhi's puritanism as pathological and socially dysfunctional. His view that '. . . (sexual) union is a crime when the desire for progeny is absent'[2] and scores of similar statements by him cannot appeal to any modern man of reason and ethical culture. Arthur Koestler once told me he thought that the only thing Gandhi resented about God was that 'He had created both man and woman'. Yet in this sense, Gandhi epitomized the central sensitivity of modern India. Perhaps each country has an area that may not be touched upon except in a stereotyped derogatory fashion; communism in America, sex in India. But such core rejections are relevant to the social anthropologist, one of whose more recent academic commitments is the study of ideology and of values in a cross-cultural perspective. Somehow, a nation's charismatic in any era must represent the nation's ideological cynosure; and there is no doubt in my mind that asceticism is India's cynosure, even if camouflaged by the canned rhetoric of technology, modernity, secularism, and the remaining forensic of India's official culture today.

I shall adumbrate the influence the *Bhagavadgītā* has had, and is having, on modern Indian thought. Along with this, I shall state its actual status in the Hindu tradition, the place this text has been given in the pre- and post-Independence political and cultural history of the land. Gandhi's interpretation of the *Gītā* will be, of course, the centre of this essay, and I shall compare it briefly with contemporary interpretations other than Gandhian, or closely aligned to the Mahatma's reading.

To begin, we have to face a paradox: students of India, both western and native, who do not know Sanskrit, and who have no firsthand knowledge of the written traditions of India, view the *Gītā* invariably as a focal, supremely significant, ubiquitous referend in India's cultural parlance; and the frequent situational interpretations of the text, made and recommended by the charismatic leaders of the Indian Renaissance, reinforce this notion. Thus, when the average modern Hindu—not villager, that is, nor the religious or cultural specialist—is asked the question 'what do you regard as the most important book representing Hinduism', he will tend to name the *Bhagavadgītā;* the more engaged might add the *Veda,* the *Purānas,* the *Rāmāyana,* and the *Mahābhārata.* The *Bhagavadgītā* is contained in the latter epic, but it has obtained its separate identity. Now, except when referred to by the experts, the term *Veda* is a pretty vague index, and though many modern Hindus may know that there are 'four *Vedas*', they tend to include *all* religious texts in them. Again, this notion was either created or reinforced by the reformers of the turn of the century. Thus, Sri Ramakrishna Paramahamsa often told his disciples stories which were obviously derived from local Bengali rural lore, for example, the tale of the *Homa*-Bird that soars high into the air, lays its eggs while in flight, which hatch in mid-air, and the chicks ascend right back to join their mother before they touch the ground. Ramakrishna prefaced this and many other stories by the phrase *bede ache* (it is in the *Veda*); but they are not. This was perhaps one of the first instances where a charismatic's generic, perfunctory use of the term *Veda* initiated a diction which has become part of the non-specialist parlance of modern Hindus.

Now when Gandhi, or Nehru, or Vijaylakshmi Pandit[3] addressed various audiences, they would often use such catchcalls as 'as our *shāstras* say'. Most of the things said—democratic and nationalistic counsel for one—were not in any *shāstra* at all. I believe that many of those speakers were not conscious of these facts—or if they were, they might have regarded such inclusions as politic and expedient. Gandhi's own case is, however, quite a bit more complex: he did know what was in the *Veda* and what was not in it; for though he had probably never studied Vedic literature properly, he had been fascinated by modern Indian commentary on the scriptural situation. For him, and to a smaller degree for the lesser national leaders, the *Bhagavadgītā* remained the spontaneous referend. Gandhi knew the *Gītā* as well as anyone ever did, and his interpretation of the text became the matrix of what his followers forthwith called 'Gandhian Philosophy'.[4] Swami B., a senior Ramakrishna Mission monk, once exclaimed with some indignation: 'I don't know why these Congresswalās always speak about Gandhian Philosophy! Gandhi's philosophy is nothing but the philosophy of the *Upanishads* and of the *Bhagavadgītā*—he has no philosophy of his own'. This statement was not so vituperative as it may sound. In the Indian setting, nothing that was not contained, however obliquely, in the traditional lore, is of much value—not excluding aeroplanes and atomic devices; for they, too, were invented and used in Vedic and Epic times as most Hindus today aver without embarrassment.

Let me summarize the points made so far. The terms '*Veda*', or '*shāstra*', as used by Gandhi and his more vocal followers, denote all religious texts including Buddhist and Jain scriptures; but the *Bhagavadgītā* stands as a single, unambiguous referend. This accounts for the inordinate importance the text has been given in comparison to other texts, which have a much higher status in the scriptural hierarchy of Hinduism; the *Veda*, together with the *Aranyakas*, *Brāhmanas*, and *Upanishads*, is canonical (*shruti*). The *Gītā*, as part of the epic, is non-canonical (*smrti*). Apart from the sociological definition of a Hindu as a person born into a Hindu *jāti* (caste), the only possible joint qualification of all Hindus is their acceptance of the authority of the *shruti* on a par with such other means of knowledge as direct perception (*pratyaksha*) and correct inference (*anumāna*). Gandhians get quite annoyed at such a definition as 'narrow-minded', superstitious, outmoded. I think we can assume without much risk that the conception of a 'Hindu' held by lay post-Gandhian Hindus is formulable: 'a Hindu is one who believes in the universality of Truth and the essential unity of all religions'. This statement is well within the scope of the totally predictable parlance of Renaissance Hinduism. The post-Gandhian assumption is obviously that every good and/or religious person *should* be called a Hindu. The scholastic notion of a Hindu as a person who accepts the authority of the *Veda*—not 'the *Veda* which is also the Bible and the Quran',[5] but the four *saṃhitās*,[6] etc.—is rejected with various degrees of indignation.

Gandhi's doctrinal strategy of eclecticism works out a rather subtle dialectical sequence, shared by Gandhian Hindus: 'superstition', in Gandhian English, supposedly translates the Indian *andhavishvās*. But *andhavishvās* does not mean 'superstition' at all—it means 'blind faith'. The Indian term, a Sanskritized neologism, was first used I believe by Dayananda in the late eighties of the last century. Since Gandhi wanted people to interiorize this sememe, 'blind faith' *is* superstition, not in the lexical sense as 'apple' is a fruit of the species *mala*, but in the semantically recommending sense like 'thinking of another man's wife *is* adultery'. Whether or not this somewhat devious semantic device was consciously created by Gandhi, I do not know. It may well be—and this would be parallel to similar semantic recommendations he made, as in a letter to Mirabehn, which starts, 'I thank you for your love-letter'.[7] He knew as well as Mirabehn or I, that hers was not a love-letter in the lexicographically accepted sense of the expression, but his use was a recommendation toward a semantic change (a love-letter *should not be* a letter documenting romantic attraction, but it *should* be a letter of the kind Mirabehn wrote to him).

Let us linger for a moment on this apparently technical point: it provides a cue, I believe, for a more incisive understanding of Gandhi's reading of the *Bhagavadgītā*. This has not been pointed out anywhere so far, in the large Gandhian literature, because most of it is either panegyric or else highly guarded. I maintain that his reading of the *Bhagavadgītā* is recommendatory, and not in any sense exegetical as it was with the medieval commentators and modern exegetes like Aurobindo, the Rama-krishna Mission Swāmis, Shivananda, and the rest of the Renaissance monastics. Gandhi wanted Indian audiences to accept the *Bhagavadgītā* as a canonical text, and regardless of whether or not he was aware of the operational distinction between *shruti* and *smṛti*, he meant business when he insisted that the *Gītā* was the gospel of Hinduism. The main reason for his insistence, I believe, should be sought in the homogeneous applicability of its tenets: for whereas it is quite impossible to interpret the *Upanishads* and the other canonical texts sociocentrically, the *Gītā* does indeed lend itself to social moralizing. Depending on the emphasis which the reader places on the central 'message' of the text, he can see in it a manual for religious devotion to a personal god (*bhakti*), or of 'work without attachment' (*karma*). One may stress the psycho-experimental, more directly *yogic* passages of the book—and this is basically Sri Aurobindo's approach—but one can just as well ignore this aspect, with impunity. As to the speculative, cognitive content of the *Gītā*, the *jñāna* element, none but the monistic doctors ever felt called upon to elaborate it; and Shamkaracharya's attempt to interpret the *Gītā* as a monistic work reads as almost pathetically contrived and farfetched. The author of the *Bhagavadgītā* had no monistic frame in mind; in fact, there is a good chance that he, or they, opposed the monistic, speculative, impersonal trend set by the *shruti* and other, earlier scriptures.

Gandhi's reading of the teachings of this *smrti* can now be succinctly stated. It is a simple, straightforward, theologically unsophisticated interpretation, one that nurtures the socio-political doctrines of twentieth century India's greatest charismatic. 'I never cite scripture unless I have subjected it to the test of personal experience'[8] is a highly revealing sentence. Its negative implication is that those parts of the *Gītā* which are not amenable to sociopolitical interpretation were not cited by him— hence the yogic and the *jñāna* elements in the text could be ignored or played down *ad libitum*. The charismatic's ignoring of a doctrinal point aids its being ignored by his audience; just as his ignoring a person or persons inside the frame of political or ideological competition tends to result in their being ignored by the charismatic's followers. The late M. N. Roy once told me in 1952: 'Gandhiji could kill a person's political ambitions by either flattering him or ignoring him to death'. This statement, however strongly phrased, might give pause to students of both Gandhi and Roy.

The links between Gandhi's chief doctrines of *satyāgraha* and *ahimsā*, seen by him as correlative terms, and the teachings of the *Bhagavadgītā* have been seriously studied by Bondurant,[9] D. M. Datta[10] and Radhakrishnan.[11] There are close to a hundred books, I would estimate, in English and in Indian languages, taking their departure from Gandhi's interpretation of the *Gītā*, but these are pious eulogies and few of them add any information to what an intelligent reading of Gandhi's own words on the *Gītā* would convey. Bondurant's and Datta's books should be read by any serious scholar who attempts to trace Gandhi's choice of the *Bhagavadgītā* as his doctrinal *vade-mecum*. Gandhi's own statements were collected in several anthologies,[12] and all this material is eminently accessible. Let me therefore present my own understanding of Gandhi's salient interpretation of the *Gītā*.

It would seem to me, in the first place, that he interpolated individual freedom, basically a humanistic notion, into the text. 'I appreciate that freedom as I have imbibed it through the central teaching of the *Gītā*, that man is the maker of his own destiny, in the sense that he has freedom of choice as to the manner in which he uses that freedom'.[13] How this is compatible with that most-quoted *Bhagavadgītā* passage (XVIII/61) *yantrārūdhāni māyayā* ('the Lord, oh Arjuna, resides in the hearts of all beings, spinning them around through his *Māyā*, like [puppets suspended] in a [puppet-] machine') escapes me. The last chapter is the 'most important', so Mr Hingorani told me in 1951; and he may have been right, because the *shāstras*,[14] by tradition, save the central *siddhānta* or 'correct teaching' for the end, having refuted opposing views in the earlier sections. The eighteenth discourse of the *Gītā* is the *bhakti*[15]-discourse par excellence, and a literal or at least an objectively uninterpreted reading of the text must convince the student, committed or uncommitted to the tradition, that *bhakti* or devotion to the personal god is indeed the core teaching, superseding both *karma* and *yoga*, and leaving *jñāna*, the impersonal, contemplative quest far behind. Now personal devotion countervails ethical and pragmatic indeterminism, and unless Gandhi intended to convey some sort of a modified determinism by this statement, he must have dissimulated the meaning of the text. It is quite unlikely that he had 'forgotten' the passage when he made this statement, and this gives me the uneasy feeling that he switched his exegetic reference where it suited him.

The manner in which a commentator handles the problem of truth reveals his main thrust to the critic. For Gandhi, the problem of truth was *not* an epistemological, but an ontological problem, as witness his constant identification of 'Truth' with 'God'. 'In the language of the *Gītā*, Chapter 10, the universe is sustained by a fraction of it (Truth). Therefore, if you replace the word "God" by the word "Truth", wherever it occurs, you will have some idea of what I mean.'[16] I do not think that this synonymity follows from the text. Indian alphabets do not have capital letters; in English, capitalizing an abstract like 'truth' identifies the term as one of greater nobility or importance than does its uncapitalized spelling. Medieval Hindu theology does indeed define the supreme being as *sat*, 'being' or 'truth', and the ontological sememe, namely 'being', 'existence', is closer to the intention of the doctors of Brahman theology. When Gandhi used 'Truth' as a synonym for 'God', he was moralizing, an activity which is much easier to accomplish in theological English than it is in theological Sanskrit or Hindi or Gujarati. Gandhi was not concerned with 'truth' in the empirical sense. In a somewhat paradoxical manner, his notion of God was a kind of Kantian notion: God as 'existent' is a theological god, God as 'Truth' is a moral god recommending moral action. I doubt whether Gandhi's sermon could have been what it was had he not had conscious or unconscious recourse to English, even when he spoke Hindi or Gujarati.

'But how is one to realize the Truth, which may be likened to the philosopher's stone or to the Cow of Plenty? By singleminded devotion (*abhyāsa*) and indifference to all other interests in life (*vairāgya*).'[17] Gandhi used technical terms of the homiletic tradition quite freely, and his rendition was based entirely on the *Bhagavadgītā*. Terms like *sannyāsa* (monastic withdrawal), *yoga, abhyāsa, vairāgya* (renunciation) have a peculiarly moralistic overtone in *Gītā* literature, primary and derived, and this seems to follow from the theistic pattern in medieval Hindu literature. Ninian Smart has shown that theistic (i.e., monotheistic) argument weakened the philosophical and speculative thrust of the Indian religious dialectic wherever it occurred.[18] The monotheistic systems (*Sāmkhya, Advaita, Bauddha, Jaina*) are elegantly autonomous, and extremely sophisticated, hence their attraction for modern cosmopolitan philosophers. But Gandhi was thoroughly antagonistic toward the style of speculation which learned Hinduism had displayed through the ages. He thought perhaps there was something immoral, frivolous, even slightly obscene about the way in which Hindu scholars had handled doctrine and argument. Here, Gandhi was very close to Swami Vivekananda, whose influence he did not admit. Vivekananda had chastised the *pandits* for 'logic-chopping'; he successfully resisted any chance of studying Sanskrit and the texts properly. Gandhi made it quite clear that he thought panditry to be redundant, to say the least, and disfunctional in the context of social reform. The highly eclectic pep-talk which the *Bhagavadgītā* is, lent itself to persistent sociocentric moralizing—no other *shruti* or *smrti* could possibly have provided these goods, even if Gandhi had sought out texts other than the *Gītā*.

We can now summarize Gandhi's reading of the *Bhagavadgītā*. All of it is eminently predictable. There are no surprises in his interpretation of the text; in fact, any sensitive scholar acquainted with Gandhian thought could make it an exercise for his own benefit and the delight of his colleagues: he could pick any *shloka* of the *Bhagavadgītā*, without checking Gandhi's rendition of it, and could guess what the Mahatma's interpretation had been. Krishna is the personal God *par excellence;* all the other *personae dramatis* are interiorized psycho-cultural entities—aspects of the human soul with its delights, desires, needs, and its short-comings. The battle of Kurukshetra was no 'real' battle where blood flowed in gallons galore, but it is the inner battle between good and evil which everyone has to fight. The *Gītā's* message is fourfold: it teaches *jnāna, yoga, nishkāma karma* (desireless action) and *bhakti*, in this ascending order of importance. *Jnāna* is intuitive knowledge of God, but not the monistic-speculative *brahman* of the classical mystics and of some

Vedantic doctors: these, Gandhi mistrusted and disliked. His attitude toward technical *yoga* was ambivalent, though I believe that he did not want to get involved with it—he certainly never spoke about Patanjali's work. In any critically valid sense, Gandhi was not a mystic; and if mysticism is to be adumbrated as a set of psycho-experimental attitudes and actions, with their concomitant intensive personal experiences as studied by Stace,[19] Underhill, [20] Zaehner[21] and by this author,[22] Gandhi was not only not a mystic, but he was quite strongly anti-mystical in his religious ideas. Among modern interpretations, his stands on one end of a continuum between a highly moralistic-pragmatic and a psycho-experimental or 'mystical' interpretation, which is represented by Sri Aurobindo Ghosh.[23]

There is a toss-up, in Gandhi's reading of the *Gītā*, between the emphasis on *nishkāma karma*, action without the desire and attachment to its results, and *bhakti*, faithful, intensive devotion to a personal God. It should be possible to tabulate statements which extol the one or the other, but I do not think that such a count would reveal any final decision on the part of the Mahatma: he either kept an intentional balance between the two emphases, or else he stressed either one according to the situational requirement. Swami Vivekananda, one of Gandhi's most important though unacknowledged ideological mentors, regarded the four kinds of *yoga* as discrete, depending on the personality of the practitioners. Thus, for no reason this author ever understood, Vivekananda regarded the Buddha as the ideal *karmayogin*, and Jesus Christ as the ideal *bhakta* (which seems justified). Gandhi would not set up mutually exclusive appellations. When he talked about the Buddha or Christ, he presented their teachings as supporting the attitudes which he was recommending just then.

Gandhi's stress on physical work and on *brahmacharyam* (chastity) were extrapolations unwarranted by the text. They find no support in the *Bhagavadgītā*. This was pointed out by Basham.[24] Krishna does indeed speak about *brahmacharyam*, but it implies, as it did in all *shruti* and *smrti* literature, a general kind of interior control, with the main function of concentrating on the Absolute within; hence the classical definition of *brahmacharyam*: he whose mind roams in the *brahman* is a *brahmachāri* (*brahmani charate yasya manah*). To use American semi-academic slang, Gandhi's 'hang-up' on sexual abstention coloured his interpretation of the text. Both the teacher and the pupil in the *Bhagavadgītā* were no doubt *brahmachāri-s* in the classical sense, men whose minds were absorbed, at times at least, in divine things; but neither of them was a despiser of women and of the joys generated by a woman's embrace. An expurgated edition of the *Mahābhārata*, without the romantic episodes involving Krishna and Arjuna, would make the epic much shorter and much less meritorious, literarily speaking.

The importance and the dignity of physical work is a western ideological import into nineteenth century India. There is no support in any Indian text—religious or secular—for this notion previous to contact with the modern West. Gandhi's insistence on it is understandable, but his reading of it into or out of the *Bhagavadgītā* was a dissimulational device, as it cannot be due to his lack of knowledge of the text. I am almost certain that Gandhi did not know the more technical reason behind the absence of concern with physical work in the *Gītā*. The famous *svadharma*[25] passage (II, 31) has been variously interpreted in favour of or against the caste rules of trade-exclusiveness. When Gandhi seemed to support the original *varna*-based division of labour, he had a Protestant configuration in mind: *varna* was a good institution because it helped people to develop skills on the basis of transmitted cultural experience. But he apparently thought there was a pedagogical link between this notion, first propounded by Swami Dayananda Sarasvati, founder of the fundamentalistic communal *Arya Samāj*,[26] and the dignity of physical labour, as an act of worship. Gandhi, like virtually all the authors of the Hindu Renaissance, ignored the lexico-semantical fact that the term *karma*, as used in the *shruti* and as implied in the *Bhagavadgītā* which quotes *shruti*,[27] does *not* mean physical labour, nor even white-collar work of any sort, but ritualistic action, particularly Vedic action, i.e, the pouring of *ghee* into the fire under Vedic incantations.

This concludes the essence of Gandhi's reading of the *Bhagavadgītā*. It is eminently pragmatic; it is also jingoistic in the sense that the austere ideals underlying his interpretation apply to the Indian scene and not to a cosmopolitan setting where hedonistic and intellectual values would have to be given status equal to that of austerity, *brahmacharyam*, vegetarianism, teetotalism, etc. It is anti-mystical in that Gandhi rejected the kind of intensive psycho-experimental involvement which mysticism generates, and from which it is derived. Gandhi was very sensitive about the standard criticism against Hinduism, expressed by western people and Indians alike: that the metaphysical involvement of the indigenous teachings of India impeded her progress and caused stagnation. The *shruti* and the Buddhist texts are quietistic, individualistic, and esoteric in the sense that they teach extrication and not involvement, rejection of social attachments and not social participation, at least for those who want to excel. Gandhi felt—and he was no doubt right—that the overwhelming preoccupation with mystical and contemplative things tends to displace mundane and social interests, at least in the Indian setting.

The question now arises whether the *Bhagavadgītā* would have the place it has, in modern India's ideology, had it not been for Gandhi's recommendation of the text as the repository of all the spiritual and ethical wealth of the land. I believe it would; and I think that Gandhi's insistence on the importance of the text worked in a confirmatory rather than in an exploratory manner. It is not within the scope of this contribution to trace the popularity of the *Bhagavadgītā* in Hindu middle class India. This is the task for a historian of ideas, and one that should be attempted. I have communicated some of my own research on the matter elsewhere in some detail.[28] I shall here outline my main points.

Western and Brahman scholars of the nineteenth century presented the *Bhagavadgītā* as the most important non-*shruti* primary text of Hinduism. The *Sacred Books of the East* series[29] was not only acknowledged by occidental orientalists and students of comparative religion; Indian scholars who read English paid their homage to the enterprise. A feedback into India continued through roughly fifty years, from 1880 to 1930. Some of the political and religious leaders of the Renaissance, particularly Vivekananda and Tilak, invoked the *Bhagavadgītā* as the scriptural pivot around which both spiritual and secular values must rally. The reasons for this choice were different for these two men. Tilak was an erudite *pandit,* a strong traditional ideologue, and a man of many intellectual and managerial resources. He cathected the heroic and the hierarchical elements of the *Gītā* in his *Gītārahasya*,[30] a treatise very much in the classical style of *tīkā*–argumentation. The crucial difference between his reading and Gandhi's lay, I think, in the interpretation of *svadharma* and of the concomitant reading of caste and its incumbent duties. For Tilak, caste was *jāti* and *varna,* a matter of birth. He had no sympathy—at least not in the *Gītārahasya*—for the newfangled interpretation of caste by qualification and achievement as opposed to caste by birth. The modernistic notion, which had come into vogue in the 'nineties, that scholarly man is a *brāhman,* a heroic man a *kshatriya,* a good and honest trader a *vaishya,* and a skilled craftsman a *shūdra,* did not find any favourable response from Tilak. He was far too knowledgeable about the primary texts, the original scriptures and commentaries to swallow a reinterpretation so popular with social reformers all over the land. I have never found any statement by Tilak criticizing Swami Dayananda, the first fundamentalist Hindu teacher to propound the idea of caste by merit and skill, but Tilak did not regard the Swami as the new prophet his followers wanted him to be.

I shall bracket another set of *Gītā* interpretations as the 'essential unity' type. It has generated the largest number of translations and editions and commentaries. It was probably inaugurated by Annie Besant; Dr Bhagavan Das was its most scholarly proponent. The Theosophical Society and the Ramakrishna-Vivekananda institutions have never been on friendly terms, ideologically speaking, but their reading of the *Gītā* does not show any important difference. When Annie Besant published her own 'translation' of the text in 1923, Gandhi was known to have read it with admiration. Besant's *Gītā*-presentation did not display any of the pseudo-esoteric inanities of Blavatsky's writings. One would expect that the theosophists might stress the *yoga* aspects above the *bhakti* and *nishkāma karma* directives of the *Gītā*, but this was not the case. The Ramakrishna Mission renditions and commentaries on the *Gītā* (e.g. by Swami Svarupananda,[31] and the famous lectures of Swami Rangana-thananda)[32] stress *bhakti* and *nishkāma karma* about evenly, yielding third and fourth place to *jnāna* and *yoga*, respectively. The fourfold, simplified scheme of *bhakti-karma-rāja-* and *jnāna-yoga*, recommended by Vive-kananda and implemented by his followers, none of whom up to this date seemed to have been aware that the scheme was Vivekananda's invention, was at the basis of the *Gītā* interpretations of the Mission; but their hierarchical recommendations—sociocentric *bhakti-and-karma* on top, individualistic *jnāna* and *yoga* at the bottom—coalesce with Gandhi's recommendations. Stress on *karma* and *bhakti*, rather than on *yoga* and *jnāna*, would be shared by neo-Vedantins, the religious *engagé* of the Hindu Renaissance, nationalists and patriots, even when they state very different aims and interests.

Anthropologists may have become impatient by now—what does the *Gītā* do to the majority of Indian people, the villagers? The answer is simple—it doesn't do much to them. Prof. Dhirendra Narain averred that the *Bhagavadgītā* was a book of the people.[33] I think he overrates the importance of the text, and the villagers' familiarity with it. In his highly perceptive study of the Hindu character, he seems to have urban milieux in mind, even though he does not identify his subjects in his long chapter on the importance of the *Bhagavadgītā*. No doubt, the village *brāhman*, some of the religiously more motivated villagers, and the itinerant *sādhu* (holy man) know the *Gītā* and many occasionally quote from it. But for the people at large, the text itself is a remotely known holy book. Perhaps all adult villagers in Hindu India have a rough idea of the epic mythology, and a high percentage of them may be aware today that the *Gītā* is part of the *Mahābhārata;* but they do not know it in any way as a set of specific rules—their sources are closer home, oral, *ad hoc*. I do not think that it is saying too much when I conclude asserting that the

Bhagavadgītā is a book for 'Great Tradition' Hindus—the literate people of the towns and the villages, *brāhmans*, merchants, and the widely ramified sectors of Indian society which could be called 'middle-class' if an approximation to western societal taxonomies were required. For the villagers in over half a million settlements on the subcontinent, it is a very indirect source of inspiration, no more perhaps than, say, the Holy Bible is to the *contadini* in Sicily and Southern Italy: the Virgin, the saints, the priests—it is they who transmit religious lore. When the villagers of India heard Gandhi speak about the *Gītā*, they heard him, not the *Gītā*, for the holy word has to be filtered through the charismatic. *He* reached the people, not the book.

NOTES

1 A. Bharati, 'Gandhi and Buddhist Atheism', *Gandhi Marg* (New Delhi), March 1961, pp. 44-49.

2 Louis Fischer, *The Essential Gandhi* (New York, 1962), p. 241.

3 Mrs Pandit addressed the students and staff of Benares Hindu University in October 1953. The author was present and took notes.

4 Harekrushna Mahatab, *Lectures on Gandhian Philosophy* (Annamalainagar, Annamalai University, 1965).

5 Bhagavan Das, *The Essential Unity of Religions* (Madras, 1954).

6 *samhita*: the central sections of the canonical Veda. The *Rk-, Sama-, Yajus-* and *Atharva-Veda samhitas* (collections) contain all the ritualistic incantations and the material for Brahmanical recitation covering the rites of passage, and a very large array of prayers, exhortations, sacred spells (*mantra*), and hymns to the Vedic deities. Whereas most Hindu scholars include the *Brahmanas* (ritualistic instructions) and the *Upanishads* (speculative interpretations of the ritual) in the canonical Veda, Swami Dayananda and the *Arya Samaj* regard the *samhita* alone as canonical.

7 M. K. Gandhi, *Bapu's Letters to Mira* (Ahmedabad, 1949).

8 Anand T. Hingorani (ed.), *The Teachings of the Gita* (Bombay, 1962), p. 69.

9 J. V. Bondurant, *Conquest of Violence—The Gandhian Philosophy of Conflict* (Berkeley and Los Angeles, 1965), pp. 112, 116-18.

10 Dhirendra M. Datta, *The Philosophy of Mahatma Gandhi* (Madison, 1968).

11 S. Radhakrishnan, *The Bhagavadgita* (London, 1948).

12 For example, Anand T. Hingorani (ed.), *All Religions are True; God is Truth;* and *The Teachings of the Gita* (all three published from Bombay, 1962); Louis Fischer, *The Essential Gandhi*, op. cit..

13 A. T. Hingorani (ed.), *The Teachings of the Gita.*

14 Although any didactic text, on any traditional topic including music and love, is called a *shastra*, the term, when used without any further specification, refers to religious texts and includes all the canonical and non-canonical literature.

15 *Bhakti* is intense, prayerful devotion to the personal god of one's choice. Its

influence was very weak in the canonical period, and became much stronger in medieval and later India, largely as a reaction against intellectualized mysticism of a monistic and pantheistic, impersonal kind.

16 *The Diary of Mahadev Desai* (Ahmedabad, 1932), p. 160.

17 Hingorani (ed.), *The Teachings of the Gita*, op. cit., p. 45.

18 Ninian Smart, *Doctrine and Argument in Indian Philosophy* (London, 1964), p. 154. See also my review of this book in *Zietschrift für Philosophische Forschung* (Meisenheim, Germany), XX, 1966, No. 1, p. 170.

19 W. T. Stace, *Mysticism and Philosophy* (London, 1961).

20 E. Underhill, *Mysticism: A Study in the Nature and Development of Man's Spiritual Consciousness* (New York, 1967).

21 R. C. Zaehner, *Mysticism: Sacred and Profane* (London, 1967).

22 A. Bharati, *The Tantric Tradition* (London, 1966).

23 Sri Aurobindo Ghosh, *Essays on the Gita* (Pondicherry, 1950).

24 Prof. A. L. Basham's lectures in the United States in 1967-68. He delivered this particular lecture at Syracuse University in December 1967. Basham went into fascinating detail to show that the notion of the dignity of physical labour was totally new in India and a direct import along with the Protestant ethic.

25 *svadharma* is literally 'one's own *dharma*' or duties, commitments one has to fulfil by virtue of one's birth in a specific social group with its specific commitments. The *Bhagavadgita* is quite clear about this—do not give up the work 'with which you are born'. Modern interpreters have interpreted the term to mean '*dharma* which is your own, by reason of your skills and qualifications'—no text bears them out in this reading.

26 See H. B. Sarda, *The Life of Dayananda Saraswati, World Teacher* (Ajmer, Vedic Yantralaya, 1946); Ch. Bawa Singh, *The Life and Teachings of Swami Dayanand Saraswati* (Lahore, 1903); and Kenneth W. Jones, 'Communism in the Punjab: The Arya Samaj Contribution', in the *Journal of Asian Studies*, vol. 28/1 (1968), pp. 39-55.

27 *shruti*: 'that which is heard', and *smrti*: 'that which is remembered'. It would be wise to ignore the etymologies of these terms—there is no connection between the logical meanings and the semantic import of these terms, and both Indian and western scholars confuse the already complicated issue. *Shruti* is the Veda; all other primary texts of religious instruction are *smrti*.

28 A. Bharati, 'The Hindu Renaissance and its Apologetic Patterns', in the *Journal of Asian Studies*, vol. 29/1 (1969).

29 The S.B.E. Series, inaugurated by Max Muller at Oxford, was completed by about 1910; all the volumes were published in Oxford, at the Clarendon Press. The first of its fifty volumes was published in 1879. This monumental series was well out of print by about 1940 and high prices were obtained by dealers who bought and sold copies, singly or in sets. In 1966 Messrs Motilal Banarsidass in Delhi projected a complete reprint of the series. Since then, they have published all the volumes— an invaluable service to Oriental studies and to serious research in comparative religion.

30 B. G. Tilak published his *Gitarahasya* in Marathi in about 1900. He also wrote an English treatise which restates, and amends, his interpretation of the *Gita* in his famous Marathi work. See B. G. Tilak, *The Hindu Philosophy of Life, Ethics, and Religion* (Poona, 1935-36).

31 Swami Svarupananda, *The Bhagavadgita* (Mylapore, The Ramakrishna Mission, 1951).

[32] Ranganathananda was President of the Ramakrishna Mission in New Delhi, where he had a cosmopolitan audience. He is now President of the Ramakrishna Mission Institute of Culture at Calcutta, the most sophisticated unit within the Ramakrishna Mission. His lectures on the *Gita* are famous among all those who speak English and listen to religion in Calcutta. He never teaches in any language but English, thereby creating and intensifying a middle-class urban audience which is highly amenable to modernistic interpretations of the *Gita*.

[33] Dhirendra Narain, *Hindu Character* (Bombay, 1957), pp. 79-108.

WESTERN INFLUENCE ON GANDHIAN THOUGHT

Adi H. Doctor

Although according to some of his admirers Gandhi's ideas and ideals were uniquely his own, Gandhi himself never claimed any originality for them. Instead, he freely admitted to the numerous influences that operated upon him. These influences were indigenous as well as western. I propose to consider here the impact and impression made by Christianity and nineteenth century western thinkers on Gandhi's philosophy of state and on his technique of non-violent resistance. At the outset, however, I wish to warn against the possible inference that Gandhi's thought was 'all second-hand'. In one sense it is true that nothing that Gandhi said had not been said before, but his originality and unique contribution lay in bringing together the teachings of various thinkers and religious and political sects. He synthesized the ideas of the Quakers, the Russian Dukhobors, socialists, anarchists and utopians, and impressed upon these his own unique stamp and conviction. In yet another respect, Gandhi stole a march over his predecessors. He evolved a technique and developed numerous tools such as fasts, boycott, *hijrat*, for the practical application of the non-violent techniques. In the political field he employed these techniques against government and in the social realm he used them to eradicate such evils as untouchability in India.

Gandhi's political philosophy has generally been described as anarchist[1] or as 'Marxism minus violence'.[2] The anarchist trend in Gandhian thinking is natural in the light of the circumstances and influences under which it developed. Gandhi's anti-state bias and his conviction that all governments are suspect and bad owed much to his early humiliating experiences in fighting an unjust government in South Africa and subsequently in India. These experiences crystallized into a conviction and philosophy of state under the influence, especially, of Tolstoy and Thoreau.

Gandhi read Tolstoy's works in 1893-94 in his first year in South Africa. Gandhi's biographer Rev. Doke informs us that during this year Gandhi read some eighty books which included Tolstoy's *The Kingdom of God is Within You, Christianity and Patriotism* and other works. In Gandhi's own words, 'I made too (*sic*) an intensive study of Tolstoy's books, *The Gospel in Brief*, *What to do?*, and such other books made a deep impression on me. I began to realize more and more the infinite possibilities of universal love.'[3] But of Tolstoy's various works, Gandhi singles out one work as having specially influenced him. In his *Autobiography* Gandhi asserts: 'Three moderns have left a deep impress on me: Raychandbhai by his living contact, Tolstoy by his book, *The Kingdom of God is Within You*, and Ruskin by his *Unto This Last*.'

But although Gandhi made a deep acquaintance with Tolstoy's thought only in 1893-94, he had by 1890, as a young student, heard of Tolstoy and was familiar with his arguments and crusading activities against all intoxicants.[4] Gandhi visited the Eiffel Tower in 1890, and in his *Autobiography* he states that Tolstoy was the chief among those who disparaged the tower as man's folly and a creation of man under the influence of tobacco.

Most of Gandhi's early writings echo Tolstoy's views on state and politics. Tolstoy considered all forms of government to be equally wicked. According to him, 'not only wars but all forms of compulsion inherent in the state are criminal'. Tolstoy refused to accept the state as a moral agent because the idea of authority implying violence could never be reconciled with morality implying willing compliance. 'Despite the unremitting efforts of rulers to conceal these facts and to attribute a different significance to authority', wrote Tolstoy, 'it simply means the rope and chain wherewith a man is bound and dragged, the lash wherewith he is flogged . . . all the requisitions of the state . . . to which men seem to yield voluntarily are always enforced by the physical threat or the reality of physical punishment. Physical violence is the basis of authority.'[5] The possession of power and authority by the state only serves to demoralize society. 'It cannot be otherwise', wrote Tolstoy, 'for not only does the possession of authority corrupt men, but either from design or unconsciously, rulers are always striving to reduce their subjects to the lowest degree of weakness, for the more feeble the subject the less the effort required to subdue him.'[6]

Tolstoy as a typical Christian anarchist considered the state futile and in order to demonstrate its futility, analyzed (in *The Kingdom of God is Within You*) the three most commonly advanced arguments to prove its necessity, namely, to maintain internal order, to promote good ends such as education and commerce, and to provide protection against foreign aggression. The argument that the state is necessary to maintain internal order, Tolstoy rejects on the ground that there are really no wicked people from whom the state need protect other people. Instead, if the people need protection against anybody, it is against the government itself. Tolstoy concedes that at times the state does check internal violence, but he immediately points out that this is invariably done by introducing into life other new forms of violence 'always increasing in intensity'. Good ends such as education and commerce can be promoted by the voluntary efforts of the people themselves. The state, if anything, has only proved a hindrance. 'Since the end of the last century every progressive movement on the part of mankind has been not only discouraged but invariably hampered by governments. Such was the case with abolition of corporal punishment, torture and slavery, with the establishing of the freedom of the press and liberty of meeting.' Finally, Tolstoy does not consider the state essential for protection against external enemies since 'every European nation professes the same principles of liberty and fraternity and therefore needs no defence against its neighbours'. On the contrary, standing armies invite war. 'It is not only that the increase of armed forces fails to protect us from danger of attack from our neighbours, it actually provokes the very attack which it deprecates.'[7]

Tolstoy advised the 'true Christian' to abstain from participation in the activities of the state. 'He must refuse conscription. He must not accept any work under the state.' At the same time Tolstoy categorically asserted that opposing the state with violence is also wicked and cannot lead to any better form of life. In his 'Letter to a Hindu', an essay written in 1908 and dealing with the subjection of India and its causes and cure, Tolstoy condemned the enslavement of two hundred million people by a 'commercial company' and advised: 'Do not resist evil [with evil], but do not yourself participate in evil—in the violent deeds of the administration of the law courts, the collection of taxes, and what is more important, of the soldiers—and no one in the world will enslave you.'[8]

The similarity between Tolstoy's views and Gandhi's is striking. Following Tolstoy Gandhi identifies the state with authority and coercive power. The state in his words 'represents violence in a concentrated and organized form. The individual has a soul, but as the state is a soul-less machine it can never be weaned from violence to which it owes its very existence'. Since the state is in essence violence it follows that the completely non-violent society will be a stateless society. 'A society organized and run on non-violence would be the purest anarchy.' (*Harijan*, 21 July 1940). In his earlier work, *Hind Swaraj*, he criticized the adoption of parliamentary government as blind acceptance of western political institutions. He compared the British parliament to a sterile woman and a prostitute. It was like a sterile woman since it had never done a single good thing of its own accord and worked only under the spur of petitions and pressures. It was like a prostitute for it had no real master, being under the control of changing prime-ministers who were more concerned with power than welfare.[9] In *Hind Swaraj* Gandhi, like Tolstoy, also condemned the army, the police and the law courts.

Gandhi's conscientious objection to majority rule is also fully in keeping with the spirit of Thoreau's and Tolstoy's writings. He repeatedly asserted that in matters of conscience the law of the majority had no place.[10] 'Swaraj will be an absurdity', he warned, 'if individuals have to surrender their judgment to a majority.'[11] Like Tolstoy Gandhi claimed conscience to be a higher court than the ordinary courts of justice; in fact, it superseded all other courts. He also considered the state to be incapable of promoting morality. Morality was a matter of inward choice. A moral action can not be performed mechanically at the behest of a state, but only voluntarily. Gandhi therefore looked upon any increase in state power with distrust, for, although state action might do some good by curbing exploitation, it did greater harm by cutting at the very root of all real development, namely, individuality.

Gandhi, however, did not merely criticize existing political institutions but also provided an alternative, namely, the decentralized state. Here one can see the marked influence of Thoreau's individualism and of the anarchist and Marxist philosophies. The non-co-operation movement brought him into close touch with Indian socialists and communists. The Marxist ideal of a classless and stateless society strongly appealed to him and it reinforced his view of the state which was deeply influenced by the individualist philosophy of Thoreau and the philosophical anarchism of Tolstoy. Gandhi did not take pains to outline in great detail the future order of society. He shared Thoreau's position: 'I heartily accept the motto "that government is best which governs least" and I should like to see it acted upon more rapidly and systematically. Carried out it finally amounts to this which also I believe "that government is best which does not govern at all"; and when men are prepared for it that will be the kind of government they will have.'[12] In a strikingly similar passage Gandhi writes: 'Political life means capacity to regulate national life through national representatives. If national life becomes so perfect as to become self-regulated, no representation becomes necessary. In such a state everyone is his own ruler. He rules himself in such a manner that he is never a hindrance to his neighbour.'[13] According to Gandhi only a society based on *purna ahimsā* (complete non-violence) can be really considered as *shāsana mukta* (administration free). But since complete non-violence is an ideal, ever to be striven for, but difficult to attain in the foreseeable future, Gandhi upheld as the immediate objective 'a predominantly non-violent state' which would be characterised by decentralization and minimum government. Thus at bottom Gandhi was an anarchist, but for all practical purposes he was willing to be content with Thoreau's individualist philosophy of minimum government.

Gandhi derived many of his economic views from Ruskin, particularly his views on money and distribution of income. Gandhi was against the use of money which he described as dirt and as the root of all evil. Its greatest evil is that it can be stored or accumulated. In the old days, wealth consisted of live-stock, food and clothes, but since they were not durable, the surplus was bartered away. There was nothing like interest. With the introduction of coins and modern currency, money could be easily accumulated and thus began exploitation and the earning of interest on capital.

Gandhi learnt of the evils of money not only from observation and experience but, as his writings show, also from Tolstoy and Ruskin. Tolstoy's views on money are best elaborated in his book *What Then Must We Do?* However, the Gandhian ideal of the minimum dependence on money seems to have been inspired mainly by Ruskin's *Unto This Last*. In *Unto This Last*, Ruskin writes: 'I want a horseshoe for my horse. Twenty smiths or twenty thousand smiths may be ready to forge it; their number does not in one atom's weight affect the question of the suitable payment of the one who does forge it. It costs him a quarter of an hour of his life and so much skill and strength of arm to make that horseshoe for me. Then at some future time I am bound in equity to give a quarter of an hour and some minutes more of my life (or of some other person at my disposal) and also as much strength of arm and skill and a little more, in making or doing what the smith may have need of.'[14] Similarly Gandhi argues: 'Coins are but a measure of labour performed. They have no other value. If I buy rupee worth of flour, I have paid for the labour of cultivation, carrying and grinding.'[15] Gandhi even tried to carry out these reforms at the Phoenix Settlement in South Africa in 1904. Gandhi's advocacy of the payment of land dues in kind, his experimenting in such institutions as grain-banks, 'hand-spun yarn currency', and a system of rural credit backed by labour instead of gold, were steps towards minimising the role of money.[16] Gandhi fully agreed with Ruskin's dictum that any science of exchange which relates to the advantage of one party is founded not on science, but nescience.

Similarly, under the influence of Ruskin, Gandhi in his early writings advocated a doctrine of absolute equality. In the *Autobiography* Gandhi confessed that he learnt three lessons from Ruskin's *Unto This Last* which he summarized thus: (a) That economy is good which conduces to the good of all; (b) a lawyer's work has the same value as the barber's in as much as all have the same right of earning their livelihood; and (c) that a life of labour—the life of the tiller of the soil and the handicraftsman— is the life worth living.[17] Following Ruskin, Gandhi argued that no work or profession is superior or inferior to any other; and all workers, whether lawyers or scavengers, should receive equal payment. Later Gandhi changed the emphasis from absolute equality to proportionate equality. He wholeheartedly and approvingly quoted the Marxist principle—from each according to his ability, to each according to his needs. He began to advocate a minimum 'living Wage' and beyond this minimum, differences were to be permitted only on the basis of differing needs.[18] At the Phoenix Settlement Gandhi drew up a programme in which every- one should labour, drawing the same living wage irrespective of colour or nationality.

A reference may here also be made to the Gandhian concept of Trusteeship which was to some extent inspired by Gandhi's study of English jurisprudence and particularly Snell's *Equity*. According to this concept the rich are to hold their surplus possessions (lands and industries) as trustees of the people and administer the same strictly for the benefit of society and not for personal gain. Gandhi himself acknow- ledged western influence in this regard when he wrote in his *Autobio- graphy*: 'My regard for jurisprudence increased, I discovered in it religion'.

Another marked feature of the Gandhian philosophy is 'simple living' and the 'back to the village' ideal, sometimes described as Gandhi's villagism. According to Gandhi 'high thinking' is inconsistent with 'the complicated material life based on high speed imposed on us by mammon worship'.[19] Here, once again, we can trace the influence of Ruskin, Tolstoy, Thoreau and others. Before coming across their works Gandhi did not much differ from the average Indian youth then leaving India for studies in the U.K. As his biographer Louis Fischer informs us he was 'aping the British gentleman on the assumption that it would raise his status and bring him into key with what he mistakenly regarded as the dominant note in British life'. While in the United Kingdom, Gandhi bought a top hat, spats, striped trousers and coat, silk shirts and a silver mounted cane. He even made an attempt at learning to play the piano and the violin.

But it did not take Gandhi's sensitive soul long to realize his folly and he soon came to the conclusion that he had no right to indulge in such luxuries while the masses of his country men starved. 'Gandhi always craved harmony with his surroundings,' writes Fischer. 'That is why, years later, he adopted the loin cloth as his garb.'[20] Gandhi gradually became convinced of the futility of wealth and realized that the path to real happiness did not lie in accumulating wealth.

The futility of wealth and the knowledge that it can bring no true happiness was also an idea that Gandhi imbibed from Tolstoy. 'The Divine Law that man must earn his bread by labouring with his own hands,' he wrote, 'was first stressed by a Russian writer named T. F. Bondareff. Tolstoy advertised it and gave it wide publicity. In my view the same principle has been set forth in the third chapter of the Gita where we are told that he who eats food without offering sacrifice, eats stolen food. Sacrifice here can only mean bread-labour.'[21]

Gandhi's denunciation in *Hind Swaraj* not only of parliaments and law-courts, but also of doctors and lawyers, and his condemnation of mechanisation in general and railroads in particular, seem to be an expansion of Tolstoy's views. According to Tolstoy, 'The Christian man may not try to gain any advantage from state institutions, he must not try to grow rich under its protection or build a career by its favour. He must not go to court, must use no industrial products, must employ in his life nothing which comes from the work of others. He must possess no property, should avoid handling money, should not travel by rail-road or bicycle, and should never vote or fill a public office.'[22]

Ruskin's work also considerably influenced Gandhi's philosophy of simple living. Gandhi read Ruskin's *Unto This Last* in 1904 overnight. Like Ruskin, Gandhi was against the vulgar show of wealth and desired to transform the upper classes. Gandhi sums up the profound impact of *Unto This Last* on his mind thus: 'This was the first book of Ruskin I have ever read . . . it brought an instantaneous and practical transformation in my life. . . . I translated it into Gujarati'.[23] According to Ruskin, society required people 'who having resolved to seek not greater wealth but simpler pleasure, not higher fortune but deeper felicity', would make self-possession their first and highest possession and 'honour themselves in the harmless pride and calm pursuits of peace'.[24] This ideal was fully endorsed by Gandhi.

Even Thoreau, whom Gandhi read in his early years, held as antithetical the possession of wealth and the acquisition of virtue. 'Absolutely speaking,' wrote Thoreau, 'the more money the less virtue; it [money] puts to rest many questions which he would otherwise be taxed to answer, while the only new question which it puts is the hard but superfluous one—how to spend it? Thus his moral ground is taken from under his feet'.[25]

Finally a word on the influence of western thought on the Gandhian method and techniques of non-violence. It is in respect of his non-violent approach to social change that Gandhi differs fundamentally from Marxists and anarchists. Gandhi's acquaintance with Christianity dates back to his student days in England. Later he came to know several Church divines like Dr Andrew Murray of the Dutch Reformed Church and Mr Coates, a Quaker, who believed in total abolition of war; he also attended Bible classes. He read Butler's *Analogy* which he found to be 'a very profound and difficult book', Madame Blavatsky's *Key to Theosophy*, Parker's *Commentary*, etc. Gandhi was also much influenced by his study of the lives of saints like St Francis of Assisi. What impressed him most was the ideal of universal compassion shared in common by Buddhism, Christianity and Hinduism. 'My young mind tried to unify the teachings of the *Gita, The Light of Asia* and the Sermon on the Mount.'

The teachings of Christ were fully in keeping with Gandhi's own nature. They reinforced the principles of pacifism and non-violence which the young Gandhi had already imbibed from the teachings of his own *vaishnava* faith and his early family upbringing. The Sermon on the Mount with its teaching, 'Resist not evil, but whosoever shall smite thee on thy right cheek, turn to him the left also', and its declaration, 'Blessed are the meek . . . Blessed are ye when men shall revile you and persecute you', Gandhi confesses, 'went straight to my heart'.[26] On the eve of the *satyāgraha* in Transvaal, Gandhi observed that he and his followers were just following the precepts of Christ.[27] At one place Gandhi even calls Christ 'the prince of *satyāgrahis*'.

Next to the Bible, Tolstoy's pacifist teachings influenced Gandhi most. Tolstoy's *The Kingdom of God is Within You* is an elaboration of the teachings of the Sermon on the Mount. Gandhi read *The Kingdom of God* at a very crucial stage in his life when, as he asserts, he still believed in violence and was passing through a crisis of scepticism. 'Its reading,' he says, 'cured me of my scepticism and made me a firm believer in *ahimsa*.'[28] Tolstoy rejected all arguments in justification of violence either as 'scientific superstition' or as 'religious fraud'. In his 'Letter to a Hindu,' Tolstoy wrote: 'Love is the only way to rescue humanity from all ills and in it you too have the only method of saving your people from enslavement. Love and forcible resistance to evil-doers involve such a mutual contradiction as to destroy utterly the whole sense and meaning of the conception of love.'[29]

Compared to the influence of the Bible and Tolstoy, Thoreau's influence on Gandhi in the development of his non-violent techniques of civil disobedience and passive resistance was less significant. According to Gandhi he came across Thoreau's *Essay on Civil Disobedience* after he had already embarked on the programme of non-violent resistance to unjust authority in South Africa. It was largely under the influence of the Bible and Tolstoy that Gandhi launched his programme of non-violent resistance. In fact, Gandhi told Rev. Doke that it was the New Testament, especially the Sermon on the Mount, which really awakened him to the rightness and the value of *satyāgraha*. The *Gītā* deepened the impression, and Tolstoy's *The Kingdom of God* gave it a permanent form. However, Gandhi borrowed Thoreau's phrase 'Civil Disobedience' to explain his struggle to English readers. Later Gandhi abandoned the phrase for the indigenous term *satyāgraha*. Nevertheless, Thoreau did exert some influence in the direction of perfecting the technique of resistance.

It is, therefore, clear that for his theory and practice of active non-violence Gandhi was heavily indebted to the West. Early British writers, like Underwood and Heiler, argued that since Hinduism was a passive religion which merely stressed non-injury to others, Gandhi's ideal of active benevolence and voluntary suffering for the sake of other people owed nothing to Hindu thought, and that his ideal was distinctly Christian. This view is patently unsound because Hinduism did preach *ahimsā* even in the sense of active love long before Christ.[30] But there should be little hesitation in admitting that among the influences that moulded Gandhi's philosophy the impact of the Bible was particularly profound and crucial. Gandhi's early upbringing in a *vaisnava* family and exposure to the pacific teachings of Jainism and Buddhism imbued him with the spirit of *ahimsā*, but it was largely the influence of the Bible and Tolstoy that transformed him into the greatest apostle of non-violence. According to Gandhi, he had not read the *Gītā* until his second year as a law student in England. His interpretation of the *Gītā* has been disputed by scholars; in any case, his commitment to non-violence took place before he could read the *Gītā* in its original Sanskrit version.

The aim of this paper has been to trace the western influences on Gandhi's philosophy and to indicate that Gandhi's ideas do not owe exclusive inspiration to Indian sources, beliefs and traditions. At the same time, nothing would explain the immense popularity of the Gandhian philosophy with the Indian masses other than the fact that its teachings strike an instinctive chord in every Indian. It would, therefore, be an exaggeration to maintain, as some scholars have done, that if one takes away from Gandhism its Indian background, what remains is merely a compound of Ruskin and Tolstoy.

NOTES

[1] See Adi H. Doctor, *Anarchist Thought in India* (Bombay, 1964).

[2] K. G. Mashruwala, *Gandhi and Marx* (Ahmedabad, 1960).

[3] Cited in Kalidas Nag, *Tolstoy and Gandhi* (Patna, 1950), p. 34.

[4] *Ibid.*, p. 27.

[5] *The Living Thoughts of Tolstoy*, presented by Stefan Zweig (Fawcett Publications, Greenwich), p. 74.

[6] *Ibid.*, p. 7.

[7] See Leo Tolstoy, *The Kingdom of God and Peace Essays* (World's Classics, O.U.P., 1951), pp. 214-20.

[8] The letter is reproduced in the Appendix of Kalidas Nag, *Tolstoy and Gandhi*, op. cit.

[9] M. K. Gandhi, *Hind Swaraj* (Ahmedabad, 1958).

[10] See *Young India*, 29 January 1925; also the issue of 15 December 1921, and 18 March 1919.

[11] *Young India*, 8 December 1921.

[12] H. D. Thoreau, 'Essay on Civil Disobedience', in *Selected Writings on Nature and Liberty* (New York, 1952), p. 10.

[13] *Young India*, 2 July 1932.

[14] 'Unto This Last' in the *Complete Works of John Ruskin*, ed. by Cook and Wedderburn (London, 1905), vol. 17.

[15] Harijan, 25 March 1939.

[16] Pyarelal, *The Last Phase* (Ahmedabad, 1956), vol. 2, p. 602.

[17] Louis Fischer (ed.), *The Essential Gandhi* (New York, 1963), p. 68.

[18] See Adi H. Doctor, *Sarvodaya* (Bombay, 1967), pp. 104-05.

[19] *Harijan*, 1 September 1946.

[20] Louis Fischer, *Gandhi, His Life and Message for the World* (New York, 1962), p. 14.

[21] See Gandhi, *From Yeravda Mandir* (Ahmedabad, 1957), ch. 9.

[22] See Stefan Zweig's Introduction to *The Living Thoughts of Tolstoy*.

[23] Cited in Kalidas Nag, op. cit., pp. 39-40.

[24] *Complete Works of John Ruskin*, vol. 17, op. cit., p. 112.

[25] H. D. Thoreau, op. cit., pp. 21-22.

[26] Cited in Fischer, *Gandhi*, op. cit., p. 15.

[27] *The Collected Works of Mahatma Gandhi* (Government of India Publication Division, Delhi), vol. 7, p. 119.

[28] Louis Fischer, *The Essential Gandhi*, p. 206.

[29] Kalidas Nag, op. cit., p. 92.

[30] One has only to remember the teachings of Jainism, Buddhism, and the *Upanishads*. *Chaitanyadeva*, the apostle of Vaishnavism, when struck by a ruffian exclaimed, 'But I shall offer you my love'.

GANDHI AND TILAK: A STUDY IN ALTERNATIVES

J. C. Masselos

On the night of Tilak's death, on 31 July 1920, Gandhi admitted to his secretary and confidant, Mahadev Desai, his feelings of loss and loneliness:

> To whom shall I go for advice now in moments of difficulty? And when the time comes to seek help from the whole of Maharashtra, to whom shall I turn? . . . it is up to me to keep Lokamanya's slogan [of Swaraj] alive and effective, it must not be allowed to sink into silence.[1]

The two had had much in common: both were leaders of men, working towards an ideal of a self-governing India. But vital differences existed in their concepts and techniques, and in their utilisation of the opportunities provided by their environment. Although it is often unproductive to indulge in contrasts and comparisons between personalities and the processes of which they were part, the method can be of value in providing an insight into their nature and function. An analysis of the parts played by Tilak and Gandhi in the second decade of the twentieth century, a period when their paths crossed, serves to highlight the basic divergences inherent in their political styles. They represent alternative courses of political action and appeal and they represent, moreover, alternative political phenomena. Although both possessed strong regional bases and strong identification with regional stereotypes, one remained bound by these factors and depended for all-India political authority upon co-operation with similarly based leaders elsewhere while the other transcended them to achieve all-India authority and a phenomenal popularity hitherto unknown in the country.

I

The ideas and behaviour of both men reflected stereotypes familiar to, and acceptable by, their region of origin. Each epitomised the local values of his area. However, while Tilak's image was less acceptable outside Maharashtra, except in the limited terms of a nationalist ideal of the dedicated patriot, Gandhi's was easily identifiable with an India-wide code of common cultural values, an association which reinforced his purely political appeal.

Tilak, militant, aggressive, the leader *par excellence*, was a man for whom the reality of politics was paramount.[2] This had been manifested in his emphasis upon agitation against alien rule, an agitation which he had actively pursued in his writings and speeches in Marathi and in the public and political turn he had given to the regional religious festival of *Ganpati* and to the celebration he had developed around the area's major historical figure, Shivaji. The same tendency had led to his association at the beginning of the twentieth century with the boycott and *swadeshi* movements and to the coining of that potent slogan: '*swaraj* [literally "self-rule"] is my birthright and I will have it'.

Tilak epitomised the *brahmanical* high tradition of Maharashtra as it had evolved over the preceding two centuries during the Maratha Confederation. The stereotype was a dual one. Culturally, it required tacit acceptance of, and certainly not public opposition to, the orthodox *brahmanical* codes of behaviour relating to social relationship and religious ritual and, positively, it enjoined features such as learning and scholarship in the religious, Sanskrit texts. These features Tilak had displayed in his acceptance of caste control in the 1890s and in his championing of the conservative position in social reform controversies whilst his study of the *Vedas* had earned him a respected position as a thinker and a scholar, but one working within the untainted confines of Hinduism.

The second aspect of the stereotype, a militant, political one, is less easy to define. It had emerged during the eighteenth century when *brahmans*, especially the *Chitpavan brahmans* to which group Tilak belonged, had assumed almost exclusive political and administrative control of the Maratha Confederation. They were men of the world, sometimes warriors as well as administrators and upholders of socio-religious values of the state; they were dynamic and activist, expert in manipulating the machine of the state. In the changed circumstances of British Maharashtra, Tilak in consolidating opposition to the new rulers performed a similar function of leadership initially amongst his own high caste community and subsequently to a broader and deeper spectrum of Marathi society.[3] There were of course challenges to his position; his leadership in Poona and the Deccan was not undisputed at several levels. Nonetheless this does not disprove the potency of his association with a high tradition in Maharashtra, nor equally the potency which his corporate image had come to assume by about 1915, particularly in this area.

Gandhi, on the other hand, epitomised a different regional tradition and a different set of values.[4] A Gujarati, a *bānia*, he possessed the frugality and simple, non-ostentatious, style of living characteristic of the *vaishya varna* in his region. But his vows of celibacy and poverty took him outside the range of this stereotype, where frugality was considered as merely the prerequisite for the acquisition and deployment of financial resources. With Gandhi the ends were ultimately ethical and religious and his mode of life, and the stated aims of his unique methods of political action, reflected this. Thus Gandhi fitted more easily into the mould of the ascetic, the *sādhu* or holy man, a mould which, it must be noted, he always took great pains to reject.[5] Yet these denials serve to indicate the extent to which he was identified with it. Thus in 1919, in celebration of his fiftieth birthday, a Gujarati poet, Nanalal D. Kavi, sang of the ascetic of Gujarat in the following, not especially mellifluous terms:

> Truth is his motto,
> Asceticism is his armour,
> His banner is of Brahmacharya, his saints' bowl,
> Inexhaustible waters of forgiveness are in,
> His skin is of forbearance,
> An heir to the Yoga of the eternal Yogi family,
> Above storm-winds of passions,
> The great living teacher of Bharata,
> He is the ascetic of Gujarat,
> The great-souled Mohandas Gandhi.[6]

The significance of this stereotype with which Gandhi was associated lay in the fact that, on the one hand, it represented to a considerable extent the values of simplicity and asceticism inherent in the high tradition of Gujarat, itself an amalgam of Jainist, Vaishnavite, and philosophical codes, and, on the other, it conformed to an India-wide high tradition of austerity and renunciation. No matter what their specific origin, Gandhi's mode of life and spiritual code were easily assimilable into familiar patterns, and the man himself could therefore be reverenced accordingly. The coin was familiar and could be valid throughout the realm once it achieved adequate circulation.

Although for purposes of analysis Gandhi in one sense can be type-cast in the ascetic mould, he and his ideas went beyond the rigid confines of any single stereotype. Unlike the traditional *sādhu* whose *sine qua non* was withdrawal from mundane activities, meditation upon metaphysical matters and perhaps discoursing on these subjects, Gandhi accepted the reality of daily affairs. In his scheme of things, no distinction was made between religion and worldly pursuits: both were coeval; what could not be pursued in day-to-day practice could not be called religion. Gandhi's views on this are best seen in his interpretation of the *Bhagavad Gītā*.[7] For Gandhi all living things, by their very nature, perform actions. The taint of, and therefore bondage to, action, can be counteracted by avoiding any desire for its fruits and rewards. Tasks must be performed to achieve their fulfilment and proper results, results being distinct from rewards. But neither result nor reward must be desired and, as he pointed out, when there was no desire for fruit, there was no temptation for untruth. Gandhi concluded that 'after forty years' unremitting endeavour fully to enforce the teaching of the *Gītā* in my own life, I have, in all humility, felt that perfect renunciation is impossible without perfect observance of *ahimsā* in every shape and form'.[8]

Thus Gandhi saw in the *Gītā* not a literal warrant for violence as some of his critics interpreted it but a philosophy of restraint, non-violence and truth. The corollary to his interpretation lay in his attitude towards politics: since the performance of action was inescapable, action must be undertaken with the ultimate ethical ends clearly in view; it was the duty of the individual to involve himself in the affairs of men and therefore in politics, but this activity must be performed through as near as possible perfect non-violence in order to achieve the desired ends of truth and salvation. Politics, therefore, and religion were inextricably inter-connected: religion must permeate political activity and conversely this very activity must be based upon sound ethical values: 'I do not believe that religion has nothing to do with politics. The latter, divorced from religion, is like a corpse only fit to be buried.'[9]

Apart from the central role that the *Gītā* had assumed as the embodiment of the evolution of Gandhi's thought, it also assumed importance as one of the more significant religious elements in his attempts to rally popular support behind him in his various campaigns. It is belabouring the obvious to emphasise the reverence for, and popularity of, the *Gītā* throughout India; in constantly referring to it in his speeches and writings, Gandhi was able to establish immediately a common and familiar frame of reference with his Hindu audience and hence to take the first step towards gaining acceptance of his own particular methods and views, again often expressed in terms of the *Gītā*. He adopted a similar technique with regard to the Muslims by talking in terms of the *Koran* but in this he was ultimately less successful, the *Koran* being less amenable to interpretation along Gandhian lines.

In addition, Gandhi utilised the *Gītā* in justifying the application of non-violence to the nationalist agitation. His analysis of the political scene in India after his return in 1915 led him to believe that the doctrine of 'tit for tat', i.e., violence, was proving increasingly attractive to the younger generation, especially to students, graduates and the more youthful members of the Indian middle class generally. Hence he considered that part at least of his task was to counteract this India-wide trend and to wean its proponents away from the doctrines of physical and non-physical violence.[10] He marshalled together his conclusions regarding the *Gītā* and his interpretation of the basis of the ancient civilization of India from which he claimed it derived, and utilised these as part of his armoury of persuasion. A specific and limited example of this can be cited in his preparation for the Bombay *hartāl* over the deportation of Benjamin Horniman, editor of the *Bombay Chronicle* and strong advocate for Indian home rule. Considerable doubt existed as to whether the *hartāl* would be non-violent after the disturbances following on the Rowlatt *satyāgraha* and Gandhi's arrest the previous month in April 1919. Consequently he issued a large number of leaflets putting forward his ethical position and justified its wide acceptance by the traditions of Indian spirituality and referred specifically in some leaflets to the *Gītā*.[11]

For Gandhi, then, the *Gītā* fulfilled a number of functions: it served as the summation of his ethical thinking but it also provided a common symbol between himself and a wider Indian audience, a symbol through which he could urge acceptance for his own doctrines and maintain the authority of, and support for, his techniques. His interpretation however was not unchallenged. It was attacked by leading moderates in 1919 and 1920 who opposed his techniques of non-violence on other grounds also. They maintained that the *Gītā* could not be interpreted in any way other than the purely literal, as a warrant for the employment of violence, and felt that its use in political agitation was a double-edged weapon which would rebound on its user.[12] In a different manner, Tilak's interpretation, despite considerable similarities, also ran counter to the tenor of Gandhi's views.

Tilak had systematised his thinking on the work during 1910-11 whilst serving his gaol sentence in Mandalay although he maintained that the finished product, *Gītā Rahasya*, represented views that he had held for at least twenty years.[13] He saw the *Gītā* as an ethical not an intuitional or mystical tract, his analysis being influenced by British ethical philosophers such as Mill, Spencer, Green, Sidgwick and others.[14]

His interpretation, like Gandhi's, emphasised that no distinction could exist between the world of daily affairs and of religion: even after an individual had achieved salvation through the paths of knowledge and devotion he remained within the realm of the mundane and had of necessity to perform action. Since the *Gītā* was preached to Arjuna for the purpose of exhorting him to action, this then was its primary message. Tilak emphasised: 'In order that the action may not bind the actor it must be done with the aim of helping [the Creator's] purpose, and without any attachment to the coming result. . . . If man seeks unity with the Deity, he must necessarily seek unity with the interests of the world also, and work for it. If he does not, then the unity is not perfect.'[15] The terminology and concepts are similar to those of Gandhi who admitted the influence of Tilak's interpretation[16] which in turn lay within the mainstream of the activist view of the work imposed upon Maharashtra by the *bhakti* saint, Dnyaneshvar, in the thirteenth century.[17]

Gandhi and Tilak however diverged over the implications to be drawn from a common acceptance of the doctrine of disinterested action. While for Gandhi truth and *ahimsā* were the highest ideals to be pursued above all else without deviation, for Tilak the ideal of action was *lokasangraha*, the promotion of the stability and solidarity of society. Social duties thus had a spiritual content within a non-dualist concept of metaphysics. Ethically, if the ends were good, then the means could not be bad. Although Tilak denied that his theory sanctioned the use of falsehood, for example against political opponents, he did accept that modifications of truth were justifiable: 'I have always maintained and do maintain that diplomacy, and not necessarily the whole truth, is expected from a statesman and this view is sanctioned both by Eastern and Western ethical writers.'[18] Similarly, violence could conform to the highest ideals of disinterested action. Like Gandhi, Tilak spoke occasionally of the pristine purity of an ancient India, a purity defiled through the ages, but Tilak accepted the revolutionary overtones inherent in the Vaishnavite theory of *avatārs* in which God incarnated himself on earth in order to destroy evil-doers and re-establish the supremacy of moral law. Thus the absolute values of *satya* and *ahimsā* which Gandhi read into the *Gītā* were denied by Tilak who put forward a more militant and aggressive view, one that was not bound by absolute spiritual ideals.[19]

Both men were devoted to politics and of both it was maintained that they applied the lessons of unselfish sacrifice embodied in the *Gītā* to their own practical politics. But, if, as it was pointed out at the time of his death, 'Politics to Tilak was his religion'[20] for Gandhi, religion was politics, the two being inextricably interconnected. Whereas for Tilak politics comprised very much the fibre of his existence, for Gandhi it comprised only a portion of his activity. Tilak had fought his battles with the social reformers in the 1890's over the issue that political progress must be paramount over other considerations of national regeneration along social, economic and even religious lines, a view that he continued to urge after his release from gaol in 1914. Gandhi, on the other hand, refused to devote himself entirely to politics in any conventional sense of the term. Issues of social reform and equality were crucial to his view of politics and he bound these together into the framework of his agitations, thereby arousing some opposition but at the same time gaining the adherence of a wider strata of the population than had been achieved previously. It was not till 1920 when he accepted the presidency of the Home Rule League that he first associated himself with an unequivocally political organisation: till that time his organisations had always been many-faceted in their approach. He even justified his membership of the Indian National Congress by claiming that it was not distinctly a political party but rather a platform or parliament for a number of different groups and policies.[21] Even this body, after he assumed control over it in 1920, altered its orientations to encompass specifically social and economic issues. It was as much this changed orientation as his personal image and the culminating of social processes in the politicisation of large lower caste clusters that accounted for the success with which Congress was able to associate new social groups (the wealthier peasantry, for example) into its body corporate in the 1920s and 1930s.

II

While Gandhi and Tilak diverged in their reading of the ethics involved in political action as well as in the image each projected, their positions in the current political scene of 1915 were equally varied. The methods with which each coped with the situation provide part at least of the explanation for Gandhi's greater success in marshalling support for himself and his policies.

Tilak had been released from gaol on 16 June 1914 after serving slightly under six years' simple imprisonment on the charge of sedition. He was then fifty-eight, suffering from diabetes and feeling his age: 'The ebb of life has set in and it is only with great care and self-restraint in diet that I have been able to keep up appearances of health.'[22]

Nonetheless he had retained his hold upon the popular affection. That he was still the *Lokamānya* ('revered by the people') was emphasised by the welcome he received when news of his release became known: the aura of Tilak *Mahārāj* was still potent within Marahashtra. At the all-India level, the prestige which his name had acquired in the years before his arrest, 1908, had been enhanced, even amongst his political rivals, by a prosecution and imprisonment which Lord Morley, Secretary of State for India, had privately characterised 'a grievous error'.[23]

But the authority as distinct from the prestige wielded by Tilak's *gadi* was more limited. Its effectiveness, and hence his manoeuvrability, was restricted by the lingering consequences of past controversies. In no sense had his six years enforced absence provided him with a clean slate upon which to work. The belligerence of his propaganda, the militancy with which he had demanded *swarāj* and the aggressiveness of his opposition to the administrative fiats of the British had previously gained him a large popular following and leadership of a core of politically activated young and not so young Maharashtrians. His 'new' or 'extremist' party had split the Indian National Congress, subsequently seceded from it and, during his imprisonment, had floundered leaderless, without direction or any significant organisation through which to further its ends. Tilak's support, largely Marathi-speaking in composition, was reconfirmed on his release but the moderate-extremist split remained a fixture in the internal politics of Western India, bolstered by the strong opposition of the leading moderate, Sir Pherozeshah Mehta, to any compromise. Hence Tilak in 1914 was denied access to the major political organisation in the country, the Indian National Congress, and to the influence and authority which corporately it was able to wield. Paradoxically, although his prestige at this time was considerable, surpassing that of any other Indian, his authority, nonetheless, was largely limited to Western India and to Maharashtrians. Hence, as he himself pointed out in his first public speech after his release, his course of action in these circumstances was not immediately apparent.[24]

Some six months after Tilak's release, on 9 January 1915, M. K. Gandhi returned to India. He was not yet the *Mahātmā* although the successful application of his novel techniques of political action to the South African situation, combined with his association with Gokhale and other Indian leaders in the later stages of negotiation and fund-raising, had earned him some fame within India. Hence the warmth of the welcome on his arrival in Bombay.[25]

At the time, Gandhi was well-known in those areas from which the South African Indians had originated, particularly Western India. This appeal was reinforced by emotional factors in Gujarat, his home region. Gujarat had not previously produced a major public figure; now it had Gandhi and Gujaratis expected much from him. Equally expectant was a younger generation of politically conscious and active Indians who were attracted by the unconventionality and anti-government tenor of his methods and even more by their demonstrable results. Institutionally, Gandhi, as a 'disciple' of Gokhale, possessed access to the major political body of the period, the Indian National Congress, and had earlier gained strong support from it during his South African campaigns. Again, through his connections with Gokhale he was associated with the moderate division of politics and was expected to associate himself with the Servants of India Society, Gokhale's special instrument for effecting social and political change. Nonetheless, his ties with the Moderates were not such as to mark him indelibly as exclusively of their persuasion. Not having previously undertaken political work in India he had neither aroused an opposition into existence nor built-up a following for himself in his own right; likewise he had avoided involvement in the acerbities of the Surat split and its aftermath whilst, when drumming up support for his own external campaigns, his appeal had been as broadly based as possible, avoiding the dangers of appealing to communal sentiments. Moderates and extremists, Muslims and Hindus equally supported his work.[26]

Thus in 1915 there was much potential for Gandhi to capitalise upon. Although he lacked any real authority or significant influence upon men or organisations in India, he possessed some, albeit limited, prestige and fame. This cut across political groupings and, despite the security of a reservoir of support in his home area, possessed all-India potential. In contrast, Tilak's potential range of authority was largely restricted by the moderate-extremist controversy while the heights of his popularity were contained within his own region.

Gandhi's initial reaction to the India which he had come to serve was to refrain from active 'politicking' and on the advice of Gokhale to spend a year in observation and preparation. He seems to have doubted the extent to which his technique of *satyāgraha* could be applied to the Indian context and he required time to establish an *āshram* and gather around him a band of followers willing to subject themselves to the almost Jesuitical strictness required.[27]

Meanwhile he continued to dissociate himself from either of the two political groups. Although his ties were closest with the moderates due to his close connection with Gokhale, these ties diminished after Gokhale's death in February 1915 when Gandhi finally took the decision not to join the Servants of India Society after strong opposition had developed within it to what was considered to be his somewhat *outré* fads and political ideas.[28] Although relationships remained equable, leading moderates tended to regard him with suspicion as possessing extremist leanings. Concurrently, feelers were put out by extremists to gain his support and inclusion within their framework.[29] These likewise came to nought. Gandhi maintained his position as a man of no party while nonetheless participating, through attendance, in functions organised by both groups and acting in one or two instances as unsuccessful mediator between the two.[30]

Although Gandhi had returned to India with the intention of devoting himself to its welfare as a whole, he had interpreted this specifically in terms of the uplift of Gujarat which at the time was considered as politically a somewhat backward province.[31] Hence he established his *āshram* in the region; likewise he encouraged activities aimed at promoting Gujarat's sense of identity, culturally, linguistically and politically. He actively promoted the first Gujarat Political Conference at Godhra and strongly associated himself with the Second Gujarat Educational Conference at Broach. His activities coincided with a political and cultural awakening that was occurring amongst the Gujarati population at the time: his work aided and subsequently continued a process that had already commenced.[32]

Concurrently he was establishing his links with the power *élite* in the area: the wealthy industrialists and merchants and the politically vocal younger generation of the middle class. Initially the process was one merely of furthering ties that had already been forged during his South African campaigns and extending their framework to cover his further activities in India. Gandhi was fully aware of the significance which wealth possessed in political agitation; it provided the sinews of war. He was equally aware of the influence which the wealthy of Gujarat wielded and was desirous of ensuring their support, a support which on the whole he was able to attract, as much through his image of sanctity as through the political ends for which he worked.[33] With regard to the younger generation, Gandhi's charm initially failed him. He arrived in India possessed of their goodwill but this was quickly dissipated on first contact. In public and in private he seemed too pedestrian, too plodding and lacking far too much in dynamism to provide the new kind of leadership which this generation desired. It was to take a couple of years and a number of successful *satyāgraha* campaigns scattered throughout the country before his methods and personal qualities were to have their full impact.[34]

Thus by the end of Gandhi's second year in India, he still remained largely an unknown quantity. Lacking any large personal following or accepted position in any political grouping he had nonetheless begun to establish for himself a strong regional basis through the minutiæ of his public activity in the area; and by means of his India-wide tours he had maintained himself in the public eye. Although in the context of respectable contemporary Indian political thought Gandhi's techniques were revolutionary in their acceptance of the idea of breaking of laws, his continued emphasis upon unswerving loyalty to the Empire and his support of the war effort, tended nonetheless to classify him as somewhat conservative.

On the other hand, the logic of Tilak's position during this period was such that it was initially necessary for him to reaffirm his loyalty to the Empire and his acceptance of constitutional reforms in terms that sounded as if the lion of Maharashtra had been finally tamed.[35] Perhaps the years of imprisonment had mellowed him and rendered him cautious but perhaps the explanation lay more in a desire to open a path for unity talks with the moderates. These did in fact follow on the appearance of his first major article in the *Mahratta* after his release but they foundered and it was not until after Pherozeshah Mehta's death at the end of 1915 that Tilak and his party were re-admitted to the Congress under a compromise agreement.

Concurrently, Tilak had been active in restoring his position within Maharashtra by means that had been earlier utilised, through the press and through speeches at conferences and other public gatherings. In addition, in 1915-16, he undertook a campaign to revive long moribund local political bodies, *zillā* and *tālukā sabhās*, in order to gain their representation on, and hence the support of a large body of adherents in, the Congress.[36]

The lingering consequences of the Surat split was thus in part largely responsible for the concentration of Tilak's activities upon re-establishing his authority within his home base. The same trend was continued after the formation of two Home Rule Leagues, one by Tilak, the other by Annie Besant, the fiery theosophical leader who rocketed to political fame during the First World War. The Leagues possessed the single objective of working for Home Rule or self-government within the Empire. They were belligerent and militant in their approach, so much so that they remained distinct entities from the Congress although membership was usually coeval. Their aim was to achieve the widest possible acceptance of the doctrine of Home Rule on the basis of a programme of mass contact and propaganda.[37]

However, while Mrs Besant's League established branches throughout India, Tilak, by agreement, limited his League to Marathi-speaking areas. Branches were created throughout the region and here, on their basis, Tilak's political authority became undisputed, the only significant challenge having been removed with the death of Gokhale in 1915, the other major Marathi public figure and his leading political opponent. Thus, by about 1918, Tilak largely controlled the public life of Maharashtra, whose ethos he in many ways so uncannily reflected. He had gained access to the Congress where his influence was considerable, due both to the forcefulness of his own personality, and to the large body of supporters in the organisation and his powerful regional support. Moreover, his association with Mrs Besant had provided him with a platform, in the form of the various branches of her League scattered throughout the country, on which to speak. These speeches had heightened his nationwide popularity, a popularity which attained unprecedented proportions. If his prestige was great and his influence consequently considerable, his authority at the all-India level in the decision-making circles of Congress remained nonetheless limited and depended for its success upon his ability to obtain co-operation and unity from other India-wide but regionally based leaders and especially from C. R. Das in Bengal.

It was at this stage that Tilak withdrew from the Indian scene in order to undertake Home Rule propaganda in England and to fight unsuccessfully a libel case against Valentine Chirol, author of *Indian Unrest*. By the time of his return in November 1919, Gandhi had established himself as a figure of undisputed major proportions. His *satyāgraha* campaigns in Champaran, Kheda and Ahmedabad had proved that his methods were applicable to the Indian context; they had created a strong impression upon public opinion throughout the country and had gained him support from regions outside his home base and from amongst the radically inclined youth of the country. The trend had been confirmed in April 1919 when Gandhi had mounted, in his Rowlatt *satyāgraha,* his first major assault against the government as a whole, the previous campaigns having been limited both in scope and in the nature of their opposition to limited grievances and limited administrative fiats. But even in the Rowlatt *satyāgraha,* despite its India-wide connotations, support had been greatest in the Punjab, in Delhi and in Gujarat. In Bombay City the backbone of the movement had derived from Gujaratis and some middle-class Marathis: the bulk of the Marathi population had not given to Gandhi the adherence that might perhaps have been expected.[38]

The Rowlatt *satyāgraha* was significant in highlighting the increased stature and wide support that Gandhi had earned. It was equally significant in emphasising that there were areas in which his writ did not hold. In no area was this more so than in the Marathi-speaking portions of Bombay Presidency. Observers such as Edward Thompson have pointed out that Marathis were on the whole disinclined to follow the *Mahātmā* as much for reasons of regional jealousies as any other.[39] Therein lay a multitude of other differences: regional traditions, as has been pointed out, differed and the non-violence of Gandhian techniques seemed a far cry from the militant tradition which Tilak had espoused. While Tilak was alive Gandhi was unable to obtain a toehold in Maharashtra in the face of the *Lokamānya's* existing popularity and strong organisational backing. Of course, in individual instances, Gandhi was able to overcome the prejudices against his techniques and the tradition which these represented (the case of Kaka Kalelkar is a prime example of this ability).[40] There was moreover a body of opinion emerging even in Maharashtra prepared to accept Gandhi by reason of his very dynamism: what Tilak was doing in words, Gandhi was putting into action.[41] Nonetheless such opinion seems to have remained limited during Tilak's lifetime and for some time afterwards.

Gandhi was aware of the limitations of his appeal in Maharashtra but he hoped gradually to have his views accepted in preference to the 'tit-for-tat' cult of which Tilak was the apostle.[42] At the same time Gandhi could not move effectively in the area without Tilak's approval, if not active support. In 1920, Gandhi was gathering his forces together to launch the largest and most significant movement of his career up to that time. To ensure maximum effect for this first non-co-operation campaign, tacit co-operation from Maharashtra was essential. Yet there was no inevitability as to what attitude Tilak would assume.

Relations between the two men had been complex. Not only were their basic concepts implicitly divergent but the differences between them were admitted and explicit. They engaged in public argument over interpretations of the *Gītā;* they publicly pointed to their differences over techniques whilst Gandhi had expressed his dislike of the tenor of the Home Rule Movement for its potential of embarrassing the Government whilst it was fighting a war.[43] In masterly understatement, an anonymous C.I.D. officer observed that 'Gandhi and Tilak have never quite hit it off as to the best methods of political propaganda'.[44]

Yet common political goals and mutual respect for each other's dedication and influence provided a basis for joint effort. Some precedents for co-operation had already been established in the preceding years. Tilak, for example, had associated himself with Gandhi on the platform of the First Gujarat Political Conference and, in 1919, from England had urged his followers to support the Mahatma. Likewise, Gandhi had associated himself with the public meetings called in protest against the treatment of Tilak at the Provincial War Conference in June 1918 by the Governor of Bombay, Lord Willingdon, and later, in June 1919, had honoured Tilak's services to the country and helped to raise funds for a Tilak Purse.[45]

Yet their responses to the immediate political situation continued to be antagonistic. This was clearly evident at the Amritsar gathering of Congress in December 1919. The atmosphere of the meeting was highly emotional and tense with the memory of the recent British massacre at Jallianwala Bagh and of their atrocities elsewhere in the Punjab. Against this background Gandhi and Tilak differed over the appropriate course of action for Congress to adopt in response to the King's Proclamation and the Reforms generally. Both were dissatisfied with what had been offered but whereas Gandhi urged outright acceptance and sincerity in working the scheme, Tilak offered responsive co-operation, an offer which seems to have envisaged participation in the reformed constitutional framework but also obstruction from within it in order to obtain further concessions. There was in addition a third, but limited, body of opinion that championed rejection of the scheme in its entirety.

Ultimately compromise was achieved but not before Gandhi had accused Tilak, according to one report of the Subjects Committee meeting, of moral turpitude and lack of truth in his acceptance of the scheme. To which Tilak replied: 'My friend! Truth has no place in politics.'[46] The different ethical viewpoints of the two men had surfaced and conflicted as had their varying styles of strategy. Significantly enough it was a gesture from Gandhi in the open session of the Congress that finally brought Tilak to accept a compromise formula: the gesture was a dramatic one, that of tossing his cap at Tilak's feet in token obeisance. This Tilak could not deny, especially in a public gathering, and he accepted the formula provided that C. R. Das of Bengal also agreed. Thus was compromise attained and likewise, thus, was Gandhi's position as one of the three or four principal leaders in the country confirmed within the power hierarchy of the Congress.[47]

During 1920 relations between the two men continued to fluctuate as did their responses to a rapidly changing political environment. Public emotions reached a high pitch as the full extent of the Punjab atrocities became widely known. A similar reaction occurred in Gandhi as his work on the Congress Sub-committee of Enquiry into Punjab affairs finally convinced him of the hollowness of the government's sincerity and morality. His speeches and writings acquired a belligerent tone hitherto lacking and one imbued with strong moral indignation:

> The present Government is immoral, unjust and arrogant beyond description. It defends one lie with other lies. It does most things under a threat of force. If the people tolerate all these things and do nothing, they will never progress.[48]

With the signing of the Treaty of Sèvres, Muslim grievances finally came to a head, again against a background of British duplicity and broken pledges. In the context of Gandhi's loss of faith in the Government, any debate over constitutional reforms must assume a secondary place if it were not in fact totally meaningless. Gandhi's focus of attention altered to encompass direct action against the Government. He began to prepare for *satyāgraha* and during the first six months of 1920 absorbed the grievances of the Rowlatt Act, the Punjab atrocities, Turkey and the Khilafat, and, finally, *swarāj*, as issues in his proposed movement. He thus widened the base of his appeal to encompass most elements of dissatisfaction in the country.

In preparing for what was to become the first non-co-operation campaign, Gandhi utilised such institutional means of ensuring maximum support as were available to him. Through his earlier preaching of Hindu-Muslim unity, through his earlier work on the Khilafat Committees and his association with Muslim 'martyrs' such as the Ali brothers, he had established some degree of influence within, and had laid down efficient lines of communication between himself and the Muslim community. His specific regional authority in Gujarat and his control over the Gujarat Congress Committee enabled him to gain its adherence to the proposed campaign and provided him with a tactical advantage in attempting to convert Congress as a whole to his method of activity. In addition, he accepted in April the Presidentship of Annie Besant's Home Rule League after her resignation and this likewise provided him with an organisational base upon which to appeal to the politically active throughout the country. This significantly extended his area of authority and reinforced his wide prestige.

In Maharashtra, however, Gandhi could do little without Tilak. In May he attempted to gain his support over the Khilafat issue and did gain some assurances to this effect.[49] With regard to non-co-operation, Gandhi claimed that Tilak stated he would not oppose it:

> I like the programme well enough, but I have my doubts as to the country being with us in the self-denying ordinance which non-co-operation presents to the people. I will do nothing to hinder the progress of the non-co-operation movement. I wish you every success, and if you gain the popular ear you will find in me an enthusiastic supporter.[50]

Yet Tilak's options remained open. In concentrating upon promoting his policy of responsive co-operation and of council entry the trend of his activities, if not his statements, was opposed to Gandhi's campaign. Thus, in April, he established a Congress Democratic Party, based in Maharashtra, and issued a manifesto which he hoped would be accepted by Congress at its next meeting. In this sense, his tactics differed little from those employed by Gandhi in utilising the Gujarat Congress Committee for much the same purpose. Gandhi, however, had reinforced the effectiveness of this technique by both capturing and creating extra-Congress organisational support, something that Tilak had not achieved. Similarly, Gandhi now possessed pockets of direct influence throughout India and was not limited merely to his home base. Nonetheless, it was only with considerable difficulty that he was finally able to gain acceptance for his program of direct, if non-violent, action by Congress in September and December 1920. He had in any case initiated *satyāgraha* on his own, through the organisations he controlled, some months earlier, on 1 August.

On the day before this occurred, Tilak died. And the first day of *satyāgraha* was converted into a day of mourning. Yet the question of his support for non-co-operation had not been definitely settled and the issue remained open. His followers in the 1920s were to pursue political paths antagonistic to Gandhi whilst the Maharastrian urban intelligentsia continued to disdain Gandhi's image and methods. Not until the 1930s was Congress in the region resuscitated along Gandhian lines and a rich middle-class peasantry persuaded to join its ranks.[51]

Despite differences in outlook, methods and ultimate ideals, Gandhi respected Tilak for what he had achieved and his feeling obituary for the man emphasises the cult-like attachment that had surrounded his life:

> No man of our times had the hold on the masses that Mr Tilak had. The devotion that he commanded from thousands of his countrymen was extraordinary. He was unquestionably the idol of his people. . . . No man preached the gospel of swaraj with the consistency and the insistence of Lokamanya. His countrymen therefore implicitly believed in him. . . . It is blasphemy to talk of such a man as dead. . . .[52]

NOTES

[1] Kaka Kalelkar, *Stray Glimpses of Bapu* (Ahmedabad, 1950), p. 50.

[2] There are numerous biographies of Tilak. The more significant include: N. C. Kelkar, *Life and Times of Lokamanya Tilak* (translated by D. V. Divekar) (Madras, 1928); D. V. Athalye, *The Life of Lokamanya Tilak* (Poona, 1921); D. V. Tahmankar, *Lokamanya Tilak, Father of Indian Unrest and Maker of Modern India* (London, 1956); T. L. Shay, *The Legacy of Lokamanya, The Political Philosophy of Bal Gangadhar Tilak* (Bombay, 1956); G. P. Pradhan and A. K. Bhagwat, *Lokamanya Tilak, A Biography* (Bombay, 1959); S. A. Wolpert, *Tilak and Gokhale:Revolution and Reform in the Making of Modern India* (Berkeley and Los Angeles, 1962); I. M. Reisner and N. M. Goldberg (eds.), *Tilak and the Struggle for Indian Freedom* (New Delhi, 1966).

[3] See Aurobindo Ghose, 'Appreciation' in *Bal Gangadhar Tilak. His Writings and Speeches* (Madras, n.d.), pp. xviii-xx.

4 The more significant of the numerous biographies of Gandhi include: B. R. Nanda, *Mahatma Gandhi. A Biography* (London, 1959); D. G. Tendulkar, *Mahatma. Life of Mohandas Karamchand Gandhi* (The Publications Division, Delhi), 8 vols.; G. Ashe, *Gandhi. A Study in Revolution* (London, 1968).

5 'Gujarat's Duty', *Navajivan*, 11 July 1920 in Mahatma Gandhi, *The Collected Works*, vol. 18 [hereafter *CW* 18], (New Delhi, 1965), p. 28.

6 The complete poem in an English translation by its author is reprinted in Government of Maharashtra, *Source Material for a History of the Freedom Movement in India, vol. 3. Mahatma Gandhi, Part 1: 1915-1922* [hereafter *HFM 3, i.*] (Bombay, 1965), pp. 561-67.

7 *Anasaktiyoga*. See Mahadev Desai's translation in *The Gospel of Selfless Action or the Gita According to Gandhi* (Ahmedabad, 1956), pp. 125-386.

8 *Ibid.*, pp. 133-34.

9 Paper read by Gandhi before the Missionary Conference, Madras, 1916, in *Mahatma Gandhi. His life, Writings and Speeches* (Madras, 1921), p. 173.

10 See *inter alia* Gandhi's speeches in Bombay, 14 March 1919 and in Trichinopoly, 25 March 1919, in *ibid.*, pp. 342, *Mahatma Gandhi. The Collected Works, vol. 15* [hereafter *CW 15*], (New Delhi, 1965), pp. 135-36, 176.

11 *HFM 3*, i, pp. 592-613.

12 *Satyagraha* Leaflet No. 18, 8 May 1919 in *ibid.*, pp. 607-08; *Young India*, 4 Aug. 1920; *Navajivan*, 8 Aug. 1920; *Young India*, 25 Aug. 1920 and 1 Sept. 1920 in *CW 18*, pp. 115-16, 125, 195-96, 219.

13 B. G. Tilak to D. V. Vidwans, 2 Mar. 1911 in M. D. Vidwans (ed.), *Letters of Lokamanya Tilak* (Poona, 1966), pp. 101-02; Speech at Amraoti, 1917, *Bal Gangadhar Tilak. His Writings and Speeches*, pp. 258-59.

14 M. D. Vidwans (ed.), op. cit., pp. 101-02, 110.

15 Speech at Amraoti, op. cit., pp. 261-62.

16 Introduction to *Anasaktiyoga*, op. cit., p. 126.

17 S. A. Wolpert, op. cit., p. 260.

18 Tilak to the President, Secretaries and members of the All-India Congress Committee, 16 Apr. 1920 in *All About Lokamanya Tilak* (Madras, 1922), p. 308.

19 Cf. *Ibid.*, pp. 343, 362, 377-81; S. A. Wolpert, op. cit., pp. 261-63; G. P. Pradhan and A. K. Bhagwat, op. cit., pp. 357-64; G. Ashe, op. cit., pp. 133-34.

20 *The Express* cited in *All About Lokamanya Tilak*, p. 51.

21 'To the Members of the All-India Home Rule League', *Young India*, 28 April 1920; *CW 17*, pp. 347-49.

22 B. G. Tilak to D. V. Vidwans, 1 February 1914 in M. D. Vidwans (ed.), op. cit., p. 176. See also pp. 119, 130, 174.

23 Cited in S. A. Wolpert, *Morley and India 1906-1910* (Berkeley and Los Angeles, 1967), p. 118.

24 G. P. Pradhan and A. K. Bhagwat, op. cit., p. 250.

25 D. G. Tendulkar, op. cit., vol. I, p. 157.

26 K. Kalelkar, op. cit., p. 21; I. K. Yajnik, *Gandhi As I Know Him* (Bombay, n.d.), vol. I, pp. 1-3; K. M. Munshi, *I Follow the Mahatma* (Bombay, 1940), pp. 1-3; D. G. Tendulkar, op. cit., pp. 110-68.

27 Weekly Report of Director, Criminal Investigation, 27 July 1915 in National Archives of India, Home Dept., Political, July 1915, 516-519 B, p. 22; *HFM 3, i*, pp. 1-39.

28 Interview with Shri D. V. Ambekar, Servants of India Society, Poona, Sept. 1962;

HFM 3, i, p. 3; K. Kalelkar, op. cit., pp. 12-13; M. K. Gandhi, *An Autobiography. The Story of My Experiments With Truth* (Boston, 1957), pp. 375-76, 385-87.

29 Cf. *HFM 3, i*, pp. 2-3.

30 *HFM 3, i*, pp. 32-33, 40; Gandhi to Tilak, 27 July 1915 in *CW 13*, pp. 121, 174; Tilak to Gandhi, July 1915 in M. D. Vidwans (ed.), op. cit., pp. 265-69.

31 *CW 15*, p. 49; M. K. Gandhi, op. cit., p. 395.

32 I. K. Yajnik, op. cit., pp. 27-29; J. C. Masselos, 'Aspects of Bombay City Politics in 1919' in R. Kumar (ed.), *Essays on the Rowlatt Satyagraha* (forthcoming publication).

33 Cf. for example, T. V. Parvate, *Jamnalal Bajaj (A Brief Study of his Life and Character)* (Ahmedabad, 1962), pp. 14-21.

34 I. K. Yajnik, op. cit., pp. 3-29; Gaganvihari Mehta, 'Meeting Gandhi' in C. Shukla (ed.), *Incidents of Gandhiji's Life* (Bombay, 1949), pp. 180-82; K. M. Munshi, op. cit., pp. 2-7.

35 *Mahratta*, 30 August 1914 cited in G. P. Pradhan and A. K. Bhagwat, op. cit., pp. 250-52.

36 Govt. of Bombay to Govt. of India, 1 June 1916, S.D. 1723 in 'Fortnightly Reports on the internal political situation in special reference to the War received from all provinces' in National Archives of India, Home Dept., Political, June 1916, 26 Deposit, p. 4.

37 See H. F. Owen, 'Towards Nationwide Agitation and Organisation: the Home Rule Leagues, 1915-1918' in D. A. Low (ed.), *Soundings in Modern South Asian History* (Canberra, 1968), pp. 159-95; 'The Home Rule Movement (A short History sketch prepared by the Government of Bombay)' in *HFM*, vol. 2. *1885-1920* (Bombay, 1958), pp. 688-94.

38 J. C. Masselos, op. cit.

39 E. Thompson, 'Gandhi: A Character Study' in S. Radhakrishnan (ed.), *Mahatma Gandhi, Essays and Reflections on his Life and Work* (Allahabad, 1944), p. 303.

40 M. Prasad, *A Gandhian Patriarch. A Political and Spiritual Biography of Kaka Kalelkar* (Bombay, 1965), pp. 68-73, 152, 160-69.

41 *HFM 3, i*, p. 202.

42 *Ibid.*, pp. 172-74; Gandhi to Manasukhlal Raojibhai Mehta, 17 Aug. 1918 in *CW 15*, pp. 25-26; Gandhi to Vinoba Bhave, 24 July 1918, in *CW 14*, p. 501.

43 *CW 15*, pp. 13-14, 261; Tilak to the Editor, *Young India*, 18 January 1920 and Gandhi's 'Comment' in M. D. Vidwans (ed.), op. cit., pp. 284-85; I. K. Yajnik, op. cit., pp. 27-29.

44 *HFM 3, i*, p. 44.

45 *Ibid.*, pp. 53-70, 144-45; *CW 14*, pp. 425-31; Tilak to Dr Sathaye, 15 May 1919 in *Sathaye Papers*, Nehru Memorial Museum and Library.

46 Cited in G. P. Pradhan and A. K. Bhagwat, op. cit., p. 335.

47 For accounts of this Congress session see *inter alia*, B. Pattabhi Sitaramayya, *The History of the Indian National Congress* (1885-1935), (Madras, 1935), pp. 303-11; I. K. Yajnik, op. cit., pp. 95-97; M. K. Gandhi, op. cit., pp. 482-86; *HFM 3, i*, pp. 249-50; D. G. Tendulkar, op. cit., pp. 271-79.

48 *CW 18*, p. 28.

49 *HFM 3, i*, p. 269.

50 Cited in D. G. Tendulkar, op. cit., p. 290.

51 R. Joshi, 'Maharashtra' in M. Weiner (ed.), *State Politics in India* (Princeton, 1968), pp. 193-94.

52 *CW 18*, pp. 110-11.

GANDHI, GOKHALE AND THE MODERATES

S. P. Aiyar

Few men in history have left so profound an impression on their contemporaries or played so controversial a role in the making of a nation as Gandhi. Indeed, his life and work provide a key to the many paradoxes of modern India. He transformed the style of political leadership in the subcontinent and thereby shaped its destiny.

Remarkable as was his role in the political transformation of India after the first world war, it must also be recalled that the techniques which he adopted were not entirely novel. Though a born strategist, he was not a very original thinker. He inherited a rich and varied political tradition which he made use of with consummate skill. He departed from the political methods of his predecessors and, even more, from their attitudes and assumptions. This departure—in some ways radical—tends to mark off the Gandhi era of Indian politics from the earlier period of moderation. However, despite the differences between these periods of Indian history, the continuity in the national development was maintained. With independence, the philosophy of the moderates returned to be embodied in the Constitution; it also underlay India's decision to be part of the Commonwealth. But, for a time, this historical continuity tended to be hidden under the dust raised by the non-co-operation movement.

A comparative study of Gandhi and Gokhale, his predecessor, will help in assessing the strength and weaknesses of the two rival methods of politics they represented. In this essay I shall try to show the fundamental differences in the outlook of Gandhi and the moderates, who were among his severest critics in the inter-war years. Such an analysis will also enable us, I believe, to view the limitations of Gandhi and Gandhism in the perspective of contemporary India.

An initial difficulty in any comparative undertaking of this kind is the mutual admiration which Gokhale and Gandhi had for each other, an admiration often expressed in an excess of verbal generosity. At his very first encounter with Gokhale at Poona in 1896 Gandhi fell in love with the man whom he was to describe later as his *guru* (teacher). This admiration was partly a personal response to his personality; he was touched by the anxiety with which Gokhale made inquiries about him. Gandhi recalled: 'It was like meeting an old friend, or better still, a mother after a long separation. His gentle face put me at ease in a moment.'[1] His impressions of Gokhale were strengthened during his stay with him at Calcutta in 1902. Gandhi greatly admired Gokhale's dedication, his truthfulness and his tender feeling towards other people. 'I believe,' Gandhi said, 'he had the capacity to cheerfully mount the gallows for the country's sake, if necessary.' He found Gokhale intensely religious by nature although the latter 'did not wear his religion on his sleeve'.

Perhaps more important were Gokhale's complete dedication to serving the country with no trace of self-interest and his insistence that politics must be spiritualized. In the preamble to the constitution of the Servants of India Society, Gokhale wrote: 'Public life must be spiritualized. Love of country must so fill the heart that all else shall appear as of little moment by its side. A fervent patriotism which rejoices at every opportunity of sacrifice for the motherland, a dauntless heart which refuses to be turned back from its object by difficulty or danger, a deep faith in the purpose of Providence which nothing can shake—equipped with these, the worker must start on his mission and reverently seek the joy which comes of spending oneself in the service of one's country.'[2] This passage undoubtedly captures the essence of Gandhi's own ideals. He saw in his master, Gokhale, the embodiment of what he wanted to be. Because of these qualities Gandhi 'installed him in his heart of hearts as his teacher in politics'.

Gokhale in turn saw in the great saga of the Indian struggle in South Africa under Gandhi's leadership the spirit and motivation which he thought ought to animate politics. In 1896 when Gandhi came to India to get support for his struggle against the iniquitous laws passed against Indians in Natal, he looked up to Gokhale for support and secured his unstinted co-operation. Thereafter, Gandhi and Gokhale were in constant communication with each other. In 1906, a law was passed in the Transvaal requiring all Indians to be registered with the police. Gandhi launched his first *satyāgraha* and courted imprisonment. In 1908 and 1909 Gokhale organised protest meetings in Bombay. On the latter occasion, addressing a mass rally at the Town Hall in Bombay, Gokhale spoke of 'the indomitable Gandhi, a man of tremendous spiritual power, one who is made of the stuff of which great heroes and martyrs are made'. One more occasion when Gokhale showered his eulogy on Gandhi may be cited. Speaking at the Twenty-fourth Session of the Indian National Congress held at Lahore on 29 December 1909 on the 'Transvaal Question' Gokhale said:

Fellow-Delegates, after the immortal part which Mr Gandhi has played in this affair, I must say it will be impossible for any Indian, at any time, here or in any assembly of Indians, to mention his name without deep emotion and pride. . . . Mr Gandhi is one of those men, who, living an austerely simple life themselves and devoted to all the highest principles of love to their fellow-beings and to truth and justice, touch the eyes of their weaker brethren as with magic and give them a new vision. He is a man who may be well described as a man among men, a hero among heroes, a patriot among patriots, and we may well say that in him, Indian humanity at the present time has really reached its high watermark.[3]

Gokhale even entertained the idea of Gandhi being his successor in the Servants of India Society.

It should also be noted that till the first world war, Gandhi like Gokhale worked for the Indian people within the framework of the Empire. In 1907, Gokhale observed:

And here at the outset, let me say that I recognise no limits to my aspirations for our motherland. I want our people to be in their own country what other people are in theirs. I want our young men and women, without distinction of caste or creed, to have opportunities to grow to the full height of their stature, unhampered by cramping and unnatural restrictions. I want India to take her place among the great nations of the world, politically, industrially, in religion, in literature, in science and in the arts. I want all this and feel at the same time that the whole of this aspiration can, in its essence and its reality, be realized within this Empire.[4]

Gokhale viewed Gandhi's work in South Africa as a struggle for equality within the Empire, a fight for the dignity of the Indian people and a vindication of the honour of the motherland.[5] At this time, despite his hostility to many aspects of Western civilization as expressed in *Hind Swarāj* (1909), Gandhi also believed that it was possible for Indians to grow to their full stature within the Empire.[6]

Stanley Wolpert has suggested that the 'unique import of Gokhale's influence upon Gandhi's life and ideas has not received the recognition it deserves, although Gandhi ungrudgingly admitted it. Perhaps the deeper currents of mental and moral identity which bound the *guru* and his disciple have been obscured by their more obvious superficial differences of dress and manner'.[7] But while the 'moral identity' underlying the

101

relationship between Gokhale and Gandhi is clear enough, in outlook the two men were poles apart. After 1919, Gandhi departed from the passive resistance of the earlier period and far from being loyal to the Empire became its greatest rebel. His techniques of political action gradually assumed forms which Gokhale would scarcely have approved. Indeed, one of the great ironies of modern Indian history is the combination of circumstances which compelled Gandhi to adopt the techniques which he did and depart radically from the spirit of Gokhale, his *guru*.

When Gandhi returned to India in 1915, the country was in the midst of war; he was still a loyal subject of the empire. He pleaded for unconditional and wholehearted co-operation in the war effort by India's educated classes. In 1915 he even refused to support Annie Besant in launching the Home Rule movement.[8] However, Gandhi was still uncertain about his plans. Gokhale had asked him to travel across the country for a whole year to get a first-hand knowledge of conditions; thereafter he could, should he so choose, seek admission to the Servants of India Society. But even before the year was out Gokhale died. Gandhi sought admission to the Society but the opposition of many members persuaded Gandhi to withdraw his application. The members of the Society perceived the fundamental differences between their outlook and that of Gandhi and felt 'that his political evolution would take him further from us'.[9]

The differences between Gandhi and the moderates were first expressed on this occasion but the stage was soon set for Gandhi to strike a new path in the politics of the time. The political climate of India was rapidly changing; the war had intensified nationalism. In 1917 Montagu announced his famous declaration of the goal of British policy in India. But the declaration was couched in language which lent itself to a variety of interpretations and although moderate opinion was quite happy with the announcement, it produced, nevertheless, diverse reactions.[10] Its scheme of dyarchy roused the suspicion of the nationalists and officials were not slow in putting an unfavourable interpretation on the meaning of responsible government. The Montagu-Chelmsford Scheme which embodied this famous announcement ran into troubled waters. The year in which the Act was passed was one of intense political unrest. The Rowlatt Act extending war-time restrictions on seditious activity, the massacre at Jallianwala Bagh, and finally the Khilafat movement, in which extremist elements among the Muslims raised the cry of *jihad* against the Government for the stringent conditions imposed on Turkey by the Treaty of Sevres—all contributed to the intensification of nationalism. Gandhi was still preaching loyalty to the Empire although he had started

102

his non-co-operation as a protest against the Rowlatt Bill. The Report of the Hunter Committee and that of the Congress Enquiry Committee which investigated the Punjab situation clearly revealed the extent to which the government had humiliated the people. Yet, Mr Montagu found himself in a position in which he had to support the administration while speaking in Parliament and the debate in the House of Lords revealed a callous indifference to the feelings, sentiments and sufferings of the Indian people. These developments shook Gandhi's faith in the British administration and he was never to recover from it again. Gandhi felt that an unarmed people needed a new technique of political action in dealing with the government. The technique which he had already used in South Africa and experimented with on a small scale in cases of isolated grievances was now to be reshaped and reconditioned for use on a national scale.

Gandhi had resolved to embark on his non-co-operation campaign on 1 August 1920, but on the previous night the great leader, Lokamanya Tilak, died. There had been fundamental differences in the political philosophies of Tilak and Gandhi. Tilak had no patience with Gandhi's insistence on Truth and non-violence. He frankly told Gandhi: 'My friend! Truth has no place in politics.'[11] And further, in a letter to *Young India*, Tilak wrote: 'Politics is a game of worldly people, and not of *sadhus*.' In reply Gandhi wrote: 'With deference to the Lokamanya, I venture to say that it betrays mental laziness to think that the world is not for *sadhus*.'[12] With Tilak's passing away, Gandhi became the natural mass leader of the Indian people. The field was now open for his experiments in non-co-operation and *satyāgraha*. In his emphasis on Truth and non-violence he departed radically from the extremists of the older school, and from Tilak in particular, but he was heir to some of the latter's techniques of mass politics. Gandhi sought, consciously or otherwise, to combine these techniques of Tilak with Gokhale's insistence that politics must be *spiritualized*. But he imparted to this process of 'spiritualization' a much wider meaning and a greater functional significance. This change was in harmony with his own view of life and progress. Gandhi's techniques of political action and his world view formed a unified whole. The understanding of this 'system' is necessary for evaluating his role in modern India, but it is also a measure of the great gap which developed between him and the leaders of the moderate school.

Gandhi was not a systematic thinker and much less a political philosopher. He sought to combine, as Ashe observes,[13] mysticism with humanism and these, welded to a shrewd capacity to bargain, constituted the foundation of his revolutionary experiments in Truth and non-violence. As a revolutionary, Gandhi was concerned more with the immediate social and political problems of the day than with the long-term reconstruction of Indian society, although the kind of society which he desired can be inferred from his voluminous writings. Gandhi had no notion of development or progress in the sense in which these terms are normally understood in the West. Modernization—the crux of development so far as India and the underdeveloped world is concerned—enters nowhere in his social thinking. His outlook was characterized by a some-what over-simplified romanticism and a desire to escape from the complexities of civilized life as well as the power structure of politics. His attitude to wealth was coloured by his admiration of Thoreau's *Walden* and he paid little attention to the problems of capital accumulation in a poor country. Gandhi emphasized the distribution, consumption and trusteeship aspects of wealth, not its rational and productive use. His study of the writings of Carlyle and Ruskin and his acquaintance with the evils of the industrial revolution—a passing phase of England's social transformation—left a permanent impression on his mind and he did little to correct that impression in the light of the social and economic changes which were taking place in England in the last quarter of the nineteenth century. A silent revolution was afoot which was soon to pave the way for the rise of the Social Service State in Britain. This was reflected not only in the political philosophy of the time but also in the growth of pamphlet literature. Gandhi's view of industrialization, and of western society in general, however, remained untouched. During his stay in London, for two years and a half, he stood aloof from English society and his views were not different from what they had been when he was an average student at Rajkot. He read the newspapers but they left little impression on his mind. He was enthusiastically drawn to the cult of vegetarianism which was popular with a group of cranks in London. Apart from this the only other interest he had was Theosophy which he learnt through Madame Blavatsky.[14]

That Gandhi had turned his mind away from the West and even more from science is evident from *Hind Swarāj* which he published in 1909. This booklet is a key to the understanding of Gandhi's world view. He held out against machinery as the greatest evil of civilization and in taking this view he was undoubtedly influenced by his knowledge of the evils of the industrial revolution. His attack on machinery and civilization was severely criticized. Professor Delisle Burns spoke of the fundamental philosophical error of Gandhi's position 'that we are to regard as morally evil any instrument which may be misused'. Gandhi later sought to clarify his position but he hardly changed his views on the subject. In 1924, asked whether he was against *all* machinery, Gandhi said: 'How can I be when I know that even this body is a most delicate piece of machinery? The spinning wheel is a machine; a little toothpick is a machine.' He thereafter argued that he was against 'the craze for machinery, not machinery as such'; he was against machinery which displaced labour and led to the concentration of wealth. He had, for example, no objection to the sewing machine, but when it was pointed out that it would take power-driven factories to produce it, Gandhi's answer was that he would nationalize such factories.[15] It is easy to see the piece of sophistry involved in this position. There is a vast and impressive literature from Ruskin to J. L. and Barbara Hammonds which draws our attention to the social costs of an industrial civilization, and modern thinking on this subject has been preoccupied with the tasks of social and economic reorganization to counter these evils. Gandhi's basic approach, however, was to do away with machinery and thus avoid the problems of modernization and industrialization.

His views on railways, lawyers and doctors are in consonance with this approach. Railways have been responsible for the spread of diseases; they have been the carriers of 'plague germs' and have destroyed 'the natural segregation' which existed before their advent; they have increased famines for they tempt people to 'sell out the food grains in the dearest markets'. Further, 'bad men fulfil their evil designs with greater rapidity. The holy places of India have become unholy'. Hospitals and doctors increase the evil in the heart of man by curing him of diseases, the results of his own negligence and indulgence. 'I have indulged in vice, I contract a disease, a doctor cures me, the odds are that I shall repeat the vice. Had not the doctor intervened, nature would have done its work, and I would have acquired mastery over myself, would have been freed from vice, and would have become happy. Hospitals are institutions for propagating sin. Men take less care of their bodies, and immorality increases.' His advice is a simple one: a doctor should 'give up medicine, and understand that rather than mending bodies, he should mend souls', and he must also understand that 'if, by not taking drugs, perchance the patient dies, the world will not come to grief and he will have been useful to them'.[16] Finally, about lawyers, he thinks they are a set of social parasites:

> The lawyers, therefore, will, as a rule, advance quarrels instead of repressing them. Moreover, men take up that profession, not in order to help others out of their miseries, but to enrich themselves. It is one of the avenues of becoming wealthy and their interest

105

exists in multiplying disputes. It is within my knowledge that they are glad when men have disputes. Petty pleaders actually manufacture them. Their touts, like so many leeches, suck the blood of the poor people. Lawyers are men who have little to do. Lazy people, in order to indulge in luxuries, take up such professions.[17]

Politically, he was not impressed by British political institutions and his understanding of parliamentary government in England may be inferred from the following passage.

> That which you consider to be the Mother of Parliaments is like a sterile woman and a prostitute. Both these are harsh terms, but exactly fit the case. That Parliament has not yet, of its own accord, done a single good thing. Hence I have compared it to a sterile woman. . . . It is like a prostitute because it is under the control of ministers who change from time to time. Today it is under Mr Asquith, tomorrow it may be under Mr Balfour.[18]

Gandhi's economic ideas, it must be conceded, had a great deal of practical significance both as strategy and as contributing to rural employment. His emphasis on *khādi* and *charkhā* not only provided valuable symbols for mass politics but they reflected his deep concern for the rural masses of India. But the relevance of his economic ideas in this sphere tended to get distorted by his inability to view the problems of agriculture and industry together and his natural hostility to the machine civilization. He saw the cities of India as the main cause for the impoverishment of the country by draining the villages dry and becoming markets for the dumping of cheap and shoddy goods from foreign lands. He was certain that India must not wear machine-made clothing, irrespective of whether it comes out of European mills or Indian mills. To these must be added his passion for equality, levelling down the rich and producing a non-violent classless society. 'A non-violent system of government,' he declared, 'is clearly an impossibility so long as the wide gulf between the rich and the hungry millions persists. A violent and bloody revolution is a certainty one day unless there is a voluntary abdication of riches and the power that riches give and sharing them for the common good.'[19] He saw in trusteeship one possible but difficult solution. At this point Gandhi's economic views and his political strategy converge. What if trusteeship failed? Gandhi sensed the hidden possibilities of non-violent non-co-operation:

The rich cannot accumulate wealth without the co-operation of the poor in society. If this knowledge were to penetrate to and spread amongst the poor, they would become strong and would learn how to free themselves by means of non-violence from the crushing inequalities which have brought them to the verge of starvation.[20]

The socialistic ideas in Gandhi's writings are too pronounced to escape attention although it must be added that there was little or no inspiration for this philosophy from a foreign source. His trusteeship theory combined with his non-violent approach appeared to Gandhi's Marxist contemporaries as a subtle apology for the protection of the interests of the bourgeoisie, and the Communist International regarded him as one who had betrayed the mass struggle to his ideal of backwardness.[21] Gandhi, however, welcomed the rise of the Socialist bloc within the Congress and occasionally professed to be a socialist and even a communist. Yet, his faith in non-violence made him shrink from a communist revolution and his dislike of large-scale machinery gave to his socialist utopia the 'character of a decentralized federation of little units'.[22]

Gandhi's world view was opposed to science and scientific outlook. He stressed that scientists could make mistakes and resort to cruelty in the name of science; he saw in the products of science—machinery and technology in general—the enslavement of man and the impoverishment of the masses. He could not appreciate, as we have seen, the discoveries of medical science. Indeed, the world-view of science which began to develop in Europe from the seventeenth century was closed to Gandhi. Even in the field of agriculture—so close to his interest and to the life of the rural masses for whom he had genuine concern—he rarely thought of what science could do to increase production and improve the lot of the agriculturist. Western education which revealed to the Indian mind the possibilities of science and progress was of little use to Gandhi. He considered this education 'mere knowledge of letters', useless for the masses:

The ordinary meaning of education is a knowledge of letters. To teach boys reading, writing and arithmetic is called primary education. A peasant earns his bread honestly. He has ordinary knowledge of the world. He knows fairly well how he should behave towards his parents, his wife and his fellow villagers. He understands and observes the rules of morality. But he cannot write his own name. What do you propose to do giving him a knowledge of letters? Will you add an inch to his happiness? Do you wish to make him discontented with his cottage or his lot? And even if you want to do that, he will not need such an education. Carried away by the flood of western thought we came to the conclusion, without weighing *pros* and *cons*, that we should give this kind of education to the people.

He maintained that the sciences he had learnt at school were of no use to him. 'I have never been able to use [them] for controlling my senses. Therefore, whether you take elementary education or higher education it is not required for the main thing. It does not make men of us. It does not enable us to do our duty.'[23]

Hind Swarāj made little impact on India when it was first published. Later, Sir Sankaran Nair tore its arguments to shreds. When it came to be more widely known in India, it estranged the moderates from its author. In spite of the admiration which the moderates originally had for Gandhi, their intellectual orientation was far removed from his. Their liberalism— a product of the western impact on Indian intellectuals—was grounded in a firm faith in progress through science and the constructive role of education. Their admiration for British institutions and their faith in the British Empire within which, in their view, India must seek equality with other independent nations is well-known and I will not therefore deal with this aspect of Indian liberalism here.[24] But two facts about the liberals require some emphasis. They were not naïve politicians who could be manipulated by the British government in India; nor were they uncritical admirers of British policy. One finds in the writings of the liberals some of the severest criticisms of British rule in India and it is no exaggeration to say that they provided the intellectual content of Indian nationalism. Secondly, it is absurd to regard them as a body of uprooted, frustrated, urban intellectuals, a small minority, who had no understanding of the real problems of India. They spearheaded the nationalist movement which was in its origins necessarily elitist in character. They cast themselves in the role of critics of the government, bringing to its attention their views on all national problems. They sought to build public opinion through enlightened discussion rather than to gain popular support through the techniques of mass persuasion. They tried to develop what we would call today a 'civic culture' and raise a citizenry conscious of both its rights and responsibilities.

The liberals saw the inter-related character of the development process in India; they paid attention to the problems of agriculture as well as of industrialization; they were preoccupied with the shaping of educational policies and moulding the minds of youths and directing their energies into constructive channels; they were concerned with the problem of unemployment and devoted attention to the diversification of the educational system through the establishment of technical and professional schools. Above all, they saw that development required a modern outlook in the country's *élite* and a gradual breaking away from some of the ideas and institutions of the traditional society. At the same time they were convinced that the country's development did not call for any total break with the past; they sought for a synthesis in which the springs of progress were firmly linked to everything worthwhile in India's tradition.

There were, to be sure, different levels of understanding of the liberal position among the followers of the school. Some were more interested in political and constitutional development; some were preoccupied with the country's economy; still others were concerned with social reform. But all of them agreed with Ranade's views on the inter-dependence of social, economic and political reform:

> You cannot have a good social system when you find yourself low in the scale of political rights, nor can you be fit to exercise political rights and privileges unless your social system is based on reason and justice. You cannot have a good economical (*sic*) when your social arrangements are imperfect. If your religious ideals are low and grovelling, you cannot succeed in social, economical, or political spheres. This interdependence is not an accident but is the law of our nature. . . . It is a mistaken view which divorces considerations political from social and economical, and no man can be said to realize his duty in one respect who neglects his duties in the other direction.[25]

There were among the liberals theists like Ranade and agnostics like Gokhale and Srinivasa Sastri and pure rationalists like R. P. Paranjpye. But they were all convinced of the possibilities of solving the country's manifold problems through education and scientific knowledge and there was hardly any aspect of India's development which escaped all of them. Even the theist Ranade was convinced of the role of science; he saw in it one of the secrets for the superiority of the west and contrasted the western intellectual tradition with the scholasticism and the narrow theological outlook of ancient Indian thinkers. Ranade saw the weakness of India's other-worldliness from the standpoint of progress and was opposed to the traditional asceticism of Hindu culture.[26] This belief in scientific knowledge and techniques characterized the liberal mind and it shows, better than anything else, how they differed from Gandhi and his world-view as expressed in *Hind Swarāj*. I may add here that most of the great leaders of the liberal school were educationists. Ranade, Dadabhai Naoroji, Surendranath Banerjea and Gokhale had been professors and Pherozeshah Mehta was closely connected with the University of Bombay where there is now a professorship instituted in his honour. Regarding Mehta's interest in education, Naoroji Dumasia has written: 'One other field in which he laboured long and fruitfully was the Bombay University Senate . . . he displayed keen interest in education even as a young man and as his power and influence grew, he spared no endeavour to fight the battle of education in the Bombay Council and in the Imperial Council too. His budget speeches invariably contained demands for more expenditure on education which he declared was India's primary, principal and most urgent necessity'.[27] Rash Bihari Ghosh, Chimanlal Setalvad, Srinivasa Sastri and Sivaswami Aiyar had been vice-chancellors in their time; C. Y. Chintamani and H. N. Kunzru did a great deal to improve the universities of Lucknow and Allahabad and R. P. Paranjpye was one of Poona's leading educationists. The liberals looked upon western education as a means for the transmission into India of the ideas and attitudes necessary for modernization and for the successful working of parliamentary institutions. For Gokhale, the greatest work of education was 'not so much the encouragement of learning as the liberation of the Indian mind from the thraldom of old-world ideas, and the assimilation of all that is best in the life and thought and character of the West . . . for this all western education is useful'.[28] Expressing similar views, Sivaswami Aiyar warned against pursuing education in the spirit of narrow inward-looking nationalist sentiments. He welcomed the invitation of foreign professors to Indian universities provided they were first-rate. As early as 1919 he drew attention to the problem of popularizing western education and encouraging the translation of standard works into the vernacular. It is even more striking—from the standpoint of current educational trends in India—that he warned against the tendency of coining equivalent words in the vernacular in the pursuit of a false patriotism. 'The realm of scientific knowledge,' he told the graduates of the Benares Hindu University, 'recognizes no exclusive distinctions of race, nationality, or country.' As early as 1912 Sivaswami Aiyar suggested that with modernization, the diversification of avenues of employment was bound to come and that managements of colleges should devote attention to the modification of courses for the changing needs of society. He called for the opening of courses in commerce and mechanical engineering.[29] The liberals also saw in western education a means through which the values of secularism could be imparted to the people of India. In the writings of both Gokhale and Sivaswami Aiyar one notices their anxiety to see a rational and scientific outlook pervade Indian society.

One of the great myths that the bureaucracy in the late nineteenth century sought to build up was that the leaders of the nationalist movement of the time, then predominantly of the moderate school, were merely a tiny, microscopic group of intellectuals who could not speak for the unlettered masses of India. The myth was reinforced during the Gandhian period. It was (and still is) frequently asserted that the liberals had no genuine interest in the problems of the rural masses. The charge was emphatically repudiated by Dadabhai Naoroji when he pointed out that it was only the educated classes of India who could at all represent the wants of the dumb millions.

> It is the educated who on the one hand can understand the advanced civilization and ideas of our rulers, and on the other hand, the ideas and wants and wishes of their countrymen. It is the educated only that can become the true interpreters, and the connecting link between the rulers and the ruled. And, moreover, it is the educated and intellectual only that can as in all countries, not England excepted, lead the van of all progress and civilization, and whom the rest of the people follow. The few earnest and talented have always, will always, be the leaders of mankind.[30]

The liberal concern for the welfare of the rural masses has, indeed, a long history. Long before Gandhi appeared on the political scene of India, liberal leaders thought and reflected on India's economic problems. They drew attention to the exploitation of India and the deepening poverty of the rural masses. They criticised the lop-sided budgets of the time and the inordinate expenditure on the defence of India; British famine policy and revenue system came in for sustained attack. R. C. Dutt's analysis of the poverty of India together with Dadabhai Naoroji's writings on the 'Drain Theory' provided some of the most powerful weapons in the armoury of the nationalists. Gokhale's speeches dealt with the problems of agricultural indebtedness, irrigation, the heavy incidence of land revenue assessment and scientific agriculture. Gokhale had sound views on co-operative credit and on ways of mobilizing small savings. He was concerned with the problem of bringing science to the service of agriculture and improving the lot of the agriculturist.[31]

But even though the moderates were concerned with the problems of rural India, these did not occupy an unduly large place in their social and economic thinking. Gandhi's emphasis on village India was lop-sided, due,

111

doubtless, to his early prejudice against large-scale industrialization. As a result of this he paid little or no attention to the problems of urban government. Municipal self-government did not interest him, perhaps due to his belief that the cities of India were 'plague spots' and parasitically dependent on the villages. The long-term consequences of this over-emphasis can easily be seen. It led to the neglect of the problems of India's cities and to the decline of municipal government. If municipal government in India is in a shambles today—two decades after independence—at least one of the principal causes for this state of affairs must be attributed to the influences of the Gandhian era.[32] Gandhi's influence was not only politically detrimental to the growth of local self-government by bringing agitational politics to municipal bodies (as the history of the Ahmedabad municipality, for example, clearly shows), but it also had an unhealthy effect on the quality of local services. Under Gandhi's influence, western educated medical officers were replaced by *āyurvedic* practitioners; in Surat, anti-vaccination campaigns were started, 'vaccination being a western abuse of mother cow'.[33]

Gandhi's technique of *satyāgraha* has been explained so frequently in Gandhian literature that it is unnecessary to deal with it here in detail.[34] It was first tried out in South Africa, and then experimented with on a small scale in isolated situations as in Champaran in 1917, before it was introduced in national politics. Psychologically, it had its origin in Gandhi's personal relationship with his wife. Gandhi confessed to John Hoyland:

> I learned the lesson of non-violence from my wife. Her determined resistance to my will on the one hand, and her quiet submission to the suffering of my stupidity involved on the other hand, ultimately made me ashamed of myself and cured me of my stupidity in thinking I was born to rule over her; and in the end she became my teacher in non-violence. And what I did in South Africa was but an extension of the rule of Satyagraha which she unwillingly practiced in her own person.[35]

It is probably because of this origin of *satyāgraha* that Gandhi insisted that the ideal *satyāgrahi* must be above sex.[36] His writings on this subject repeatedly stress the moral qualities which all *satyāgrahis* must possess and he laid down guide-lines for a successful *satyāgraha*. His insistence on non-violence not only underlined the moral qualities of the struggle but called for special qualities in the participants. He repeatedly asserted that *satyāgraha* was not for the weak-willed and he warned that in the long run violence cannot lead to lasting solutions. For Gandhi, Truth must be discovered in action; it emerges in a non-violent encounter in which the opponent is persuaded, even 'morally compelled', to see it. Truth reveals itself to both parties in the conflict—owing, doubtless, to their common humanity—and transforms them.[37] A certain degree of analysis of griev-ance situations was undoubtedly present in Gandhi's *satyāgraha* campaigns; he formulated his demands carefully and communicated them to his opponents. Yet, the conception of Truth is one of the most mystifying elements in Gandhi's philosophy of non-violent resistance. Truth, he claimed, was revealed to him through a subtle process of intuition which he described as his 'Inner Voice'. His statements on Truth, couched in the language of theology, paralyzed the thinking of his admirers and confused his critics. The uncomfortable fact of it all seems to be that Gandhi himself was the victim of some confused thinking. This is apparent in his answers to Sir Chimanlal Setalvad who questioned him as member of the Hunter Commission:

> *Sir Chimanlal*: However honestly a man may strive in his search for truth, his notions of truth may be different from the notions of others. Who then is to determine the truth?
> *Gandhi*: The individual himself would determine that.
> *Sir Chimanlal*: Different individuals would have different views as to truth. Would that not lead to confusion?
> *Gandhi*: I do not think so.
> *Sir Chimanlal*: Honestly striving after truth is different in every case.
> *Gandhi*: That is why the non-violence part was a necessary corollary. Without that there would be confusion and worse.
> *Sir Chimanlal*: Must not the person wanting to pursue the truth be of high moral and intellectual equipment?
> *Gandhi*: No. It would be impossible to expect that from every one. If A has evolved a truth by his own efforts which B, C and others are to accept, I should not require them to have the equipment of A.
> *Sir Chimanlal*: Then it comes to this—that a man comes to a decision, and others of lower intellectual and moral equipment would have to blindly follow him.
> *Gandhi*: Not blindly.[38]

Gandhian *satyāgraha* subsumed several techniques of action such as civil disobedience, non-co-operation, boycott and fasting. Underlying these techniques was his world view which gave them their distinct quality. Gandhi's non-violent non-co-operation meant withdrawal of loyalty to the British system of government in India; it involved the abandonment of schools and colleges, courts and councils and a boycott of foreign goods. These weapons Gandhi presented to his people as means for the attainment of *swarāj;* to them it conveyed the notion of independence in an indigenous idiom but he himself gave it a special meaning. It meant self-reliance, 'the ability to regard every inhabitant of India as our own brother and sister', 'the abandonment of the fear of death'. Further, he even said, 'There can be no Swaraj without our feeling and being the equals of Englishmen'. Gandhi's program of revolution—that is what it was—concealed an attempt to set up a parallel government which would, ultimately, tilt the 'balance of loyalty' in favour of the native 'government'.[39] Gandhi contemplated a program of progressive non-co-operation in which the intensity of the movement would be in consonance with the growing strength of the masses.[40]

Satyāgraha was launched in a variety of situations and on a number of occasions from 1916 to 1942, but a detailed study of these from the standpoint of crowd psychology has not yet been attempted. Did Gandhi realize that his experiments with the mobilization of the masses could get out of control and result in violence and anarchy? Accused of responsibility for the occurrences in Madras, Bombay and Chauri Chaura, Gandhi said:

> I knew that I was playing with fire. I ran the risk and if I was set free I would still do the same . . . I wanted to avoid violence. Nonviolence is the first article of my faith. It is the last article of my faith. But I had to make my choice. I had either to submit to a system which I considered has done an irreparable harm to my country or incur the risk of the mad fury of my people bursting forth when they understood the truth from my lips.[41]

The reactions of the Indian liberals to Gandhi's experiments in mass politics stemmed from their fear that the movement would get out of control, despite the declarations of non-violence and the hold which Gandhi had over the masses. They also feared that violence and disobedience to constituted authority would become a habit and, ultimately, produce an ungovernable nation. Their faith in constitutional agitation was rooted in their firm belief that the foundation of law and order is the first condition of civilized life. They also saw in constitutional agitation a technique through which the public could be educated in its rights as well as its responsibilities.[42] It must not be thought that the moderates were naïve in their adherence to constitutional methods. In fact, they were realistic enough to argue that the forms of agitation must be modified according to circumstances, constitutional methods being the normal avenues for the redress of grievances. Speaking in 1925, the liberal, C. Y. Chintamani, said:

> The Liberal party does not swear by constitutional methods as if they were the Vedas or the Bible. If in a given situation the Liberal party should find that there are methods other than the constitutional which could be employed effectively with greater chance of success, and with no risk of doing more injury to the country itself than to the opponent, I have not the slightest doubt whatever that the Liberal party will unhesitatingly discard on such an occasion what is called the constitutional method, and adopt other methods which it may believe to be more effective.[43]

In his presidential address to the All India National Liberal Federation, Sir P. S. Sivaswamy Aiyar pointed out that one of the great difficulties of non-co-operation and non-violence is in maintaining their non-violent character. In his 'Thoughts on the Political Situation' (1930) he argued that the greatest danger of Gandhi's mass movements through civil disobedience was that revolt against constituted authority would become rooted in the mental make-up of the masses. He said: 'The advocates of civil disobedience imagine that the spirit of lawlessness, of law-breaking, once roused can be laid to rest when the right occasion has passed. This attitude is of course intelligible in a disciple of Tolstoy, the Anarchist genius'.[44]

The liberals' fears of the dangers inherent in Gandhi's disobedience were justified in Gandhi's own life time. Gandhi's moral posture and his insistence on non-violence were lost in mob fury; habits of disobedience spread and they ceased to be *civil*. By 1942, the mass revolt acquired a momentum of its own and Gandhi admitted his inability to control events and absolved himself of any responsibility for the breakdown of order and the violence which took place. After a long and painful experiment which had wrought incalculable harm to individual lives as well as to the nation, Gandhi realized the relevance of the warnings which Gokhale and the later moderates had given. Geoffrey Ashe, Gandhi's recent biographer, writes:

> In their correspondence Gandhi assured the Viceroy that his last essay in national Satyagraha was a closed chapter. The reasons for this retreat were not merely strategic. Events had proved that the

non-violence which he supposed the masses to have learnt from him was in most cases superficial, and an outcome of weakness rather than strength. It worked when he was favourably placed to make it work. In 1930 he had got the movement off on the right lines himself, and retained a high degree of control even from prison. But in 1942 the rising had been independent of him, and no real Satyagraha had occurred. A minority had been violent, a majority did nothing. Gokhale's warning long ago—that he made demands beyond people's capacity—sank in at last.[45]

There was one other aspect of Gandhi's mass movements to which attention must be drawn. He departed radically from the secular temper which had characterized the earlier phase of the national movement and the Congress organization. The moderates had a secular outlook; it was this which separated Gokhale from Tilak. With Gandhi, the social conservatism of the nineteenth century was further strengthened. Gandhi combined religion and politics. The language and idiom in which he expressed his political aspirations and his concepts of politics were Hindu: *satyāgraha, hartāl, harijan, Rām Rājya*, etc. In the eyes of many Muslims, consequently, he seemed to appear in the guise of a Hindu politician rather than as a national leader. It was the tragedy of Gandhi's life that his efforts to bring the Hindus and the Muslims together through non-violence and build a united India only resulted in widening the gulf which had existed between the communities for several centuries. To add to the irony of it all, the final decision on the partition of India was taken without so much as consulting him. Thus in the two great ends of his life—non-violence and Hindu-Muslim Unity—Gandhi failed, and he spent the evening of his life in disillusionment and experiments in *brahmacharya*.[46]

Gandhi left behind no constructive corpus of ideas on which a government could be built. The Constitution of India was framed on principles and ideas rooted in western constitutionalism, the bedrock of Indian liberalism. Gandhi's ideas were virtually brushed aside as of little relevance in constitution-making for a twentieth-century state. However, although Gandhi's ideas found no place in the constitutional structure of free India, his political techniques were quickly learnt by the masses, but the spirit of non-violence and the moral temper of Gandhi were readily forgotten. This perverted inheritance from the Gandhian period is now one of the principal challenges to the future of liberal constitutionalism in India.

NOTES

[1] Stanley Wolpert, *Tilak and Gokhale: Revolution and Reform in the Making of Modern India* (Berkeley and Los Angeles, 1962), p. 143.

[2] D. G. Karve and D. V. Ambekar (eds.), *Speeches and Writings of Gopal Krishna Gokhale* (Bombay, 1966), vol. 2, p. 182.

[3] *Ibid.*, p. 420.　　　[4] *Ibid.*, p. 217.　　　[5] *Ibid.*, p. 413.

[6] See S. R. Mehrotra, *India and the Commonwealth 1885-1929* (London, 1965), pp. 112-13.

[7] Stanley Wolpert, op. cit., p. 143.

[8] S. R. Mehrotra, op. cit., p. 113.

[9] P. Kodanda Rao, *The Right Honourable V. S. Srinivasa Sastri, A Political Biography* (Bombay, 1963), p. 17.

[10] The differences between the Indian National Congress under Gandhi and the Moderates underlay the different attitudes to the Empire and the Commonwealth during this period. See S. P. Aiyar, *The Commonwealth in South Asia* (Bombay, 1969).

[11] Stanley Wolpert, op. cit., p. 291.

[12] *Ibid.*, p. 292.

[13] Geoffrey Ashe, *Gandhi, A Study in Revolution* (London, 1968), p. 389.

[14] It is worthwhile exploring the nature of Gandhi's personality as revealed in his choice of authors, his pre-occupation with vegetarianism and in related childhood and adolescent experiences mentioned in his *Autobiography* and other writings. A major breakthrough in our understanding of Gandhi may come one day through the application of psycho-analytical tools. See in this connection the interesting exploratory analysis by P, Spratt, *Hindu Culture and Personality* (Bombay, 1966), Appendix 1.

[15] M. K. Gandhi, *Hind Swaraj or Home Rule* (Ahmedabad, 1958), p. 7.

[16] *Ibid.*, pp. 45, 59, 102.

[17] *Ibid.*, p. 55.　　　[18] *Ibid.*, p. 31.

[19] Nirmal Kumar Bose, *Selections From Gandhi* (Ahmedabad, 1948), pp. 77-78.

[20] *Ibid.*, p. 79.

[21] Geoffrey Ashe, op. cit., p. 249.

[22] *Ibid.*, pp. 332-33.

[23] Gandhi, op. cit., p. 87. In response to criticism from several quarters Gandhi restated his views on education in later writings. See N. K. Bose, op. cit., ch. 17. Gandhi's later views, however, are not much of an improvement on his earlier statements. His criticism of western education was that it was based upon a foreign culture and carried out in a foreign language; that it 'ignores the culture of the heart and the hand and confines itself simply to the head'. He was opposed to paying for higher education through the general revenue. He conceded the need for degrees in mechanical and other branches of engineering, but what such graduates would do in his utopia is far from clear. But dangerous and reactionary, in my opinion, was his view that academics should not be allowed to decide on either the medium of instruction or the subjects taught. 'Theirs will be the privilege of enforcing the nation's will in the best manner possible.' See Bose, op. cit., pp. 265-66.

[24] The admiration of the liberals for parliamentary institutions and their 'loyalty' to the Empire and Commonwealth returned as guiding factors to Indian leadership

after independence. They determined India's decision to remain in the Common-wealth. Jawaharlal Nehru's views in 1948 were precisely those of the liberals and of his father two decades earlier. For an elaboration of this theme see my book *The Commonwealth in South Asia* mentioned in Note No. 10.

25 M. G. Ranade, 'Liberate the Whole Man' in T. N. Jagadisan (ed.), *The Wisdom of a Modern Rishi* (Madras, n.d.), p. 149.

26 See P. J. Jagirdar, *Studies in the Social Thought of M. G. Ranade* (Bombay, 1963), p. 104.

27 Naoroji Dumasia, 'Sir Pherozeshah Mehta' in L. F. Rushbrook Williams (ed.), *Great Men of India* (Bombay, n.d. but probably 1939), p. 308.

28 *Speeches of Gopal Krishna Gokhale* (Madras, 1920), p. 135.

29 'Benares University Convocation Address', in K. A. Nilakanta Sastri (ed.), *A Great Liberal, Speeches and Writings of Sir P. S. Sivaswami Aiyar* (Bombay, 1965), p. 14.

30 C. L. Parikh (ed.), *Essays, Speeches, Addresses and Writings of Dadabhai Naoroji* (Bombay, 1887), pp. 360-61.

31 See T. M. Joshi, 'Economic Thought of Gopal Krishna Gokhale' in A. B. Shah and S. P. Aiyar (eds.), *Gokhale and Modern India* (Bombay, 1966), pp. 92-94. Also, B. N. Ganguli, 'Gopal Krishna Gokhale: His Economic Ideas' in C. P. Ramaswami Aiyar and others, *Gokhale the Man and His Mission* (Bombay, 1966).

32 The harmful effect of the nationalist movement on the growth of local self-government is suggested by Hugh Tinker, *Foundations of Local Self-Government in India, Pakistan and Burma* (Bombay, 1967). Practically all the earlier moderates were interested in the problems of municipal government and many had direct experience of working in urban bodies.

33 *Ibid.*, pp. 144, 289.

34 See in particular, Joan V. Bondurant, *Conquest of Violence* (Bombay, 1959); N. K. Bose, *Selections from Gandhi*, op. cit.; and Gene Sharp, *Gandhi Wields the Weapon of Moral Power* (Ahmedabad, 1960).

35 Geoffrey Ashe, op. cit., p. 182.

36 *Ibid.*, pp. 180-81. See also the illuminating observations of P. Spratt, op. cit., p. 81.

37 Erik H. Erikson, *Insight and Freedom* (Cape Town, 1968), pp. 12-13.

38 Cited by Geoffrey Ashe, op. cit., pp. 196-97.

39 *Ibid.*, pp. 210-11.

40 N. K. Bose and P. H. Patwardhan, *Gandhi in Indian Politics* (Bombay, 1967), p. 24.

41 Sankaran Nair, *Gandhi And Anarchy* (Madras, 1922), Appendix XXI.

42 For Gokhale's ideas on constitutional agitation see my discussion in A. B. Shah and S. P. Aiyar, *Gokhale and Modern India*, op. cit.; also my *Liberalism and the Modernization of India* (Ahmedabad, 1967).

43 Speech to the United Provinces Liberal Association, published in the *Leader*, 22 January 1925.

44 K. A. Nilakanta Sastri (ed.), op. cit., p. 438.

45 Geoffrey Ashe, op. cit., p. 358.

46 *Satyagraha* had its origin, as already noted, in a very intimate relationship which partly explains his insistence that the *satyagrahi* should conquer his sexual impulses. Gandhi's own admission of the failure of *satyagraha* probably led to further experiments in self-effacement and the conquest of his 'biological self'. His experiments in *brahmacharya*, described in some detail by Geoffrey Ashe, may be of some significance in unravelling the mysteries of Gandhi's personality from the psychological angle.

TAGORE-GANDHI CONTROVERSY

Sibnarayan Ray

'I started with a disposition to detect a conflict between Gurudev [Rabindranath Tagore] and myself,' said Gandhi in reply to an anxious question during his last visit to Santiniketan in December 1945, 'but ended with the glorious discovery that there was none.'[1] The 'discovery' was typical of the Mahatma. His Indian disciples have also generally tended to play down the differences between these two great men by stressing their mutual admiration for and affinity with each other. Jawaharlal Nehru, who knew both of them intimately and suffered from a divided loyalty, found comfort in maintaining that 'they seemed to present different but harmonious aspects of India and to complement one another'.[2] K. R. Kripalani repeats the same point: 'Unlike Tolstoy and Lenin, who seem to challenge and repudiate each other and represent a balance of contrary forces in the development of Russian civilization, Tagore and Gandhi have confirmed and upheld each other and represent a fundamental harmony in Indian civilization'.[3] In his foreword to a collection of documents relating to Tagore-Gandhi controversy Kaka-saheb Kalelkar asserts that 'basically there was no distinction or difference of opinion between the two and . . . the whole thing was a case of mis-understanding and of a difference of emphasis'.[4]

It is, of course, true that Tagore and Gandhi held each other in high esteem. Gandhi invariably addressed Tagore as *Gurudev* or the divine teacher, and Tagore acclaimed his younger contemporary as *Mahātmā* or the great soul. Gandhi sought Tagore's blessing before commencing his historic fast in September 1932; and a year before his death Tagore appealed to Gandhi to take Visva-Bharati under his protection.[5] Neverthe-less they disagreed time and again in public, and the issues were more often than not quite fundamental. The record is worth reviewing before it is further obscured by well-meaning exercises in hagiographic recon-ciliation.

I

Tagore and Gandhi met for the first time at the former's *āshram* at Santiniketan in 1915. Tagore, then fifty-four, was already a world figure.

The award of the Nobel Prize for literature in 1913 had brought belated recognition to modern India's most original poet and thinker. His phenomenal output in Bengali was, of course, accessible only to those who knew the language, but between 1912 and 1914 he had also published in English eight volumes of his writings, and his travels in England and the United States in 1912-13 had made a profound impact on western intellectuals. Tall, slender but powerfully built, gifted with fine and expressive features, his noble face framed by abundant wavy hair and a flowing graceful beard, Tagore's appearance was in perfect harmony with the majestic beauty of his genius.

His guest, who was eight years younger, was, on the other hand, a relatively obscure individual who had recently returned to India (9 January 1915) after nearly twenty-one years in South Africa. Rather frail and medium sized, sporting a dark moustache on an otherwise clean shaven face, inconspicuous looking except for his penetratingly honest eyes, Gandhi was still trying to find his bearings in India where he was almost a stranger. His experiences and experiments in South Africa which had shaped his personality, ideas and techniques of collective action were but vaguely known to sections of the Indian public. Reverend Doke's biographical sketch of Gandhi, first published in London in 1909, did not have an Indian edition till 1919.[6] Gandhi's only major work so far, *Hind Swaraj*, originally written in Gujarati in 1909 and translated shortly after into English, had been banned by the Bombay government in 1910; and although it did receive Tolstoy's commendation, in India Gandhi's *guru*, Gopal Krishna Gokhale, 'thought it so crude and hastily conceived that he prophesied that Gandhi himself would destroy the book after spending a year in India'.[7] In fact, Gokhale had advised him on his return to devote a year to acquainting himself with the Indian reality; he had also promised him help in establishing an *āshram* of his own in Gujarat. But Gokhale died in February, and thus when Gandhi visited Tagore his position in the country was far from certain.

The meeting was brought about by a common friend, Charles Freer Andrews, who till his death in 1940 would continue to function as the most intimate personal link between the two great men. Andrews came to India in 1904 to work as a missionary teacher at St Stephen's College, Delhi.[8] Gradually he discovered his life's vocation which was to serve the Indian people and to work towards a reconciliation of races, religions and cultures. In 1912 during a visit to England he met Tagore at the house of William Rothenstein where he heard him read from *Gitanjali*. He was then forty-one, and the meeting proved to be the turning point of his life. On his return to India he visited Santiniketan several times in 1913 and

120

decided to make it his home. However, before he could do so he was sent by Gokhale to South Africa to study the situation and assist Gandhi, and as his biographers record, 'within two or three days they were "Mohan" and "Charlie" to one another'.[9] There he spoke lovingly to Gandhi of Tagore and his marvellous vision; he also wrote long letters to Tagore vividly describing Gandhi's personality and various activities.

Returning from South Africa Andrews went to live and work at Santiniketan (June 1914). He kept in touch with Gandhi, and when the latter, having disbanded his Phoenix settlement and school in South Africa, decided to send the inmates to India in advance of his own return, Andrews persuaded Tagore to offer them temporary accommodation at Santiniketan. Gandhi himself came to Santiniketan on 17 February 1915 but did not meet Tagore who was away in Calcutta. On 6 March he came again to stay for six days and it was then that the two first met.[10]

Andrews apparently had good reasons to expect that the two men he admired most would find much to share with each other. They were both deeply religious but unorthodox in their approach to Hinduism; both had a high regard for Christ and his ethic of universal compassion, and were critical of western materialism and power-lust; both loved India but rejected aggressive nationalism. Moreover, had not Tagore anticipated in his writings many of Gandhi's ideas and practices? He had repeatedly argued that the heart of India lay not in its cities and towns but in its neglected villages, that the nationalist movement should give its first priority to rural reconstruction through agricultural improvement, cottage industries and co-operatives, that power-oriented politics was sterile and had to be replaced by patient community endeavour dedicated to service, reform and education. He had urged the Congress leaders to come out of their elitistic exclusiveness, to abandon their mendicant pursuit of concessions from foreign rulers, and to take up instead the much more challenging task of preparing the common people to run their affairs themselves. He had found much to appreciate in England but had opposed British rule because it emasculated the Indian people, exploited their divisions, and ruined the countryside. He had advocated *swadeshi* (production and use of indigenous goods), national education, and Hindu-Muslim reconciliation, and raised his voice against religious bigotry, social taboos, and in particular, untouchability.[11] Three years before Gandhi started his Phoenix settlement he had founded the *āshram* at Santiniketan (1901) where young students were to be trained in simplicity and courage, harmony and dedication, co-operative living and spiritual freedom.

Tagore had also consistently rejected violence in all its forms and even formulated the ideal of non-violent resistance to wrongs and injustice. His *brāhma* upbringing and love of *vaishnava* poetry had developed in him a strong distaste for Bengal's popular cult of *Kāli*-worship which involved sacrifice of innocent animals to a dark deity invoked as the mother goddess. His first two novels, *Bouthākurānir Hāt* (1883) and *Rājarshi* (1887), show his pre-occupation with the ideal of non-violence. According to his own account the theme of the second novel was suggested by a dream in which he saw 'a father and a girl before the temple. Blood was running out over the steps, and the girl was deeply pained. "Why is this blood? Why is this blood?" she kept asking and tried to wipe it away. Her father was very troubled, and couldn't answer her, so tried to silence her, really to silence his own mind. I woke up, and determined to put this in my story'.[12] Three years later (1890) he returned to this theme in a moving tragedy, *Bisarjan*, where the young hero voluntarily sacrifices himself to prove the superiority of non-violence to violence.[13]

During the first decade of the present century when in the wake of the Bengal Partition (1905) militant Hindu nationalism began to turn to revolutionary ideologies and terrorist methods, Tagore took an open stand against this development which made him extremely unpopular with the nationalist Hindu intelligentsia.[14] Besides stressing the crucial importance of constructive activities to a movement for social and political emancipation, he also offered in the play, *Prāyaschitta* (1909), his alternative of open non-violent resistance to oppressive political power. Its plot is derived from his first novel, but it introduces a new character, Dhananjay Bairagi, who leads the peasants in a non-violent no-rent campaign against their tyrant king. In this character Tagore portrayed what in Gandhian language would be called a true *satyāgrahi*, ten years before that word was to gain national currency in India.[15]

Thus a meeting of minds could be expected when Gandhi came to see Tagore. In fact, in his first letter to Gandhi thanking him for sending his Phoenix boys to Santiniketan, Tagore expressed the hope that they (the Phoenix boys) would 'form a living link in the *sādhana* of both of our lives'.[16] But he had not reckoned with the younger man's missionary zeal. Gandhi was not content to be a mere guest; he spoke to Tagore about the behavioural shortcomings of Santiniketan; he even presumed to suggest that Tagore's *āshram* would improve morally by adopting the much more austere principles of his recently disbanded settlement at Phoenix.[17] Tagore was thus given his first uncomfortable experience of Gandhi's strait and self-confident rectitude. Perhaps he spoke about it to Andrews, for sometime later when Gandhi sent Andrews a copy of the proposed rules for his own *āshram* at Kochrab, the latter warned him against the risk of spiritual emasculation involved in the vow of celibacy. Andrews also 'argued vehemently with Gandhi about his "moral tyranny".'[18] Emasculation and moral tyranny—the words already anticipate what later on would become two of Tagore's principal charges against Gandhi.

II

The two had little contact during the next four years. Gandhi was fully occupied with his *āshram* (moved to a new site on the bank of Sabarmati in 1917), his campaign against indenture labour, and limited *satyāgraha* at Champaran, Ahmedabad and Kheda. Gradually he was gaining recognition as a new type of leader in Indian public life. These were also crucial years in the development of Tagore's thought and literary style. In collaboration with Pramatha Chaudhuri he launched a vigorous and sustained attack in the pages of the literary monthly, *Sabujpatra* (*Green Leaves*), on various aspects of Hindu orthodoxy—its obscurantist outlook and oppressive institutions, gerontocratic mores and puritanic values. The uncompromisingly radical approach to society and human relations which now began to characterise his novels and short stories provoked wide and bitter criticism in Bengal which, in its turn, intensified his alienation from the tradition-bound community. In his poems and plays the accent was increasingly on the dynamic aspects of reality—on life's *élan* and ever-changing forms, its movement and fluidity, its inexhaustible youth and energy, its urge for freedom and adventure.[19] From May 1916 to March 1917 he was abroad on his fourth foreign tour visiting Japan and the United States. What he saw there deepened his distrust of nationalism which he openly condemned as 'a cruel epidemic of evil that is sweeping over the human world of the present age, and eating into its moral vitality'.[20] Like Goethe he became an exponent of cosmopolitanism and world culture in almost lonely opposition to the rising ideological tide of the period. In 1918 he formulated the idea of an international university at Santiniketan, and on 22 December the foundation-stone of Visva Bharati was laid with proper ceremony.

1919 was a year of fast and far-reaching developments. Gandhi, who had profoundly shocked Tagore in 1918 by his recruiting campaign in support of the war,[21] was by now completely disillusioned with the British. In protest against the notorious Rowlatt Bills he called upon the people to observe a nation wide *hartāl* or suspension of all activities (originally fixed for March 30, but subsequently changed to April 6). It received unprecedented public response but also led to several outbreaks of mob violence. On 5 April Gandhi wrote to Tagore seeking from him 'a message of hope and inspiration for those who have to go through the fire'. Tagore's reaction was mixed. He felt that resistance to the bills was necessary; he also fully agreed with Gandhi that it had to be non-violent; but he feared that in the given circumstances a mass movement was almost certain to intensify race-hatred and the spirit of revenge. On 12 April he wrote an open letter to Gandhi addressing him as 'Dear Mahatmaji'. Welcoming Gandhi's ideal of courageous non-violence, he nevertheless warned him that 'passive resistance . . . is not necessarily moral in itself', that without adequate spiritual preparation of the people the movement might 'degenerate into fanaticism', that under its self-deceptive cover violence might reassert itself.[22] The Jallianwala Bagh massacre took place the following day. Tagore received the details from Andrews, and on 30 May 1919 wrote his historic letter to the Viceroy, Lord Chelmsford, renouncing his Knighthood, and 'giving voice to the protest of the millions of my countrymen surprised into a dumb anguish of terror'.[23] Meantime Gandhi had decided on temporary suspension of the movement on April 18. He admitted the point of Tagore's warning: 'My error lay in my failure to observe this necessary limitation. I had called upon the people to launch upon civil disobedience before they had thus qualified themselves for it, and this mistake of mine seemed to me to be of a Himalayan magnitude.'[24]

In spite of his Himalayan mistake, the *hartāl* marked the beginning of Gandhi's emergence as the supreme leader of the Indian nationalist movement. During the later part of 1919 he organized the Congress inquiry in the Punjab, presided over the Khilafat Conference in Delhi, and was entrusted with the drafting of the new constitution of the Congress. He also assumed editorship of two weeklies, *Navajivan* and *Young India* (October 1919). In April 1920, he invited Tagore to Ahmedabad to address the Gujarati Literary Conference where the poet had an opportunity to hear Gandhi expound his Tolstoyian view that literature was for and about the masses, that its true aim was to educate the people in the principles of virtuous living.[25] In May Tagore left India on his fifth foreign tour during which he travelled extensively in England, Europe and the United States where he spoke repeatedly on the meeting of the East and the West and his ideal of universalism and creative unity.[26] He did not return till July 1921 although he kept in touch with the dramatic turn of events in India, mainly through his correspondence with Andrews.

The turn came with the launching of the all-India non-co-operation campaign by Gandhi on 1 August 1920. He persuaded the Congress to adopt his resolution at a special session at Calcutta (September 1920), and then to ratify it at the session at Nagpur (December 1920). The constitution of the Congress was radically altered by making it a mass organization; its objective was declared to be the attainment of *swarāj*; and it was committed to non-violent non-co-operation on a national scale. From this point Gandhi's leadership of the Congress became virtually absolute.

Andrews was drawn to non-co-operation although he had strong reservations about Khilafat. He 'dreaded to be cold and indifferent in such an atmosphere as we have at present'.[27] His letters, however, were causing great anxiety to Tagore not only because he wanted Santiniketan to be saved from 'the whirlwind of our dusty politics'[28] but also because he saw in non-co-operation a serious threat to all his cherished ideals and aspirations. He wrote repeatedly to Andrews cautioning against the negative character of the movement and urging that the energies released by Gandhi be directed to constructive activities. In one of his early letters on the subject (Paris, 18 September 1920) he expressed himself in unambiguous terms:

> I find our countrymen are furiously excited about non-co-opera-tion. . . . Such an emotional outbreak should have been taken advantage of in starting independent organizations all over India for serving our country. Let Mahatma Gandhi be the true leader in this; let him send out his call for positive service, ask for homage in sacrifice, which has its end in love and creation. I shall be willing to sit at his feet and do his bidding if he commands me to co-operate with my countrymen in service and love. I refuse to waste my man-hood in lighting fires of anger and spreading it from house to house.
>
> It is not that I do not feel anger in my heart for injustice and insult heaped upon my motherland. But . . . it would be an insult to humanity if I use the sacred energy of my moral indignation for the purpose of spreading a blind passion all over my country. It would be like using the fire from the altar of sacrifice for the purpose of incendiarism.[29]

In subsequent letters he reminded Andrews of Rammohun Roy 'who had the profound faith and large vision to feel in his heart the unity of soul between the East and the West' (20 December 1920); warned against the sacrifice of 'the complete man . . . to the patriotic man, or even to the merely moral man' (14 January 1921); and expressed his fear that he would be 'rejected by my own people when I go back to India' (8 February 1921).[30] Then in three successive letters (2, 5, and 13 March) he developed his critique of non-co-operation which he described as 'political asceticism'. 'It has at its back a fierce joy of annihilation, which at its best is asceticism, and at its worst that orgy of frightfulness in which human nature, losing faith in the basic reality of normal life, finds a disinterested delight in an unmeaning devastation.' 'We are to emancipate Man from the meshes that he himself has woven round him—these organizations of national egoism.' His ideal, he explained, was *mukti*, emancipation, which 'emphasized the fact of *ānanda*, joy, which had to be attained', and not Buddha's *nirvāna*, which 'emphasized the fact of *dukkha*, misery, which had to be avoided'. Co-operation was the law of man's growth, and India's aim should be to achieve 'one grand harmony of all human races'. 'Our present struggle to alienate our heart and mind from the West is an attempt at spiritual suicide.'[31]

The three letters were published in the May 1921 issue of India's leading English monthly, *The Modern Review*. Gandhi's reply appeared next month in his own journal *Young India*, and the great debate was started. Gandhi argued that his 'struggle is being waged against compulsory co-operation, against one-sided combination, against the armed imposition of modern methods of exploitation masquerading under the name of civilization'. He further pointed out that 'rejection is as much an ideal as the acceptance of a thing', that weeding is as necessary to cultivation as sowing, that '*mukti* is as much a negative state as *nirvana*'. He assured Tagore that 'non-co-operation is intended to pave the way to real, honourable and voluntary co-operation based on mutual respect and trust'.[32]

Tagore returned to India on 16 July, and in August he gave several public lectures developing his arguments against non-co-operation and his alternative perspective of India's development. He was particularly disturbed by Gandhi's call for boycott of schools and his total rejection of modern western thought and culture.[33] In his first lecture under the title '*Shikshār Milan*' he pointed out that 'the freeing of the soul from the oppression of the material universe' was essential to spiritual growth, that 'secular knowledge is today in the possession of European thinkers and scientists and we in the East who need it must seek their help', that while India should reject 'the greed that is now enthroned in the heart of European civilization', 'if we are biased against Western science just because it is of the West, we shall not only deprive ourselves of the principles it has to teach, but pull down our own eastern spirituality'. Instead of boycotting schools in a spirit of arrogant nationalism, India should seek to develop educational centres where 'the unity of spiritual and scientific knowledge' would be cultivated.[34] When this view was sharply attacked by his younger contemporary, Saratchandra Chattopadhyay, at that time Bengal's most popular novelist and an ardent supporter of non-co-operation, Tagore replied at full length in his next public lecture, 'Satyer Ahwān' (29 August 1921). He expressed his deep faith in Gandhi's 'capacity for love' which 'has captured the heart of India', but he maintained that the movement launched by Gandhi was not in consonance with the spirit of freedom and truth. It rejected reason and refused to teach people that swarāj was 'a vast enterprise involving complex processes and needing as much study and clear thinking as impulse and emotion'. Its dogmatic stress on the charkhā or spinning wheel as the key to swarāj would in no way solve India's problems of poverty, ignorance, or stagnation; instead, it would only obscure the need for scientific research and creative enterprise in diverse directions. What was worse, 'there is a tyranny in the air', for the movement with its demand for uniformity and unquestioning obedience had made its participants intolerant of all criticism. India's freedom would not be achieved by surrendering free inquiry to blind faith in a short cut solution. Her awakening which was 'a part of the awakening of the world' required reinstating 'reason on its lost pedestal'. The emphasis should be not on the burning of foreign cloth but on creation of new wealth, not on isolation and conflict, but on reconciliation and unity in diversity.[35]

In September Gandhi came to Calcutta, and on 6 September he met with Tagore for four hours, Andrews being the only other person present. During the discussion Gandhi's supporters organised the burning of foreign cloth in Tagore's courtyard to register their protest against Tagore's unpatriotic attitude.[36] Andrews wrote subsequently: 'What seemed most evident . . . was a difference of temperament so wide that it was extremely difficult to arrive at a common intellectual understanding, though the moral ties of friendship remained entirely unbroken.'[37] The English version of Tagore's second lecture ('The Call of Truth') and Gandhi's reply to it were both published in October. Gandhi described Tagore as 'a sentinel warning us against the approach of enemies called Bigotry, Lethargy, Intolerance, Ignorance, Inertia and other members of that brood'. However, he argued that his 'plea for the spinning wheel is a plea for recognising the dignity of labour', the charkhā would rescue the poor millions of India from hunger and enforced idleness, the burning of foreign cloth was an act of self-purification, non-co-operation was 'a retirement within ourselves' and 'Indian nationalism is not exclusive, nor aggressive, nor destructive'.[38]

It was not a reply that could satisfy Tagore, particularly since in the following months the proneness of the non-co-operation movement to mob violence became agonisingly obvious. In November there were terrible communal riots in Bombay in the wake of boycott, and Gandhi went on a fast of penance. However, in December the Congress decided to launch mass civil disobedience after investing Gandhi with 'sole executive authority'.[39] Tagore, who was then occupied with the establishment of a rural reconstruction centre near his *āshram*, wrote an open letter on 1 February 1922 cautioning that a political movement involving 'an immense multiple of different traditions and stages of cultures' was unlikely to remain non-violent for long, that *ahimsā* was incompatible with the stirring up of 'blind forces' which it would not be able to control, that *satyāgraha* to be fruitful required patient education of the people in its ethical principles, and that a movement without such a preparation could only bring disaster.[40] The letter was published on 3 February; the terrible events at Chauri Chaura occurred on 5 February, when twenty-two policemen were burnt alive by an infuriated mob. On 12 February Gandhi suspended the movement and undertook a five-day fast of penance.[41] He was arrested on 10 March, tried on charge of sedition, and sentenced to six years' imprisonment. He spent two years in jail and was released unconditionally in February 1924.

III

Tagore's fear that mass civil disobedience, even under Gandhi's leadership, would inevitably lead to mob violence was tragically confirmed by Chauri Chaura. It was not that he did not admire Gandhi's ideal of non-violent resistance to tyranny and injustice. In fact, in his play *Muktadhārā*, written shortly before Chauri Chaura, he upheld this very ideal.[42] Later in December 1922 when with Andrews he briefly visited the *āshram* at Sabarmati he paid eloquent homage to Gandhi's dedication and self-sacrifice, his moral courage and compassion.[43] However, he was not persuaded that non-violence was compatible with a mass movement which was actuated largely by negative sentiments and a desire for quick results. In 1923, he wrote several articles in which he pointed out that there was no short-cut solution to India's complex problems, that the primary need was to educate people in rational thinking and constructive activities, that the people's reliance on the Mahatma to achieve freedom by some miraculous means only showed their slave mentality, that Hindu-Muslim unity would not be achieved without a radical change in the attitudes of the two communities.

In December 1924 the Congress under Gandhi's presidentship made spinning a qualification of membership, and reaffirmed its faith in the *charkhā*. In an effort to win Tagore to his point of view Gandhi visited Santiniketan on 29 May 1925, but was unsuccessful. Shortly after the meeting Tagore wrote a long article under the title 'The Cult of the Charkha' explaining his disagreement with Gandhi. Life, he argued, expresses itself in many forms which 'in death . . . merge into sameness'. In India 'this ominous process of being levelled down into sameness has long been at work' so that in the end the people have 'acquired a distaste for very existence'. For India's emancipation what was needed was a revitalization of man's creative intelligence, his ability to discover 'the wealth of diversity' within himself. Gandhi's cult of the *charkhā*, on the contrary, would impose blind uniformity on the people; it would reinforce their slavish habit of 'everlasting recapitulation'; instead of removing poverty or achieving Hindu-Muslim unity, or leading to *swarāj*, it was more likely to paralyse the reasoning power of the people and perpetuate their habit of reliance on the *guru* or some magical *mantram*. Tagore pleaded for the development of the spirit of rational thinking and inventiveness which would inspire enterprise in various fields of activity, and promote unity in diversity.[44]

In his brief rejoinder Gandhi first cautioned his readers that 'the Poet's criticism is a poetic licence and he who takes it literally is in danger of finding himself in an awkward corner'. He then pointed out that he did not 'want everybody to spin the whole of his or her time to the exclusion of all other activity', that all he wanted was that every Indian should give 'every day only thirty minutes to spinning as sacrifice for the whole nation'. However, 'the Charkha is intended to realize the essential oneness of interest among India's myriads'. He also stressed that 'round the Charkha . . . a national servant would build up a programme of . . . hundreds of other beneficial activities'.[45]

Another significant issue on which Tagore and Gandhi differed basically in 1925 was that of birth control. Gandhi's opposition to artificial methods was well-known to his associates and followers; but it was in March 1925 that he dealt publicly with this issue. He stated categorically:

> There can be no two opinions about the necessity of birth control. But the only method handed down from ages past is self-control or brahmacharya. It is an infallible sovereign remedy doing good to those who practise it. . . . The union is meant not for pleasure but for bringing forth progeny. And union is a crime when the desire for progeny is absent.
>
> Artificial methods are like putting a premium upon vice. They make men and women reckless. . . . Adoption of artificial methods must result in imbecility and nervous prostration . . . if artificial methods become the order of the day nothing but moral degradation can be the result.[46]

129

Greatly distressed by Gandhi's attitude Margaret Sanger wrote to Tagore (12 August 1925) seeking his view. Tagore's statement was equally forthright:

> I am of opinion that Birth Control movement is a great movement not only because it will save women from enforced and undesirable maternity, but because it will help the cause of peace by lessening the number of surplus population of a country scrambling for food and space outside its own rightful limits. In a hunger-stricken country like India it is a cruel crime thoughtlessly to bring more children into existence than could properly be taken care of, causing endless suffering to them and imposing a degrading condition upon the whole family. . . . I believe that to wait till the moral sense of man becomes a great deal more powerful than it is now and till then to allow countless generations of children to suffer privations and untimely death for no fault of their own, is a great social injustice which should not be tolerated. I feel grateful for the cause you have made your own and for which you have suffered.[47]

The only other major public debate between the two took place in 1934, but Tagore's difference with Gandhi found expression on a number of occasions. He wrote two stories, 'Nāmanjur Galpa' (1925) and 'Sanskār' (1928), satirizing the skin-deep egalitarianism of the supporters of non-co-operation. In 1929 reviewing a newly-published book on his own political philosophy he again stressed that true *swarāj* would be achieved not by agitational politics but through patient education of the people in co-operative activities and self-government.[48] While he fully supported Gandhi's movement against untouchability and in September 1932 gave his 'blessing' to the 'epic fast' at Yeravda jail (he was present when Gandhi broke his fast and he paid his homage to the Mahatma in moving words),[49] he expressed his doubts next year about the consequences of the Yeravda Pact, and when in May 1933 Gandhi again decided to undertake a fast of self-purification, Tagore advised him against it.[50] In 1937 Gandhi published his scheme of Basic Education, which with minor modifications was adopted by the Congress in 1938. Tagore, who possibly more than any other Indian had worked unremittingly in the cause of educational reforms, criticised the scheme because it 'seems to assume that material utility, rather than development of personality is the aim of education'. He objected to the idea of an education which would train people 'to view the world . . . in the perspective of the particular craft they are to employ for their livelihood'.

He also considered it basically unfortunate 'to give . . . a vested interest to the teachers in the market value of the pupils' labour'.[51] Instead he pleaded for an approach to education 'which takes count of the organic wholeness of human individuality that needs for its health a general stimulation to all faculties, bodily and mental'. The keynote of modern education, he insisted, is free and harmonious development of man's creative potentiality.

Tagore was also greatly distressed by the growing rift in the Congress during the late 'thirties, but even more by the authoritarian attitude and conduct of Gandhi towards Subhash Chandra Bose. When at the Tripuri Congress a leading Gandhian, Seth Govinda Das, demanded unquestioning obedience to the Mahatma after comparing him in glowing terms with Mussolini, Hitler and Stalin, Tagore protested in an open letter warning against fascist tendencies in Indian politics.[52] He repeatedly voiced his opposition to all forms of totalitarianism and to the Munich spirit of appeasement.[53] In this his attitude was closer to that of Nehru and M. N. Roy, and in contrast to the somewhat ambiguous position of Gandhi.

Tagore's sharpest attack on Gandhi during the 'thirties, however, came when shortly after the terrible earthquake in Bihar in 1934 the Mahatma issued a public statement (24 January) asserting that the calamity was 'a divine chastisement sent by God' for the sin of untouchability. Tagore pointed out that such an explanation not only assumed God to be morally inferior to civilized men and women since the so-called punishment made no distinction between the guilty and the innocent (the victims included many children and untouchables), but it was also completely unscientific in holding cosmic phenomena to be dependent on human custom and behaviour. He considered it singularly unfortunate that Gandhi should in this way strengthen the elements of unreason, already so very powerful in India—'unreason, which is a fundamental source of all the blind powers that drive us against freedom and self-respect'. Gandhi, however, was adamant. 'I cannot prove the connection of the sin of untouchability with the Bihar visitation,' he replied, but 'the connection is instinctively felt by me'. 'Visitations like droughts, floods, earthquakes and the like, though they seem to have only physical origins, are, for me, somehow connected with man's morals. . . . With me the connection between cosmic phenomena and human behaviour is a living faith that draws me nearer to my God.' On this Nehru commented a year later: 'This was a staggering remark. . . . Anything more opposed to the scientific outlook it would be difficult to imagine.'[54]

IV

Such then, in brief, is the record. Gandhi's glorious discovery notwithstanding, Tagore disagreed with him on virtually every major issue—mass civil disobedience and non-co-operation, *charkhā* and the burning of foreign cloth, Khilafat and the approach to Hindu-Muslim unity, *brahmacharya* and birth control, fasting, basic education, and the relation between science and morality. But the difference was more fundamental than the record of their public dispute alone would indicate. Romain Rolland noted this quite early when, comparing Gandhi and Tagore, he wrote: '[They] are as much apart . . . as a sage can be from an apostle, or as Plato can be from Saint Paul. On the one side, we have the genius of faith and charity, which wishes to be the leaven of a new humanity, and on the other, the genius of intelligence, free, vast and serene, which comprehends the totality of all existences'. Rolland admired both, but he confessed that 'with all veneration to the Mahatma, I am with Tagore'.[55]

The difference, when analysed, shows many facets. In contrast with Gandhi's tradition-bound Gujarat, Tagor's Bengal had always been notorious for its heretical spirit. Gandhi was deeply influenced by the ascetic ideals of Jainism which never made any appeal to Bengal; instead, the Bengali mind has always been characterised by an ambient eroticism.[56] Gandhi belonged to the *bānia* caste from which he imbibed a mixture of utilitarianism, organizational efficiency and devotional sentiments. Tagore, on the other hand, came of an aristocratic *brāhman* family with a reputation for intellectual curiosity, aesthetic refinement and adventurous individualism. Gandhi's mother with her austere vows and endless fasts of penance and purification provided him with his archetype of saintliness. Tagore's mother was a shadowy figure, but from his father, the Maharshi, he acquired a contemplative religion which saw virtue in harmony and self-unfolding, and which had a strong distaste for any variety of masochistic morality.

They were both eclectic in their approach to the Indian cultural heritage, but they selected very different elements. Gandhi's knowledge and appreciation of ancient and classical India was patently narrow and marginal; this in a way made it easy for him to make an interpretation of the *Gītā* which was arbitrary and personal. But the main source of his spiritual nourishment was the *Rāmāyana* of Tulsidas. His predilection was for the didactic and devotional aspects of medieval Hinduism. Tagore, on the contrary, was introduced very early in life to the speculative grandeur of the *Upanishads*. His own poetic temper responded eagerly to the notion of God as the great artist who fulfilled himself in the endless creation of beautiful forms. He also found in classical India a fullness of spirit which was akin to his own. His mind dwelt lovingly on the wondrous poetry of Kalidasa, the delicate murals of Ajanta, the extraordinary combination of grace and vitality in Hindu-Buddhist sculpture, and the music and dancing and seasonal festivals which made life in the classical age so very vivid and colourful before attenuation set in with the triumph of taboos and proliferating restrictions. He too admired some of the saint-poets of medieval India, but what drew him to them was not their didacticism but their intensely lyrical intuitions of transcendence and their rejection of conventional morality.

They also responded differently to western culture and civilization. Gandhi rejected most of it, but 'the Sermon on the Mount . . . went straight to my heart', and the Christian notion 'that renunciation was the highest form of religion appealed to me greatly'.[57] He was influenced by some of the ideas of Carlyle, Ruskin and Tolstoy which stressed austere living, manual labour, simplicity, purity and non-violence. But Europe's impressive achievements in arts and letters, science and philosophy, political freedom and material well-being, had no attraction for him. Christ greatly appealed to Tagore also, but he had little sympathy for the obscurantism, authoritarianism and puritanism of the Church. What he admired most in the west was its spirit of intellectual inquiry and its commitment to liberty and creative self-expression. Against Sparta's sterile dictatorship he upheld the fruitful liberalism of Periclean Athens;[58] he wrote repeatedly in praise of the humanism of the European renaissance; in Goethe's dynamic universalism he found an ideal which was very similar to his own *weltanschauung*. There was much in the West which he condemned—its aggressiveness and greed, its unscrupulous pursuit of power and profit—but he also believed that the West had a historic role to play in the revitalisation of Asian societies. He valued not only science and technology but Europe's art, literature and music, its inexhaustible curiosity and inventiveness, its mobility and self-energising power.

Consequently Tagore felt a strong affinity with such nineteenth century Indian humanists and rationalists as Rammohun Roy, Iswarchandra Vidyasagar and M. G. Ranade who had welcomed the western impact on India because of its liberalizing significance.[59] Gandhi was never in tune with these champions of modernization; his spiritual predecessors in modern Indian history belong to the opposite camp which includes immensely popular figures like Dayananda and Vivekananda. He, in fact, went beyond them in his opposition to western cultural infiltration of India. He thus attracted to his movement nationalists, revivalists and populists while Tagore found himself increasingly estranged from the ideological climate of the country.[60]

Central to it all was the difference in personality of these two great men. It is not simply that Tagore was a poet and Gandhi a political leader; for many poets including not a few in Bengal became Gandhi's disciples while a political leader like Nehru sent his daughter to Santiniketan for her education. But Tagore, like Goethe, was much more than a poet; he was modern India's *uomo universale*. Poet, playwright, novelist, philosopher and social critic, educationist and organiser of rural co-operatives, painter and composer, he expressed himself in a spectacular variety of activities. They were all nourished by the almost inexhaustible resources of his creative genius, and it is not surprising that he found in creativity the purpose and meaning of human existence. Whatever contributed to the development of the creative personality of every individual was in his view good; anything that restricted this development was evil. Freedom was essential to creation; so were knowledge, sensitiveness, joyous acceptance of life, love, harmony with nature and co-operation with fellow human beings. 'Deliverance is not for me in renunciation. I feel the embrace of freedom in a thousand bonds of delight'. (*Collected Poems and Plays of Rabindranath Tagore,* London, 1958, p. 34.)

Gandhi too was not a mere political leader. His polity was grounded in morality, which in its turn was guided by his religious faith. But his religious ethic involved on the one hand the ideal of 'freeing my soul from the bondage of the flesh', and on the other, seeking salvation 'through incessant toil in the service of my country and of humanity'.[61] The first of these two pursuits brings out most sharply the contrast between him and Tagore. Tagore celebrates the body—its potential for beauty, joy, love, intelligence and creation. To Gandhi on the contrary 'the human body, with its lusts and sins, is . . . an evil, not a good. Only by complete severance from this human body can perfect deliverance be found. . . . [He] is one with the medieval saints in a passionate belief in celibacy as practically the only way to realize the beatific vision of God'.[62] With this asceticism went a profound distrust of reason, art, science, and in general, most elements of civilization.

Tagore admired the second pursuit—service of humanity—but in Gandhi's personality even this was inextricably tied with self-mortification. To be able to serve, Gandhi believed, one must acquire full control over all one's passions, and this required austere living, *brahmacharya,* fasting, etc. Gandhi's experience taught him that such practices gave to the practitioner a great store of energy which would then be available for service. In effect, it was a deliberate narrowing of interests and feelings to be able to discipline, fortify and eventually direct the individual's will to a specific purpose. In contrast with the richness of sensibility in Tagore, Gandhi's personality was distinguished by extraordinary will-power which, though dedicated to service, was unmistakably authoritarian. Even Nehru recognised this; but it was M. N. Roy who analysed this aspect at some length, and following Erich Fromm's study of Luther and Calvin, suggested that at the heart of the Gandhian religious ethic was the Mahatma's 'fear of freedom'.[63]

The antinomy is clear; nevertheless, their mutual regard was not a matter of superficial courtesy. To Gandhi intellectual disagreements were of little consequence; he appreciated in Tagore his 'singular purity of life'. He consistently refrained from initiating any controversy; instead, he stressed their common commitment to non-violence, decentralisation, and the inter-dependence of ends and means. Besides, after the death of Gokhale (1915) and Tilak (1920), Gandhi's position became increasingly one of lonely eminence in Indian public life; he had many followers and a few political rivals; but in Tagore he found 'the great sentinel' who offered him friendship with disinterested criticism. However, I doubt if he could ever engage in a genuine 'dialogue' with Tagore in Martin Buber's meaning of that word.[64] With Tulsidas' devotional didacticism as his model of good poetry and old Tolstoy's rigorism as his guide in the world of art, he could hardly be expected to sympathise with Tagore's eudemonic humanism, or genuinely to appreciate the rich multi-formity of his creative genius.[65] C. F. Andrews vainly tried to introduce him to the glories of Tagore's *The Cycle of Spring*, but the only compositions of Tagore which really moved Gandhi were some of his devotional songs. He saw in Tagore what he wanted to see, his *'tapashcharya'* or 'single minded devotion', his ability to 'represent the mass mind of India'. It is consequently not surprising that on the occasion when he spoke of his discovery of the absence of any real conflict between himself and Tagore he could advise Tagore's followers 'to make Santiniketan hum with the music of the [spinning] wheel' since that was how he interpreted the ideal of Tagore.[66]

Tagore's attitude was obviously more complex, sensitive, and, I suspect, basically ambivalent. To him the polarity was too real to be conveniently played down. In Gandhi's puritanical politics he saw a threat to creative imagination very similar to the one made by Plato in the *Republic*.[67] 'Will our Indian Swaraj, when it comes to exist', he wrote to Andrews in 1921, 'pass a deportation order against all feckless creatures who are pursuers of phantoms and fashioners of dreams, who neither dig nor sow, bake nor boil, spin nor darn, neither move nor support resolutions?'[68] He found no scope for compromise with Gandhi's asceticism and opposition to science, his exploitation of the 'irrational force of credulity in our people', his insistence on ritual and discipline, his creed of the *charkhā*, or his negative attitude to modernization and the west.

But at the same time there was much in Gandhi which he genuinely admired—his unconquerable spirit and freedom from selfishness, practice of non-violence and of morality in politics, dedication to service and identification with the common people. Most of all, he valued Gandhi's 'energizing power', 'the great life force of the complete man who is absolutely one with his ideas, whose visions perfectly blend with his whole being'.[69] It was this inner unity and moral dynamism which made it possible for Gandhi to move the traditionally passive people of India and draw them into the campaign of non-violent non-co-operation. Tagore who always aspired to be able to awaken in the people their dormant courage and self-confidence, their capacity for dedication and constructive work, but who also knew that the task was beyond his own resources, could not but be profoundly impressed by the phenomenal response of the Indian masses to Gandhi's leadership.

And yet his apprehensions were never altogether allayed. For the man who was 'completely one with his ideas' was also a puritan whose ideas were strait and inflexible, and in his phenomenal rapproachement with the people there were insidious elements of irrationality and messianism which could lead to what, in Talmon's language, might be called 'totalitarian democracy'.[70] Tagore, therefore, could not share the privilege of Gandhi's glorious discovery; instead he preferred an attitude of anguished ambivalance to the naïve optimism of *mauvaise foi*.

NOTES

[1] Pyarelal, *The Santiniketan Pilgrimage* (Ahmedabad, 1958), p. 25.

[2] Jawaharlal Nehru, *The Discovery of India* (Bombay, 1966), p. 361.

[3] K. R. Kripalani, *Gandhi, Tagore and Nehru* (Bombay, 1949), p. 8.

[4] R. K. Prabhu & R. Kelekar (ed.), *Truth Called Them Differently* (Ahmedabad, 1961), foreword, p. x.

[5] For Tagore's appeal and Gandhi's reply see *Harijan*, 2 March 1940, and *Visva-Bharati News*, April 1940.

[6] Joseph J. Doke, *M. K. Gandhi, An Indian Patriot in South Africa* (first Indian edition, Natesan, Madras, 1919; repr. Govt. of India Publications Division, Delhi, 1967).

[7] D. G. Tendulkar, *Mahatma, Life of Mohandas Karamchand Gandhi* in 8 vols., hereinafter *DGT* (Delhi, 1960-63), vol. 1, p. 109. For Tolstoy's commendation, *ibid.*, p. 329; Kalidas Nag, *Tolstoy and Gandhi* (Patna, 1950), p. 67; *Collected Works of Mahatma Gandhi* (Govt. of India Publications, Delhi), vol. 10.

[8] For his biography see Benarsidas Chaturvedi and Marjorie Sykes, *Charles Freer Andrews* (London, 1950). Andrews edited and published several volumes on Tagore and Gandhi which contain many details of his relations with both: *Letters to a Friend* (London, 1928); *Thoughts from Tagore* (London, 1929); *Mahatma Gandhi's Ideas* (London, 1929); *Mahatma Gandhi: His Own Story* (London, 1930); and *Mahatma Gandhi at Work* (London, 1931).

[9] Chaturvedi and Sykes, op. cit., p. 95.

[10] Krishna Kripalani, *Rabindranath Tagore: A Biography* (London, 1962), pp. 245-47. For a more detailed account see Prabhatkumar Mukhopadhyay, *Rabindra-Jibani*, vol. 2, pp. 367-68, 376-78. This monumental Bengali biography of Tagore in 4 vols., hereinafter *PKM* (Calcutta, rev. and enlarged ed. 1946-56) has not yet been translated into English.

[11] Tagore presented these views and arguments in various essays and addresses collected in the volumes: *Atmashakti* (1905), *Raja O Praja* (1908), *Samuha* (1908), *Swadesh* (1908) and *Samaj* (1908). See *Rabindra-Rachanabali*, hereinafter *RR* (Collected works of Tagore in Bengali, published by Visva-Bharati, Calcutta, vols. 1-26, 1939-48; vol. 27, 1965), vols. 3, 10, 11 and 12. For English version of some of these essays, Rabindranath Tagore, *Towards Universal Man* (London, 1962).

[12] Edward Thompson, *Rabindranath Tagore, Poet and Dramatist* (London, 1948), p. 54. Gandhi also recorded his shock at the sight of blood and animal sacrifice at the Kali temple, Calcutta. See M. K. Gandhi, *An Autobiography* (Ahmedabad, 1959), pp. 171-72.

[13] For the two novels and the play see *RR*, vols. 1 and 2. An English version of *Bisarjan* under the title *Sacrifice* (London, 1917) was dedicated 'to those heroes who bravely stood for peace when human sacrifice was claimed for the goddess of war'.

[14] He had briefly participated in the anti-partition movement but withdrew after discovering its violent and destructive tendencies. For his anguished disillusionment with revolutionary nationalism see in particular his two later novels, *Ghare-Baire* (publ. 1916; *RR*, vol. 8; English tr. *The Home and the World*, London, 1919), and *Char Adhyay* (publ. 1934; *RR*, vol. 13; English tr. *Four chapters*, Calcutta, 1950).

[15] See *RR*, vol. 9. For a thoughtful discussion of the contemporary significance of *Prayaschitta* see *PKM*, vol. 2, pp. 173-76.

[16] *PKM*, vol. 2, p. 368; also G. D. Khanulkar, *The Lute and the Plough: A Life of Rabindranath Tagore*, tr. by Thomas Gay (Bombay, 1963), p. 197.

[17] Gandhi's own account (*An Autobiography*, op. cit., p. 281) shows no awareness that he was imposing upon his host's courtesy. *PKM*, vol. 2, pp. 377-78, gives a more objective account. Earlier at Poona Gandhi had caused embarrassment to Gokhale and resentment among the members of the Servants of India Society by 'starting one morning the work of cleaning the latrines of the society's colony'. *DGT*, vol. 1, p. 159.

[18] Chaturvedi and Sykes, op. cit., p. 110.

[19] Tagore's published works of this period include: *Phalguni* (1916, Eng. tr. *The Cycle of Spring*, London, 1917), play; *Balaka* (1916) and *Palataka* (1918), verse; *Ghare-Baire* (1916) and *Chaturanga* (1916), novels; *Galpasaptak* (1916) and *Paylanambar* (1920), short stories, and *Sanchay* (1916) and *Parichay* (1916), essays. See *RR*, vols. 7, 8, 12, 13, 18, and 23. For Pramatha Chaudhuri see Buddhadev Bose, *An Acre of Green Grass* (Calcutta, 1948), ch. 2.

137

20 Rabindranath Tagore, *Nationalism* (London, 1950), p. 16. First publ. London, 1917.

21 C. F. Andrews, *Mahatma Gandhi's Ideas* (London, 1929), p. 252.

22 Full text of Tagore's letter in *The Collected Works of Mahatma Gandhi*, hereinafter *CWMG* (Govt. of India, Publications Division, Delhi, 1958—; 29 vols. published so far covering 1884-1926), vol. 15, appendix 1, pp. 495-96. For Gandhi's letter, *ibid.*, pp. 179-80.

23 For text of letter and related details, Amal Home, *Purushottam Rabindranath* (Calcutta, 1955), pp. 41-65. Also see C. F. Andrews, 'Gandhi and Tagore', *The Hindu* (Madras), 10 April 1924.

24 *DGT*, vol. 1, p. 260. Also see *CWMG*, vol. 15, pp. 104-05 (telegram and letter to Andrews, 25 Feb. 1919), pp. 243-45 (press statement on suspension of civil disobedience, 18 April 1919).

25 Speech at Gujarati Sahitya Parisad, 2 April 1920, in *CWMG*, vol. 17, pp. 301-03. In *Hind Swaraj* Gandhi listed six non-fictional works of Tolstoy including *What is Art* which he advised all to read. *CWMG*, vol. 10, p. 65. In his book of recollections, *Among the Great* (Bombay, 1950) D. K. Roy has recorded his discussions with Gandhi about the latter's Tolstoyian views on art (pp. 61-68; 78-82).

26 Rabindranath Tagore, *Creative Unity* (London, 1922).

27 C. F. Andrews to Rabindranath Tagore, 15 November 1920, quoted Chaturvedi and Sykes, op. cit., p. 160 from C. F. Andrews papers at Rabindra Sadan, Visva-Bharati, Santiniketan. Andrews opposed 'the Khilafat doctrine of a Turkish empire . . . which involved the refusal of independence' to the Arabs and the Armenians. Letter to Gandhi, 23 September 1920. For Gandhi's replies to Andrews' criticism of Khilafat see *CWMG*, vol. 17, pp. 498-501; and vol. 18, pp. 72-74. For Andrews' support of non-co-operation see his pamphlets and compilations published during 1921-23: *Non-Co-Operation* and *The Meaning of Non-Co-operation* (Tagore & Co., Madras); *Independence, the Immediate Need* and *A Case for India's Independence* (Ganesan, Madras). Also see Nehru, *An Autobiography* (Bombay, 1962), pp. 66-67.

28 Tagore's letter to Andrews, 3 October 1920. During Tagore's absence Gandhi visited Santiniketan and addressed the inmates on 17 September 1920. *CWMG*, vol. 18, pp. 264-66. For the turmoil at Santiniketan and Andrews' role in it see *PKM*, vol. 3, pp. 59-63.

29 Rabindranath Tagore, *Letters to a Friend* (London, 1928), pp. 95-96. Tagore's letters to Andrews written during May 1920 to July 1921 were originally published in a volume under the title, *Letters from Abroad* (Ganesan, Madras, 1924). *Letters to a Friend* was a revised and enlarged edition of this volume containing his letters to Andrews from 1913-22.

30 *Ibid.*, pp. 109, 115, 123.

31 For these three letters, *ibid.*, pp. 127-37; also *The Modern Review*, vol. 29, No. 5.

32 'The Poet's Anxiety', *Young India*, 1 June 1921; *CWMG*, vol. 20, pp. 161-64.

33 For Gandhi's various articles and speeches on boycott of schools in 1920-21 see *CWMG*, vols. 18-21. At Santiniketan he reaffirmed his belief that 'Western civilization is the work of Satan'. *Ibid.*, vol. 18, p. 264.

34 Original Bengali text published as a pamphlet, Calcutta, August 1921; English version, 'The Union of Cultures', *The Modern Review*, November 1921; 'The Unity of Education' in *Towards Universal Man*, pp. 231-51.

35 Original Bengali text in *Kalantar*, RR, vol. 24; English version in *The Modern*

Review, October 1921; 'The Call of Truth' in *Towards Universal Man*, pp. 252-73. For Chattopadyay's attack see his volume of essays *Swadesh O Sahitya* (Calcutta, n.d.), pp. 20-41.

[36] Leonard Elmhirst, 'Personal Memories of Tagore' in *Rabindranath Tagore, A Centenary Volume* (Sahitya Akademi, New Delhi, 1961), pp. 14-15. Also see Kripalani, *Rabindranath Tagore*, op. cit., pp. 292-93.

[37] C. F. Andrews, *Mahatma Gandhi's Ideas*, p. 256.

[38] 'The Great Sentinel', *Young India*, 13 October 1921; *CWMG*, vol. 21, pp. 287-91.

[39] *DGT*, vol. 2, p. 72. To the rural people Gandhi was already an *avatar*, or incarnation of the deity; pictures representing him as Shri Krishna were on sale everywhere; his criticism of the practice only intensified the devotional feeling of the masses towards him. See *DGT*, *Ibid.*, p. 59, and *CWMG*, vol. 20, p. 361.

[40] Published in *The Bengalee*, 3 February 1922. Andrews had also repeatedly cautioned Gandhi against the tendency of the non-co-operation movement towards mob violence. In particular he opposed Gandhi's encouragement of the burning of foreign cloth—'You are doing something violent, distorted, unnatural'—and like Tagore, he too was not satisfied with Gandhi's explanation. See Andrews, *Mahatma Gandhi's Ideas*, pp. 269-75; *DGT*, vol. 2, pp. 54-56; and *CWMG*, vol. 20, pp. 499-500; vol. 21, pp. 41-44, 206-07.

[41] Explaining why he decided to suspend the movement Gandhi wrote to Nehru on 19 February 1921 that even before Chauri Chaura he had reports from Madras, Calcutta, Allahabad and other places that 'our people were becoming aggressive, defiant and threatening, that they were getting out of hand and were not non-violent in behaviour . . . if the thing had not been suspended we would have been leading not a non-violent struggle but essentially a violent struggle'. *A Bunch of Old Letters written mostly to Jawaharlal Nehru and Some by Him* (London, 1960), pp. 23-24.

[42] *RR*, vol. 14; English tr. in *The Modern Review*, May 1922; tr. by Marjorie Sykes in *Three Plays of Rabindranath Tagore* (Bombay, 1950).

[43] *Young India*, 21 December 1922.

[44] *The Modern Review*, September 1925; original Bengali version in *Sabujpatra*, July-August 1925.

[45] 'The Poet and the Charkha'. *Young India*, 5 November 1925; *CWMG*, vol. 28, pp. 425-30. Curiously Gandhi in his reply referred to Tagore as 'Sir Rabindranath' although Tagore had renounced his knighthood more than six years ago.

[46] *Young India*, 12 March 1925; *CWMG*, vol. 26, pp. 279-80. Also see in the same volume, pp. 446-53.

[47] Tagore's letter of 30 September 1925 in *Birth Control Review*, quoted *PKM*, vol. 4, p. 44.

[48] For the two stories, *RR*, vol. 24; English tr. of 'Namanjur Galpa' (Rejection Slip) in Lila Ray (ed. and tr.), *Broken Bread* (Calcutta, 1957). For Tagore's review of Sachindranath Sen's *The Political Philosophy of Rabindranath*, *RR*, vol. 24.

[49] See Rabindranath Tagore, *Mahatmaji and the Depressed Humanity* (Calcutta, 1932); also in Bengali, Rabindranath Tagore, *Mahatma Gandhi* (Calcutta, 1948); *RR*, vol. 27, pp. 289-312. Also see *DGT*, vol. 3, pp. 167, 175-77.

[50] *DGT*, vol. 3, p. 201; *PKM*, vol. 3, p. 355 and 361, vol. 4, p. 162; 'Dr. Tagore disowns Poona Pact', *The Statesman*, 26 July 1933.

[51] *Visva-Bharati News*, January 1938, pp. 51-53. For Gandhi's scheme and other

details, see *DGT*, vol. 4, pp. 186-203, and for Tagore, see *PKM*, vol. 4, pp. 107-21. Tagore, *Towards Universal Man* includes several of his essays and addresses on education. *Visva-Bharati Quarterly*, vol. 13, parts 1 & 2, 1948, 'Education Number', has a detailed bibliography of Tagore's writings on education.

52 Tagore's letter to Amiya Chakravarty, 17 March 1939, published in *Prabasi*, Baishakh, 1346 (May 1939).

53 Tagore was President of the League against Fascism and War, and Honorary President of the Indian Civil Liberties Union. For general discussion of his anti-totalitarian views see Rajendra Verma, *Tagore Prophet Against Totalitarianism* (Bombay, 1964), and Sachin Sen, *The Political Thought of Tagore* (Calcutta, 1947). Among his many statements and letters attacking fascism, the following may be mentioned: 'Philosophy of Fascism', *Manchester Guardian*, 5 August 1926; revised version, *Visva-Bharati Quarterly*, October 1926; 'Fascism in Spain: Appeal for checking the tide', *The Statesman*, 3 March 1937; 'Poet Denounces Japan' and 'The Danger of Fascism: Warning to Britain', *Amritabazar Patrika*, 11 October 1937; 'Tagore's Message: Japanese Imperialism Denounced', *Amritabazar Patrika*, 27 June 1938; 'Onslaught of Maniacs: Tagore on Fate of Czechoslovakia', *Hindusthan Standard*, 10 November 1938; *Poet to Poet* (correspondence between Tagore and the Japanese poet Yone Noguchi on the Sino-Japanese Conflict), published by Sino-Indian Cultural Society (Pamphlet 5), Calcutta 1939.

54 Nehru, *An Autobiography* (Bombay, 1962; original edition 1936), p. 490. For statements by Gandhi and Tagore, *Harijan*, 2 and 16 February 1934. Also see *DGT*, vol. 3, pp. 247-51.

55 Romain Rolland, *Mahatma Gandhi: A Study in Indian Nationalism*, tr. from French by L. V. R. Aiyar (Ganesan, Madras, 1923), p. 78 and p. 98 fn. Also see Rolland, 'Homage from a Man of the West to Gandhi' in S. Radhakrishnan (ed.), *Mahatma Gandhi: Essays and Reflections on His Life and Work* (Bombay, 1956), pp. 197-99.

56 See R. C. Majumdar (ed.), *The History of Bengal* (Dacca, 1963), vol. I, Chapters 13, 14 and 15. Also Nihar Ranjan Ray, *Bangalir Itihas Adi Parva* (History of the Bengali people—First Phase) (Calcutta, 1952), Chapters 11, 12 and 15.

57 Gandhi, *An Autobiography*, p. 49.

58 Tagore, *Towards Universal Man*, p. 267.

59 *Ibid.*, 133-34; *Charitrapuja* (1907) in *RR*, vol. 4, pp. 477-523. To Gandhi's derogatory observations on Rammohun Roy (*Young India*, 24 April 1921) Tagore reacted strongly. *Letters to a Friend*, pp. 164-65, and 'The Cult of the Charkha'.

60 I have discussed this elsewhere. See my essays, 'Decline of the Indian Intellectuals' and 'Rabindranath Tagore and Modern Bengal' in *Quest* (Calcutta), Oct.-Dec. 1958 and May 1961, respectively.

61 See C. F. Andrews, *Mahatma Gandhi: His Own Story* (London, 1930), pp. 337-38. Also *CWMG*, vol. 23, 'My Mission', pp. 346-49. 'My national service is part of my training for freeing my soul from the bondage of the flesh'.

62 C. F. Andrews, *Mahatma Gandhi's Ideas* (London, 1929), pp. 343-44. In his remarkable book *Eros Denied* (London, 1965), Wayland Young has discussed, in the context mainly of western civilization, some of the disastrous consequences of this anti-humanistic view of the human body and the act of sex.

63 M. N. Roy, *Problems of Freedom* (Calcutta, 1945). For Erich Fromm's analysis of Luther and Calvin, see his *The Fear of Freedom* (London, sixth impression, 1952), pp. 53-84. Nehru in his *Autobiography* (op. cit., p. 129) spoke of 'a kingli-

ness' in Gandhi 'which compelled a willing obeisance from others. Consciously and deliberately meek and humble, yet he was full of power and authority, and he knew it, and at times he was imperious enough, issuing commands which had to be obeyed'. Also see Erik Erikson's recent study, *Gandhi's Truth* (New York, 1969).

64 Martin Buber, *Between Man and Man*, tr. by R. G. Smith (London, 1947).

65 In this connection, Mahadev Desai's record of a conversation between Gandhi and Ramachandran, a student of Tagore and Andrews, is illuminating. See C. F. Andrews, *Mahatma Gandhi's Ideas*, ch. 20, 'A morning with Gandhi', pp. 331-42. For the Renaissance notion of 'multi-formity' see Ernst Cassirer, *An Essay on Man* (London, 1944), and his essay on Giovanni Pico Della Mirandola in *Journal of the History of Ideas*, vol. 3, no. 2, April 1942.

66 Pyarelal, *The Santiniketan Pilgrimage*, pp. 16, 18, 27. Re. *The Cycle of Spring*, see Chaturvedi and Sykes, op. cit., p. 299.

67 For a brilliant critique of Plato's illiberal philosophy, see Karl R. Popper, *The Open Society and its Enemies* (Princeton, 1950).

68 *Letters to a Friend*, p. 145.

69 'Gandhi the Man' in Prabhu and Kelekar, op. cit., p. 135.

70 See, J. L. Talmon, *The Origins of Totalitarian Democracy* (London, 1952).

GANDHI AND NEHRU

I. W. Mabbett

Gandhi was a dreamer, divorced from the real world of political decision-making, an idealist whose visions of what the independence struggle ought to be blinded him to what it actually was. Alternatively, he was an intensely practical man of action who time and time again jolted the conscience of India with startling and decisive actions, a determined leader with an uncanny knack for sensing the right thing to do while others merely debated. He was an arch-hypocrite with a peculiarly unctuous brand of sanctimony. He was a saint, fired with a burning honesty and imbued with profound gentleness, natural courtesy, dignity, charm. He was an extremist who carried his egregious doctrines to their logical conclusion. He was a middle-of-the-road compromiser, sometimes ready to betray the principles for which his followers stood in a deal with his opponents. He was a fiery revolutionary, an antediluvian conservative.

Nehru was a vacillating politician, prey to conflicting loyalties, ever ready to commit himself to a policy and slide out the next minute at the prompting of a fresh claim on his duty. Alternatively, he was a man of principle, standing upright for an ideal and a goal, and going to prison for them, while other men signed away their souls. He was a perennially youthful romantic who charged brashly into the politics of nationalism, his father reluctantly cast as Sancho Panza; he was a realist with a consistent and clear vision of the road to independence and the means to power. He was a tough and sometimes bitter protagonist in the political drama, a sensitive introvert who was fundamentally unsure of himself.

These are some of the stereotypes of two men who tower over the history of modern India, and they are all true, in a way. Clearly the two are complex characters, and any account of the relationship between them must take account of their complexity. Clearly, too, when there are so many perspectives, there will be material to support an infinity of comparisons and contrasts between the two men, and an attempt to sketch the relationship in the language of everyday psychology runs the risk of becoming a mere *jeu d'esprit*. Gandhi and Nehru had widely divergent views about the role of religion, about socialism, about means and ends in the independence struggle, we might say, stringing banal facts together, but the bond between them was cemented by a shared commitment to a single unwavering goal, an ardent love of their country, an unshakeable conviction of the rightness of their cause.

But perhaps the complexity is just as much in the circumstances that shaped their careers as in their characters, and perhaps, as is suggested here, their relationship is best understood in the light of the course of events that threw them together and made them colleagues in one venture. What follows is a brief account of their responses to each other through the period of this venture.

Nehru and Gandhi met for the first time at the Lucknow Congress in 1916. Nehru was a young man with his school and university career in England only a few years behind him; Gandhi was in his forties, recently returned from his career in South Africa where he first worked out his political style and made his name. There ·being no record of the impression that Nehru made on Gandhi, we can only speculate, as does Nehru's biographer, Frank Moraes: 'To Gandhi, clad in a coarse cotton *dhoti* and long coat and wearing his native *Kathiawadi*, or turban—he was to adopt his famous loincloth only in 1921—Nehru must have seemed equally distant and different. Perhaps, being a good judge of men, he noted the purpose behind the petulance of the young man's mouth. The patrician stared from the proud dark eyes, but there was sensitivity in them.'[1] As for Gandhi, he struck Nehru at first as a rather distant and alien figure, unfamiliar in the world of young nationalist politicians.

At the time Nehru had yet to make his mark; it was with his father that Gandhi had more business, for Motilal was one of the dominating figures in Congress in the decade or more following the war. In the 'twenties, the three men—Motilal, Jawaharlal and Gandhi—came between them to hold a position of commanding influence in the counsels of Congress, an oddly contrasting trio. An elder statesman of towering presence, an impetuous young revolutionary, and a pious *sādhu*—these were the men who so largely shaped the course of nationalist politics. Jawaharlal came to see the other two as the most important influences in his development. In his autobiography he discussed the character and the influence on him of his father and Gandhi. The two, he acknowledged, were very different, and yet some things they had in common, the very things that attracted and compelled Jawaharlal himself. Significantly, he quoted his father's praise of Gandhi's manliness, not superficially the most obvious of Gandhi's attributes but in Motilal's eyes the key to his strength, and added: 'Evidently he wanted to stress the fact that he did not admire Gandhiji as a saint or a Mahatma, but as a man. Strong and unbending

143

himself, he admired strength of spirit in him. . . . There was a royalty and kingliness in him which compelled a willing obeisance from others. Consciously and deliberately meek and humble, yet he was full of power and authority, and he knew it, and at times he was imperious enough, issuing commands which had to be obeyed.'[2]

It was Gandhi's strength of spirit that attracted both the Nehrus to him, and made of them more than colleagues. To Jawaharlal, Gandhi was Bapu, father. In 1919, when the promulgation of the Rowlatt Bills seemed to Congressmen to promise intolerable curtailments of the liberty of Indians, Jawaharlal was among the most vehement advocates of resistance and vigorously supported Gandhi's programme of non-violent resistance when it was mooted, a programme that offered the likelihood of imprisonment to its participants; but it was as a family friend that Gandhi advised him to keep his enthusiasm in check for his father's sake. Only slowly and haltingly did Motilal follow his son along the road that led to voluntary sacrifice, comparative poverty, and jail.

1920 was Gandhi's year. He dominated Congress, and the launching of civil disobedience was from his inspiration and under his management. Reluctantly and with considerable heart-searching the older Nehru followed his lead; as Jawaharlal remarked in his autobiography Motilal was the only prominent Congress leader of the older generation to come out openly for Gandhi's policy right from the beginning, knowing that it would commit him to the virtual abandonment of his lucrative legal practice.[3] From this point on, circumstances drove them step by step to a total commitment. Caught between his love for his son and his keen sense of what was right for India, Motilal followed behind Jawaharlal, who threw himself heart and soul into the cause of non-violent resistance.

It therefore came as a brutal shock, not the only one that was to test his faith in Gandhi, for Jawaharlal Nehru to learn while in prison in 1922 that Gandhi had suddenly called off the programme of civil disobedience. For him, as for his father and other organisers who had accepted jail sentences as part of the programme, civil disobedience represented the only way ahead. Boats had been burned.

The attitudes of Nehru and Gandhi to the suspension of civil disobedience are different and revealing. For Gandhi, what mattered was the moral purity of the conduct of the programme; any violence nullified it completely. For Nehru, what mattered was the result that was to be looked for—the destruction of the power of the government.

An episode that occurred in the *hartāl*, general strike, of 1919, shows us Gandhi's thinking. Demonstrations in Bombay got out of hand and there were charges by mounted police, causing casualties. Gandhi later remonstrated with the Police Commissioner responsible, asserting that it had been unnecessary to break up the procession as the people were 'not by nature violent but peaceful'.

> And thus we argued at length. Ultimately Mr Griffith said, 'But suppose you were convinced that your teaching had been lost on the people, what would you do?' 'I should suspend civil disobedience if I were so convinced.'[4]

Thus civil disobedience should be used as a weapon only so long as it was used in the right spirit, that of the man who tries by non-violence to shame his opponent into a recognition of the truth. This principle had to be supreme. So when in 1922 the campaign was marred by wanton violence and murder in the village of Chauri Chaura, this came as the last straw to him; for long he had been seeing evidence that those who were putting civil disobedience into effect did not see it as he did. He wrote to Nehru: 'I received letters both from Hindus and Mohammedans from Calcutta, Allahabad and the Punjab, all these before the Gorakhpur incident, telling me that the wrong was not all on the Government side, that our people were becoming aggressive, defiant and threatening, that they were getting out of hand and were not non-violent in demeanour.'[5]

Nehru's attitude contrasts strikingly. For him, Gandhi's technique of non-violence, *satyāgraha*, was a means to an end; and, if there should be sporadic violence arising from the imperfection and ignorance of the Indians professing it, this was to be regretted but it need not destroy the effectiveness of *satyāgraha* as a political weapon. The non-violent method 'could only be a policy and a method promising certain results, and by those results it would have to be finally judged'.[6] From this point of view it was wayward and perverse of Gandhi to abandon the policy simply because of an outbreak in one village. On reflection, Nehru was able to justify Gandhi's action to himself, but not on moral grounds. The real justification lay, he thought, in Gandhi's intuitive sense of the situation, realising that with so many Congress leaders in prison the civil disobedience movement was losing its orientation and was now a spent force. What mattered was not Gandhi's own rationalisation of his actions but his instinctive feeling. 'He reacts to this instinctive feeling and fashions his action accordingly, and later, for the benefit of his surprised and resentful colleagues, tries to clothe his decision with reasons.'[7]

Nor was this the only issue on which Nehru and Gandhi did not see eye to eye. The big issue of the later 'twenties was the definition of the objective of Congress. This, under Gandhi's influence, had been defined as *swaraj*, independence, but the precise implications of this independence were not spelled out. The vagueness of the definition seemed dangerous to the more radical spirits like the younger Nehru, who insisted absolutely upon a form of independence that would be a complete break with Britain. Older leaders such as Motilal were at first prepared to allow dominion status or something like it to figure as India's final destination, a policy that had some chance of gaining the acquiescence of the British government. 'Dominion status' was the prime bogey in the 'twenties— unnecessarily, as it may seem from hindsight, since Jawaharlal himself as the first Prime Minister after independence was ready enough to keep India in the Commonwealth. The difference between complete independence and dominion status seemed real enough in 1927 however, when Jawaharlal gained approval at the annual Congress for a resolution declaring complete independence as the goal. This provoked fierce disagreement, the two Nehrus finding themselves in opposite camps. The following year the older Nehru was responsible for a report that set out the aims of Congress in a way that secured the maximum of support from the various disparate groups in the nationalist movement, and included a reference to dominion status. The next annual session of Congress approved it, but, after much wrangling, with the qualification that if the government did not offer dominion status in one year then complete independence would become the goal. Torn between conflicting loyalties, Jawaharlal stayed away from the meeting that passed this resolution.

Gandhi was upset by Jawaharlal's seeming haste in all this and wrote a letter rebuking him; but it was done in love and friendship.

> I see quite clearly that you must carry on open warfare against me and my views. For, if I am wrong I am evidently doing irreparable harm to the country and it is your duty after having known it to rise in revolt against me. Or, if you have any doubt as to the correctness of your conclusions, I shall gladly discuss them with you personally. The differences between you and me appear to me to be so vast and radical that there seems to be no meeting ground between us. I can't conceal from you my grief that I should lose a comrade so valiant, so faithful, so able and so honest as you have always been; but in serving a cause, comradeships have got to be sacrificed.[8]

This was written in January 1928, weeks after the Madras session had shown a serious threat to the authority of Gandhi; later in the letter he suggested that there should be an open confrontation between the two men in the pages of Gandhi's periodical *Young India,* and we can see that in dramatising the disagreement in this way, Gandhi was, whether consciously or not, staking the loyalty his colleagues gave him on a piece of moral blackmail. The confrontation did not eventuate, and as we saw the next session produced an unhappy compromise.

The personal relationship between them was strengthened if anything. In the very month of the 1928 session Gandhi wrote to Nehru congratulating him on his part in the demonstrations against the visiting British Simon Commission, in the course of which he suffered a beating at the hands of the police. 'My love to you. It was done bravely. You have braver things to do. May God spare you for many a long year to come and make you His chosen instrument for freeing India from the yoke.'[9] In 1929 Gandhi engineered the election of Nehru as president of Congress for the year. Nehru's political biographer Michael Brecher sees this as a shrewd move to appease the younger radicals represented by Nehru. Revealing, perhaps, is the assurance given by Gandhi to placate his personal following that Nehru as president was much the same as himself as president.[10] It was typical of Gandhi's technique to act as kingmaker behind the scenes, causing others year by year to occupy the presidency according to his will. However we regard it, it is clear that Gandhi could count on Nehru's loyalty. Writing to refute the idea that there was ganging up against Gandhi among the leaders of the Congress at the time of the 1931 Round Table Conference which Gandhi attended, Nehru claimed in his autobiography that among the members of the Committee 'had grown up friendship and camaraderie and regard for each other. They formed not a coalition but an organic unity, and it was inconceivable for any one to intrigue against the other. Gandhiji dominated the Committee, and every one looked to him for guidance'.[11]

Further shocks to Nehru's loyalty were in store. In 1932, while he was in prison, he learned that Gandhi had announced a 'fast unto death' in protest against the Communal Award, the government decision to devise separate electorates for minorities in future Indian elections. What Gandhi objected to was the principle of hiving off the untouchables into their own electorates, even though it guaranteed them representation, because it seemed to him to perpetuate old and evil social divisions. For Gandhi the moral issue was supreme; to Nehru it seemed irresponsible to jeopardise the greater issue, the independence struggle, to say nothing of Gandhi's own life, for the sake of what he regarded as a side issue.

> I felt angry with him at his religious and sentimental approach to
> a political question, and his frequent references to God in connection

147

with it. He even seemed to suggest that God had indicated the very date of the fast. What a terrible example to set!

If Bapu died! What would India be like then? And how would her politics run? There seemed to be a dreary and dismal future ahead, and despair seized my heart when I thought of it.[12]

Yet once again on reflection Nehru came round to the view that in some uncanny way Gandhi knew instinctively what was the right thing to do, and that his fast must be in the true interest of the independence struggle. The reactions throughout India to the fast, the sense of urgency about the evils of untouchability, seemed to confirm this. A telegram came from Gandhi, seeking his opinion and delighting him by the way Gandhi thought to give bits of family news amid his travail. Soon afterwards an agreement was reached with the government and Gandhi seemed to be vindicated.

But Nehru was unhappy about Gandhi's way of preoccupying himself with social evils like untouchability, which seemed to him to cloud the real issues. In 1933 came the twenty-one day fast against untouchability. 'How I wish I could feel that you had understood the absolute necessity of it,' wrote Gandhi, trying to persuade him of the paramount importance of cleansing Hinduism.[13] But there was a fundamental difference of outlook. Nehru was shocked and disheartened once again in 1934 when Gandhi called off civil disobedience. That the campaign would have to be wound up he was prepared to accept, but the reasons for doing so that Gandhi gave at the time seemed trivial and irresponsible. A colleague was reluctant to serve his time in prison as *satyāgraha* required, and Gandhi blamed himself for blindness in not seeing the imperfections of those around him. 'Even if it was a serious matter,' wrote Nehru, 'was a vast national movement involving scores of thousands directly and millions indirectly to be thrown out of gear because an individual had erred?'[14] Subject to the tensions of prison life, Nehru was overwrought, and his disappointment in Gandhi brought on a crisis of doubt. An anchor seemed to have gone, and he was oppressed by a terrible feeling of loneliness.

Nehru was often unhappy at having to witness the unpredictable doings of Gandhi from inside prison, where he spent much of the early nineteen-thirties; he was unhappy too when he came out and entered the thick of Congress politics, preparing to contest elections. He found himself as Congress secretary working with colleagues who were not sympathetic to him. Increasingly, he felt that what India needed was far more than even complete political change; it was thorough-going social and economic change, in the direction of socialism. He was impatient of the jobbery he discerned among too many of his colleagues, who seemed to want independence for the sake of power for themselves rather than as a means to a programme of reform and industrialization for the country. His opposition to the evils of social traditions and to religious sectarianism coincided of course with Gandhi's, but with his socialism he was at the opposite pole from Gandhi's arcadian vision of a self-sufficient village India bettering itself with handicrafts. There were rumours of a rift between him and Gandhi, who felt constrained to write in his periodical *Harijan*: 'No doubt there are differences of opinion between us. . . . They were clearly set forth in the letters we exchanged some years ago. But they do not affect our personal relations in any way whatsoever. We remain the same adherents to the Congress goal, that we have ever been.'[15]

The years that led up to the war were a period of strain for the Congress leaders. The gulf between the old guard and the younger radicals became increasingly difficult to cross. Gandhi was preoccupied with the 'constructive programme', the work of moral and social reform which for him was more important than the purely institutional changes for which Nehru was ultimately working. Nehru himself suffered deepening gloom, finding himself increasingly hindered by uncongenial colleagues and by communalism and pettiness in the nationalist movement at large.

The Japanese threat raised acutely the question whether Gandhi's non-violence could be used by a sovereign state as a technique of foreign policy. Driven by the logic of his faith, Gandhi felt obliged to answer yes. Nehru, and all those who thought as he, disagreed. Gandhi at that time may have seemed a utopian, an idealist, something of a has-been. Nehru wrote:

> So for the first time, he went one way and the Congress Working Committee another. There was no break with him for the bond was too strong, and he will no doubt continue to advise in many ways and often to lead. . . . In recent years I have found a certain hardness creeping into him, a lessening of the adaptability that he possessed. Yet the old spell is there, the old charm works, and his personality and greatness tower over others.[16]

Gandhi's domination over Congress was far from ended. It was he who inspired a resolution passed at the 1942 Allahabad session of Congress in favour of non-violent resistance to the Japanese. Though Nehru and Gandhi stood together behind the resolution, the situation was a further strain on his loyalty: his instinct was for armed resistance, and he was reluctant to accept that non-violence was practical and efficient as a

149

technique. He was placed under an even greater strain when Gandhi issued his famous demand that the British should quit India, handing over power to an independent Indian government. He was ready to co-operate with Britain by offering bases, but only on terms of sovereignty and equality. Implicit in the demand was a threat of civil disobedience if the government refused to grant independence, and this is what confronted Nehru with the same agonising conflict of loyalties that so often beset him and thrust him into awkward compromises, for the last thing he wanted was full-scale civil disobedience at a time when it was likely to cripple the resistance of India to Japan. For months he struggled, and in the end his loyalty to Gandhi won. In August 1942 he put his name to the 'Quit India' demand of Congress.

Once the issue was joined, the old doubts and tensions became irrelevant; the conflict was between Congress and government, which acted swiftly and vigorously. Before long all the Congress leaders were back in jail, and it was not until the end of the war that Gandhi and Nehru could again play central roles. In 1946, despite the popularity of Vallabhbhai Patel, Gandhi contrived the election of Nehru to the Congress presidency. In this capacity, Nehru was shortly afterwards asked to form an interim government of India; thus Gandhi's action in securing his election virtually represents him as Gandhi's choice as first Prime Minister of independent India.

What we may notice about the period leading up to independence is not the tortuous progress of negotiations with the British but the response of the two men to the most important events of the time—the communal riots and massacres that marred the birth of modern India and Pakistan. Both men were staunch opponents of communalism in any form, both impatient of the sectarian spirit that devilled relations between educated leaders as well as villagers. Both of them—Gandhi by instinct, Nehru originally by self-training—were at home in the villages where they spoke a language that people could understand. Both of them were thus equipped to show themselves at their best in the time of riots, touring the afflicted areas and appealing for commonsense and toleration. Brecher points to the contrast in their approaches, Gandhi speaking without recrimination straight to the heart of each individual, Nehru more ready to scold and hector,[17] but the similarities are at least as important. Both were unsparing of themselves, both carried the message of peace.

Gandhi's elevation of Nehru to the presidency perhaps showed great prescience in equipping India with a leader whose background and westernised outlook fitted him to conduct the final negotiations with the British. Besides this, it was a happy accident that Nehru and the last Vice-

roy, Lord Mountbatten, should understand each other so well, to the point
of striking up a deep and lasting friendship. Independence came more
speedily than might otherwise have been, and India was launched upon a
new career with Nehru at the head of government and Gandhi, as was his
wont, giving authoritative guidance from behind the scenes.

Right up to the end, Gandhi was preoccupied with moral and social
justice, with the setting of the right example, rather than with the management of institutions, and it was his uncompromising moral stand that led
to his death at the hands of a Hindu extremist. The assassination was a
bitter personal blow to Nehru.

Despite the frequent strains upon his loyalty to Gandhi, he had always
come back to the fold, always been captivated by 'the old charm', always
been refreshed and soothed by his contacts with the older man. 'We
always feel a little younger and stronger after meeting him and the
burdens we carry seem a little lighter,' he had said as recently as 1948.[18]
Nothing had been able to break the bonds that were formed in the early
days of civil disobedience. No natural orator, Nehru was moved to simple
eloquence when he broadcast to the country the news of Gandhi's death.

> The light has gone out of our lives and there is darkness every-
> where and I do not quite know what to tell you and how to say it.
> Our beloved leader, Bapu as we call him, the father of our nation, is
> no more. Perhaps I am wrong to say that. Nevertheless, we will not
> see him again as we have seen him these many years. We will not
> run to him for advice and seek solace from him, and that is a terrible
> blow not to me only but to millions and millions in this country.
> And it is difficult to soften the blow by any advice that I or anyone
> else can give you.[19]

The evidence of the affection that bound Nehru and Gandhi is
impressive. There is more, of course, from Nehru's side than from
Gandhi's, in a host of books, speeches and letters. Gandhi was more
reticent, but from his treatment of Nehru throughout his career as well
as from his letters and a limited number of public statements it is easy to
see that the attachment was mutual. Perhaps, for him, Nehru represented
things that he did not possess or from which, though still half-consciously
hankering after them, he had deliberately turned away—comparative
youth, worldly success, a modern western outlook, vanity, personal
ambition—things that Gandhi had wanted as a very young man before he
abandoned the quest from a feeling of inadequacy. Nehru was a blend
of his own youthful worldliness and his own maturer dedication, and

151

perhaps to symbolise the unity of the disparate parts of his own mind he needed to carry Nehru with him.

Right to the very end, he succeeded in carrying Nehru with him, not simply as a friend but as a political ally, despite the reservations that involved Nehru in agonising compromise. As everybody attested, Gandhi had a great personal charm that one cannot sense from his writings alone, which worked a magic spell on Nehru whenever the two were together, however much disappointment, shock and even resentment his wayward actions and pronouncements might produce in Nehru.

Certainly the differences in temperament were profound. For Gandhi, his gospel of non-violence was more than a means to political independence—it was a way of life, a religious creed, a doctrine of suffering. 'The question is whether you are capable of every suffering that may be imposed upon you or may be your lot in the journey towards the goal. Even whilst you are suffering, you may have no bitterness—no trace of it—against your opponents.'[20] This was rather the religious goal of self-purification than a political programme, convinced though Gandhi was that the right moral attitudes were necessary if *satyāgraha* was to achieve political success. Nehru, on the other hand, though he acknowledged the virtue and piety implicit in Gandhi's approach, saw it essentially as a means to an end, and the end was more important. Gandhi frequently admitted that he was more interested in the means, and his whole attitude to the nationalist movement was governed by his preoccupation with the spiritual health of Indian society. Hence he spent much of his time on what seemed to others as side-issues. His fasts, directed against untouchability or communalism, clouded the central political issue for Nehru, but for him caste and religious attitudes were the central issue.

The goals of the two men were quite different. Nehru wanted to break down caste and religious prejudice as part of a programme of modernisation, industrialisation, socialism. Gandhi wanted to do the same things for the moral benefit of the people of India, and he could visualise a future where happy contented villagers cared for their own wants and had no need of industries. To Nehru he sometimes seemed like an old-style revivalist, playing on unhealthy and irrational instincts. He appalled Nehru when he saw an earthquake as a divine judgment on the practice of untouchability.[21] Gandhi's approach in Nehru's eyes discouraged the people of India from thinking, let them see him as a magician who would win for them what they wanted; and Gandhi's insistence that independence, vaguely defined as *swarāj*, was a thing in the mind—that India would be free when Indians thought themselves free—smacked of woolly mysticism.

Not that Nehru failed to see Gandhi's point that India as a nation would gain strength and self-respect as soon as its people realized that they could achieve anything by genuine solidarity. Nor did he despise the moral elements in Gandhi's teachings. He did not see village handicrafts as the salvation of an independent India's economy, but he recognised the campaign to encourage hand-spinning as a link for the leaders with the masses and as a therapy for his own soul. Many hours he spent in prison spinning. Again, he did not see non-violence as an end in itself, but he was deeply imbued with its principles. He shared Gandhi's complete freedom from any taint of religious intolerance and like him gave priority to combatting the twin evils of untouchability and communalism. Like him too, Nehru was deeply rooted in the western ideals of efficiency and clean administration, and was intolerant of all forms of jobbery and corruption.

The two men had other traits in common. Unlike the debating-chamber politicians that were so numerous in both their generations, both throve on contact with villagers, drawing strength in different ways from touring country areas and addressing large informal meetings. For Gandhi, there was an instinctive attraction to poverty and simplicity in this; for Nehru, it was an exercise that helped to rid him of his inner uncertainty of himself and bolstered his confidence, perhaps as he would admit his vanity too; but both of them really cared for the people of the villages with a deep earnestness, and this is what matters. Both men were completely committed to their cause. Both men made sacrifices for it. Both were hard workers, unsparing of themselves and exacting a high standard from those around them. Nehru as Prime Minister was notorious as a finicky administrator, insisting upon handling minute details himself and spending perhaps too much time on dealing with his own correspondence. Gandhi lived like a clock, mercilessly challenging himself with an ever austerer regimen.[22]

But to understand the nature of the relationship between them we need to do more than list their similarities and differences and decide that the first outweighed the second. It is easy to slip into the way of describing things in isolation and treating them statically, because this is convenient; but personalities and events in history change and grow and cannot be understood outside their contexts. It would be wrong to describe the independence movement in India as the doings of a number of individuals dealing with the government, because the real protagonists in the drama were huge and inexorable social forces. In the same way it would be wrong to describe the relationship between Gandhi and Nehru from static pictures of their personalities alone, for this relationship was itself moulded in part by the same forces, which gripped hold of the men who participated in the affairs of the nation and compelled them to respond with all the resources of their being. What threw Gandhi and Nehru together in spirit was above all the affinity of the responses they were making in the nationalist predicament.

Gandhi began his career as a would-be westernised lawyer, and found himself constantly exposed to situations with which he could not cope. When in South Africa he found the road to follow, a passionate striving to impose his will on outward circumstances by first imposing his will on himself lay at the heart of his campaign. This produced his preoccupation with virtue rather than with political action; as L. I. and S. H. Rudolph point out his autobiography contains a record of surprisingly many private activities and family problems precisely because his 'experiments with truth' began with his inner life and worked out to politics.[23] It followed from this preoccupation with will-power that, for all his humility, Gandhi was in many ways an autocratic figure.

Nehru was very different. He lived through other people, was ready always to identify himself with other people, was pulled hither and thither by his relationships, and thus he was changeable in views and behaviour, affectionate, often touchingly so, to those in his immediate circle, and, he would admit, vain, seeing himself through others' eyes all the time. It was therefore natural that he should see India as a being with a life of its own, and take passionately to heart its grievances and the cause of its self-respect. He was not in his early life subject to constant humiliation by the British, but he identified himself cordially with the poor and ignorant who, in his eyes, were so humiliated, and waxed bitter on behalf of Mother India. 'It is curious how one cannot resist the tendency to give an anthropomorphic form to a country. . . . India becomes Bharat Mata, Mother India, a beautiful lady, very old but ever youthful in appearance, sad-eyed and forlorn, cruelly treated by aliens and outsiders, and calling upon her children to protect her.'[24] Vicariously humiliated, he sought for India the dignity that Gandhi, with his quiet courage, epitomised.

For both men, the freedom movement meant a battle with cowardice and the cultivation of courage. It was a peculiar relationship that grew between them. Gandhi, with his iron determination and with the closed mind that Nehru detected behind his courtesy, represented a country's self-respect, and in this capacity he could lay almost any claim on Nehru, who, fascinated despite himself, allowed himself to be manipulated. 'And then Gandhi came,' he wrote. 'He was like a powerful current of fresh air that made us stretch ourselves and take deep breaths, like a beam of light that pierced the darkness and removed the scales from our eyes.'[25]

NOTES

[1] F. Moraes, *Jawaharlal Nehru* (New York, 1957), pp. 4-5.

[2] J. Nehru, *An Autobiography* (London, 1936), p. 129.

[3] *Ibid.*, p. 64.

[4] M. K. Gandhi, *An Autobiography, or the Story of my Experiments with Truth* (Ahmedabad, 1940), p. 344.

[5] J. Nehru, *A Bunch of Old Letters* (Bombay, 1960), p. 23.

[6] J. Nehru, *An Autobiography*, p. 84.

[7] *Ibid.*, p. 85.

[8] J. Nehru, *A Bunch of Old Letters*, p. 59.

[9] *Ibid.*, pp. 70-72.

[10] M. Brecher, *Nehru, A Political Biography* (London, 1959), p. 137.

[11] J. Nehru, *An Autobiography*, pp. 287-88.

[12] *Ibid.*, p. 370.

[13] J. Nehru, *A Bunch of Old Letters*, p. 113.

[14] J. Nehru, *An Autobiography*, p. 505.

[15] *Harijan*, 15 July 1936.

[16] J. Nehru, *An Autobiography*, p. 610.

[17] M. Brecher, op. cit., pp. 320-21.

[18] *Hindustan Times*, 31 December 1946.

[19] *Homage to Mahatma Gandhi* (Government of India, Ministry of Information and Broadcasting, New Delhi, 1948), pp. 9-10.

[20] *Young India*, 19 March 1925.

[21] J. Nehru, *An Autobiography*, p. 490.

[22] See L. I. and S. H. Rudolph, *The Modernity of Tradition* (Chicago, 1967), p. 222,

[23] *Ibid.*, p. 169.

[24] J. Nehru, *An Autobiography*, p. 431.

[25] J. Nehru, *The Discovery of India* (New York, 1960), p. 274.

GANDHI AND ROY: THE INTERACTION OF IDEOLOGIES IN INDIA

Dennis Dalton

Over a century ago, Thomas Carlyle remarked in his lecture on 'The Hero as Prophet' that 'the most significant feature in the history of an epoch is the manner it has of welcoming a Great Man'.[1] Today, the social sciences pursue the study of the great man in history from a number of angles: through psycho-historical personality analysis;[2] in related sociological studies of charismatic leadership;[3] and through historical analysis of an individual leader's ideology.[4] Such works have sought not only to reach deeper than Carlyle ever envisaged into the psyche and social milieu of the great man; they have also directed our attention, as Carlyle advised, to the significance of the *response* made to him. In this respect, the social sciences have made us realize how much the study of the great man involves an understanding of the attitudes and needs of those around him.

The purpose of this essay is to suggest the significance of Gandhi, one of the few great men of his epoch, through an analysis of the response made to him. The particular response analyzed in this case will not be that of the Indian masses, but rather that of a single individual, M. N. Roy, who was known for many years in India as Gandhi's severest critic. The importance of Roy's response will be seen not only in the content of his criticism, but also in the evolution of his view of Gandhi. For in the example of Roy's changing response and movement towards Gandhi, one perceives the gradual confluence of two distinct streams of thought. There emerges ultimately, in these two men, a common pattern of ideas, a similar way of thinking, on issues concerning freedom and authority, leadership and revolution, ethics and politics, and the right organization of the social order. This resultant conceptual 'cluster' of assumptions and attitudes is not peculiar to Gandhi and Roy: it has been shared, in modern India, by a long line of her ideologists, and it will be seen here as forming the core of a 'great tradition' of ideology in nationalist India. Therefore, Roy's response to Gandhi may be seen in a larger sense as a response to the ideological tradition of 19th and 20th century India. Gandhi fulfills

Carlyle's conception of the great man in the sense that he is representative of a tradition of ideas which had a major role in the formation of modern India's national culture. When Roy criticized Gandhi, he was, then, not attacking a mere *mahātmā*, but a national tradition. And as a part of that tradition, he was sometimes fighting himself.

Manabendra Nath Roy (1887-1954) was born into a Bengali *brāhman* family in a village outside of Calcutta.[5] Twenty-eight years later, as a terrorist revolutionary, he left India for an adventurous career in the Communist international movement. These initial twenty-eight years in Bengal were decisive for the shaping of his personality and thought. Three components of this early experience deserve mention. First, there was the influence of Roy's *brāhmanical* family background and outlook. This inspired and reinforced his penchant for theory, his elitism, and his strong moral temper.[6] Second, there was Roy's early, intense belief in Hinduism. His religious frame of mind, like his *brāhmanical* spirit, never left him, but prodded him on in his quest for 'those abiding, permanent values of humanity'.[7] Third, in this first generation of his life, the ideology of Indian nationalism exerted an immense influence on Roy as it did on many of his contemporary Bengali intellectuals and students.

'An ideology,' writes Edward Shils, 'is the product of man's need for imposing intellectual order on the world. The need for ideology is an intensification of the need for a cognitive and moral map of the universe. . . .'[8] Roy's quest for an adequate ideology began during his youth in Bengal. It continued throughout his next phase as an orthodox communist and later as a Marxist revisionist. Then, still later, having abandoned Marxism for what he called 'Radical Humanism', his search intensified for 'a cognitive and moral map of the universe'. It ended not in satisfaction, but only with his death in 1954. Yet, in this last phase of his thought, Roy had come closer to the fulfilment of his needs, to realization of his identity through the construction of an ideology, than he had ever approached in his earlier phases. The outlines of Roy's cognitive and moral map had been determined in his youth by the combined influences of a *brāhmanical* outlook, a Hindu creed, and the nationalist experience in Bengal. Yet, unlike Gandhi, Roy never came to terms with the demands of his early formative period; unlike Gandhi, he remained alienated until the end from large segments of his own tradition. It is for this reason that the evolution of Roy's thought, which represents a continuing response to the demands of Gandhi and the Indian nationalist tradition, forms an important part of this analysis.

The year 1915 is a key one in the Gandhi-Roy story. In that year, Roy, a terrorist schooled under Jatin Mukherjee and Aurobindo Ghose, left

Calcutta on a revolutionary mission to obtain German arms for the struggle against the Raj. In that same year, Mohandas Gandhi returned to India after twenty-one years in South Africa. He soon began his extraordinary rise to power in the Congress. By 1920 he had come to dominate the Indian nationalist movement with a sure sense of leadership that reached a dramatic peak with the Dandi Salt March of 1930. During these fifteen years of Gandhi's eminence, Roy acquired his reputation of being 'undoubtedly the most colourful of all non-Russian Communists in the era of Lenin and Stalin'.[9] From 1915 until December 1930, Roy moved about on various revolutionary missions, from Mexico to Moscow to Berlin, and then Paris, Zurich and Tashkent. In Mexico, Roy was converted to Communism and reputedly helped form the first Communist Party there. In Moscow, he contributed to revolutionary strategy for communist activity in the colonial areas.[10] In Europe, he rose to a position of authority in the Comintern, published a series of books and pamphlets on Marxist theory, and edited a communist newspaper. Therefore, the achievements of both Gandhi and Roy during this period were spectacular.

Yet, for all their respective achievements, there was never anything like a balance of power between these two figures. It was Gandhi and never Roy who dominated the Indian nationalist movement with his unparalleled genius for mass leadership. Whereas Roy would struggle long and hard to gain power in India, Gandhi acquired authority with ease and kept it. While Roy necessarily remained, throughout this fifteen year period, preoccupied with Gandhi's power, the latter never mentions Roy in his writings or speeches. Even after Roy's return to the political scene in the late 'thirties, Gandhi took scant notice of him. Roy, then, remained both a cultural and political outsider and suffered as a result. Gandhi, after his return to India in 1915, became rooted in the nationalist tradition and developed a style of political behavior which gained for him personal confidence as well as political power. Thus, while Roy, out of touch with his tradition, never ceased in his effort to come to terms with Gandhi and all that the Mahatma personified, Gandhi, secure in his surroundings, could remain aloof. In this sense, a consideration of Roy's view of Gandhi becomes part of a larger problem, that of the relationship of the Indian intellectual to his tradition.[11]

The first detailed Marxist critique of Gandhi appeared in Roy's first major book, *India in Transition*, which was written in Moscow in 1921. The book grew out of discussions which Roy had with Lenin and other communist figures at the Second Congress of the Communist International. At this Congress, Roy had argued against Lenin that communist policy in the colonial areas must be to support proletarian rather than bourgeois movements. Lenin contended that bourgeois nationalist organizations like the Indian Congress could be considered revolutionary, and since no viable Communist parties existed, these organizations deserved the support of the International. Roy replied that the Congress and similar agencies could only betray the revolution: an Indian proletariat existed, and must be mobilized behind a communist vanguard. Liberation from imperialism could only come under communist leadership. The Roy-Lenin controversy was clearly over fundamental issues, and had innumerable implications for communist strategy in the future.

Roy later reflected back upon his differences with Lenin and concluded that 'The role of Gandhi was the crucial point of difference. Lenin believed that, as the inspirer and leader of a mass movement, he was a revolutionary. I maintained that, a religious and cultural revivalist, he was bound to be a reactionary socially, however revolutionary he might appear politically.'[12] In Roy's view, 'The religious ideology preached by him [Gandhi] also appealed to the medieval mentality of the masses. But the same ideology discouraged any revolutionary mass action. The quintessence of the situation, as I analyzed and understood it, was a potentially revolutionary movement restrained by a reactionary ideology.'[13] 'I reminded Lenin of the dictum that I had learnt from him: that without a revolutionary ideology, there could be no revolution.'[14] These arguments formed the basis of the position on Gandhi that was developed by Roy in *India in Transition*.

'The most serious defect of *India in Transition*,' writes a leading biographer of Roy, 'is its under-estimation of Mahatma Gandhi's political potential.'[15] Roy begins his critique of Gandhi in this book with the confident assertion that Gandhism has now 'reached a crisis' and its 'impending wane . . . signifies the collapse of the reactionary forces and their total alienation from the political movement'.[16] Roy's confidence was rooted in the classic Marxist belief in the inexorable march forward of western civilization. Gandhism was seen as a temporary obstacle in the path of history, which would soon be swept aside: not by the Raj, but by the masses themselves, once they became conscious of the progressive movement of history. Whatever Gandhi may tell the masses, 'post-British India cannot and will not become pre-British India'. Therefore, 'Here lies the contradiction in the orthodox nationalism as expressed of late in the cult of Gandhism. It endeavours to utilize the mass energy for the perpetuation or revival of that heritage of national culture which has been made untenable by the awakening of mass energy. . . . Therefore, Gandhism is bound to be defeated. The signs of the impending defeat are

159

already perceptible. Gandhism will fall victim to its own contradictions.'[17]

Roy admits that under Gandhi's leadership, through the effective use of *hartāl* and non-co-operation, 'For the first time in its history, the Indian national movement entered into the period of active struggle'.[18] Yet, here as elsewhere Roy remains confined within his Marxist categories. Gandhi's success in 1920, he says, simply revealed that 'the time for mass-action was ripe. Economic forces, together with other objective causes had created an atmosphere' which propelled Gandhi into power. Roy seeks to drive home his argument against Lenin by stressing the potential role of the Indian proletariat, portraying it as an awakened and thriving revolutionary force. Roy's conception of the proletariat was as fanciful as was his anticipation of 'the imminent collapse of Gandhism'.[19] In each of these miscalculations, one sees repeated the old error of an inappropriate application of Marxist doctrine to an unfamiliar political context.

However, Roy's mistakes cannot be explained wholly in terms of his doctrinaire Marxism. Rather, his Marxism may be explained as part of a desperate search for a new ideology, which was in turn prompted by a quest for a new identity. The identity that Roy sought in the critical period of his youth, was that of an urbane, cosmopolitan type, entirely at home with western civilization, fully equipped to appreciate and assist in its historical forward movement. Yet, he required as well an ideology that would allow him to criticize those aspects of western civilization which were responsible for the subjugation of his own people. The ideology must, in short, serve to liberate him from the sense of inferiority instilled by imperialism, and at the same time arm him in his struggle for the liberation of India. Marxism suited this purpose exactly. His total affirmation of Marxism, therefore, followed immediately after his total rejection of nationalism, and from this there emerged his total and unreasoning denial of Gandhi as a lasting political force in India. In this sense, *India in Transition* offers a clear example of an intellectual determined to reject his tradition. Not only Gandhi, but also extremist leaders like Tilak and Aurobindo, who only five years earlier had commanded Roy's allegiance, are now dismissed with contempt as examples of 'petty-bourgeois humanitarianism'.[20] For the next ten years, until his imprisonment in 1931, Roy struggled to affirm himself in his new identity as an international Marxist revolutionary.

Throughout the 'twenties, as Roy rises to the peak of his authority in the Comintern, his view on Gandhi set forth in 1921 is refined and elaborated. A series of excellent articles and pamphlets by Roy and his first wife Evelyn are devoted to Gandhism. In *One Year of Non-Co-operation*, for example, the Roys distinguished five 'grave errors' or 'great

160

defects' of Gandhism. The 'most glaring defect' is the absence of an intelligent programme of economic reform. Next, there is Gandhi's 'obstinate and futile' emphasis on social harmony instead of a frank recognition of the real necessity of class conflict. Then, they find a senseless 'intrusion of metaphysics into the realm of politics'. The revolt against the Raj, they emphasize, 'is a question of economics, not metaphysics'. Further, they deplore Gandhi's reactionary view of history, his desire 'to run from the Machine-age back to the Stone Age'. Finally, they criticize the total lack of any revolutionary quality in Gandhi's approach to social change; they see only a 'weak and watery reformism, which shrinks at every turn from the realities of the struggle for freedom'.[21] The entire critique is made with exceptional clarity and forcefulness, and it, together with other writings by the Roys on Gandhi, represent the most incisive communist criticism of him during this period.

For a variety of reasons Roy soon fell out of favour with Moscow, and in December 1929 he was officially expelled from the Communist International. He reacted by persuading himself that he could seize control of the revolutionary movement in India, and a year later he returned home. He was soon arrested, and he remained a political prisoner until November 1936. These five hard years in jail witnessed a substantial change in Roy's ideology, and this eventually had its effect upon his view of Gandhi.

While in prison, Roy, like Gandhi and Nehru, read and wrote voluminously. His three volumes of 'prison diaries' refer often to Gandhi. Indeed, it might be argued that there is no better index to the extent to which Gandhi's presence dominated the Indian scene than the jail reflections of his harshest critic.[22] Roy had inherited from his early nationalist experience and religious outlook a moralist's predilection for seeing the world in categorical terms of right and wrong and he had acquired from his *brāhmanical* spirit a corresponding intellectual tendency to construct the required moral categories. Although Gandhi was never a theorist of this type, he nevertheless shared with Roy a strong taste for moralizing and a passionate concern for the ethical well-being of society. Eventually, in his Radical Humanist phase, the morality in Roy will prevail, just as it had always prevailed in Gandhi, and Roy will abandon Marxism because he finds it devoid of ethics. However, even as early as the 'thirties, a first glimpse of the way in which Roy's moral outlook will erode his Marxism can be seen in his prison diaries. This appears in his reflections on the two concepts of freedom and revolution. Both of these ideas were to become key themes of Radical Humanism, and the basis of their later development is found here, in the diaries.

When Roy wrote about freedom and revolution as an orthodox

161

Marxist in the 'twenties, he conceived them as economic categories. Freedom would come with the necessary changes in the economic mode of production, and revolution would be achieved through a violent seizure of power by the Party and the masses. Now, in the 'thirties, Roy begins to perceive other dimensions in these two ideas. In regard to freedom, he says that his aim is to 'indicate the way to real spiritual freedom offered by the materialist philosophy'.[23] For the first time in Roy's writings, the supreme goal of 'spiritual freedom' is distinguished from the lesser aims of 'political freedom, economic prosperity and social happiness'.[24] It should be obvious that Roy, a Marxist, is not using the term 'spiritual freedom' here consciously in a metaphysical sense. Yet the term does not derive from Marxism; and it cannot be a mere coincidence that it was used often by both Vivekananda and Aurobindo, whom Roy had at one time read closely. The significant change in Roy's concept of revolution is evident in his increasing preference for the term 'Indian Renaissance', which means for him a 'philosophical' and 'spiritual' as well as economic revolution. His concluding essay, 'Preconditions of Indian Renaissance',[25] in the second volume of the jail diaries emphasizes the need for a new philosophical outlook in India.

The above analysis of Roy's prison diaries is not meant to suggest that a reader of these volumes in the 'thirties, with no possible knowledge of the way Roy's thought would develop, could have perceived the affinities between Gandhi and Roy which eventually appeared. The fact, however, that these ideas can be found in the diaries in embryonic form indicates that Roy's movement towards a Gandhian way of thinking did not occur overnight. What did occur was a long and painful intellectual journey in which Roy gradually yielded, point by point, to the force of an ideological tradition until substantial similarities with Gandhi and with earlier Bengali nationalists were established. Moreover, if it were not for Roy's untimely death, the journey towards reconciliation might well have continued further.

On the other hand, while it is necessary to appreciate this degree of continuity in Roy's thought, it is equally important to recognize the sharp contrasts, especially in his view of Gandhi, between the 'thirties and the late 'forties. The ruthlessness of Roy's attack on Gandhi in the diaries reaches a climax in an essay entitled 'India's Message'. The critique begins with a contemptuous dismissal of Gandhism as a political philosophy. Far from positing a philosophical system, Roy finds in Gandhism only 'a mass of platitudes and hopeless self-contradictions' emerging from 'a conception of morality based upon dogmatic faith'. As such, it is religion, not philosophy; a religion which has become politicized and thus serves as 'the ideological reflex' of India's 'cultural backwardness' and 'superstition'.[26]

Roy's attack on Gandhi in 1922 was largely content to write Gandhism off as a medieval ideology at the mercy of inexorable economic forces. Now, however, Roy concentrates on the moral virtues which Gandhi idealized and refutes them at length. Roy argues that 'admirable virtues' like 'love, goodness, sacrifice, simplicity, and absolute non-violence' when preached to the masses by Gandhi only serve to emasculate them. Overthrow of the ruling classes becomes impossible, and the result can only be 'voluntary submission of the masses to the established system of oppression and exploitation'. The worst of Gandhi's tenets is his 'cult of non-violence', the 'central pivot' of his thought, 'holding its quaint dogmas and naive doctrines together into a comprehensive system of highly reactionary thought'. Far from serving any noble purpose, *ahiṃsā* in politics only tends to support the forces of violence and exploitation. 'Therefore, those who preach non-violence [to and for] . . . the exploited and oppressed masses, are defenders of violence in practice.' If Gandhi's non-violence were practised, capitalism would remain entrenched and 'the Juggernauth of vulgar materialism' would emerge triumphant. 'Love, the sentimental counterpart of the cult of non-violence, thus is exposed as mere cant.' Finally, Roy asserts that Gandhi's values are based on 'blind faith' and offer only 'the message of mediaevalism' which idealizes 'the savage living on the tree'. In this way, Gandhi inhibits real progress, which Roy sees in terms of the 'dynamic process' of 'modern civilization' that 'must go forward'. For Roy, then, the light is in the West: in the forces of rationalism, technology, modern science, and 'an economy of abundance'.[27] This latter position was maintained by Roy until the end, and it will always distinguish him sharply from Gandhi.

Soon after his discharge from prison, Roy decided that the sole route to political success in India lay in co-operation with the Congress. This meant a much more conciliatory attitude towards Gandhi. Subhas Bose had opposed Gandhi in the Congress with some initial success, but Roy, unlike Bose, had neither mass appeal nor a strong regional base of power in Bengal. Therefore, Roy made a brief but futile attempt to rise in the Congress through co-operation with the Gandhians. His article of this period entitled 'Gandhiji, A Critical Appreciation' reflects this spirit of conciliation. He begins with the claim that 'I appreciate Gandhiji's greatness better than any of his ardent admirers'. Gandhi, he says, is a great 'political awakener' of the masses and the highest tribute that one can pay him 'would be to regard and respect Gandhiji as the embodiment of the primitive, blind, spontaneous spirit of revolt of the Indian masses'. While

Roy does mention, incidentally, that Gandhism may in the future come to stifle the revolution rather than promote it, he concludes that at present 'let us admire, respect, and properly appreciate him for the great services that he has rendered to the struggle for freedom'.[28] This article does not present a sincere statement of Roy's view of Gandhi at this time. As his personal correspondence shows,[29] Roy regarded Gandhi in this period as his arch-enemy, who should be destroyed as quickly as possible. The significance of this 'critical appreciation' by Roy lies in its indication of the extent to which Roy, in his effort to influence the Congress, was prepared to compromise his real view of Gandhi as a hopeless mediaeval reactionary. In the months ahead, Roy made a desperate attempt to gain power, but he failed miserably. No single factor was more responsible for this than his utter inability to come to grips, not merely with Gandhi, but with the nationalist culture that Gandhi represented and to which Roy remained so much an outsider.

In 1946, Philip Spratt, a close associate and strong admirer of Roy, wrote an appreciative foreword for Roy's latest series of speeches, which were published under the significant title of *New Orientation*. Spratt reviewed Roy's position on Gandhi and then concluded:

> Roy was highly critical of Gandhism from the very start, in 1920, and has never altered his opinion. . . . Yet it is true, I think, that he has failed to make his criticisms intelligible to the Indian reader. His approach to Gandhism seems that of an outsider, an unsympathetic foreigner. He has never tried to get under the skin of the Mahatma or his admirers and see where that extraordinary power comes from.[30]

This remark constitutes a good indication of the nature of Roy's difficulties with Gandhi during a generation of observation and criticism. Yet, precisely at the moment of Spratt's writing, we can see now in retrospect that significant changes were occurring in Roy's thinking about several key theoretical issues: fundamental questions concerning the nature of power and authority, revolution and history, politics and leadership. And with this fundamental reassessment of basic issues, which Roy called his 'New Orientation', there eventually followed a drastic change of view on Gandhi.

Several factors influenced Roy's sweeping intellectual re-appraisal in 1946. First, Roy's Radical Democratic Party, established in opposition to the Congress, was resoundingly defeated in the Indian general elections held throughout the country in the spring of 1946. If the historical importance for India of these general elections was to demonstrate that the League controlled the Muslims and the Congress the Hindus, then their importance for Roy was to show that his party, given the nation's polarization, was nowhere in sight. It meant the end of his political career. A second factor which affected his thinking concerned the direction and behaviour of the world communist movement under Stalin. Abroad, the brutal aspects of his leadership were becoming crudely clear; at home, Roy had long been under attack from the Communist Party of India and it became evident that neither practical nor theoretical reconciliation with Communism was possible. Roy expressed the nature of his dilemma in stark terms when he told his followers that they must beware of 'two psychoses' prevalent in India, those of Communism and of nationalism. 'Radicalism,' he declared, 'is not camouflaged Communism. We shall have to get over the major nationalist psychosis as well as the minor Communist psychosis, if we believe that we have something new to contribute to the political thought and practice, not only for our country, but of the world as a whole.'[31]

An ideologist abhors nothing more than a moral vacuum, or what Roy liked to deplore as the 'moral and cultural crisis'[32] of our time. For such a vacuum or 'crisis' suggests basic uncertainty over the rightness and wrongness of fundamental moral values, and it is the element of moral certainty which the ideologist seeks above all else. In this respect, Gandhi was no less an ideologist than Roy; but whereas Gandhi had achieved certainty on such matters during his experience in South Africa, Roy underwent a series of such crises, the last and most serious in 1945-46. The final phase of his life, from 1946-53, represents a period of gradual resolution in which Roy delved deeply into his personal resources, trying to form a coherent pattern of thought to meet the demands before him. A close examination of Roy's prolific writings during this period could tell us much about problems relating to the intellectual between tradition and modernity or the relation of ideology to the quest for personal identity. The main purpose of the concluding section of this essay will merely be to suggest how Roy, while trying to purge himself of the 'nationalist psychosis', nevertheless moved far away from Marxism into a way of thinking which is significantly akin to Gandhi and other nationalist figures like Vivekananda and Aurobindo.

On 16 August 1946, while Roy, residing in Dehra Dun, was appraising and reappraising his New Orientation, and Gandhi was busily commenting on Nature Cure from Sewagram, there occurred in Calcutta the worst catastrophe that British India had known. The Muslim League's 'Direct Action Day' in Calcutta was accompanied by unprecedented communal riots: the great Calcutta killing lasted until 20 August, and in these four tragic days, 4000 Hindus and Muslims were slaughtered. The event marks a horrific watershed in the study of the Partition; and its consequences were to have a profound effect upon Roy's view of Gandhi.

Gandhi's reaction to the Calcutta killing, unlike that of Nehru or Jinnah, was to perceive immediately the disastrous social implications and then to act courageously, in an attempt to quell the violence. Just as the Jallianwala Bagh massacre twenty-seven years earlier had shocked Gandhi into realizing the injustice of the Raj, so the Calcutta killing forced him to see the abyss of violence within his own society. When he learned of the appalling scope of the Calcutta tragedy, he exclaimed: 'Would that the violence of Calcutta were sterilized and did not become a signal for its spread all over!'[33] However, when the virus spread into Noakhali and Bihar, he moved fast and effectively. The ensuing fifteen months, culminating in his assassination, contain the finest hours of his entire career. During this period, he scored two brilliant triumphs for his method of *satyāgraha* in his Calcutta and Delhi fasts against communal violence. Less dramatic than these, but equally impressive, were his 'walking tours' in Noakhali and his ingenious use of the prayer meeting to restore trust in a series of strife-torn villages. These final acts moved nearly everyone in India—British, Hindu, and Muslim, alike—to a higher appreciation of Gandhi's greatness. Roy in this case was no exception.

'What changed Roy's attitude [towards Gandhi],' writes Philip Spratt, 'was Gandhi's campaign against the communal massacres, which came at the time of his own final disillusionment with Communist political methods.' Spratt observes the similarity in Roy's and Gandhi's mutual opposition to Partition, and the common spirit of their response to the communal riots. He remarks that on hearing the news of Gandhi's assassination, 'Roy was deeply moved . . . henceforth a new respect for Gandhi showed in his writing.'[34] There was indeed a striking change in Roy's attitude towards Gandhi following the assassination. In two articles of February and April 1948, entitled 'The Message of the Martyr' and 'Homage to the Martyr', Roy sets forth for the first time the extent of his ideological agreement with Gandhi. He now discovers that Gandhi's revivalist nationalism was neither the essential nor the greatest element in Gandhi's teaching. 'Essentially, [Gandhi's message] is a moral, humanist, cosmopolitan appeal. . . . The lesson of the martyrdom of the Mahatma is that the nobler core of his message could not be reconciled with the intolerant cult of nationalism, which he also preached. Unfortunately, this contradiction in his ideas and ideals was not realized by the Mahatma until the last days of his life.' In Gandhi's final phase, what Roy repeatedly calls the 'moral and humanist essence of his message' appeared, and it is precisely this which is 'needed by India never so very urgently as today'. Thus, Indians can do justice to their Mahatma when they learn 'to place the moral and humanist core of his teachings above the carnal cult of nationalism and power-politics'.[35]

There are those who argue that Roy's tributes to Gandhi after the assassination were merely sentimental outbursts, entirely inconsistent with the main line of his thought. This argument is mistaken for several reasons. First, when Roy was attacked by some of his readers for calling Gandhi a humanist and cosmopolitan, he admitted that he had written the article while 'deeply moved' by the crime, 'in an emotional state'. But then he went on to defend his position with vehemence, deploring the 'insensitivity of the logical purists' who attacked him, and refusing categorically to retract a word that he had written. Gandhi, he insisted in this later article, 'sincerely wanted politics to be guided by moral considerations', and his 'endeavour to introduce morality into political practice was the positive core of Gandhism.'[36] This made Gandhi, like Roy, a humanist. A second reason why this argument is mistaken has already been seen: glimpses of Roy's movement away from Marx and towards Gandhi can be found as early as in the prison diaries, and are clearly manifest two years before the assassination in the ideological changes of his 'new orientation'. Finally, far from Roy's tribute to Gandhi being a sporadic outburst, his changed attitude takes a permanent form in his later writings: as Philip Spratt remarked, a 'new respect' for Gandhi now infuses his thoughts. This can be seen clearly in an article which Roy wrote on Gandhi a full year after the assassination. In this piece, Roy pays respect to 'the immortality of his [Gandhi's] message' and then sums up the significance of Gandhi's thought in these remarkable words: 'Practice of the precept of purifying politics with truth and non-violence alone will immortalise the memory of the Mahatma. Monuments of mortar and marble will perish, but the light of the sublime message of truth and non-violence will shine forever.'[37] The passage signifies a total departure from Roy's earlier denunciation of Gandhi. Equally important, though, is the relationship which Roy suggests here between the values of truth and non-violence on the one hand, and the goal of purifying politics on the other. For the formation of this conceptual relationship indicates a nexus of ideas in Roy's mind familiar to Gandhi's way of thinking, especially on the themes of politics and power, and the relation of the means to the ends of action.

'The implication of the doctrine of non-violence,' Roy now believes, 'is the moral dictum that the end does not justify the means. That is the core of the Mahatma's message—which is not compatible with power-politics. The Mahatma wanted to purify politics; that can be done only by raising political practice above the vulgar level of a scramble for power.'[38] This passage represents those ideas which Roy began to develop at a feverish pace in the last five years of his life. In a characteristically Gandhian manner, Roy wants now to purify politics by purging it of both the 'struggle for power' and the party system itself. 'Humanist politics,' he says, must be a moral force; 'it must get out of the struggle for power of the political parties'.[39] Only in these circumstances can political power be transformed into moral authority. Leadership must come not from corrupt party bosses, but rather from 'detached individuals, that is, spiritually free men [who] cannot be corrupted by power . . . it is possible for the individual man to attain spiritual freedom, to be detached and thus to be above corruption. Such men would not hanker after power'.[40] This preoccupation with the corruptibility of political power and the need for establishing a moral basis for leadership was, as Roy acknowledged, at the heart of Gandhi's thought. Moreover, their common preoccupation emerges from a similar set of ideological assumptions about the moral nature of men, and the possibility of creating a perfect social order of spiritually free men. The implications of this way of thinking for politics are far-reaching: they range from a vision of the ideal political leader as a *karmayogin* type, above the lust for power, occupying a position of pure moral authority, to a theory of social organization which urges party-less politics, and a highly decentralized system of government. This is a way of thinking which is fraught with paradoxes. There is a strong element of elitism or moral authoritarianism mixed with a marked strain of not only populism but a peculiar variety of Indian anarchism. Yet it is this paradoxical quality which makes the ideology of modern India so fascinating: as appealing, in its way, as the equally paradoxical thought of Calvin, or Rousseau, or Marx.

The aim of this essay has been to trace the development of Roy's view of Gandhi, and to argue that the significance of the radical changes which occurred may be attributed not only to the dominant force of Gandhi's personality and leadership but, at a deeper level, to the impact on Roy of a 'great tradition' of attitudes and ideas which runs throughout the Indian nationalist movement. Gandhi's embodiment, to a large extent, of this ideological tradition draws our attention to him, as both a leader and as an ideologist. Through Gandhi we may come to understand a way of thinking about man in society which reinforced Indian nationalism. Through an analysis of Roy's response to Gandhi we may detect the force of an ideological tradition which was articulated, in its various aspects, by a number of other Indian thinkers in the 19th and 20th centuries. Bankim Chandra Chatterjee, Vivekananda, Aurobindo, Bepin Chandra Pal, Rabindranath Tagore, Vinoba Bhave and Jayaprakash Narayan all may be seen as having contributed in some way to this tradition of ideas.

It should be stressed in conclusion that the perception of a great tradition of ideas in modern India need not detract from the variety of little traditions of thought which co-exist beside it. Nor are the latter necessarily subsumed within the former. There is much in Roy's thought, for example, that is not encompassed by Gandhi. Radical Humanism as set forth by Roy and developed by his associates cannot be fairly presented as merely a variation on Gandhism. For Roy's persistent emphasis on atheistic humanism, rationalism, and materialism must distinguish him from Gandhi, indeed, from any other tradition of thought in modern India. The focus of this essay has been on an ideological movement of congruence and not divergence. It is this movement of thought, shared to a notable degree by such apparently divergent figures as Gandhi and Roy, that can be seen as the dominant ideology of modern India.

NOTES

[1] Thomas Carlyle, *On Heroes, Hero-Worship and the Heroic in History* (New York, 1898), p. 42.

[2] Erik Erikson, *Young Man Luther* (New York, 1958) will be followed in 1969 by the publication of a psycho-historical analysis of Gandhi.

[3] Especially the superb analysis of Gandhi as a charismatic leader in Lloyd and Susanne Rudolph, *The Modernity of Tradition* (Chicago, 1967), part two.

[4] Stuart Schram, *The Political Thought of Mao Tse-tung* (a revised edition is forthcoming, published by Praeger Press). The Introduction to this work is invaluable for an understanding of Mao's ideology.

[5] L. A. Gordon, 'Portrait of a Bengal Revolutionary', *Journal of Asian Studies*, vol. 27, no. 2 (February 1968), pp. 197-216.

[6] Roy acknowledges the *brahmanical* influence in his *Memoirs* (London, 1964), pp. 163-64.

[7] Roy, *New Orientation* (Calcutta, 1946), p. 27.

[8] Edward Shils, 'Ideology' in *The International Encyclopedia of the Social Sciences*, vol. 7, p. 69.

[9] Robert C. North and X. L. Eudin, *M. N. Roy's Mission to China* (Berkeley and Los Angeles, 1963), p. 1.

[10] *Ibid.* North believes that 'Roy ranks with Lenin and Mao Tse-tung in the development of fundamental Communist policy for the underdeveloped . . . areas of the globe'.

[11] See the comment on Roy's relation to his tradition by Edward Shils in 'The Culture of the Indian Intellectual', University of Chicago Reprint Series, pp.

15-16. (Reprinted from *Sewanee Review*, April and July 1959.)

12 Roy, *Memoirs*, p. 379.

13 *Ibid.*, p. 543.

14 *Ibid.*, p. 413.

15 G. D. Overstreet and Marshall Windmiller, *Communism in India* (Berkeley and Los Angeles, 1959), p. 40.

16 Roy, *India in Transition* (Geneva, 1922), p. 205.

17 *Ibid.*, p. 207.

18 *Ibid.*, p. 235.

19 *Ibid.*, p. 208.

20 *Ibid.*, p. 209.

21 M. N. Roy and Evelyn Roy, *One Year of Non-Co-operation* (Calcutta, 1923), pp. 56-58.

22 See especially: M. N. Roy, *Crime and Karma, Cats and Women: Fragments of a Prisoner's Diary*, vol. 1 (Calcutta, 1957), pp. 112-19; *India's Message: Fragments, etc.*, vol. 2 (Calcutta, 1950).

23 Roy, *India's Message*, p. 307.

24 *Ibid.*, p. 189.

25 *Ibid.*, pp. 237-307.

26 *Ibid.*, pp. 210-11.

27 *Ibid.*, pp. 214, 215, 216, 222, 228, 236.

28 *Independent India*, 16 October 1938, p. 453.

29 At precisely the time when Roy says he was expressing his 'appreciation' of Gandhi to one of the Mahatma's colleagues, we find him writing to a Marxist comrade abroad: 'Our real fight is against the right wing which is still very powerful thanks to the popularity of Gandhi. . . . I am striking at the very root. Gandhist ideology must go before the nationalist movement can develop its enormous revolutionary potentialities. And Gandhi has recognized in us his mortal enemy. As a matter of fact, in his inner circle I am branded as the enemy No. 1.' (Roy to Jay Lovestone, 19 October 1937, Bombay.) Exactly one year after writing his appreciation, Roy wrote to an Indian associate for help in the great effort 'to destroy this curse of Gandhism'. (Roy to Makhan Lal Sen, 12 September 1939.) The quotations are from correspondence preserved in the M. N. Roy Archives of the Indian Renaissance Institute, Dehradun, U.P., India.

30 P. Spratt, 'Foreword' in Roy, *New Orientation* (Calcutta, 1946), p. xv.

31 Roy, *New Orientation*, p. 56.

32 Roy, *Reason, Romanticism and Revolution* (Calcutta, 1952), vol. 1, p. v.

33 Gandhi as quoted in *The Statesman* (Calcutta), 27 August 1946.

34 Philip Spratt, 'Gandhi and Roy', unpublished article.

35 *Independent India*, 22 February 1948, p. 67.

36 *Independent India*, 18 April 1948, p. 176.

37 *Independent India*, 30 January 1949, p. 37.

38 *Independent India*, 22 February 1948, p. 67.

39 Roy, *Politics, Power and Parties* (Calcutta, 1960), p. 121.

40 *Ibid.*, pp. 81-82. Compare this view with Gandhi's address to the Hindustani Talimi Sangh Group in December 1947, recorded in D. G. Tendulkar, *Mahatma* (Delhi, 1963), vol. 8, pp. 227-32.

NON-CO-OPERATION, 1920-22

Hugh F. Owen

I

Surely, so much has been written about Gandhi's non-violent non-co-operation, including the movement of 1920-22, that nothing much remains to be said. So at least it might be argued. But in fact there is still much that we need to know about non-co-operation. Old assumptions need to be re-examined and tested, and further detailed research needs to be done. Three questions in particular need fuller answers than they have received so far. What were Gandhi's aims in launching non-co-operation? How successful was he in achieving them? To what extent and in what ways did Indians respond to him, and why?

In one sense Gandhi's aims were obscure. He refused to plan out his programme in detail, even to himself, and took the Christian words 'one step enough for me' as a *mantra*.[1] As a religious man seeking after truth, he clung to the belief that a good deed must produce a good result.

Yet, in the tide of words which Gandhi wrote and uttered at this time certain fundamental goals emerge. Probably most fundamental of all, he was aiming at the salvation of his soul.[2] In this-worldly, political and social terms he had two fundamental goals. The first of these was to inculcate *satyāgraha*—non-violent resistance, even non-violent coercion—as the means of solving conflict. He wrote later that when he returned to India in 1915 he 'wanted to acquaint India with the method I had tried in South Africa',[3] and in 1920, when his ideas for his forthcoming campaign were maturing, the District Magistrate of Ahmedabad paraphrased a statement by Gandhi to him as follows:

> . . . the fight was really a bigger one than a mere struggle with the Government of India or Great Britain. It was a fight between soul-force and brute-force and in waging it he had the good of England and Europe as much in mind as that of India. His object was to prove that a new force had been born into the world before which fleets and armies and all the methods of material civilization would prove useless. He believed India was better fitted than any country in the world to receive this new teaching, and if he could

carry the country with him he believed that the victory of soul-force over brute-force was assured; and that this victory would open the eyes of the world and ultimately convert them to his way of thinking.[4]

Here the important thing was to change the mentality of the Indian people: to make them self-reliant and fearless, and to prepare them for self-sacrifice, so that they might offer resistance to the government (and in due course to other social groups) and bear the suffering involved without relapsing into violence. Secondly, and related to this, in order to revitalise and restore India he wanted to turn her people back from their flirtation with modern, 'material civilization' to the traditions and institutions of their past. In the course of his successful struggle to convert the Subjects Committee of the Calcutta Special Congress to his programme of non-co-operation, Gandhi clinched his argument by asserting that 'he believed in the ancient ideals of the East and not in the modern and advanced ideals of the West'.[5]

Non-co-operation was designed and developed in order to further these inter-related aims of inculcating *satyāgraha* among as many Indian social groups as possible, and detaching them from the western or modern institutions introduced by the British Government. In the course of elaborating his programme, Gandhi distinguished and stressed certain more precisely-defined goals, notably the involvement of both Muslims and Hindus in the campaign, and the reconciliation of these two communities; the uplift of socially and economically depressed groups; and the attainment of *swarāj* or 'self-government'. Muslim-Hindu unity had already been spotlighted by Gandhi as a primary aim in his Rowlatt Act *satyāgraha* of 1919, and the 1920-22 movement carried forward the issues, the organisation and the agitation launched then. The depressed groups whose position was to be improved comprised primarily the untouchables, and the impoverished—particularly in the countryside—but also included womenfolk generally. Gandhi had already begun efforts to improve the status of untouchables, and now focussed on the use of the *charkhā*, or spinning wheel, and the wearing of *swadeshi* (Indian made), hand-spun, hand-woven materials (*khādi*) as a means of fostering cottage industry and reducing the lowest classes' sense of dependence on others, especially foreigners.[6] *Swarāj* was usually understood as meaning national self-government (with or without an imperial link to Britain), but while Gandhi used it to mean that, he also used it to mean any government responsible to the people, and even to mean the acceptance of non-violent non-co-operation which would give the nation the self-confidence necessary for exerting its will over the government.[7]

Gandhi's immediate objective was, in fact, to bring as many as possible of the numerous groups comprising Indian society into the movement he was leading. To do so, he appealed to the discontents and grievances of a number of these groups—or took the initiative in reminding them of grievances they were in danger of forgetting! Even more, he raised as issues government decisions, policies or institutions, which flouted religiously-sanctioned social mores, beliefs, or ideals or injured the pride and self-respect of groups within Indian society or of Indians as a whole. But in order to reassure the more timid among his countrymen and those who had more to lose from disturbances, Gandhi incorporated planks in his programme which provided plenty of activity while involving no head-on collision with the government. This not only helped in his inculcation of non-violence, but also enabled him to postpone the more aggressive activities in the non-co-operation programme and so reduce the likelihood of Government repression while the movement was in its formative stage. Throughout the 1920-22 non-co-operation movement Gandhi was engaged in balancing his call to non-violent arms with restraint.

From his suspension of the Rowlatt Act *satyāgraha* in April 1919 to the end of the non-co-operation movement early in 1922 Gandhi was feeling his way forward. Within the broad framework of the goals outlined above he built up his programme in a pragmatic fashion, now stirring, now restraining, and generally seeking to do both at once.

In May 1919 the national movement was like a fire which had partly burnt itself out and had been partly doused: it was in some danger of going out altogether, but there was even more danger that if Gandhi fanned it then it would flare up uncontrollably once more. He therefore kept promising those who were dissatisfied with the suspension of the movement that *satyāgraha* would be renewed within the next few months or even weeks.[8] In July, however, recognising the danger of violent outbreaks if civil disobedience were renewed, he suspended it indefinitely. He now focussed attention upon the mistreatment of Indians in South Africa, and in a restrained way upon the viciousness of the Punjab martial law administration, and enjoined hand-weaving and spinning upon his followers.[9] Through his work in the Congress Punjab Inquiry Committee he acquired within the existing nationalist organisation a strong position, which he further strengthened at the Amritsar session.[10] By participation in the Punjab Inquiry, he associated himself with the most inflammatory issue of the time; but at the same time his voice 'was always for moderation and restraint'.[11] Gandhi's exercise in equipoise was epitomised in his rallying, on the one hand, of the somewhat reluctant Khilafat

173

Committee, and his insistence, on the other, that the Amritsar Congress pass resolutions regretting the Indian excesses of the preceding April and welcoming Montagu's Reforms.

II

Already during the last two months of 1919 he had begun moving toward non-co-operation, and during the next six months he continued to evolve his programme. He first proposed non-co-operation in an All-India Khilafat Conference in Delhi on 23 and 24 November 1919, when he suggested that Indian Muslims should 'withdraw co-operation from the Government' if the temporal embodiment of the Khilafat, the Ottoman Empire, were dismembered by Britain and her allies in the Peace Treaty.[12] A Khilafat leaders' conference in January 1920 empowered him, together with Maulana Abul Kalam Azad and Hakim Ajmal Khan, to draw up a programme of non-co-operation, but it was not until March that Gandhi started to put forward detailed proposals.[13] These were crystallised at an informal Khilafat Conference in Delhi on 22 March and promulgated as four successive stages: first, the renunciation of titles and honorary posts; secondly, the gradual withdrawal from service by government employees including menial servants; thirdly, the withdrawal from service of police and military; and last, and most remote, the suspension of payment of taxes.[14] Gandhi was not satisfied, however, with this programme, and nor apparently were some government servants, since it would affect few apart from them except title-holders! Early in June at a series of important meetings of the Central Khilafat Committee in Allahabad Gandhi expounded a much more elaborate first stage of non-co-operation, which would include (in addition to the renunciation of titles) the boycott of government schools and colleges, the boycott of law courts, and—at the insistence of Hazrat Mohani and others—the buying of *swadeshi*, to the exclusion of foreign, goods. The withdrawal of government servants was allowed to slide into the background, and stages three and four were relegated to the future.[15] Gandhi justified the boycott of courts and schools on the ground that it was 'sinful' to co-operate with, or receive anything from, a government which had shown itself to be evil by its treatment of the Punjab and its attitude to the Khilafat.[16] Indeed, for Gandhi the whole system of the government and its institutions was 'inherently corrupt'; the very magnitude of Indian lawyers' fees was 'sinful'; and government-aided education was thrice-blighted—it was taught in a foreign language, inculcated a foreign culture, and emphasised literary at the expense of manual training.[17] Gandhi had already argued in similar vein in *Hind Swaraj*, as long before as 1908,[18] and was now glad, doubtless, of an opportunity to win Indians back to their own, superior civilization. More immediately in 1920 he wanted to attack the authority of the government by shaking these twin pillars. Echoing the arguments used by Tilak and Aurobindo in their call for passive resistance in 1907, he reasoned that the government established its authority through the courts and manufactured clerks through the schools, and that both these props should be knocked away.[19] Although wary of the vindictiveness of Hazrat Mohani's proposal to boycott British goods, Gandhi laid stress more positively on the use of *swadeshi* goods—something he had long encouraged—on the three grounds that the use of what is indigenous is somehow good in itself; that it would enable the educated to reach the masses; and would help alleviate poverty.[20]

He rounded out his programme early in July by adding the boycott of the Legislative Councils to the first stage of non-co-operation. His advocacy of the reformed Councils had never been very enthusiastic: before the Amritsar Congress he had said 'the reforms . . . will be worthless', and in May 1920 he had suggested that many need not 'trouble about entering the councils'.[21] As with British law and education, he found something intrinsically unhealthy about parliaments.[22] When, therefore, Lala Lajpat Rai, returning home from voluntary exile, was so shocked by what he saw and heard of government repression in his native Punjab that he suggested Indians should boycott the reformed legislatures,[23] Gandhi welcomed the idea. 'Needless to say,' wrote Gandhi, 'I am in entire accord with Lala Lajpat Rai.'[24]

III

Gandhi set out to win the support of the Muslims first of all for his programme, and indeed it was devised largely with them in mind. That an aspirant for all-India leadership should start by wooing the Muslims is striking, since national leaders up to now had experienced great difficulty in winning their support. But the task was less difficult for Gandhi than for many others, since he was deeply religious but had worked out his religious position independently for himself,[25] and was therefore able to comprehend the Muslims' religious standpoint and appeal to it. Furthermore, the Muslims were particularly susceptible to such an appeal at this stage, since their holy lands and the Khalif of the Sunnis were under attack. Gandhi had identified himself with the resulting Pan-Islamic feeling which was rising toward the end of the First World War, and Muslims joined Hindus in his Rowlatt Act *satyāgraha* in March-April of 1919.[26] The initial Khilafat Committee (later the Central Khilafat Committee) was founded during that agitation by a number of Muslim businessmen of Bombay, led by the wealthy Mian Muhammad Chotani.[27] This committee suffered from the general political decline when Gandhi called off the Rowlatt movement, but as news of the unfavourable peace terms being devised for Turkey leaked through during 1919 the Committee revived. Under the inspiration of more fervent Pan-Islamists in the United Provinces it eventually arranged an all-India Khilafat Conference at Lucknow for 21 September. At a public meeting in Bombay on 18 September, Gandhi assured the 25,000 Muslims present that 'they had 21 crores [210 million] of Hindus at their back' and urged them to 'put their heart and soul into the agitation' and adopt 'the satyagraha spirit'.[28] Thus encouraged, the Lucknow Conference resolved to set up a network of Khilafat Committees and to observe 17 October as Khilafat Day by fasting and mourning.[29] When Gandhi urged Hindus to join Muslims in a *hartāl* on that day, the Khilafat Committee gratefully let him take over most of the preparatory work for the Day in Bombay. Stressing non-violence, Gandhi prescribed mass demonstrations, and the *hartāl* was widely observed in cities and towns, thanks largely to the lieutenants, Muslim as well as Hindu, whom he had recruited in his earlier campaigns.[30]

This peaceful *hartāl* marked a considerable advance in Gandhi's drive for Muslim support. Both the ardent and the more cautious were attracted to *satyāgraha*, and Gandhi was invited to attend the next All-India Khilafat Conference on 23-24 November in Delhi organised by the local Khilafat Committee. Here once again the more ardent Pan-Islamists from the United Provinces, such as Hazrat Mohani, Abdul Bari and Abdul Ghaffar, pressed for vigorous action; the Conference voted to boycott the Peace celebrations, and they were effectively boycotted throughout the country.[31] The balance in Muslim ranks was swung in favour of the more aggressive Pan-Islamists by the release from detention of the Ali brothers in December 1919[32] and of Azad in January 1920. A rash of Khilafat conferences ensued, especially in Azad's home province, Bengal, and in March one conference in Calcutta called for a further *hartāl* on 19th of that month, which the Central Khilafat Committee meekly endorsed.[33] Gandhi was now becoming quite as concerned with restraining as with stimulating the movement, and sought to curb the language of the Ali brothers and others and to prevent attempts to involve turbulent urban working-class groups.[34] An informal Khilafat Conference in Delhi in the same month accepted Gandhi's programme for non-co-operation as it stood.[35] Muslim feeling continued to mount: in April conferences of the *ulema* and of Khilafat Workers initiated a *hijrat* (flight by Muslims from oppression) to Afghanistan.[36] In May Gandhi was formally elected to the

Central Khilafat Committee.[37] At Allahabad on 1 and 2 June that Committee decided to put non-co-operation into effect, and to do so appointed a sub-Committee, consisting of the Ali brothers, Azad, Hazrat Mohani and Dr Kitchlu of Amritsar, with Gandhi as a 'sort of dictator'.[38]

Gandhi thus launched non-co-operation on 1 August under the auspices of an influential, widespread Muslim organisation. But Muslim acquiescence had by no means been automatic, nor was it complete. Four kinds of opponents to Gandhi's programme may be distinguished among the Muslims: the secular nationalists; certain Muslim regional leaders, particularly in the Muslim-majority provinces, Bengal and the Punjab; the timid; and those who objected to certain planks in Gandhi's programme. The 'nationalists', mainly in the Muslim League and typified by Jinnah and the Raja of Mahmudabad, opposed the appeal to religion as obscurantist and potentially divisive of Indian society; they were outnumbered, however, at the Khilafat meetings and at the Muslim League sessions.[39] Important regional leaders in Bengal and the Punjab had fallen out with the Muslim League over the terms of the Lucknow Pact: the Punjab Muslim League under Sir Muhammad Shafi was disaffiliated, and in Bengal Syed Nawab Ali Chowdhry resigned from the League and founded his Indian Moslem Association.[40] After some hesitation in mid-1920, these bodies rejected non-co-operation,[41] following the innately conservative bent of their members, and recognising that their provincial communalism would be submerged in the broader stream of Pan-Islamism. Numbers of timid Muslims held aloof or resigned from the Khilafat committees in 1920,[42] but Gandhi's emphasis on non-violence reassured others. Those who opposed specific items of the programme, as Fazlul Huq of Bengal opposed the educational boycott for example, were generally carried along by Gandhi's determination, Shaukat Ali's bluster, and their own acceptance of non-co-operation in principle.[43]

No Muslim could actively oppose the Khilafat without thereby labelling himself a 'bad Muslim'.[44] Gandhi and the Pan-Islamists were in a very strong position, and Muslims fell in behind them or lay low.

Gandhi could not afford to rest, however: to put the Khilafat Committee's decision into effect he and Shaukat Ali toured the Punjab, Sind, Tamilnad and Malabar in July and August calling Muslims to defend the Khilafat, others to help them, and all to non-violence.[45]

IV

Having won Muslim endorsement, Gandhi was well situated to carry Congress. Here he encountered stiff opposition, nevertheless, from older nationalist leaders and regional elite groups. As with Muslims, some opposed specific planks as inimical to youth or their group interests.[46] Many Hindus were averse to taking such a serious step over a Muslim communal issue unrelated directly to India, and the Pan-Islamists reinforced this aversion by welcoming the possibility of an Afghan invasion.[47] The Congress leaders' most immediate quarrel with Gandhi was that he was trying to divert them from the Indian legislatures just when these bodies were obtaining some real power—and at a time when other social groups were starting to challenge the regional *élites* which dominated the longer-established Provincial Congress Committees. Ambition and jealousy were undoubtedly involved: Tilak and Das especially aspired to all-India leadership which Gandhi was rapidly assuming. Even more, Gandhi was challenging their provincial positions and those of the socially-dominant groups they represented. The dominance of the *chitpavan Brāhmans* in Maharashtra, represented by Kelkar, Khaparde and Moonje, was threatened by the Marwaris and depressed castes, to whom Gandhi appealed, and by the cultivating castes, the bitterness of whose anti-Brahmanism Gandhi sought to assuage;[48] the Hindu *bhadralok*, who dominated politics and society in Bengal, feared that Gandhi's call to rouse mass peasant groups, Muslim or Hindu, would sweep them away;[49] in the Punjab, the Hindu trading castes, exemplified by Lala Lajpat Rai, might be unenthusiastic about helping to stimulate Muslims, urban or rural, to a more active political role; and in Madras, Gandhi's programme provided a further issue in a struggle for dominance within Congress.[50]

The first test came at the All-India Congress Committee (A-ICC) meetings in Banaras on 30-31 May. Gandhi's opponents found it difficult to oppose him point blank in view of his popularity with the Congress rank and file and elements among the masses. Gandhi called on their sense of outraged honour over the Punjab—indeed the meeting had been delayed to consider the Hunter Committee's report on the Punjab[51]—and they could not reject non-co-operation outright without seeming to rebuff the Muslims. Furthermore, by taking up a more aggressive position than theirs Gandhi had manoeuvred any who opposed him into the position of crypto-Moderates or crypto-'Besantines'. At the suggestion of some Madras members the Committee sought to evade the issue by deferring a decision to a Special Session of Congress at Calcutta early in September.[52]

At this Special Congress Gandhi carried his programme against the opposition of 'the leaders as a whole'.[53] First, they were confronted pretty well with a *fait accompli*: the Muslims had already begun non-co-operation on 1 August, and Gandhi made it clear it would continue with or without Congress backing.[54] Furthermore, feeling over the Punjab had not subsided, as those who had proposed the session had hoped: quite the reverse, for Gandhi had reminded his audiences of this, and the British played into his hands, the House of Lords exonerating and praising General Dyer.[55] Boycotts in Egypt, too, provided an example.[56] More important, some members of the regional *élites* had decided to place national above group loyalties: such were Gangadharrao Deshpande and S. M. Paranjpe in western India, and Jitendralal Bannerjee in Bengal.[57] Gandhi's lieutenants from his earlier campaigns supported him vigorously at the Special Congress. Even before it, Rajendra Prasad persuaded the Bihar Provincial Conference to commit itself to Gandhi's programme, and Vallabhbhai Patel did likewise (with Gandhi's personal assistance) at the Gujarat Provincial Conference.[58] The All-India Home Rule League had supported Gandhi's Rowlatt Act *satyāgraha*: in April 1920 its council elected Gandhi as chairman and in July backed non-co-operation.[59] Gandhi's lieutenants and the officers of the League arranged for trains to bring Gandhi's supporters from Madras and Bombay, and they elected as many as possible of 'the Khilafat people' to the Calcutta Subjects Committee.[60] The Khilafatists apparently disciplined their members within the Committee, too: 'Mr Fazlul Huq was actually seen to be physically removed from one lobby to another'.[61] The major issue was the Council boycott, and here Gandhi had outflanked his opponents. They agreed on the need to do battle with the British, and most had even agreed to non-co-operation in principle, while hoping to obstruct its implementation.[62] They were thus in a very weak position to resist Gandhi's call to put non-co-operation into practice. As at the 1919 Amritsar Congress, Gandhi suggested that Das, his chief opponent, was somewhat less than honest—this time in seeking election to the Councils in order to obstruct from within.[63] He clinched his victory by accepting *swarāj* as one of the goals of non-co-operation, thus winning Motilal Nehru's support; and by agreeing that the boycotts should be 'gradual'—which Das and others took to mean that they marked only an 'ideal':[64] his programme was carried in the Subjects Committee by 148 votes to 133. In the open session between one-third and one-half the delegates abstained from voting, suggesting they disliked all or part of Gandhi's programme but felt Das and Pal offered them no adequate alternative. Here the *imprimatur* of the Subjects Committee upon the resolution and Gandhi's popularity and superior organisation told, and the voting was approximately 1855 to 873.[65]

Gandhi now called for full implementation of the first stage of non-co-operation. The boycott of law courts and educational institutions was indeed 'gradual', although Motilal Nehru gave up his lucrative practice, and some students crossed from government to 'national' schools in Gujarat and Calcutta.[66] The main effort was naturally concentrated upon boycotting the forthcoming elections. The branches of the Home Rule League and Congress and Khilafat Committees exhorted voters to abstain,[67] and in Bombay for example only 15 per cent of electors voted.[68] Gandhi's continuing tours spread his fame among urban and rural folk;[69] after some hesitation Das, Kelkar and Rai, and after longer delay the Madrasi leaders decided that popularity, if not loyalty to Congress, dictated the withdrawal of their candidatures.[70]

At the Nagpur Congress at the end of 1920 Gandhi's opponents rallied again.[71] Nagpur was in 'Tilak territory' but numbers of the late Lokamanya's followers now followed Gandhi, and Das' tactic of bringing a large party opposed to Gandhi was matched by the Bengal Khila-fatists.[72] Above all, by boycotting the elections Gandhi's opponents had weakened their case further, and they still had no clear alternative to Gandhi's programme.[73] Recognising this, Das, Rai and Pal capitulated and supported non-co-operation.

V

Gandhi was now in overall command of the nationalist movement. From January 1921 to March 1922 he guided it through four phases, each of which in its way contributed to his aims of stirring while restraining.

The first phase ran from the Nagpur Congress to the A-ICC meeting at Bezwada (Vijayawada) on 30 March-1 April 1921. During these months Gandhi concentrated upon implementing the first stage of non-co-operation and mobilising large demonstrations against the Duke of Connaught, who had come to inaugurate the reformed Councils. The tension experienced by those who had worked for the adoption of non-co-operation was released in action, and new groups were involved.

The proportion of pleaders who threw up their practices was not large,[74] but spectacular examples, such as Motilal Nehru and Das, gave the whole non-co-operation movement impetus. *Panchāyats* were established to provide alternative means of settling cases, and litigants did use them—sometimes under the threat of social ostracism—notably in the Punjab, Bihar and Central Provinces.[75] The renunciation of honours by title-holders tarnished the 'glory' of government favours.[76]

The boycott of educational institutions was probably the most successful plank in the programme, especially in Bengal and in Bihar, Orissa and Assam, where students were affected by the Bengali example, but also in virtually every other educational centre.[77]

After some hesitation, it was agreed that municipal and other local government bodies would not be boycotted, and non-co-operators succeeded in capturing control of numbers of such bodies, notably in Madras, Gujarat and the Punjab.[78] Attention was also given to the internal organisation of the movement. Gandhi's streamlining of the upper level of the Congress structure was matched by the revival of local Congress and Home Rule *sabhās* and the establishment of new Congress and Khilafat Committees. Pleaders and students who had left their institutions were enrolled as volunteers to speak on non-co-operation, hand-spinning and -weaving.[79]

The agitation encouraged people both in the towns and the country to look forward to civil disobedience, especially in the form of non-payment of taxes. The temper of the agitation of the tenants of the United Provinces against their landlords prompted Gandhi to remind them that 'we are not at the present moment offering civil disobedience'.[80]

The second phase occupied the period from early April to 30 June. At the Bezwada A-ICC session Gandhi announced that he would no longer concentrate on the boycott of lawcourts, titles and schools, since 'the Congress had achieved the real object of the propaganda, namely the demolition of the prestige of these institutions of the bureaucratic Government'.[81] This may have been partly so, but Gandhi probably felt that few spectacular successes remained to be won along these lines. Instead, Congress should aim for ten million members, for a fund of ten million rupees, and to have two million *charkhās* in use, by 30 June.[82] These goals would call for plenty of hard work while deflecting 'non-co-operators' from themes likely to bring them into conflict with the government, at least after the hartals for 6 and 13 April in National Week, which were very widely observed:[83] furthermore, they would provide the organisational and financial sinews for civil disobedience when it came.

Gandhi intended the *charkhā* as a symbol and agent of economic and social uplift of the depressed, as well as a testimony to Indians' pride in their common identity.[84] He now demanded equality of treatment for untouchables by nationalists.[85]

Liquor shops were also vigorously picketed. This had not been part of the non-co-operation programme, but Gandhi felt 'God has sent the movement to us unsought'.[86] It not only contributed to the uplift of the depressed, but appealed to Muslims and Hindus, and indeed to many 'who otherwise are opposed to non-co-operation'.[87] This liquor boycott deprived the governments of much excise revenue—and if they protected liquor sellers against intimidation they could be accused of compelling people to drink![88] More localised discontents also contributed to the strength of non-co-operation—notably among the Sikhs, the tea-plantation labour in Assam, and the *kisāns* (peasants) of the United Provinces.[89]

The governments met these movements with prosecution or prohibition, which led in a number of instances to clashes with excited crowds.[90]

By a great effort on the part of Gandhi and his committees the ten million rupees were collected by 30 June,[91] and although the full complement of members had not been enrolled, Gandhi felt it necessary to move on to new targets to maintain the impetus of the movement—and so inaugurated the third phase, June-mid October. He now reinforced his appeal to use the *charkhā* with a call for the boycott of foreign cloth,[92] and underlined his message by adopting the loin cloth.[93] The western-educated (and their wives) especially were asked to burn their foreign clothes, and merchants to abjure trade in foreign cloth. Some Marwari commercial associations and more devoted followers of Gandhi did so, but the general response was disheartening.[94]

The outbreaks of violence in the previous phase prompted Gandhi to emphasise the need for non-violence[95] and for improved organisation. The recruitment of volunteers and establishment of Congress Committees begun earlier continued.[96] Gandhi's success in inculcating non-violence was reflected in the lack of violence when the Ali brothers were arrested in mid-September.

By this time, however, the movement had decidedly lost way, and in mid-October Gandhi moved to revive it, and so launched the fourth and final phase. Taking up the statements for which the Ali brothers as well as a number of *ulema* had been prosecuted, Gandhi called on government servants and soldiers to resign.[97] The proscribed statements were repeated broadcast. After a slow beginning, numbers of government officers, police and *chaukidārs* resigned.[98] Nationwide *hartāls* were called to mark the arrival of the Prince of Wales on 17 November.[99] Provincial governments agreed the *hartāls* were 'unexpectedly complete', and the Government of Bengal observed that it was 'now clear that the non-co-operation movement has built up an organisation of very real power, and this it will be necessary to break'.[100] Already on 4 November the A-ICC had authorised the Provincial Congress Committees to launch civil disobedience.[101] Expectancy rose *pari passu* with government attacks on the organisations: Bardoli, Guntur, Kaira, Kamrup and other districts prepared to refuse payment of taxes.[102] Gandhi, however, was concerned lest repression, excitement and lack of commitment to *ahimsā* result in violence.[103] His anxiety had been deepened by clashes during the November *hartāl* in Bombay, and, as is well known, he called the movement off following the murders of policemen at Chauri Chaura in February.

VI

May the non-co-operation movement be said to have failed then? In so far as Gandhi called it off, it may. Furthermore, Das, Motilal Nehru, Kelkar and others were soon to show that they could not resist the 'deadly trap' of the legislatures. And the mutually antagonistic aspects of Muslim and Hindu communalism, submerged by the Khilafat campaign, reappeared.

Nevertheless the organisational links which had been forged in 1919-22 were not destroyed by repression and imprisonment and were repaired when Congressmen re-emerged from jail. Gandhi might congratulate himself, too, on the extent to which nativism had been inculcated among his fellow-countrymen, though others might regret this as backward-looking. Non-violence had been imbibed and practised to a remarkable degree. And Gandhi's own mystique was clearly established. People had been stirred to follow his programme in most parts of India: to understand why this was so we need, above all, more detailed studies of Indian regions, individual cities and districts.[104]

NOTES

[1] Article, 29 Dec. 1920, in *Young India, 1919-1922* (Madras, 1922), pp. 337-38.

[2] See Bombay Presidency Police: Abstracts of Intelligence [hereinafter such abstracts will be referred to thus: (name of Province) Police (year)], 1921, paragraphs 337 (7), 382 (8), in N. R. Phatak (ed.), *Source Material for a History of the Freedom Movement in India*, vol. 3 'Mahatma Gandhi, part I: 1915-1922' (Bombay, Government [of Maharashtra], 1965) [hereinafter *HFMB*, vol. no.], pp. 370, 374. I am indebted to a former student, Mrs P. Simpson, for drawing to my attention M. K. Gandhi, *An Autobiography: the Story of My Experiments with Truth* (London, Cape, 1966), p. xii.

[3] *An Autobiography* (London, Cape, 1966), p. 330; cf. 'The Satyagrahashrama', 16 February 1916, in *Speeches and Writings of Mahatma Gandhi* (Madras, 1933), pp. 377-90.

[4] Bombay Police 1920, par. 879 (x), in *HFMB* 3, p. 281.

[5] *The Hindu* (Madras), 8 September 1920, p. 5; cf. M. K. Gandhi, *Hind Swaraj or Indian Home Rule* (Ahmedabad, 1939), especially pp. 16-17, 31-38, 44-45, 58-66; 'Hind Swaraj', 26 Jan. 1921 in *Young India*, op. cit., pp. 1101-04.

[6] For examples of women's response to Gandhi, see Government of India, Home Department Political file [hereinafter such files will be referred to thus: Home Poll] Deposit March 1920, no. 2, p. 3.

[7] D. G. Tendulkar, *Mahatma: Life of Mohandas Karamchand Gandhi* (Delhi, 1961), vol. 2, pp. 73-74; see *Young India*, op. cit., 22 Sept. and 29 Dec. 1920, pp. 1089, 1095.

[8] *Young India*, [10] May 1919, p. 6b; 2 June 1919, p. 7d; Home Poll B June 1919, nos. 701-4, p. 15; *ibid.* Deposit [hereinafter Dep.] July 1919, no. 48, p. 14; *ibid.*

Aug. 1919, no. 51, pp. 6-8; M. K. Gandhi Papers, held at Sabarmati Ashram, Ahmedabad, photocopies at National Archives, Delhi [hereinafter Gandhi Papers Sabarmati], items nos. S 6618, 6628, 6649; *Qaumi Report,* 8 and 20 May 1919, in Madras Native Newspaper Reports, 1919, pp. 772, 849.

9 *Young India,* 5 July 1919, p. 2a; 11 June 1919, p. 3; 12 July 1919, p. 2a; articles reproduced in *Young India 1919-1922 (Supplement)* (Madras, 1924), pp. 1240-46; 1268-93.

10 See H. F. Owen, 'The Leadership of the Indian National Movement, 1914-20' (Canberra, unpublished Ph.D. thesis, 1965), pp. 453-55.

11 M. R. Jayakar, *The Story of My Life* (Bombay, 1958), vol. 1, p. 321.

12 *Young India,* 3 Dec. 1919, p. 8; cf. Gandhi, *An Autobiography,* p. 401.

13 *Young India,* 10 March 1920, p. 4; A. K. Azad, *India Wins Freedom: An Autobiographical Narration* (Calcutta, 1959), p. 9; Home Poll Dep. March 1920, no. 89, p. 16; *ibid.* April 1920, no. 103, p. 13; *ibid.* July 1920, no. 89, pp. 11-12.

14 Home Poll Dep. April 1920, no. 103, pp. 11-14; *Young India,* 5 May 1921, pp. 247-48.

15 See Home Poll B July 1920, no. 109, Accompaniment C; *ibid.* Dep. July 1920, no. 13, pp. 5-6.

16 *Young India,* 29 Sept. 1920, pp. 425-26.

17 *Young India,* 29 Sept. and 6 Oct. 1920, 1 Sept. 1921, pp. 425-26, 411-13, 451-55.

18 *Hind Swaraj* (1939), pp. 55, 88, 99.

19 *Young India,* 11 August 1920, pp. 407-08; cf. Tilak, 'Tenets of the New Party', 2 Jan. 1907, in *All About Lok. Tilak* (Madras, 1922), pp. 502-03; Sri Aurobindo, *The Doctrine of Passive Resistance* (Pondicherry, 1966), pp. 25-29.

20 See Gandhi, *An Autobiography,* p. 400; 'Swadeshi', 14 Feb. 1916 in *Speeches and Writings of Mahatma Gandhi,* pp. 336-44; *Young India,* 3 Dec. 1919, p. 8.

21 *Navajivan,* 26 Oct. 1919, translation in *Young India,* 5 Nov. 1919, p. 4; *Young India,* 19 May 1920, p. 396.

22 *Hind Swaraj* (1939), pp. 31-33.

23 In his Urdu paper, *Bande Mataram,* cited [in English] in *Young India,* 30 June 1920, p. 5b.

24 *Young India,* 7 July 1920, p. 8b.

25 A point made to the writer by Professor N. R. Phatak, Bombay, 24 April 1963.

26 For an examination of this, see the writer's 'Who Knows How It All Came About?' in R. Kumar (ed.) *India in 1919* (forthcoming).

27 Bombay Police 1919, pars. 503, 529, 575, 603, 628.

28 *Young India,* 20 Sept., *Mufid e Rozgar,* 23 Sept., *Muslim Herald,* 26 Sept. 1919, in Bombay Native Newspaper Reports, 1919, pp. 342, 375, 420; Home Poll Dep. Nov. 1919, no. 15, pp. 4-5.

29 United Provinces Police 1919, pars. 2116, 2164, 2320; C. Khaliquzzaman, *Pathway to Pakistan* (Lahore, 1961), pp. 47-48.

30 Home Poll Dep. Nov. 1919, no. 14, pp. 7-8; Bombay Native Newspaper Reports, 1919, pp. 449, 474-77, 496-98.

31 United Provinces Police 1919, pars. 2360, 2457, 2458; Bombay Police 1920, par. 168 (h), in *HFMB* 3, pp. 237-41; Home Poll Dep. Jan. 1920, no. 5; Bombay Native Newspaper Reports, 1919, pp. 633-35.

32 United Provinces Police 1920, par. 18; Bombay Police 1920, par. 242; Khaliquzzaman, op. cit., p. 51.

33 Home Poll Dep. March 1920, no. 89, pp. 16-26; *ibid.* April 1920, no. 103, p. 13; *ibid.* July 1920, no. 89, pp. 3, 11-13; *ibid.* no. 90, pp. 5-6.

[34] *Young India*, 10 March 1920, p. 3; Bombay Police 1920, pars. 453 (f) (j) 549 (x), in *HFMB* 3, pp. 257-61.

[35] G. S. Khaparde, *Diary* (extracts held at *Kesari-Mahratta* Trust, Poona), 22 March 1920; A. K. Azad, op. cit., p. 10.

[36] See Home Poll Dep. July 1920, no. 94, p. 25; *ibid.* no. 106, p. 26.

[37] *Ibid.*, June 1920, no. 112.

[38] Home Poll B July 1920, no. 109; *ibid.* Dep. July 1920, no. 13, pp. 5-6.

[39] C. Khaliquzzaman, op. cit., pp. 47-49; United Provinces Police 1920, par. 18.

[40] Bihar and Orissa Police 1917, par. 143; J. H. Broomfield, *Elite Conflict in a Plural Society: Twentieth-Century Bengal* (Berkeley, 1968), pp. 125-29.

[41] Home Poll Dep. Dec. 1920, no. 59; *ibid.*, no. 66.

[42] See B. A. Koor to Chotani, 12 May 1920, in Home Poll Dep. June 1920, no. 112, Accompaniment 'A'; Bombay Native Newspaper Reports, week ending 29 May 1920, pp. 11, 14.

[43] See M. A. Ansari to Gandhi [1 April 1920], no. S7143. Gandhi Papers Sabarmati; Home Poll Dep. July 1920, no. 105, p. 5; Bombay Police 1920, par. 1043 (v), in *HFMB* 3, p. 291.

[44] See Home Poll B July 1920, no. 109, Accompaniment 'C'.

[45] Bombay Police 1920, pars 1043 (g), 1103 (c) (i), 1131 (E) (F) (H) (S); *ibid.* pars. 1072 (z), 1131 (d) (m) (z), 1163 (XXIII) (XXIV), 1238, in *HFMB* 3, pp. 292, 298-302, 306-20.

[46] See M. R. Jayakar, op. cit., vol. 1, p. 339; G. I. Patel, *Vithalbhai Patel: Life and Times* (Bombay, Laxmi Narayan Press, n.d.), vol. 1, pp. 449 ff.

[47] Home Poll B July 1920, no. 109, Accompaniment 'E'; *Young India*, 23 June 1920, p. 255.

[48] See M. A. Ansari to Gandhi [1 April 1920], no. S7143, Gandhi Papers Subarmati.

[49] Though see differences on this, Home Poll B June 1919, nos. 494-97, pp. 4-7.

[50] See A. Rangaswami Iyengar to C. Vijiaraghavachariar, 4 May 1920, C. Rajagopalachar to C. Vijiaraghavachariar, 7 July 1920, Vijiaraghavachariar Papers.

[51] See A. Rangaswami Iyengar to Gokaran Nath Misra, 14 May 1920, File 2/1920, A-ICC Papers.

[52] See C. Rajagopalachar to C. Vijiaraghavachariar, 16 June 1920, Vijiaraghavachariar Papers.

[53] *Hindu*, 4 Sept. 1920, p. 3.

[54] Home Poll Dep. Sept. 1920, no. 70, p. 6.

[55] *Ibid.* July 1920, no. 97, p. 15; House of Lords *Debates*, vol. 41, cols. 222-307, 311-78; *Amrita Bazar Patrika* (Calcutta), 23 July 1920, p. 6, 24 July 1920, p. 6; Bombay Native Newspaper Reports, weeks ending 24 July 1920, p. 10, 31 July 1920, pp. 13-14; Bombay Police 1920, par. 982.

[56] Madras Native Newspaper Reports, 1920, pp. 1161, 1198-99.

[57] G. Deshpande, *Autobiography* (Bombay, 1960) [kindly translated for the writer by Dr U. Mahajani], pp. 328-31, 337-38, 342-46; interview with Prof. S. Mukherjee, Rampur Hat, 27 Aug. 1963.

[58] *Searchlight* (Patna), 29 Aug. 1920, p. 8, 3 Sept. 1920, p. 4; K. K. Datta, *History of the Freedom Movement in Bihar* (Patna, 1957), vol. 1, pp. 302-03; N. D. Parikh, *Sardar Vallabhbhai Patel* (Ahmedabad, 1953), pp. 110-15.

[59] *Young India*, 28 April 1920, p. 1; Circular from General Secretaries, All-India Home Rule League, 10 April 1920, Adyar Archives; Home Poll Dep. Aug. 1920, no. 31.

60 *Hindu,* 6 Sept. 1920, p. 5; Home Poll Dep. Aug. 1920, no. 110, p. 30; *ibid.* Sept. 1920, no. 70, p. 5.

61 *Hindu,* 8 Sept. 1920, p. 5.

62 *Mahratta,* 29 Aug. 1920, in Bombay Native Newspaper Reports, week ending 28 Aug. 1920, p. 13; *Amrita Bazar Patrika,* 6 Sept. 1920, p. 6; *Hind*u, 6 Sept. 1920, p. 5, 8 Sept. 1920, p. 5; Harkishen Lal to S. Satyamurti, telegram, 28 Aug. 1920. Satymurti Papers; see J. H. Broomfield, 'The Non-Co-operation Decision of 1920: a Crisis in Bengal Politics', in D. A. Low (ed.), *Soundings in Modern South Asian History* (London, 1968), p. 250.

63 *Hindu,* 6 Sept. 1920, p. 5.

64 *Hindu,* 7 Sept. 1920, p. 5; *Amrita Bazar Patrika,* 9 Sept. 1920, p. 6.

65 *Hindu,* 10 Sept. 1920, p. 5.

66 *Searchlight,* 24 Sept. 1920, p. 8; Home Poll Dep. Dec. 1920, no. 59; *ibid.* no. 67; *ibid.* no. 84.

67 'Instructions to the Branches of the Swarajya Sabha, lately the All-India Home Rule League, Oct. 1920', no. S7327, Gandhi Papers Sabarmati; Bombay Police 1920, par. 1523 (32); *ibid.* 1339 (s), 1450 (15), in *HFMB* 3, pp. 328-29, 335-36.

68 Home Poll Dep. Jan. 1921, no. 33.

69 C. F. Andrews to R. Tagore, 15 Oct. 1920, C. F. Andrews Papers; Home Poll Dep. Dec. 1920, no. 66; *ibid.* Feb. 1921, no. 35.

70 *Swadesamitram,* 10 and 28 Sept. 1920, in Madras Native Newspaper Reports 1920, pp. 1067, 1161; Home Poll Dep. Oct. 1920, no. 51, p. 3.

71 Statement by C. R. Das, enclosure in B. S. Moonje to V. J. Patel, 5 Dec. 1920, A-ICC Papers.

72 G. S. Khaparde, *Diary* (extracts held by the History of the Freedom Movement Office, Bombay), 3 Dec. 1920; Home Poll Dep. Feb. 1921, no. 35.

73 See N. R. Alekar to C. Vijiaraghavachariar, 11 Nov. 1920, Vijiaraghavachariar Papers; Vijiaraghavachariar, Presidential Address, Nagpur Congress, in *Congress Presidential Addresses* (Madras, 1935), vol. 2, pp. 502, 505-18.

74 [A-ICC] Civil Disobedience Enquiry Committee, *Report* (Madras, 1922), p. 36, estimates 1200 to 1500 did so.

75 Home Poll Dep. April 1921, no. 43, pp. 13, 15; *ibid.* June 1921, no. 12, p. 10; *ibid.* no. 65, pp. 7, 8, 9.

76 [AICC] Civil Disobedience Enquiry Committee, *Report,* p. 39.

77 N. C. Kelkar to Gandhi, 28 January 1921, no. S7446, Gandhi Papers Sabarmati; N. C. Kelkar, *A Passing Phase of Politics* (Poona, 1925), pp. 42-46; Home Poll Dep. April 1921, no. 41, pp. 9, 13; *ibid.* no. 42, pp. 4, 15, 21-22, 23; *ibid.* no. 43, pp. 6, 20; *ibid.* June 1921, no. 65, pp. 1, 2, 9, 11; *Hindu,* 15 Feb. 1921, p. 6.

78 Home Poll Dep. April 1921, no. 42, p. 4; *ibid.* June 1921, no. 45, p. 3; *ibid.* no. 65, pp. 1, 2.

79 *Ibid.* April 1921, no. 43, pp. 6, 9, 15-16, 18; *ibid.* June 1921, no. 12, pp. 10, 12, 13; *ibid.* no. 45, pp. 1, 2, 17; *ibid.* no. 65, pp. 8, 9; *Hindu,* 8 Feb. 1921, p. 5.

80 *Young India,* 9 March 1921, p. 772; see Home Poll Dep. April 1921, no. 42, p. 7; *ibid.* no. 43, pp. 4, 12, 18; *ibid.* June 1921, no. 12, p. 8; *ibid.* no. 45, p. 2; *ibid.* no. 51, p. 12

81 *Hindu,* 1 April 1921, p. 5.

82 *Ibid.;* for the ratios fixed for each linguistic province of Congress, see K. K. Datta, op. cit., vol. 1, pp. 368-69.

83 Home Poll Dep. June 1921, no. 51, pp. 3, 7-8, 10, 12, 13, 16, 18, 21-22, 25, 31, 38; *HFMB* 3, pp. 391-92.

84 See speech, in *Hindu*, 16 Sept. 1921, p. 3.
85 *Young India*, 27 April 1921, 25 May 1921, pp. 641-52, 800; Bombay Police 1921, pars. 359 (12), 382 (8) (10), 391 (2), 424 (8), 461 (18), 474 (10), in *HFMB* 3, pp. 371-74, 377-78, 381, 393-94, 400-03; Home Poll Dep. June 1921, no. 46, p. 23; *ibid*. no. 51, p. 4.
86 *Young India*, 25 May 1921, p. 801.
87 Report of Government of Bihar and Orissa, Home Poll Dep. June 1921, no. 64, p. 20.
88 Home Poll Dep. June 1921, no. 51, p. 13; see also *ibid*. no. 13, pp. 9, 10, 12-13, 28; *ibid*. no. 46, pp. 6, 16; *ibid*. no. 63, pp. 3, 7, 11, 16, 18, 19, 28; *ibid*. no. 64, p. 10.
89 *Ibid*. no. 51, pp. 18, 22; *ibid*. no. 13, pp. 7, 9, 34-35; *ibid*. no. 63, pp. 11, 13, 88; *ibid*. no. 46, pp. 14, 25; *ibid*. no. 64, pp. 3-5, 16.
90 *Ibid*. no. 13, pp. 8, 11, 27-28, 35, 51; *ibid*. no. 46, pp. 6, 13-14, 28; *ibid*. no. 63, pp. 18, 23, 26; *Young India*, 2 March, 25 May, 15 June 1921, pp. 852, 868, 870.
91 See, e.g., Bombay Police 1921, pars 511 (7) (8), 391 (11), 511 (12) (18) (52), 523 (14) (30) (38), 548 (5) (6) (14), 552, *HFMB* 3, pp. 403-19; Home Poll Dep. June 1921, no. 63, pp. 13, 21, 23; *ibid*. no. 64, p. 19; Home Poll 1921, file no. 18, Report for July 1921, pp. 2, 6, 9.
92 *Young India*, 6 July 1921, pp. 509-10, 555-56.
93 *Hindu*, 23 Sept. 1921, p. 5.
94 *Hindu*, 16 Sept. 1921, p. 3, 17 Sept. 1921, p. 3, 19 Sept. 1921, p. 5; Home Poll 1921, file 18, July, pp. 2, 6, 11, 12, 15, 18; *ibid*. [Aug.]-Sept., passim.
95 *Young India*, 28 July, 1 June, 15 June 1921, pp. 717-21, 802-04, 808-16; Home Poll 1921, file 18, Sept., p. 8.
96 Home Poll 1921, file 18, July, pp. 6, 12, 14; *ibid*. [Aug.]-Sept., pp. 18-19, 50-51; *ibid*. Oct., pp. 12, 16, 19, 22, 43, 58, 59.
97 'A Manifesto', *Young India*, 6 Oct. 1921, pp. 934-35.
98 Home Poll 1921, file 18, Nov., pp. 12, 14, 19-21, 41, 46-47, 50, 53; *ibid*. Jan. 1922, pp. 2-3, 5-6, 12, 48.
99 *Ibid*., Nov., pp. 12-14, 41, 50, 53, 55-56, 58, 60, 75.
100 *Ibid*., p. 13.
101 *Young India*, 10 Nov. 1921, pp. 936-42.
102 Bombay Police 1921, pars 1263 (27), 1330 (13); *ibid*. 1922, pars 10 (1), 27, in *HFMB* 3, pp. 452, 454-57; Home Poll 1921, file 18, Dec., passim; ibid. 1922, Jan., pp. 9, 18-19, 48, 53.
103 See *Report of the 36th Indian National Congress, Ahmedabad, 1921* (Ahmedabad, 1922), pp. 31-36; Bombay Police 1921, par. 1324 (12); *ibid*. 1922, par. 10 (10), in *HFMB* 3, pp. 454, 456.
104 For beginnings in this direction, see Broomfield's article mentioned above; R. Kumar (ed.), *India in 1919* (forthcoming); and for the more recent period, M. Weiner, *Party Building in a New Nation: the Indian National Congress* (Chicago, 1967).

The primary source materials, on which this paper on Non-Co-operation, 1920-22 is based, were collected with the research assistance of my wife, Thérèse, on two visits to India: the first in 1962-63, with financial assistance from the Australian National University; and the second in 1967-68, with assistance from the Social Sciences Research Council of Australia and the University of W.A. Much help has also been given by the National Library of Australia, Canberra, and by my own University Library.

187

GANDHI AND THE HINDU-MUSLIM QUESTION

A. B. Shah

Next to freedom, Hindu-Muslim unity and the liquidation of untouchability were the two most important goals of Gandhi's public life in India. He succeeded in considerable measure in undermining, if not liquidating, untouchability. A great deal no doubt remains to be done, but it is clear that public opinion in India has for some decades past been unreservedly committed to the abolition of untouchability. This commitment has also been reflected in the Indian Constitution, which was drafted by B. R. Ambedkar, himself a leader of Indian untouchables and a scholar of comparative religion and constitutional law. Art. 17 of this Constitution declares that the practice of untouchability is an 'offence punishable in accordance with law'. Arts. 330, 332 and 335 provide reservations for the Scheduled Castes (by which name castes which were formerly untouchable are now known) in the legislatures and services in proportion to their population. And, finally, Art. 338 provides for the appointment of a Special Officer for promoting the welfare and rapid social and cultural advancement of the Scheduled Castes. Also, apart from these constitutional provisions, students belonging to these castes receive free-studentships and scholarships up to the highest stage of education regardless of the economic status of their parents, and State or Union cabinets generally include at least one representative of the Scheduled Castes.

Despite these measures untouchability persists, mainly in rural areas; nor is it surprising that it should. Evils which are centuries old and which have their roots in the social structure and religious tradition of a people cannot be exorcised by legislation and administrative measures alone. What is significant is the fact that except for a small lunatic fringe associated with the Shankaracharya of Puri,[1] no section of the Indian intelligentsia nor any political party—not even the Jana Sangh or Hindu Mahasabha—is in favour of untouchability. Fifty years ago that was not so, and the credit for bringing about this transformation in the Hindu mind would go to Gandhi more than anyone else. It is true that Gandhi's task was facilitated by the work of a succession of social reformers, but their influence was generally confined to the educated middle class.[2]

Gandhi alone could devise and apply a method of taking their message of the basic equality of men to all the strata of Hindu society. The problem now is not one of carrying conviction but of implementation, which is a function of economic growth and the accompanying modernisation of Indian society.

By contrast, Hindu-Muslim unity evaded Gandhi throughout his active life except for a brief spell during the Khilafat agitation.[3] Not only that; in spite of his ceaseless effort to prevent it, the country had to accept partition as the price of freedom. And soon after Independence Gandhi had to die at the hands of a Hindu fanatic, though he alone among the top leaders of the Indian National Congress was unreconciled to partition.

Gandhi's failure to bring about Hindu-Muslim unity raises some interesting questions. Why did Gandhi fail in spite of his patent sincerity and willingness to go more than half way to allay the fears and suspicions of the Muslims? How was it that Gandhi, who asked the British to hand over power—if they did not trust the Congress to give a fair deal to the non-Hindus—to Jinnah but quit, came to be increasingly isolated not only from the Muslims but also from his own followers in his quest for unity? And why, after twenty-one years of partition which was expected to solve the problem of Hindu-Muslim relations in the sub-continent, does it still exist, in the sense that India is even now groping for a theoretically valid solution of it? What, indeed, is the nature of the problem? Is it just a question of ensuring for India's Muslim citizens, as for other weak groups like the Scheduled Castes, security from persecution, social equality and adequate facilities for rapid advancement; or is it something more basic of which tension in the political field is merely an expression? In the two decades that have elapsed since Gandhi's death these questions have not been seriously examined by the leaders of India's political or intellectual life, and the universities have perhaps been the worst defaulters in this respect. It is only now, during the last two years, that the entire history of the Hindu-Muslim question in India is being subjected to a radical scrutiny by a small group of Hindus and Muslims, mostly of the younger generation, based at Bombay and, significantly, at Aligarh. The members of this group look upon the Hindu-Muslim problem from the standpoint of the sociology of religion and regard it as an aspect of the larger problem of the modernisation of a traditional society. What follows is an examination of some of the questions formulated above from this point of view.

II

A satisfactory discussion of these questions would require an examination of Gandhi's philosophy of life, his theory of social change and, most important of all, the nature of the Hindu and Islamic traditions, the types of mind that they mould and their interaction in India over a period of nearly a thousand years. We shall consider only a few of them here and that too in a highly selective manner.

Gandhi was essentially a philosophical anarchist in his view of man and did not subscribe to the idea of original sin. On the contrary, he believed that man was 'essentially' good, with a spark of the divine in him, and no one was beyond redemption even though the struggle for self-realization was bound to be arduous and long. He therefore approached the problem as a well-meaning, persuasive, non-sectarian nationalist. He worked on the assumption, based on his experience in South Africa, that if Hindus and Muslims could be brought together in joint constructive endeavour they would see that unity was in their common interest and would learn to live together in peace and harmony.[4] (This was, in a sense, begging the question, for coming together in a joint undertaking would presuppose the realization that unity was in mutual interest. However, the difficulty is only verbal; it does not exist on the plane of action, where besides logical reasoning, sudden changes of mood contribute to the decision to act. The Khilafat agitation is an example.) To this end he sought to project the universal human values preached by all major religions, including Hinduism and Islam, and hoped that in the course of time the forces of unity would triumph over those of separatism. For, according to Gandhi's way of thinking, 'true' religion could only join, not keep separate, men of different faiths. If Hindus and Muslims regarded themselves as essentially separate people the fault, Gandhi thought, lay not in the beliefs and practices enjoined by their scriptures or in the history of the two communities in India, but in a defective understanding of their 'real' message.[5]

This is a noble view of man and religion. But it overlooks the fact that man, as a product of evolution, is a union of good and evil just as it overlooks the historically determined character of his culture and institutions. Consequently, Gandhi missed the deeper, social and cultural, roots of the Hindu-Muslim conflict in India. Instead, following Tilak,[6] he attributed its origin to the wily British, who certainly were interested in preventing the Muslims 'from joining the seditious opposition'.[7] Gandhi did not see that Muslim separatism was 'a direct logical development of the policies Sayyid Ahmad Khan had stood for and preached, and which had won the adherence of Muslim opinion during his lifetime'.[8] The British encouraged and exploited the separatist sentiment, but they certainly did not create it.

Lacking a historical perspective on the question, Gandhi was satisfied that 'given a sufficient number of Hindus and Musalmans with almost a fanatical faith in everlasting friendship between the Hindus and Musalmans of India',[9] sooner or later the masses would realise the suicidal implications of religious conflict and work together for freedom from foreign rule. I would call this approach the Rama-Rahim approach, since it tacitly assumed that Hindus and Muslims could live together in peace without a fundamental modification of their attitude to religion. Such an approach was bound to fail. It did not take into account the hold that religion with its dogma, tradition, custom, ritual and historical memories has on the minds of men in a pre-modern society. Gandhi also assumed that the Muslims in India subscribed to the idea of territorial nationalism and would be willing to subordinate to it their sense of separate identity based on religion. True, he knew some Muslims who lent plausibility to this assumption, but they were unrepresentative of the Muslim community. On the contrary, right since the days of the Wahabi movement, Indian Muslims were used to thinking in terms of pan-Islamism and felt nearer to fellow-Muslims outside India than to their non-Muslim countrymen. There were exceptions like Sir Syed Ahmad Khan, who were separatist in relation to Hindus but who placed loyalty to the British above their pan-Islamic sentiment. But while 'the separatist line taken by Sayyid Ahmad Khan in relation to Hindu-Muslim politics was accepted by the Muslim consensus in India . . . his loyalism was rejected when it came into conflict with pan-Islamic sympathies'.[10] This trend continued in the twentieth century and was forcefully expressed by Mohammad Iqbal, the most important leader of Muslim thought in India since Syed Ahmad Khan. Iqbal was opposed to nationalism because he saw in it 'the germs of atheistic materialism' and because 'Islam, as a religion, has no country'.[11] The term 'pan-Islamic sentiment' provided the motive force behind the Khilafat movement. Gandhi made it a national issue in the hope that thereby he would win over the Muslims to the nationalist cause.

Gandhi's support for the Khilafat agitation did bring the Muslims closer to the nationalist movement for the time being. But it was a unity born of expediency. The Congress and the Muslims, though they were united against the British, were fighting for different things. The temporary unity forged between them soon began to show cracks even as the Khilafat agitation was on. The Moplah riots of 1921 showed that an appeal in the name of Islam, even if directed against the British, could easily release anti-Hindu passions and reduce to nought the efforts of well-meaning leaders to bring about Hindu-Muslim unity.[12] Gandhi and the Khilafat leaders tried hard to ensure that the riots did not do lasting damage to hard-created communal harmony. But the abolition of the Khilafat by the Turkish National Assembly in 1924 cut the ground from under their feet, and Hindu-Muslim relations were once again back where they stood five years earlier. Indeed, in a sense the new situation was less favourable to the growth of unity. As a reaction to the Moplah riots and the refusal of Khilafat leaders to condemn the atrocities against the Hindus, there came into existence a movement for the consolidation of the Hindu society under the leadership of Madan Mohan Malaviya and Swami Shraddhanand Saraswati.[13] The Rashtriya Swayamsevak Sangh (R.S.S.), a para-military volunteer organisation whose members are systematically indoctrinated into fanatical devotion to Hindu culture and the idea of a Hindu nation, was started by Dr K. B. Hedgevar in 1927 and was the logical culmination of this reaction.[14]

Nor was this the only legacy of the Khilafat agitation. It also gave a new turn to Muslim politics in India. Till the end of World War I, only the upper classes of Indian Muslims—the feudal aristocracy and the small group of professional men—were interested in politics. With the exception of a few liberals like Jinnah, they were hostile to the Congress and favoured the continuation of British rule in India. They justified their separatist stand more in terms of history and culture than of a threat to Islam.[15] The Khilafat movement politicized the Muslim masses under the leadership of the *ulema* and reduced the League to impotence in Indian politics. Liberal Muslims like Jinnah had no place in this new type of mass politics and were alienated from the nationalist agitation. On the other hand, the *ulema* who supported the Congress were not interested in the growth of secular nationalism in India. Consequently, once the Khilafat issue was dead, many of them like Mohammed Ali parted company with the Congress. Maulana Abul Kalam Azad was the only prominent leader of the Khilafat movement who came to accept the idea of a composite nationalism and developed a theoretical justification for it through his own interpretation of the *Quran*.[16] For the rest, the anti-British struggle was only a stage in the ultimate Islamization of India. They were opposed to the demand for Pakistan, for the creation of Pakistan would restrict the scope for missionary activities by generating 'passions of hatred and antagonism'. Maulana Husain Ahmad Madani, leader of the Jamiyat-ul-Ulama-i-Hind—an organisation of 'nationalist' Muslims sponsored by the Deoband *ulema*—made this point clear in the following words in the course of a speech he delivered at Delhi on 19 September 1945.

It is the non-Muslims who are the field of action for the '*tabligh*' of Islam and form the raw material for this splendid activity. Today,

192

by propagating hatred towards the Hindus, this field is being closed and this material wasted. . . .

Our object is to bridge the gulf of hatred which is being created by the protagonists of the scheme of Pakistan; we are opposed to the idea of limiting the right of missionary activities of Islam within any particular area. The Muslims have got a right in all the nooks and corners of India by virtue of the great struggle and grand sacrifices of their ancestors in this country. Now it is our duty to maintain that claim and try to widen its scope, instead of giving it up.[17]

Thus, except opposition to British rule, the 'nationalist' Muslims had nothing in common with the essentially secular leadership of the national movement. It is true that the latter also, especially Gandhi, talked the language of religion—more precisely, what W. H. Morris-Jones has called the saintly idiom. But Gandhi's conception of religion, as expressed in his speeches and programmes of social reform among the Hindus, was non-doctrinaire and non-conformist. That of the 'nationalist' Muslims, on the other hand, was crudely sectarian and therefore incompatible with the emergence of an integrated Indian society. In relations to the Hindus, they were as separatist as the Muslim League. The difference between the two was not regarding the *fact* of the distinct identity of the Muslims but regarding the *nature* of that identity. For the League, as remarked earlier, this identity was mainly defined by culture and history, and only secondarily by religious belief. It exploited religion in the pursuit of a secular goal, first for winning a privileged position and then for carving out a separate state for the Muslims of India. For the 'nationalist' Muslims, secular goals had only an instrumental value in the spread of Islam throughout the subcontinent. Certain statements in Jinnah's speech to the first meeting (11 August 1947) of the Pakistani Constituent Assembly[18] provide a striking contrast to Madani's argument quoted above. That Pakistan developed in altogether a different direction from what Jinnah had envisaged is a different question. As we shall see below in the Indian context, the failure of Jinnah's vision of Pakistan merely shows that political solutions are not enough in dealing with problems which are essentially social and cultural.

The issue raised by the separatism of the Muslim League was resolved by recourse to partition, though the solution did not work as satisfactorily as its authors had thought at the time. As it turned out, partition merely internationalised certain aspects of the Hindu-Muslim problem without touching its real cause. Also, the problem inherent in the position of the

Deoband *ulema* has in recent years been assuming a serious form. The impossibility of attaining their religious goal in the foreseable future seems at last to have been realised by them. Like Maududi in Pakistan,[19] they now appear willing to adopt a policy of gradualism and concentrate on lesser goals. At the same time, many Muslims who formerly subscribed to an anti-separatist position have of late started demanding separate, Muslim-majority districts and even States within the Indian Union for safe-guarding Muslim interests. They have joined hands with separatist organisations like the Muslim League and the Tameer-e-Millat as well as with the obscurantist Jamaat-e-Islami Hind, and all are actively co-operating with the communists, particularly in Bengal and Kerala. Indeed, one witnesses in recent developments in Muslim politics in India all the features of the pre-partition period, with the difference that practically all the Muslim groups are this time united on a single platform, that of the Muslim Majlis-e-Mushawarat.

III

The Gandhian approach was saintly in the main and precisely on that account it was bound to fail. But it was also akin to the Marxist, in the sense that it assigned a derivative role to the cultural factor. Gandhi believed that the urge for freedom would enable the Muslims to take an enlightened view of their religion. This, however, presupposes that a certain measure of individuation has already taken place in the culture system known as Islam, and Gandhi assumed that it had. This was perhaps a natural assumption, for the Hindu mind is basically individualistic, indeed narcissistic,[20] so that it is easy for it to transcend intermediate loyalties and take to the path of individual salvation. It is therefore difficult for a Hindu to visualise, except by a special effort of reason and the imagination, a mind that is almost totally lacking in the conception of the individual and derives the significance of human life solely from his membership of the collectivity. This, however, seems a characteristic feature of almost all cultures based on revealed religion. If Christian culture appears to be different in this respect, that is because from its inception Christianity was influenced by the Greek tradition. It was the revival of this tradition that led to the Renaissance and the rise of Protestantism with its stress on personal interpretation of the Holy Writ. The humanisation of Christianity, with the consequent growth of a secular conception of individuality, was thus a direct outcome of its interaction with the Greek tradition. It is worth noting in this connection that unlike the People of the Book, the Greeks were not blessed with a prophet nor, unlike the Hindus, with incarnations of God. They had

194

therefore to rely on reason and observation alone for discovering the nature of things. Also, they were polytheist and their gods were hardly distinguishable from human beings: they had superhuman powers but entirely non-transcendental interests. Consequently, the Greeks could develop a tradition of critical inquiry and a climate of tolerance necessary to let 'a hundred flowers bloom and a hundred schools contend'.

The Greeks had also another advantage. They had no counterpart of the *Vedas*, which the Hindus regarded as eternal and uncreated by man. They were therefore free from the burden of unchanging Truth and able to create science as an expression of man's spiritual quest, and the rudiments of scientific method as providing a tool of inquiry as well as a criterion for the validity of its findings. The Greek tradition might have had a similar effect on Islam to what it had on Christianity. But by the time Islam came in contact with it—in the reign of al-Māmun (813-833)— the latter had already lost its élan and Islam too had outgrown its formative stage. More important still, Islam arose in a society that was riven with inter-tribal feuds. It had no state worth the name and did not hesitate to subject dissent to tribal persecution. The founder of Islam had therefore to found a state before its message was fully delivered, still less developed in contact with a more advanced culture without the arbitrament of force. The rapid and spectacular expansion of Islam during the hundred years following the Prophet's death over the stagnant and decadent societies of the surrounding region also had an inhibitory effect on its future development. Continued victory over others strengthened the Muslim's conviction that his faith was not only perfect but superior to others and its doctrine, infallible.[21] Dissent, when it arose, was as ruthlessly put down in Islam as in medieval Christianity, so that even the finest Muslim scholars were careful to avoid saying anything that might appear as questioning the fundamental tenets of the faith. Thus the Mutazillites, who made use of Greek ideas in the exposition and defence of Islamic theological doctrine, 'were regarded as heretical by the main body of Sunnite Muslims' and were treated as such.[22] Even Ibn Sina, one of the few really great Muslim philosophers, was criticised by authorities of the Muslim tradition for 'limiting the power of God to a predetermined logical structure' and for 'diminishing the sense of awe of the finite before the infinite'.[23] Nor is that all; Ibn Sina himself in his later years seems to have turned—or posed as—a devout gnostic. Indeed, as H. A. R. Gibb observes, 'it comes as something of a shock to be confronted with the thickening web of "irrational" elements in the writings of such a personality as Avicenna'.[24]

This is not to suggest that Islam is unique in its record of intolerance in the past. It is, rather, that Islam still exhibits the same intolerance of free inquiry and dissent as it did in less enlightened times.[25] What little possibility there might have been of the softening of this attitude through the development of science and philosophy after mutual persecution by the Mutazillites and their orthodox opponents was effectively frustrated by al-Ghazāli for centuries to come.[26] His work ensured that no renaissance would ever take place in Muslim society unless, as in Turkey, it were imposed from above. Muslim scholars look upon al-Ghazāli as the greatest thinker Islam has produced. It would be truer to say that, like Shankara to Hinduism, he was the greatest disaster that befell Islam after the death of the Prophet.

So great has been the hold of orthodoxy on the Muslim mind that nowhere has Muslim society so far been able to throw up, in the natural course, an articulate class of liberal Muslims committed to modern values and all that such a commitment implies in the fields of criticism and social action. Such a class alone can subject the tradition of Islam to a critical scrutiny and prepare the ground for the entry of Muslim society into the modern age. For, as the experience of developing countries in the post-war period shows, efforts to modernize the political and economic systems in the absence of social and cultural modernization accompanying, if not preceding, them can only result in frustration or perversion. The persistence of Hindu-Muslim tension in India, the anti-Kadiani riots in Pakistan in 1953, the growing influence of Maududi's Jamaat-e-Islami in that country as well as in India, and the repeated attempts to assassinate President Nasser by the Muslim Brotherhood in Egypt in the name of Islam—all go to suggest that the conflict between tradition and modernity in Muslim society cannot be resolved until the very ethos of Islamic culture has undergone a qualitative change.

That Gandhi did not see the Hindu-Muslim problem in this light is not surprising in view of his outlook and background. But as the years passed he did realize that it would be unwise to make a solution of this problem a pre-condition for the withdrawal of the British from India.[27] He came to believe that once the Hindus and Muslims were faced with the prospect of managing the affairs of the country in the absence of a third party, they would hammer out an agreement satisfactory to both. Meanwhile, he continued working in his own way for Hindu-Muslim unity and reassuring the Muslims that his conception of *swarāj* did not visualise any religious group dominating over others. However, the scales were already heavily loaded against him, and whatever chance of success he might have had was effectively nullified by the British policy of 'divide and rule'.

196

IV

Many students of Indian affairs have blamed Gandhi for the religious overtones of his approach and considered it the main cause of the Muslims' alienation from the Congress. In the light of the early history of the problem this seems to be a gross exaggeration. For as early as 1867, Sir Syed Ahmad Khan held the view that Hindus and Muslims could not form a single nation.[28] Except for a brief period around 1880, he always maintained that the two communities were separate nations. For instance, in a letter written in 1888 to Badruddin Tyabji, third President of the Congress, he observed: 'I do not understand what the words "National Congress" mean. Is it supposed that the different castes and creeds living in India belong to one nation, or can become a nation, and their aims and aspirations be one and the same? I think it is quite impossible. . . . I object to every Congress in any shape or form whatever which regards India as one nation'.[29] Earlier, writing in 1860 soon after the Mutiny in which Hindu and Muslim sepoys fought together, he had advised the British to reorganise the Indian army on religious lines with a view to segregating Hindu soldiers from the Muslim.[30] Sir Syed maintained this attitude till his death in 1898, and the tradition of Muslim separatism that he developed was carried on by Aligarh in the succeeding decades. Syed Ameer Ali, another modernist Muslim leader from Bengal, also held similar views.[31] And Mohammad Iqbal, father of the Pakistan idea, also believed that Hindus and Muslims could not constitute a single nation. He believed, ideally, in a single state of the Muslim people, but since the idea was not likely to be acceptable to Muslims who already had their own national identities, he proposed a League of Islamic nations. The Pakistan idea, acccording to which Muslims of north-west India would have a separate state of their own, was part of this larger conception.[32]

Jinnah was the only non-orthodox Muslim leader of note who was actively associated with the Congress for a considerable period of time. But his role was not so much that of combating the separatist influence of the Muslim League, with which also he was associated, as of bringing about a compromise between the Congress and the League. Thus the so-called Lucknow Pact of 1916, to which Tilak was a party and according to which the Congress conceded to the Muslims separate electorates, weightage and the power of vetoing legislation affecting their community, was drafted by Jinnah and, indeed, for some time was also known as the Jinnah-Tilak pact. He left the Congress at the time of the Khilafat agitation in 1920 and never went back to it in later years. Even then he continued trying to bring about an understanding between the

197

two organisations and participated in the deliberations of the All Parties' Conference called by the Congress in 1928 to draw up a constitution for India that would be acceptable to all parties. The Conference appointed a Committee with Molital Nehru as chairman and the Committee submitted its report, popularly known as the Nehru Report, in August 1928. By this time the Congress leadership had come under Gandhi's influence and its ideas of secular, territorial nationalism had been crystallized to a considerable extent. Thus the Nehru Report talked of the fundamental rights of the citizen but rejected the Muslim demand for separate electorates.

When the All Parties' Conference met at Calcutta in December 1928 to consider the Report, Jinnah moved certain amendments to its recommendations. On the amendments being turned down by the Conference, the Muslim League withdrew from it. A few days later a Muslim All Parties' Conference was held at Delhi, which was attended even by some 'nationalist' Muslims and which declared that no constitution that did not incorporate their demands would be acceptable to the Muslims. Soon thereafter, Jinnah formulated his 'fourteen points'. According to these demands, besides a weak Centre and separate electorates:

4. In the Central Legislature Muslim representation should not be less than one-third [the Muslim population in India being about 25 per cent of the total].

8. No Bill or Resolution or any part thereof shall be passed in any legislature or any other elected body if three-fourths of the members of any community in that particular body oppose it as being injurious to the interests of that community.

13. No cabinet, either central or provincial, should be formed without there being at least one-third of Muslim Ministers.

14. No change shall be made in the Constitution by the central legislature except with the concurrence of the States constituting the Indian Federation.[33]

From this time on, Jinnah appeared as an uncompromising separatist and dubbed the Congress as a Hindu organisation, thus deliberately refusing to distinguish between the secular nationalism of the Congress and the incipient Hindu nationalism of the Hindu Mahasabha and the R.S.S. Later, in the 'thirties, he began steadily playing up the danger that the Congress conception of nationalism was supposed to pose to Islam as well as Muslim interests. The Pirpur Committee's Report, detailing the alleged acts of discrimination and atrocities against the Muslims in provinces under Congress rule just before the war, was part of this propaganda offensive. The Report was based on distortion and fabrication. The Congress cited the opinions of the British Governors, under whom its ministries worked, to rebut the charges and offered to accept the verdict of an independent inquiry.[34] However, Jinnah was no longer interested in arriving at an understanding with the Congress. His sole aim was to politicize once again the Muslim masses as Gandhi had done in the days of the Khilafat agitation and to rally them under his banner for a final show-down with the Congress. If for this, he had to distort truth and exploit religion, or even to manipulate Hindu-Muslim riots, he was prepared for it.

Still Jinnah did not demand a separate state for the Muslims though already from 1930 onwards such a demand was being put forward by a section of Muslim opinion. He realized that there was no visible prospect of the withdrawal of British power from India. In such a situation, by asking for a separate state he would merely appear as a political romantic. However, with the first signs of power being transferred to Indian hands in the near future, he came out with the famous Pakistan resolution which the Muslim League adopted at its Lahore session in March 1940.

Apologists for the Muslim League have maintained that Jinnah became a separatist only after continued frustration in his attempts to persuade the Congress to allay the Muslims' sense of insecurity in a predominantly Hindu society. What has been stated above would show that not fear of Hindu oppression but the strongly separatist Muslim attitude was primarily responsible for the tragic denouement of Hindu-Muslim relations in India. The demand for Pakistan was only the final expression of this separatist attitude under British rule; but its roots go back to the earliest period of Islam as a socio-cultural system not only in India but also in Medina where the Prophet founded the first Muslim state. For, in this context, 'separatism' means an insistence on the recognition of one's community as a national or quasi-national group which, *qua* such a group, is entitled to special consideration and privileges. It thus indicates a certain attitude to other groups and is reflected in obstinate resistance to any process of interaction that may ultimately lead to the emergence of a common national identity cutting across the old lines of division. Separatism in this sense has always been a characteristic of Muslim society wherever Muslims are in a substantial minority, and Indian Muslims are no exception in this respect. Historically, it has expressed itself in different demands in different periods, their nature and content varying with the changing balance of forces at a given moment. In India, Muslim separatism has been particularly strong because of the memories of Muslim rule for nearly eight hundred years before the Sepoy Mutiny in 1857. How deep-rooted this attitude is among Indian Muslims, regardless of the degree to which they are orthodox, is illustrated by the fact that both the Muslim League and the 'nationalist' Muslims were united in their demand for reservations, weightage and special treatment in matters of language, personal law and employment under government. Even after partition most of these demands continue to be pressed by practically all Muslim organisations in India. And, like Jinnah, they too do not make a distinction between secularists who demand the modernization of Muslim society along liberal lines and the Hindu chauvinists who claim that India belongs to the Hindus and should become a Hindu state in which non-Hindus, including Muslims, would be permitted to live as 'guests'.[35] In the eyes of the Muslim leadership, 'both [the secularists and the Hindu chauvinists] are equally dangerous to Muslims, untouchables and other minorities'.[36] However, Muslims need not feel pessimistic about their future. 'A single Muslim is nobler and higher than a thousand Hindus. The only need for him is to become awake and regard himself as a Muslim. He goes with Allah's blessings. It is a holy deed when his dagger rushes into the heart of aliens; and he is the victor.'[37]

It is true that liberal Muslims would disown such sentiments. However, their number is small and they lack the moral courage and organization to combat this attitude even by so much as publicly dissociating themselves from it. On the other hand, many educated Muslims have, in discussion or correspondence with the present writer, sought to offer an apologia for it in terms of the real or imaginary persecution to which Muslims are being subjected by the Hindus.

V

The preceding discussion should not be taken to imply that Gandhi and the Congress were blameless in every respect. However, their mistakes were of a different type and stemmed from the Hindu tradition of which they were a product. This tradition put a premium on woolly thinking, the idea of consensus and an essentially narcissistic approach to reality. These features of the Hindu attitude were responsible for much confusion and blurring of issues, and they still plague India not only in the political field but also in others, including those of education, development and social reform. They were, inevitably, reflected in the Congress approach to the Hindu-Muslim problem and were bound to render it self-defeating. Only, neither Gandhi nor any other leader of the national movement was able to foresee and prevent its consequences in time. Even today, most leaders do not understand where the Congress went wrong and how.

The social structure and cultural tradition of the Hindu were such as to render him incapable of integrating non-Hindus into a single nation. The caste structure of Hindu society and the negative attitude of its dominant tradition to problems of secular life leave him with only two basic loyalties: loyalty to the caste or kinship group and, when he begins to think of the other world, loyalty to his own self. Consequently, he fails to develop a hierarchically ordered system of loyalties and the civic virtues indispensable for nation-building in the modern sense. Since he accepted caste as a legitimate unit of the social organisation, he did not see anything seriously wrong in conceding the *prima facie* validity of the Muslims' demand for the recognition of their collective political identity. We thus find Hindu leaders of the Congress agreeing to disproportionately large Muslim representation in the legislatures and the services by separate electorates and reservation of seats. By granting to each community separate legislative powers as the Lucknow Pact did, they nourished Muslim separatism and, by implication, recognised the Muslim claim that they were a separate society, if not a separate nation. Such concessions did not matter much in the case of the Sikhs and the Christians since the idea of territorial nationalism did not conflict with their religious beliefs. Nor did they suffer from that pathetic combination of a feeling of insecurity and a sense of superiority which generally characterises a community—the Maharashtrians, for instance, among the Hindus —that has once enjoyed power and has now fallen low. And as if these factors were not enough the Hindu's fear of pollution, associated with the caste system which is being secularised only during the last three decades, was an additional barrier that caused understandable resentment among the Muslims. It persuaded even the best of them that their separatism was, after all, a justified reaction to Hindu obscurantism. Even a few Hindu progressives, notably the Royists and the communists, who had a bad conscience over the evils of caste and looked upon Tilak and Gandhi as the embodiments of Hindu reaction, took the same view of Muslim separatism. In reality, they could not perceive the essentially secular approach of Gandhi beneath his saintly idiom, knew little of Tilak and still less about Islam as a culture and theory of society.

That Tilak should have been regarded as 'revivalist and anti-Muslim' by apologists of the Muslim League is not surprising.[38] But it is a sad commentary on the world of academic scholarship[39] that it still goes by the stereotype of Tilak that journalists like Valentine Chirol, who were working in collusion with the British Government of the day, deliberately frabricated for reasons of state.[40] As a matter of fact, in the entire body of Tilak's writings there is not one sentence that may be considered hostile to the Muslims. Nor, as is popularly believed, was he a leader of the cow-protection movement. On the contrary, he was of the view that just as Muslims should not be permitted to slaughter a cow in a Hindu locality, Hindus too should not be permitted to prevent a Muslim from killing it in a slaughterhouse. If either party violated this norm, which was sanctified by custom, the government should, according to Tilak, punish it in the interests of peace and good-neighbourliness.[41] And as to the Muslim demand for separate electorates and weightage, Tilak was more 'pro-Muslim' than Gandhi, who was opposed to separate electorates though he was prepared to give them weightage in order to allay their fears and suspicion.

If Tilak and Gandhi were not responsible for the rise and growth of Muslim separatism, neither can it be traced to the neo-Hindu revival symbolized by Swami Vivekananda and Aurobindo Ghosh. Both had a highly sophisticated conception of religion and held no brief for the shortcomings of what passed as Hinduism in their days. On the contrary, Vivekananda was full of admiration for Islam and was 'firmly persuaded that without the help of practical Islam, theories of Vedantism, however fine and wonderful they may be, are entirely valueless to the vast masses of mankind'.[42] Aurobindo, before he retired to Pondicherry, belonged for a few years to the terrorist movement which hardly had anything to do with Hindus or Muslims *per se*, as its only aim was to bring about a violent overthrow of British rule. What he did after turning *yogi* was merely to develop a universal philosophy of the coming 'Supermind' and offer refuge to those who wished to lead a life of quiet spirituality away from the hurly-burly of the work-a-day world.

Indeed, the only Hindu leader who can be charged with having promoted anti-Muslim feelings was Swami Dayanand Saraswati and the Arya Samaj that he founded for the revival of the 'pure' Vedic religion.[43] However, Dayanand symbolised the beginning of a Hindu reaction to aggressive Muslim proselytization rather than a cause of it. It is interesting to note that the Arya Samaj made headway only in regions like the Punjab, where the proselytizing activities of the Muslims were strong, or the old Hyderabad State where Muslims were the ruling community and treated the Hindus as second-class citizens. Elsewhere, for instance, in Bengal and Maharashtra, the Arya Samaj, like the Jana Sangha till 1967, has practically no following.

The neo-Hindu revival was thus directed more to the reform of Hindu society than to building up an anti-Muslim movement. All the three important leaders of this revival—Dayanand, Vivekananda and Aurobindo —were opposed to untouchability and were primarily concerned over the degeneration of Hindu society or with the further refinement of Hindu speculative thought. Of the three, Dayanand was the only one interested in the Hindu-Muslim question from what might be considered the political standpoint and, as mentioned above, his was primarily a reaction to the expansionism of Islam.

It is true that the terrorist movement adopted *Vande Mātaram* and the worship of *Kāli*, a Hindu goddess, as a religio-political ritual. The terrorists also drew inspiration from the history of Hindu resistance to the Muslim conquerors of an earlier age. But all this had only allegorical significance in their effort to build up a resistance movement against the British and, at least to the terrorists, carried no anti-Muslim implications for their own age. In any case, with the growth of Tilak's influence and later the appearance of Gandhi on the scene, the terrorist appeal rapidly declined without leaving any lasting effect on the mind of the average Hindu.

VI

We are thus left with only one explanation of Muslim separatism in India and Gandhi's failure to bring about Hindu-Muslim unity. Muslim separatism, like Hindu insularism, is *sui generis* and in its contemporary form dates back to the 'sixties of the last century. While each fed the other, neither originated as a reaction to the other. As early as 1880 the effective leadership of the Muslim community in India rested with separatist elements. There was no Hindu Mahasabha nor an allegedly Hindu-oriented Congress in 1888 or 1906. The deputation of Muslim leaders that waited on Lord Minto, then Viceroy of India, at Simla in October 1906 was got together by the British Principal of Sir Syed Ahmad's Aligarh Muslim-Oriental College after prior consultation with Lord Minto's advisers.[44] Earlier, even Lord Curzon's decision to partition Bengal had finally come to be taken on considerations of 'divide and rule' rather than of administrative convenience.[45] Nationalist opposition to the decision was exploited by the British to drive a further wedge between the two communities. But it would be wrong to attribute this opposition to Hindu revivalism even if Hindu leaders of the Congress used terms like 'vivisection' to describe the partition. As a matter of fact, the Nawab of Dacca was himself opposed to it in the earlier stages of the opposition and presided over public meetings, attended by Muslims as well as Hindus, to condemn Lord Curzon's decision. And Tilak's own articles on

the question show that he was moved only by nationalist considerations.[46]
By the time Gandhi assumed the leadership of the nationalist movement,
Muslim separatism was already a recognised force in Indian politics. Only,
the Muslim argument in justification of the demand for special treatment
had shifted its emphasis from considerations of 'political importance' to
those of fear and insecurity in a predominantly Hindu society. By constant repetition, this latter argument had so sunk into the Hindu mind that
even the Marxists, who prided themselves on their historical approach,
failed to see its separatist inspiration till Jinnah came out with the demand
for Pakistan. By that time it was too late to turn the tide back unless the
Congress were willing to face the prospect of a civil war. Gandhi was
prepared for it. According to Nirmal Kumar Bose, he remonstrated with
Nehru and other members of the Congress Working Committee against
their acceptance of the Mountbatten plan. Replying to the argument that
if instead of accepting partition the Congress were to launch a fresh civil
disobedience movement in order to win freedom for undivided India, the
Muslim League might 'start Hindu-Muslim riots all over India', Gandhi
is reported to have sharply asked: *Is se dar gaye? Kitne log mare gaye
hain—ek lākh, do lākh? Hindustān ki āzādi ke liye do, chār, das lākh nahi
marenge aur āzādi ā jāyegi?* (Are you frightened by this [prospect]?
How many persons have lost their lives [so far]—one lakh, two lakh? Do
you imagine that India will become free without two lakh, four lakh,
[even] a million people dying for it?)[47]

Gandhi's advice was not heeded by the 'tired men'[48] who constituted
the leadership of the Congress party. In their rejection of Gandhi and
acceptance of partition lies the greatest and most poignant failure of his
public life. Soon after, he was assassinated, preaching Hindu-Muslim
unity at a prayer meeting and planning a goodwill tour of the Punjab,
where one of the worst massacres of modern times had taken place.

If Muslim separatism is *sui generis* and not a reaction to Hindu revivalism, it still remains to trace it to its roots. I would suggest that it is
inherent in the religion and culture of Islam. This is not the place to
enter upon an analysis of Islam as a culture beyond what has already been
said in Section III of this article. What is important for our purpose is
to note that unlike Christian society some five hundred years ago and, to
a significant extent, Hindu society in the nineteenth century, Muslim
society in most parts of the world has had no renaissance of its own. Consequently, even the modernists among Muslim intellectuals have so far
shown themselves unwilling to subject their religion to the type of critical
appraisal that characterised the beginning of the modern age for the
Christian or Hindu society. Thus even an eminent scholar like Professor

204

M. Mujeeb finds it useful to begin an otherwise magnificent study of Indian Muslims with the following obeisance to orthodoxy:

> It is the author's firm belief that the Indian Muslims have, in their religion of Islam, and in the true (sic) representatives of the moral and spiritual values of Islam, the most reliable standards of judgment, and they do not need to look elsewhere to discover how high or low they stand.[49]

One may add that even Muslim intellectuals, particularly of the post-1947 generation, who profess Marxism scrupulously avoid criticizing their community's culture and religion for reasons of expediency. Till this situation changes there can be no satisfactory solution of the Hindu-Muslim problem, which at heart is an aspect of the problem of modernisation of the Indian society. Indeed, the basic issue that almost all Muslim societies face today is that of coming to terms with the modern age. Hindu society has for many decades past presented a differentiated picture of value committments and intellectual attitudes on the part of its educated élite. Muslim society, on the other hand, still presents a practically homogeneous picture in this respect. As a result, in two decades after partition once again one witnesses a gradual rebirth of pre-partition Muslim politics in India, with the only difference that for obvious reasons no demand for a second partition is likely to be made this time. The growing strength of the Jana Sangh in terms of electoral support, and particularly the increasing sympathy with which the average well-meaning Hindu has begun to look upon it, indicates the nature of the Hindu reaction to this phenomenon. It is clear that neither the Gandhian nor the Marxist approach is likely to help in forestalling the Hindu-Muslim confrontation that the present trends imply. Only a radically secular approach based on the refinement of religion and its relegation to the personal sphere of life will suffice. In the words of Sir Jadunath Sarkar, 'If India is ever to be the home of a nation able to keep peace within and guard the frontiers, develop the economic resources of the country and promote art and science, then both Hinduism and Islam must die and be born again. Each of these creeds must pass through a rigorous vigil and penance, each must be purified and rejuvenated under the sway of reason and science'.[50] Such death and rebirth of religion would have been necessary even if India were a purely Hindu or a purley Muslim society. For the multi-religious society that it is, Sarkar's prescription can be rejected only at the peril of great human suffering and prolonged stagnation. Though Gandhi did not try it, I have a feeling that had he been alive today he would have endorsed the historian's point.

NOTES

[1] Cf. the Shankaracharya's interview published in *Free Press Journal*, Bombay, 18 April 1969.

[2] The only exception was Jyotiba Phule, who belonged to the *Mali* ('gardener') caste in Maharashtra and founded the *Satyashodhak Samaj*, Society for the Discovery of Truth. His followers were almost exclusively non-Brahman.

[3] The agitation was started by Indian Muslims in 1919 against the terms imposed by the Allied Powers on the Ottoman Sultan at the end of World War I. Incidentally, the Khilafat Committee started then is still in existence in India.

[4] *Young India*, 25 February 1920.

[5] *Harijan*, 8 June 1940.

[6] See N. C. Kelkar (ed.), *Lokmanya Tilak's Articles from Kesari* (4 vols. in Marathi), (Poona 1922-30).

[7] The words occur in a letter sent by an official to Mary Minto, wife of the Viceroy, Lord Minto, after the latter had received a Muslim deputation led by the Aga Khan on 1 October 1906. See Ram Gopal, *Indian Muslims: A Political History 1858-1947* (Bombay, 1964), p. 100.

[8] Aziz Ahmad, *Islamic Modernism in India and Pakistan 1857-1964* (Oxford, 1967), p. 66.

[9] *Young India*, 16 March 1922.

[10] Aziz Ahmad, op. cit., p. 126.

[11] Quoted from the *Speeches and Writings of Iqbal* in Sachchidanand Sinha, *Iqbal: The Poet and His Message* (Allahabad, 1947), p. 79. See Mohammed Iqbal, *Javidnama* (translated by A. J. Arberry) (London, 1966), pp. 55-58.

[12] For details, see Ram Gopal, op. cit., pp. 154-60.

[13] *Ibid.*, p. 157.

[14] See *Why Hindu Rashtra?* (Bangalore, 1962) and *Bunch of Thoughts* (Bangalore, 1966), both by M. S. Golwalkar, *Sarsanchalak* (Chief Director) of the Rashtriya Swayamsevak Sangh.

[15] See M. A. Jinnah's presidential address at the Lahore session of the Muslim League, reproduced in part in C. H. Philips and B. N. Pandey (eds.), *The Evolution of India and Pakistan 1858-1947* (Oxford, 1962), pp. 353-54.

[16] M. A. Karandikar, *Islam in India's Transition to Modernity* (Bombay, 1968), pp. 238-39; Aziz Ahmad, op. cit., pp. 184, 188-89.

[17] Quoted in Ziya-ul-Hasan Faruqi, *The Deoband School and the Demand for Pakistan* (Bombay, 1963), p. 117. Also see M. A. Karandikar, op. cit., pp. 256-60 for further light on the attitude of the Deoband School and its political arm, the Jamiyat-ul-Ulama-i-Hind.

[18] Eg., '. . . in [the] course of time Hindus will cease to be Hindus and Muslims will cease to be Muslims, not in the religious sense, because that is the personal faith of each individual, but in the political sense as citizens of the State . . .', quoted in *Report of the Court of Inquiry constituted under Punjab Act II of 1954 to enquire into the Punjab Disturbances of 1953* (Superintendent of Government Printing, Lahore, 1954), p. 202. Hereinafter *Munir Commission Report*.

[19] Aziz Ahmad, op. cit., p. 217.

[20] See P. Spratt, *Hindu Culture and Personality* (Bombay, 1966), and 'Tradition and Modernity in India' in A. B. Shah, *Planning for Democracy and Other Essays* (Bombay, 1967).

[21] Cf. 'Since every action or saying of a prophet is, in the case of our own Holy Prophet it certainly was, prompted by Allah, it has the same degree of inerrancy as the formal revelation itself, because prophets are *ma'sum*, incapable of doing or saying something which is opposed to Divine wishes. These sayings and actions are *sunna* having the same infallibility as the Quran'.—*Munir Commission Report*, p. 205. Whether and to what extent the two learned judges believed in their statement is less important than the fact that they considered it necessary to make it.

[22] W. Montgomery Watt, *What is Islam?* (2nd ed.) (Chicago, 1953), pp. 102-05.

[23] Seyyed Hossein Nasr, *An Introduction to Islamic Cosmological Doctrines* (Harvard, 1964), p. 214.

[24] H. A. R. Gibb in the Preface to Seyyed Hossein Nasr, op. cit.

[25] As contemporary instances, mention may be made of Dr Fazlur Rahman's resignation from the directorship of the government-sponsored Islamic Research Institute at Karachi and Dr Taha Husain's dismissal from the University of Cairo, both under pressure of popular wrath over attempts to give a modern interpretation of Islam. See A. Guillaume, *Islam* (London, 1966), pp. 156-58. Also *Munir Commission Report*, op. cit.

[26] For a sample of al-Ghazali's views, see W. Montgomery Watt (tr.), *The Faith and Practice of al-Ghazali* (London, 1953), especially pp. 34, 36, 65, 70.

[27] *Young India*, 29 October 1931.

[28] Aziz Ahmad, op. cit., pp.33-34.

[29] *Source Material for a History of the Freedom Movement in India*, collected from Bombay Government Records, vol. 2, p. 71; quoted in Ram Gopal, op. cit., p. 67.

[30] Ram Gopal, *How India Struggled for Freedom* (Bombay, 1967), pp. 78-79.

[31] 'We form a nationality as important as any other. . . . If the vast masses of low caste people who are nominally Hindus were excluded from the Hindu figures, certainly the disparity which now appears between the Hindu and Mohammedan population would not strike as so great or so disproportionate.' Ameer Ali in a speech introducing the Muslim League deputation in London to Lord Morley, Secretary of State for India in January 1909; quoted in Ram Gopal, *Indian Muslims*, p. 193.

[32] Mohammed Iqbal, *Six Lectures on the Reconstruction of Religious Thought in Islam* (Lahore, 1930), p. 223; also *Javidnama*, pp. 55-56.

[33] For a complete list of the demands, see C. H. Philips and B. N. Pandey (eds.), op. cit., p. 236. For the additional thirteen demands made by Jinnah a decade later, see M. A. Karandikar, op. cit., p. 252.

[34] M. A. Karandikar, op. cit., p. 251.

[35] M. S. Golwalkar, *Why Hindu Rashtra?*, p. 8.

[36] Editorial in *Nida-e-Millat*, 12 January 1969; quoted in *The Secularist*, no. 1 (April 1969), Quarterly Bulletin of Indian Secular Society, Bombay, p. 8.

[37] Khalilullah Hussaini, President, All-India Tameer-e-Millat, in a speech at Aurangabad on 12 May 1968; reported in *The Secularist*, no. 1, p. 5.

[38] K. K. Aziz, *The Making Of Pakistan* (London, 1967), p. 29.

[39] Aziz Ahmad, op. cit., p. 164.

[40] Ram Gopal, *Indian Muslims*, pp. 88-89.

[41] N. C. Kelkar, op. cit., vol. 1, pp. 214-15, 228, 277.

[42] *The Complete Works of Swami Vivekananda* (Calcutta, 1963), vol. 6, pp. 415-16.

[43] See Dayanand Saraswati, *Satyartha Prakash* (in Hindi); *Introduction to the Commentary on the Vedas*, translated from the Sanskrit by Pandit Ghasi Ram. (Delhi, 1958).

44 For supporting evidence, see Ram Gopal, *Indian Muslims,* pp. 98-100.

45 Ram Gopal, *How India Struggled for Freedom,* ch. 8, especially pp. 140-42.

46 N. C. Kelkar, op. cit., vol. 3, pp. 74 and following pages.

47 N. K. Bose and P. H. Patwardhan, *Gandhi in Indian Politics* (Bombay, 1967), p. 52. *Lakh* = one hundred thousand.

48 The words are Jawaharlal Nehru's, quoted in Leonard Mosley, *The Last Days of the British Raj* (London, 1961), p. 248.

49 M. Mujeeb, *The Indian Muslims* (London, 1966), p. 24.

50 Jadunath Sarkar, *A Short History of Aurangzib* (Calcutta, 3rd edn., 1962), p. 449.

GANDHI AND THE COMMUNISTS

P. Spratt

Gandhi returned to India from South Africa in 1915, and became the effective leader of the nationalist movement in 1919. He retained the active leadership down to 1946, when it became clear that the struggle for independence had succeeded. The Communist International was formed in 1919 and issued its first appeals to India and the other Asian countries in 1920; the Communist Party was formally established in India in 1925. Though in Gandhi's lifetime the Party never attained great strength, its ideas exerted considerable influence, and it is possible to speak of a competition betwen the two sets of ideas.

The Communist Party accepts the model for the future of India presented by Russia. This is to be attained by a revolutionary dictatorship. The system will be technologically progressive and promises eventually a high material standard of life, but the model has not as yet substantially relaxed its political and cultural dictatorship. Because of its illiberal character it has lost much of the support which it formerly enjoyed among idealists throughout the world.

The model for the future presented by Gandhism is not so clear. In his *Hind Swaraj*[1] (1909) Gandhi made a complete and uncompromising statement of his utopia, and in particular rejected parliamentary democracy, but those who accept the doctrine of this book have always been a negligible minority. He never deceived himself about this, and in a Preface to it dated January 1921 he said that he was working for 'parliamentary Swaraj'. The communists also realised from the start that his utopia had no practical significance: two of their early pronouncements said, 'Gandhism is more and more becoming an ideology directed against mass revolution'; 'Gandhism . . . preaches and defends the interests of the Indian capitalists'.[2] The practical effect of Gandhi's policy is to make possible an evolution towards the model of a technologically advanced society presented by the liberal capitalist or the social-democratic countries.

However, until 1947 the immediate issue between Gandhi and the communists was the relative effectiveness of their policies for the preliminary purposes of achieving national independence. As against the constitutional-

209

ists, Gandhi held that it was necessary to mobilise power by mass non-co-operation; the communists went a step further and said that a revolutionary seizure of power was necessary. The question lost practical importance in 1947, when India achieved independence, but discussion on what might have been did not cease.

The Montagu-Chelmsford constitutional reform of 1919 made the 'transferred' half of the provincial governments responsible to elected legislatures. This responsibility to an electorate was decisive, says V. P. Menon, 'the movement towards democratic self-government had acquired irresistible momentum; all that the Second World War did was to quicken the pace'.[3] Against this it can be argued for the Gandhians that the Government of India Act of 1935 conferred a larger quantum of responsibility on both the provincial and the central governments only because of the Non-co-operation of 1920-21 and the Civil Disobedience of 1930 and 1932-34. The communists, however, point out that despite the Act of 1935 the British were still in control in 1947, and contend that what then compelled them to go was revolutionary activity, 'the unprecedented growth of anti-imperialist forces . . . demonstrations for the release of Indian National Army prisoners; militant mass struggles led by the Communist Party; and above all the Royal Indian Navy revolt'.[4]

However, the fact is that the majority of the British Establishment were prepared to relinquish power when the 1935 Act was passed. The Conservative opposition in Parliament argued that the Act yielded to the Indian ministers so much power that the British Governor-General would be unable to maintain any position against national sentiment, and an early transition to full self-government by convention could be foreseen. The majority had no answer to this, and it must be supposed that they accepted it. 'It remains incontrovertible that the 1935 Act . . . was the final major, constructive achievement of the British in India. . . . It would be wrong to conclude from the failure of the central federal structure to materialise that the 1935 Act had failed itself. On the contrary, later in his life Nehru told me that it proved to be an organic connecting link between the old and the new.'[5]

The situation of India during the Second World War was very much like that of Ireland during the First. In 1913 the Asquith Government passed a Home Rule Act which the Irish Parliamentary Party and other representatives of Irish opinion accepted. The other Dominion Prime Ministers sent their official congratulations. Implementation was postponed because of the war, and of disagreement over Ulster which it was expected would be resolved. All concerned were surprised by the rebellion in 1916, which however led events in a quite different direction.

Thirty years later there was a rebellion in India. On 16 August 1946, the Muslim League launched 'Direct Action' against the Hindus. 'The general situation in the country was alarming. . . . In further communal disorders it was doubtful if the loyalty of the Army and the Services could be relied upon.'[6] Hence Attlee's decision, announced on 20 February 1947, to withdraw by June 1948. Mountbatten brought the date forward to August 1947 for the same reason. 'The Services began to take sides, especially in the Punjab, and the army, the last instrument to hold the situation in the hands of the Government, would also be contaminated before long by the communal virus. The Viceroy . . . decided to advance the date of the handing over of power.'[7] It was not the hatred of the Indians for the British, or of the poor for the rich, but of the Muslims for the Hindus and vice versa, that gave the quietus to the British régime.

Nevertheless the Gandhians can claim that their actions did hasten the change in the British attitude in the 1930s and thus achieved independence. The Communists, however, argue that it would have happened twenty years earlier if Gandhi had not been so afraid of violence as to halt all activity, as a result of which Non-co-operation ceased, because some rioters had killed twenty-two policemen in the village of Chauri Chaura on 4 February 1922.[8]

It is possible to guess what might have happened. If the agitation had been continued, further violent outbreaks would probably have occurred. Minor disturbances were taking place almost every day. In November 1921, when the Prince of Wales arrived in Bombay, there had been a grave outbreak, in which about fifty were killed and 400 wounded, mainly by police firing. But the outbreak at Chauri Chaura was more alarming than the usual quick-tempered flare-up, which dies down quickly without much damage done. This attack on the police showed a bitter vengefulness which if it had spread would have led to much bloodshed. The movement would have lost the sympathy of large sections of Indian opinion, and the British would have felt free to use the force at their command. Gandhi was no doubt right to put an end to it, and though Nehru disagreed at the time, he came to that conclusion later: 'As a matter of fact the suspension of civil resistance in February 1922 was certainly not due to Chauri Chaura alone, although most people imagined so. That was only the last straw. . . . Our movement was going to pieces'.[9]

If, on the other hand, the agitation had continued without much violence, the British would probably have made a political offer sufficiently attractive to induce Gandhi to negotiate. Then the communal problem would have arisen. V. P. Menon says: 'It is a moot point whether, if the agitation had succeeded in wresting some big concession from the British, the two communities would have continued to co-operate. Perhaps not; for, in my honest opinion, to put it mildly, the Khilafat leaders were not non-communal . . . if things had reached the stage of detailed constitutional discussions, it is hardly conceivable that a split would have been averted.'[10]

The communists do not admit the force of such considerations. Their remedy for the communal trouble was to raise the pitch of joint mass agitation against the common enemy. 'A dynamic movement of the people, based on their own vital interests, was the sovereign remedy for communal aberrations.'[11] But if the agitation had been powerful enough to compel the British to enter into negotiations, we do not know what constitutional scheme the communists would have supported. In the last years before 1947, when this problem dominated public discussion, the Communist Party made detailed proposals not designed to lead to a bourgeois democratic constitution under which Hindus and Muslims might live in peace and freedom, but intended to lead to a socialist revolution.[12]

It is relevant therefore to consider the solution enforced after the socialist revolution in Russia to the analogous problem there. The persecution of Christianity began two months after the revolution and continued till shortly before the Second World War. Many thousands of priests and monks were killed, and the great majority of the churches were closed. During the war and since then, however, the Orthodox Church has been tolerated and used for the purposes of official propaganda. Persecution of the Muslim religion began about 1928, after the Central Asian provinces had been reconquered. 'In Turkestan 14,000 mosques were closed, in Idel-Ural 7000, in the Caucasus 4000, and in the Crimea 1000. By 1938 there was not a single mosque in the Crimea.'[13] In the North Caucasus, 'whereas in 1921 there had been 4000 mosques, 2000 religious schools, and more than 10,000 mullahs . . . by the end of the 1930s there were only 150 empty mosques and 150 aged mullahs and muezzins. The Arab religious schools had been prohibited in 1925-26; in 1929 the mosques were closed, while the Moslem priests . . . were physically exterminated.'[14] Lest it be thought that the obdurate Muslims brought this persecution upon themselves, it should be mentioned that Buddhism in Russia has been completely wiped out as an organised religion.[15]

After this experience, the Muslims have not been obstreperous. A recent well-informed attempt to sum up the situation speaks of 'a well-disciplined and reasonably well-fed, well-clothed and well-educated population . . . there are, however, other circumstances which preceded or accompanied the present state of material well-being: the rigours of the original Tsarist conquest, of the Civil War and of the collectivisation period; the drop of nearly a million in the Kazakh population between 1926 and 1939; the deportation a thousand miles from their homes of nearly a million Muslims during the Second World War; the presence in the Muslim lands of over six million Russian colonists; the regimentation of native culture; the retention by Moscow of control over the defence, foreign policy and economy of the Muslim republics; and the great preponderance of Russians in research posts and the teaching profession. . . . There are many indications that the authorities are dissatisfied with and even apprehensive about the attitude of the Muslims towards the régime. Summary dismissals of Muslim republican ministers and party officials are fairly frequent, and as recently as 1956 the First Secretary of the Azerbaydzan Communist Party was executed. . . . There are some signs of resentment at interference with traditional culture and customs and at the preferential treatment accorded to non-Muslims in the matter of higher education and appointments. Generally speaking, however, the present attitude is one of passive acquiescence.'[16]

Thus the communist solution to the communal problem is quite unacceptable to civilised people. It is a problem to which there is no easy solution, and in a free society containing different religious communities it is likely to persist, causing more or less serious trouble from time to time. But this is better than suppression of the problem by terror.

It may be concluded that the communists' retrospective criticism of Gandhi's leadership of the Non-Co-operation movement lacks plausibility.

The Civil Disobedience of 1930 and 1932-34 was similar to Non-Co-operation, except that fewer Muslims took part. Though suppressed more rigorously, it was kept up at a high pitch of intensity for a long time, and this demonstration persuaded the British Government to omit the intermediate step recommended by the Simon Commission and proceed at once to make India self-governing except for defence and foreign affairs. The Congress contested the provincial elections in 1937, and alone or with minor allies formed governments in eight of the eleven provinces. The provisions of the Act of 1935 relating to the Government of India were not enforced, because a sufficient number of princely states did not accede before the outbreak of the war in 1939.

The Act had been passed when the liberal, conciliatory Baldwin was Prime Minister. Chamberlain, efficient, practical and unimaginative, and involved in the war which he had so much feared, took a simple, legalistic view of Indian affairs. The British Government was still responsible for foreign policy, so it declared India at war, without consulting those who in slightly different circumstances would have been in power in Delhi. This blunder provoked another of equal magnitude. The Congress leaders took it as evidence that there had after all been no change of heart in Britain, and ordered their eight provincial governments to resign. Thus was set going the fateful chain of reactions which led on to the unnecessary Quit India campaign, the political vacuum which made possible the rise of the Muslim League, and the partition of India.

After his release from internment in 1944 Gandhi had prolonged discussions with Jinnah. He was ready to accept a large degree of autonomy for Muslim-majority areas, but Jinnah insisted on the total separation of the Muslim-majority provinces, including their Hindu-majority districts. There was thus no agreement. Thenceforth, though Gandhi was consulted, he took a less active part in the negotiations which ended three years later in partition and independence. But when communal violence broke out in Bengal in 1946 he went to that province, walking through the villages and trying to persuade the people to live in peace. After independence he performed a public fast in Calcutta, and later another in Delhi, and these were effective in checking the mutual massacres. This work of the last two years of his life is regarded as among his greatest achievements.

The Communist Party opposed the Civil Disobedience movement. Until June 1941 it opposed India's participation in the war and criticised the Congress opposition as half-hearted. After the war the Congress Working Committee sent to the Communist members of the All-India Congress Committee a statement of charges, mentioning their 'unqualified support of the Muslim League's claim for Pakistan', and quoting a statement of March 1940: 'Once Gandhism held the fate of British rule in its hand. Today it pursues the logic of unconditional co-operation with the same Government. . . . Gandhism has entered into its decadent phase . . . it is acting as a fetter on our national struggle. . . . Gandhi would not use England's difficulty to win India's freedom . . . it is the line of the cowardly and compromising bourgeoisie. Gandhism . . . is seeking to use its position to overtake and imprison the rapidly growing forces of revolution.' But after Germany attacked Russia the Communist policy changed and the Party opposed the Quit India campaign; in particular the responsibility for the August disturbances was placed by the Communists on the Congress Working Committee in September 1942, long before the publication of Tottenham's [the Home Member] pamphlet on the subject'.[17]

That the communists gave unqualified support to the demand for

Pakistan is not quite true. That demand, adopted by the Muslim League in 1940, appealed to the Muslim masses, and the communists hoped that it could be used for revolutionary purposes. But the communist theory does not contemplate self-determination for religious groups; so, as Overstreet and Windmiller explain it, the communists took up the doctrine that India consists of a large number of nationalities, of which some are Muslim, and if all were granted self-determination, this would satisfy the Muslim masses.[18]

In 1942 the Central Committee of the Communist Party adopted a resolution mentioning sixteen Indian nations. But it proceeded: 'the recognition of the right of separation need not necessarily lead to actual separation. On the other hand, by dispelling the mutual suspicions, it brings about unity of action today, and lays the basis for a greater unity in the free India of tomorrow. National unity . . . strengthened in the course of joint struggle in the defence of our motherland is bound to convince the peoples of all Indian nationalities of the urgent need to stick together'.[19]

What the communists were doing was to try to repeat Lenin's policy. 'Lenin had insisted on making self-determination for all the national components of the Empire part of bolshevik doctrine. . . . The promise was progressively modified as soon as national minorities began to take advantage of it to assert their claims to independence. . . . The bolshevik organisations established in the borderlands during the period of the Provisional Government were used, with the support of troops prepared to follow the bolsheviks, to overthrow . . . the newly-established national governments.'[20]

Thus it does not matter how far the communists went to conciliate the Muslim League, or whether they added the words 'the urgent need to stick together' in the second edition of the resolution quoted above.[21] The whole policy was intended to be a deception far graver than that. Before the revolution the communists promise the land to the tiller: after they are safely in power they nationalise the land. Before the revolution they promise a higher standard of life for the worker: after it they lower the worker's standard of life by fifty per cent in order to provide a surplus for investment. The nationalities policy is of the same type. Moreover, the Communist Party of India adhered to it consistently; its Election Manifesto of January 1946 said, 'Full and real sovereignty shall reside in the National Constituent Assemblies',[22] and the resolution later presented by Mr Somnath Lahiri to the Constituent Assembly said, 'The people of each such unit will have the unfettered right . . . to decide . . . whether they will join the Indian Union or form a separate state'.[23]

The communist policy on this matter was more consistent than Overstreet and Windmiller suggest, and was not unqualified support for the Pakistan demand. It was intended to divert the mutual hostility of the Muslims and Hindus into a common revolutionary struggle against the British. However, it never gave any promise of success. During the massacres of 1946-47 British people were seldom if ever attacked. If Gandhi's policy on the Hindu-Muslim problem failed, there is no reason to think that the communists' policy would have done any better.

When Gandhi was assassinated, the communists did not change their attitude towards him. Their survey of the first year of independence began: 'The year of freedom . . . saw the ghastly murder of Mahatma Gandhi, plotted by those who were certified as patriots only a few days ago. . . . The death of Mahatma Gandhi at this junction symbolises, however, the end of an epoch . . . that phase of India's struggle in which the bourgeois leadership headed the struggle to use it as a weapon of compromise . . . non-violence . . . was nothing but a formula of emasculation of the national struggle. . . .'[24] Overstreet and Windmiller discern in some phrases in R. Palme Dutt's article in the *Labour Monthly* (London) of March 1948 a suggestion for a 'new line' on Gandhi, but concede that there were few other signs of such a thing.[25] In the third edition of *India Today*, of which the Preface is dated October 1948, Dutt mentions the assassination but makes no comment on it, and retains the adverse criticisms of Gandhi of the earlier editions: 'the best guarantee of the shipwreck of any mass movement which had the blessing of his association. This Jonah of revolution, this general of unbroken disasters. . . .'[26] (The communists did not at that time admit that India had gained independence: they considered the independence of August 1947 bogus.)

Some change in the content and tone of references by communists to Gandhi appeared in the 1950s. During their visit to India in 1955 Khrushchev and Bulganin spoke of him as an 'outstanding leader' and 'glorious patriot and friend of the people'. The Russian experts on India then began to revise their opinion on him. 'Our unconditionally negative attitude towards Gandhi's non-violent tactics has been refuted by the facts.'[27] In April 1961 the press published a statement by another Russian student of Indian affairs that 'progressive and even revolutionary movements can develop under religious slogans'. A commentator interprets this as part of the effort by the Russian Government to improve relations with India.[28] The Soviet Government is to celebrate the Gandhi centenary. Some welcome this change as a manifestation of common sense and human feeling; others fear it as a retreat in preparation for a renewed advance towards the long-cherished aim of the communist conquest of India.

Gandhi often discussed their ideas with communists. As with all opponents, he wished to maintain good relations. He was appreciative, and professed to accept their ultimate aim of equality, though he never abandoned his objection to violence and untruth, which imply a breach of good relations. Non-violence however has further implications. Together with the harmony of means and ends, and the preference for 'one step enough for me', it teaches a doctrine of social empiricism. Hiren Mukerjee protests that those who condemn communists for adopting bad means to good ends are hypocritical.[29] He is of course right. Trotsky in *Terrorism and Communism* made the same answer, and gave the analogy of surgery, which inflicts pain in order to achieve health. Admittedly this criticism of the communist doctrine is often pushed too far, and Gandhi's principles are expressed too simply. Nevertheless a difference remains.

Surgery is fairly scientific. People trust the doctor's prediction as to the outcome of an operation, and his warning as to the consequences of not having the operation, though mistakes do happen. But can the communist surgeon be trusted in the same way? They predict supreme happiness if society undergoes the operation, and dire consequences if it does not: there is no other way to salvation. But Marxism has proved to be wrong on many important matters. It failed to predict the main features of the later development of western capitalist society, the society which Marx specially studied—the ever faster advance of technology, the continued prosperity of capitalism, the levelling out of the trade cycle, the success of democracy, the effectiveness of the trade unions, the expansion of the middle class, the liquidation of the colonial empires without fatal consequences to the metropolitan countries, the rise and fall of fascism, the persistence of nationalism (under both capitalism and socialism), etc. Thus the prediction as to the fate of the patient who refused to undergo surgery has proved very faulty. What of the patient who had his operation? At any rate his supreme happiness has been a long time coming, and his suffering in the post-operative period has been severe. Mukerjee is indignant about the Jallianwalabagh massacre in 1919, in which 379 people were shot dead.[30] It was indeed a horrible affair. But it strikes one as incongruous that an admirer of communism should be so upset by it. If the British had perpetrated a Jallianwalabagh massacre every day from 1919 till they left in 1947, they would have liquidated only a fraction of the number which Lenin's and Stalin's police liquidated in the same period.[31]

This drastic communist policy would be justified only if it were known with virtual certainty that its predictions about the future of capitalism and the consequences of a socialist revolution were true. In fact it can be said with confidence that both predictions are false. The claim of Marxism to be scientific is true only with many qualifications. It has some validity as a guide for leaders who want to detect the weak points of a society with a view to seizing power. As a guide to the establishment of a good society afterwards it has no validity at all. On the record hitherto, a capitalist economy under a constitutional democracy is far superior.

As a corrective to the dogmatic over-confidence of the communists, Gandhi's cautious empiricism has great value. It is imprudent to use bad means for good ends because it is so seldom possible to be sure that the good end will materialise, and in fact bad means tend strongly to corrupt the end. Since we know so little about society, and can do so little to control it, a short-range empiricism is the only reasonable policy.

Next to non-violence, communists condemn Gandhi's support for property. 'His theory of trusteeship, his insistence on certain moral values, . . . all these proved in actual practice to be of enormous help to the bourgeoisie. . . .'[32] Those who do not accept socialism can regard the doctrine of trusteeship in a different light. Property has been justified in the general interest in the past, and there is no reason to think that its usefulness is exhausted. It is, in particular, a probably indispensable safeguard of liberty, which is enjoyed by both owners and non-owners. In this age liberty and property have lost popular esteem and are apt to be lightly sacrificed. Gandhi's approval of property, expressed in the doctrine of trusteeship, strengthens its defence against envious attacks, and reassures property owners against mistaken promptings of conscience about it. He was also quite unequivocal in his refusal to countenance attacks on property. 'I do claim that by constant practice we shall come to a state of things when lawful possessions will command universal and voluntary respect.'[33] 'I shall be no party to dispossessing propertied classes of their property without just cause.'[34]

His defence of property is quite consistent with his general ideas about society. He was aware that men are unequal in natural endowment and in social conditioning. Even after he abandoned the defence of caste, he upheld *varna*, the ancient division of society, supposedly according to aptitude; though he wanted it freed from ideas of high and low. 'In this conception of the law of *varna*, no one is superior to any other. All occupations are equal and honourable.'[35] He also continued to stress *swadeshi:* 'I must not serve my distant neighbour at the expense of the nearest',[36] which however broadens out into a doctrine that one's responsibility to others varies according to the relations in which one stands to them. He was aware, in short, that society has a structure, and this is

218

opposed to the assumption of the communists that men are an undifferentiated mass, that any economic difference is due to exploitation, and that the claim of the poor to an equal share is more urgent than all other claims. 'The true source of rights is duty', Gandhi said. 'If leaving duties unperformed we run after rights, they will escape us.'[37] This stresses the ethical autonomy of the individual, which clashes with the communist doctrine that man is wholly a product of his environment. The contrast appears in Gandhi's instructions to the workers whom he once led in a strike: 'never to resort to violence, never to molest blacklegs, never to depend upon alms, and to earn bread, during the strike, by any other honest labour. . . . The labourers pledged themselves not to resume work. . . .'[38] All this, including the pledge, emphasises the individual's reliance on his own resources, in contrast to the communists' emphasis on mass solidarity. *Satyāgraha*, as Gandhi conceived it, has a strongly emphasised individualistic character. He was often called an anarchist, and he certainly expressed the anarchist's suspicion of the state: 'I look upon an increase in the power of the state with the greatest fear because . . . it does the greatest harm to mankind by destroying individuality, which lies at the root of all progress'.[39]

Gandhi's ethics derives from the Hindu tradition, which exalts the individual soul and only after long training, at the summit of spiritual attainment, identifies it with the universe. Up to that point the soul is taught to isolate itself. Much of this stress on individual self-development remains in Gandhi's teaching and example. Most people, immersed in their communities and inadequately individualised, need such teaching and example. The communist doctrine and activity, on the other hand, encourage dependence on the community and favour an undifferentiated mass society, wholly dependent on and subject to a political élite. Gandhi's doctrine tends to develop a liberal, individualised, democratic order; the communist doctrine produces a mass society under a dictatorship.

Since 1947 policies inspired in part by the pre-revolutionary and agitational, and the post-revolutionary and constructive, example of communism have competed with policies inspired by Gandhi, and have done so all too successfully. Large funds have been invested in big, capital-intensive, nationally-owned concerns. The state has taken over a considerable proportion of economic enterprise, and deprived large groups of their property. The centre has prevailed over the periphery, the city over the village. Austerity has given way to ostentation, and hard work is discouraged by over-staffing, inflation, and general carelessness and permissiveness. It might have been hoped that Gandhi's teaching would play the inspiring and constructive part in Indian economic development which, according to Weber's analysis, that of Calvin did in Europe. Any hope of such a thing must now be abandoned. India has tried to enjoy a twentieth-century welfare system on the strength of an economy wholly inadequate for that purpose. Expansion has therefore been starved, while inequality has increased and discontent is rising. Communism made little progress when it confronted Gandhi directly, but it seems to be well on the way to success by confusing the minds of his heirs.

NOTES

[1] All Gandhi's books are kept in print by the Navajivan Publishing House, Ahmedabad.

[2] Quoted at length by M. R. Masani, *The Communist Party of India* (London, 1954), pp. 21, 43.

[3] V. P. Menon, *An Outline of Indian Constitutional History* (Bombay, 1965), p. 49.

[4] E. M. S. Namboodiripad, *Note for the Programme of the Communist Party of India* (New Delhi, n.d.), pp. 1-2.

[5] Lord Butler, *Jawalharlal Nehru and the Struggle for Independence* (London, 1966), p. 23.

[6] V. P. Menon, *The Transfer of Power in India* (Calcutta, 1957), p. 338.

[7] V. P. Menon, *An Outline of Indian Constitutional History*, p. 72.

[8] Hiren Mukerjee, *Gandhiji: a Study* (2nd ed., Bombay, 1960), p. 69.

[9] Jawaharlal Nehru, *An Autobiography* (Delhi, 1962), p. 85.

[10] V. P. Menon, *An Outline of Indian Constitutional History*, p. 28.

[11] Mukerjee, op. cit., p. 128.

[12] G. D. Overstreet and M. Windmiller, *Communism in India* (University of California Press, 1959), pp. 490-98.

[13] *Genocide in the USSR* (Munich, 1958), p. 199.

[14] *Ibid.*, p. 41.

[15] *Ibid.*, p. 191.

[16] G. Wheeler, *Racial Problems in Soviet Muslim Asia* (London, 1960), pp. 60-62.

[17] P. C. Joshi, *Communist Reply to Congress Working Committee's Charges* (Bombay, 1945), part 1, pp. 2, 5, 6, 10.

[18] Overstreet and Windmiller, op. cit., pp. 492-93.

[19] G. Adhikari (ed.), *Pakistan and National Unity* (Bombay, 1944), pp. 15-16.

[20] L. Schapiro, *The Communist Party of the Soviet Union* (London, 1960), pp. 220-21.

[21] Overstreet and Windmiller, op. cit., p. 497.

[22] *Election Manifesto of the Communist Party of India* (Bombay, 1946), p. 4.

[23] *Declaration of Independence* (People's Publishing House, Bombay, 1946), p. 8.

[24] *One Year of Freedom* (People's Publishing House, Bombay, 1948), p. 1.

[25] Overstreet and Windmiller, op. cit., p. 515.

[26] R. Palme Dutt, *India Today* (Bombay, 1949), p. 334.

[27] Quoted by Overstreet and Windmiller, op. cit., p. 521.

[28] *Thought* (Delhi, 7 December 1968), p. 11.

[29] Mukerjee, op. cit., p. 209.

[30] *Ibid.*, p. 48.

[31] A. D. Sakharov, *Peaceful Coexistence and Intellectual Freedom* (Delhi, 1968), p. 14: 'At least ten to fifteen million people perished in the torture chambers of the N.K.V.D., in camps for exiled kulaks . . .'. R. Conquest, *The Great Terror* (London, 1968), p. 533: '. . . Twenty million dead, which is almost certainly too low and might require an increase of 50 per cent or so, as the debit balance of the Stalin régime.'

[32] E. M. S. Namboodiripad, *The Mahatma and the Ism* (Bombay, 1958), p. 190.

[33] *Harijan*, 22 February 1942.

[34] *Amrita Bazar Patrika*, 2 August 1934.

[35] *Young India*, 17 November 1927.

[36] *Young India*, 12 March 1925.

[37] *Young India*, 8 January 1925.

[38] M. K. Gandhi, *An Autobiography* (Ahmedabad, 1959), p. 315.

[39] Quoted by Mukerjee, op. cit., p. 207.

'EVEN AS UNTO THEE'

An inquiry into Gandhian consistency

Hugh Tinker

The last years of Gandhi's life have given a great deal of trouble to his interpreters. It is true that the Noakhali peace-making and the Calcutta fast find him fulfilling his pilgrimage towards truth and non-violence. But what are we to make of his apparent acquiescence in the negation of so many of his hopes? We are told that he supported the use of Indian troops in Kashmir: even that he was prepared to fight Pakistan over the issue of Abdul Ghaffar Khan's imprisonment. But these are nothing compared to his acquiescence in the partition of India and the acceptance of 'two nations', Muslims and Hindus. Most Gandhian studies pass these matters by.[1] During those last years, Gandhi was misunderstood both by supporters and antagonists. Jinnah became so baffled by his encounters with Gandhi that he could only conclude that the latter was attempting to weave some involute plan to undo him. The British leaders were almost equally exasperated. Wavell's assessment of the political situation in May 1946 went thus: 'Over it all broods the influence of Mr Gandhi, a pure political opportunist, and an extremely skilful one, whose guiding principle is to get rid of the hated British influence out of India as soon as possible'. At almost the same moment A. V. Alexander observed to his Cabinet Mission colleagues: 'Gandhi has two objects: to humiliate the British government, and to promote a policy of scuttle, and secondly to secure power without a constitution coming into being so as to abandon the just claims of the Muslim League'. A year later, even one as sympathetic as Lord Mountbatten could express himself 'astounded' and 'shocked' by what Gandhi proposed.

Some have explained his apparently inexplicable attitudes at this time in terms of the contradictions which we find in most great men. 'Faults?' asks Carlyle, writing of 'The Hero as Prophet', 'The greatest of faults, I should say, is to be conscious of none.' And so we accept in a Churchill or a De Gaulle that if he is petty, this merely sets off his nobility; if he is silly, this only emphasises his wisdom; if he is self-indulgent, this only reminds us of his service and sacrifice. Doubtless we can find such paradoxes in Gandhi's personal life, but we don't find (as we do in Churchill) these contradictions in his national leadership. Indeed, I have written elsewhere: 'Few political leaders have been so fundamentally consistent as Gandhi, with a consistency impossible of achievement, even for the Mahatma himself'.[2] But Gandhi functioned (consistently) on different political planes—at different levels, as one writer observes.[3] The level which was fundamental was that of individual experience, realised through participation and co-operation in social action. But there was also the level of mass political activity through the Indian National Congress, and the level of British government and policy. Gandhi distinguished carefully between the appropriate responses at these different levels. His fundamental level is that of the non-violent, stateless society. At that level, the State is an unnatural and undesirable system of authority: in Gandhi's words, 'Violence in a concentrated and organised form'. If, then, an independent Indian State emerges, it is pointless to expect this to be expressed in non-violent terms. The non-violent State is a contradiction: and Gandhi, accepting the necessity for an Indian State as a transitional system (one that may last a long time, given the Indian people's unreadiness for non-violence) is prepared to accept the use of force by such a State.

His attitude to the British government is capable of a similar explanation. If an Indian State is merely a transit camp on the road to the non-violent society, even more, the British government is a staging post, to be left behind as soon as possible: Indians cannot begin to change themselves while under the domination of alien rule. However, so long as the British government lasts, Gandhi acknowledges the necessity to deal with it in its own terms. And so, his famous statement to Judge Broomfield: 'I am here, therefore, to invite and submit cheerfully to the highest penalty that can be inflicted upon me for what in law is a deliberate crime and what appears to me to be the highest duty of a citizen'.[4] In his last days, Gandhi was asked to take part in negotiations to draft a constitutional settlement for independence in India. Nothing could be more artificial to Gandhian ideas than a series of proposals and counter-proposals all concerned to fashion a new structure of government. But at one level, Gandhi accepted this procedure as a necessary preliminary to terminating British rule in India. Because its values were so removed from Gandhian values, he could not be expected to participate eagerly in the process: and, indeed, his part became smaller and smaller and eventually faded altogether. But there were moments when Gandhi found himself involved in the minutiæ of negotiation. Then he behaved appropriately, like an English-style constitutional lawyer.

It was not surprising that the British and the Muslim League found these different attitudes at different levels impossible to comprehend. It had been Gandhi's role twice before to negotiate a constitutional settlement: with Smuts in South Africa, and with Irwin (Halifax) after the second civil disobedience movement. In both these situations, Gandhi had achieved much in creating an individual human relationship, and less in securing a workable political compromise. After the second world war, there was no scope for Gandhi to conduct political negotiations through personal relationships: he found himself but one of many actors on a stage (even though the greatest of the actors). At first, British and Indians looked to him as an arbiter. But Gandhi found himself unable to contribute effectively to the constitutional tussle. He could not draw others up to his desired level, that of individual realisation through co-operation. He could not grasp the implications of what was happening at the levels of Indian and British political and party confrontation. He was elbowed into the position of a spectator. And he found fulfilment not on the national and international political level but, finally, through non-violence, at the level of social action.

We may doubt whether Gandhi would have wished to spend much time on the present inquiry. When American visitors questioned him about apparent contradictions in his teaching he replied: 'Consistency is a hobgoblin'. In his life-long pursuit of truth, perception was realised through experience. The experiences of his last years led him to revise many of his assumptions: particularly about the capacity of the Indian people and their leaders to realise his goal of *ahimsā, satyāgraha,* and *sarvodaya* within calculable time. His desire to live 125 years in order to participate in the attainment of the ideal vanished when he realised that much more than half a century must elapse before independent India attained the true *swarāj.* Gandhi's last intervention in politics—the exertion of influence and power—was made in August 1946. Thereafter he sought only non-political solutions (some would say spiritual solutions).

When the Cabinet Mission arrived in India at the end of March 1946, they at once turned to Gandhi and asked for his advice. Gandhi replied that he would rather that their question was put to the authorised representatives of the Congress. Gandhi warned the ministers that they would have a much greater measure of difficulty than any previous mission. He pleaded for gestures of conciliation: in particular, release of political prisoners still in detention (like Jayaprakash Narayan)[5] and removal of harsh measures like the salt tax.

Turning to the Pakistan demand, Gandhi said that he had passed eighteen days with Jinnah [in 1944] but he had never been able to extract a concrete definition of what constituted Pakistan. 'The substance of

Pakistan, as he understood it, was independence of culture and a legitimate ambition. . . . If this was what Mr Jinnah meant, he accepted it, and did so in writing. . . . The two nation theory is far more dangerous. The Muslim population is a population of converts—only a microscopic minority are not. They are descendants of Indian-born people. Jinnah is sincere, but his logic is utterly at fault, especially as a kind of mania possesses him. He himself was called a maniac, and he therefore honoured Mr Jinnah for his mania. In eighteen days he [Gandhi] failed to be convinced of this two nations theory. He asked Jinnah whether his own son [Harilal] who had gone over to the Muslim religion changed his nationality by doing so?'

Gandhi emphasised that the Cabinet Mission must carry the problems inherited from the past: 'They must lie on the bed they had prepared'. But also, 'Wrong does not become right to give it a new lease of life. If you have undone the past you must write on a clean slate'. There must be a considerable interim period before an agreed constitution would emerge. To bridge this period, Gandhi put forward a proposal designed to reconcile the contestants among the Indian leadership: 'Let Mr Jinnah form the first government and choose its personnel from elected representatives in the country. . . . If he does not do so then the offer to form a Government should be made to Congress. . . . The interim government must be absolutely national. Mr Jinnah would choose who he liked for his Government. They would be subject to the vote of the Assembly from which they were drawn.'

Lord Pethick Lawrence made the obvious objection that Jinnah could not command a majority: either at the centre, or in most of the provincial legislatures. If he had to choose ministers, most of them would have to be drawn from parties other than his own.

It may be that Gandhi had envisaged this condition as a necessary means of obtaining a consensus of opinion in the interim government, whoever was the leader. He contented himself with observing that it was inescapable that the Congress had a majority in most of the legislatures. He concluded by insisting that he did not under-rate the difficulties of the situation. 'If he were not an irresponsible optimist he would despair of any solution.'[6]

At this meeting, on 4 April 1946, Gandhi speaks as an elder statesman, above the party political battle. To him the total arena of Indian politics is represented by the Congress. Jinnah is a prodigal son of the Congress who may be brought back into the family by generous dealing; and, as Gandhi says in conclusion, there are seen to be grounds for optimism.

At his next encounter with a junior member of the Cabinet Mission team, Woodrow Wyatt M.P., Gandhi speaks as a prophet of doom. It is little more than a week later (13 April) but Gandhi announces that Britain cannot make a decision: 'There may well have to be a blood-bath in India before her problems are solved. He would urge non-violence on Congress, but he does not expect them to observe it. The only thing that he expects from Congress is that they will fight decently.' Five days later, Gandhi and Nehru met Stafford Cripps. The interview confirmed the growing impression of the British ministers that there was no basis for agreement.[7] The Cabinet Mission discarded their first approach—to act as brokers between the Congress and the League—and turned to considering how they might themselves evolve a compromise solution. Two weeks later Cripps again met Gandhi, and also Azad and Jinnah. On 26 April: 'Azad asked Cripps for an interview and then spontaneously said that he thought that he could get the Congress Working Committee to agree to negotiate with the Moslem League on the basis of an all-India Union confined to foreign affairs, defence and communications, with a legislature which would meet in two parts to deal with optional subjects.' Azad made his move as President of the Congress: but this was a personal initiative, unsupported by his colleagues. It appears that Gandhi only heard of Azad's offer indirectly. According to Sudhir Ghosh's account of this episode, Cripps provided him with a copy of a letter containing the Maulana's proposals. Ghosh goes on to say that Gandhi then interviewed Azad and asked him 'whether he had written any letter to the Viceroy about the negotiations that were going on. The Maulana flatly denied having written any letter at all. He did this while the letter in original was lying in front of Gandhiji'.[8]

There seems to be a basic misunderstanding about what was suggested by Azad in his personal capacity as a *ballon d'essai*, and what he wrote to the Mission as President of the Congress.

On 27 April, Lord Pethick Lawrence wrote to Azad and Jinnah suggesting a conference on the basis of 'A Union Government dealing with the following subjects: Foreign Affairs, Defence and Communications. There will be two groups of Provinces, the one of the predominantly Hindu Provinces and the other of the predominantly Muslim Provinces. . . .'

To this Azad replied the same day: 'The Congress has never accepted the division of India into predominantly Hindu and predominantly Muslim provinces. It however recognises that there may be provinces which are willing to delegate to the Central Government subjects in the optional list while others may agree to delegate only compulsory subjects like Foreign Affairs, Defence, and Communications.' Azad went on to ask that a clause referring to the Provinces having 'residuary sovereign rights' be omitted: if that were conceded, he promised to place the Mission's proposals before the Working Committee. This he did, and next day wrote a further letter on behalf of the Working Committee which defined their objective as 'a Federal Union of autonomous units'. In these exchanges, Azad does not appear to have written to the Viceroy: it therefore seems that his denial to Gandhi was perfectly genuine, and that Sudhir Ghosh had been given some other letter: perhaps that written to Pethick Lawrence.

The next move was the Simla Conference between the Cabinet Mission, Nehru, and Jinnah (with their colleagues). This left both sides as far apart as before, and the Mission had no alternative but to issue their own proposals on 16 May. Gandhi had observed the Simla Conference for himself, but continued to comment as though beyond the battle, urging the parties to come together. His reaction to the scheme of 16 May was to align himself more closely alongside the Congress Working Committee and to scrutinise the proposals of the Cabinet Mission as a working politician. He seized upon the most important feature of the scheme: that it was not an 'award', imposed by the British upon the disunited Indian leaders but a 'recommendation': which was therefore negotiable. Writing to the Mission on 19 May he asked: 'Do you regard a recommendation as obligatory on any member of the contemplated constituent assembly? There is such a ring about the quotation [of constitutional measures]. Can those who enthusiastically welcome the paper but are discerning enough to repudiate, for instance, grouping, honourably seek to educate the country and the communities against the grouping clause?' Gandhi had at once served notice that the proposed north-western group of provinces and the eastern group—the putative basis for Pakistan—could not come into being if the North-West Frontier and Assam were unwilling to enter. Grouping, in his view, must be voluntarily accepted by the participating provinces. Next day he wrote another letter, making detailed points about contingent subjects. Among these he insisted on the departure of British troops: or else independence 'is either insincere or a thoughtless cry'. He also rejected the formula of 'parity', as between Congress and the Muslim League in the proposed interim government: 'The best and incorruptible . . . are wanted'.

The Cabinet Mission were alarmed by almost all Gandhi's points which were endorsed by a Congress resolution of 24 May. They issued a statement emphasising that grouping was 'an essential feature of the scheme' as indeed it was, if the assent of the Muslim League was to be secured.

Meanwhile, Gandhi reverted to his role of detached observer. Writing in the issue of *Harijan* for 26 May he said: 'My conviction abides that it [the Cabinet Mission scheme] is the best document the British Government could have produced in the circumstances. It reflects our weakness, if we could be good enough to see it. The Congress and the League did not and could not agree. We would grievously err if, this time, we foolishly satisfy ourselves that the differences are a British creation.' But, Gandhi went on: 'In my opinion the voluntary character of the statement demands that the liberty of individual units [provinces] should be unimpaired.'

There followed three weeks of intensive discussions in which Gandhi remained close at hand to the actual participants. On 11 June he had an interview with Wavell in which the Viceroy stressed the need to accept an interim government in which Congress and League each took a half share as an expedient to get over immediate difficulties. He asked for a generous gesture from the Congress, and Gandhi appeared to respond: 'He agreed that a coalition was necessary. What was required was a homogeneous team which would work together'. Seemingly inspired by his vision of co-operation, Gandhi went on to urge Wavell to see Nehru and Jinnah together. 'He would advise me [Wavell] to pin them down to make a government and not allow them to leave the room until they had done so. Parity was of no account, nor whether the members belonged to the League or the Congress or anyone; provided they were the best men available.'

However, two days later Gandhi addressed a letter to the Viceroy which seemed to contradict his talk of a coalition. He wrote: 'You must make your choice of one horse or the other. So far as I can see you will never succeed in riding two at the same time. Choose the names submitted either by the Congress or the League. For God's sake do not make an incompatible mixture and in trying to do so produce a fearful explosion'. This letter followed two days of high-pressure activity in which Wavell and his Cabinet colleagues held meeting after meeting with the Indian leaders to try to obtain an acceptable formula for a coalition. Perhaps they should have accepted Gandhi's advice that the two political groups were no longer capable of being yoked in double harness. But the British leaders were still clinging to the twin propositions: no Pakistan, and an equal role for League and Congress in a united India. They persevered with the construction of a government on paper.

When the British leaders next met Gandhi on 16 June he was in favour of their proposals for bridging the gap. A week went by, with the stalemate unresolved. By now Gandhi was participating fully as a Congress decision-maker. It was in this role that he met the Cabinet ministers and the Viceroy on 24 June, accompanied only by Sirdar Patel.

At the morning meeting Gandhi could not speak, as it was his day of silence; so he returned at 8 p.m. in the evening when his lips could utter. The purpose of the British leaders was to insist upon 'grouping' as the essential basis of their scheme. Gandhi still dissented. He said that eminent lawyers agreed with him. 'It was clear that the Delegation were the law-givers and could not interpret their own law. It must be the Federal Court which would interpret the meaning of the statement. . . . The Indian people would have to work this Constituent Assembly which had no statutory existence. It would be a difficult thing to do as the Delegation had created this Statement which had no legal existence. There were bound to be differences of opinion. . . . The Congress, the Muslim League and the British Government used the same terms to mean different things. For example, to the Congress independence meant independence now. To the Delegation it meant independence "when this Charter is passed". But it would only become a Charter if the people went for it and the British Government afterwards legalised the charter.'

On this occasion Gandhi was obviously speaking at the level of the lawyer, and his British listeners might be forgiven for feeling confused. As recently as 12 June, Gandhi had written to Pethick Lawrence, specifically describing himself as a 'detached observer'. Gandhi went on to suggest that if there were a change of government in Britain there might be a change of policy, a suggestion that reveals that Gandhi imagined that negotiations might be drawn out till 1950 when the Labour Government's term of office expired. This was too much for Pethick Lawrence who interrupted Gandhi to observe: 'It was not the practice of British Governments to repudiate definite pledges given by their predecessors. . . . He thought that Mr Gandhi would be the first person to object if the Delegation could only be set up by Act of the British Parliament'.

Although unconvinced, Gandhi lent his weight to endorsing the Cabinet Mission's scheme at the crucial meeting of the All-India Congress at Bombay on 7 July. He now realised that many in the Congress imagined that because the British government was willing to grant independence the cause of freedom had been won. He commented (in *Harijan*) on 'the smug satisfaction that the Congressmen, having suffered imprisonment, have nothing more to do to win freedom, and that a grateful organisation should reward their service by giving them first preference in the matter of elections and officers'. This was his comment on those who had accepted the scheme in order to obtain power; but those who had opposed acceptance arguing that the Congress must *fight* for independence were also rebuked. 'Is independence to be bought at the price of a bloody revolution? . . . They have to tread a very dangerous path in openly making the Congress such an institution. My argument has no force if subterranean activity is a doctrine of universal application. . . . The very thought repels me.'

If Gandhi rejected the office-seekers and the men of force alike, where would he find his true *swarāj*? He knew that 'the Congressmen in general certainly do not know what kind of independence they want. . . . In true democracy, every man and woman is taught to think for himself or herself. How this real revolution can be brought about I do not know except that every reform, like charity, must begin at home'. Once again, Gandhi recognised that there could be no substitute for the long, uncertain and painful path of self-education and self-regeneration which all must tread. India would receive independence long before Indians could attain freedom.

The gap between the immanent and the immediate was horribly revealed by the great Calcutta killing in which more than four thousand perished. Once again in *Harijan* Gandhi drew the lesson, which was as unpalatable to him as to his readers: 'Unfortunately for us we are strangers to the non-violence of the brave [the courage to face death without revenge] on a mass scale. Some even doubt the possibility of the exercise of non-violence by groups, much less by masses of people. They restrict its exercise to exceptional individuals. Mankind can have no use for it, if it is always reserved only for individuals. Be that as it may, this much is clear, that if the people are, probably, not ready for the exercise of non-violence of the brave they must be ready for the use of force in self-defence'.

Gandhi's disillusionment was shared by many, including the Viceroy, who now came to believe that Britain could no longer hold the ring, and must pull out, while still maintaining some control. After visiting Calcutta, Wavell asked Nehru and Gandhi to call on him; they met on the evening of 27 August. Wavell appealed to his visitors to co-operate in re-opening the way to a coalition government by agreement to a formula which would accept the grouping principle until after a constituent assembly had done its work. He asked them to sign the following document:

> The Congress are prepared in the interests of communal harmony to accept the intention of the Statement of May 16th that provinces cannot exercise any option affecting their membership of the sections, or of the groups if formed, until . . . the first general elections have been held.

The two leaders refused to sign the document, and entered into many hours of what V. P. Menon calls 'legalistic arguments'.[9] One can only explain this refusal, on Gandhi's part, by suggesting that for him the 'grouping' formula existed on the level of constitutional law, and not on the level of *satyāgraha*. This was to be Gandhi's last intervention at that level. Without doubt he now realised that he had nothing more to contribute as a lawyer and party leader. Throughout his life he had alternated between periods of involvement in party organisation and policy, in which he dwelt at the centre of public affairs, and other periods in which he turned his back on the leaders and the cities and immersed himself among the little people of the remote countryside. The cycle of participation and withdrawal is seen in the lives of other leaders who combine social action with contemplation; it is most evident in the life of Christ. Now Gandhi quit Delhi for the remote interior of rural Bengal, Noakhali. This did not mean that he abandoned the search for freedom, but that he now expected to find this by entirely different means. And so, when he was asked why he did not concede Pakistan to the League, as no other solution had been found, he replied: 'Only after independence has been won can there be a question of Pakistan. . . . Until and unless India is free, there cannot be any other question.'

When asked, 'Now that there was neither Pakistan nor peace, what would be his solution?' Gandhi made this reply: 'That is exactly what I am here for and what I am trying to find out in Noakhali. The moment I find it I will announce it to the world.'[10]

Gandhi's unavailing search lasted four months, from 6 November 1946 to 2 March 1947. He had been made aware of the fury of Hindu-Muslim hatred, and also of the continuing links which joined members of the warring communities together. On 22 March, the new Viceroy, Lord Mountbatten, arrived in India. He immediately asked to see Gandhi, who was moving among the victims of communal violence in Bihar. Gandhi at once came to Delhi, and met Mountbatten on 31 March. The Viceroy set himself to win Gandhi's confidence; with considerable success, for at subsequent meetings on 1 and 4 April, a plan was produced to overcome the deadlock between Congress and League. It was the successor to the plan which Gandhi had placed before the Cabinet Mission at his first meeting with them. It went even further in trying to create trust by showing trust. 'This plan left the selection of the new Cabinet entirely to Mr Jinnah who could either have Muslim League representatives only, or, if he felt so inclined, Pandit Nehru and other Congress leaders . . . the Congress Party with their majority in the Legislative Assembly was to guarantee to co-operate fairly and sincerely in all matters which the new Cabinet brought forward, and were in the interests of the Indian people as a whole.' Mountbatten was to act as referee or umpire, with power to rule on what were 'the interests of the Indian people'. The Viceroy raised the question as to what would happen on his departure. Gandhi's answer was to speak of C. F. Andrews and his life of service to India. Would Mountbatten be prepared to do the same: to serve, not as a British Viceroy but as the Head of an independent Indian state? Perhaps not surprisingly this proposition astonished the Viceroy. He replied that he could not give an immediate reply, and he asked that Gandhi ensure that any such commitment would be supported by Congress. Gandhi said he sincerely hoped to be able to secure Congress backing, but in a letter dated 11 April he was obliged to report that he had been unable to obtain agreement from the Congress leaders, and so had to withdraw his proposed solution.

Mountbatten then went ahead with his own plan 'designed to place the responsibility of dividing India conspicuously on the Indians themselves'. When Gandhi was invited to meet Mountbatten on 5 May to discuss these proposals he expressed complete disagreement. Once again he called on the Viceroy to turn the whole of India over either to the League or to Congress on the basis of immediate Dominion status. In Mountbatten's view this was a formula for civil war, and he said he was shocked to hear such a suggestion from a man of peace. Gandhi submitted his plan in the form of a note on 10 May:

> There shall be no division of India until the British have left: i.e., it is for the Congress and the League to settle the question, and not for Britain to impose anything.
>
> The Indian Government shall be composed either of Congress, and persons of their choice, or the League, and persons of their choice. The present lack of team-spirit is deplorable.
>
> If you want not to leave a legacy of chaos in the land you must make your choice and make over power of the whole country including the States to one party.

However, Mountbatten had created an impetus, a momentum, which carried both Congress and League forward to the decision to divide the subcontinent. When the Mountbatten plan was announced on 2 June, the Viceroy again saw Gandhi and found him gloomy. Mountbatten, in his breezy way, said his plan was the 'Gandhi Plan', insisting that 'all the salient ingredients, such as leaving the choice of their future to the Indian people themselves, avoiding coercion, and transferring power as soon as possible were suggested by him'. We may doubt whether Gandhi was as sanguine as to accept this argument entire, but when he was asked next day (5 June) if he would undertake a fast against the plan he refused. 'Fasts could not be undertaken out of anger. Anger was a short madness. He must therefore undertake the fast only when the still small voice within him called for it.'

At this time, Gandhi made his apparently quaint comment on Nehru's leadership: 'Jawaharlal cannot be replaced today whilst the charge is being taken from the Englishmen. Jawaharlal, a Harrow boy, a Cambridge graduate, and a barrister, is wanted to carry on the negotiations with Englishmen.' He went on to indicate that when India was free the leader need not know English, but might come from the countryside. Perhaps this was the most explicit statement by Gandhi of his conception of different levels of politics, and the need to adopt different styles to suit the different levels. It also indicated a realisation that Nehru, not he, was the leader for this hour.

As the political leaders rushed forward to receive the transfer of power, Gandhi made some last efforts to arouse his countrymen to the implications of the decisions they were taking. The Indian Army was to be divided between the two new states. Gandhi insisted: 'This creation of two opposing armies out of one, hitherto with one and a common goal (whatever it was) must frighten every lover of India. Will the two armies be created not in order to face and fight a common danger but to destroy one another?' He called upon his countrymen to renounce a future army, thus creating strength out of weakness. Of course, no one listened, and so Gandhi accepted the logic of the decision: if armies were to be retained then one must not quibble if armies were employed in the business of war. Gandhi emphasised that his commitment to non-violence was a personal one: 'Non-violence is my creed. It never was of the Congress. With the Congress, non-violence has always been a policy. A policy takes the shape of a creed while it lasts: no longer.' He concluded: 'If the Congress was pledged to the policy of non-violence then there would be no army supported by it. But she supports an army, which may eat up the civilians and establish military rule in India, unless the people listen to me. . . .'

At the last, Gandhi knew that the people were not listening. Words were not enough; only action would suffice, and this must be the act of sacrifice. Gandhi knew that partition would mean bloodshed. He went to Calcutta, meaning to move on to Noakhali or Punjab or wherever the situation demanded. On 31 August 1947, there was a demonstration against his peace mission. Gandhi's interpretation was that this was a sign and a warning from God: 'The situation calls for sacrifice on the part of top-rankers.' Next day he knew what to do: 'To put [in] an appearance before a yelling crowd does not always work. It certainly did not last night. What my word in person cannot do, my fast may. It may touch the hearts of all the warring elements. . . . I therefore begin fasting from 8.15 tonight, to end only if and when sanity returns to Calcutta. . . .'

The Calcutta fast did restore sanity to Calcutta. The ordinary people responded. But Gandhi's prophecy of the consequence of the Congress and India adopting a system of government and power based upon force was soon realised at the national level. Gandhi announced that such a system must employ its force in order to secure justice from Pakistan in relation to Kashmir. 'In a state run by him there would be no police and no military. But he was not running the Government of the Indian Union. . . . If one party [Pakistan] persisted in wrong-doing . . . the only way left open was that of war.'

However, before long, Gandhi came to believe that the wrong was being done by India as well as Pakistan; and so he entered on his last fast, in order to win over the Indian government to a policy of friendship towards Pakistan and to recreate harmony between all the communities within India. Gandhi's first triumph as a young lawyer was to bring about a conciliation between estranged relatives.[11] His last triumph was to promote concilation between the estranged peoples of the sub-continent: 'I will give unto this last even as unto thee. . . .'

He had ceased to be the leader and organiser of a great political party. He had even ceased to be the leader of the Indian national movement. He devoted his last efforts to warning India of the dangers ahead and of the imperative necessity for moral regeneration. Most great men who live to a ripe age seem to decline into anti-climax. Age diminishes them. If we think of those with whom Gandhi may appropriately be compared— Gladstone, Garibaldi, Tolstoy—we almost wish to draw a veil over their last years. To Gandhi was given a last apocalyptic vision. 'My eyes have now been opened. I see that what we practised during the fight with the British under the name of non-violence was not really non-violence. God had purposely sealed my eyes, as He wanted me to accomplish His great purpose through me. That purpose being accomplished, He has restored my sight.' Gandhi knew that his moral ascendancy had induced the British to grant independence. Independence was the doorway to freedom. As a younger man he had believed in the British Empire, as the vehicle for freedom and justice for all. That belief had died. Now his faith in the Congress as the vehicle died also. 'We must recognise the fact that the social order of our dreams cannot come through the Congress of today. Nobody knows what shape the constitution will ultimately take. I say, leave it to those who are labouring at it. . . .'

Once again, Gandhi affirmed that a non-violent state was a contradiction in terms: then let the party politicians create a constitution fit for party politics! Once again he recognised that the different levels of thought and action could only be reached by responses appropriate to those levels. Gandhi could not hope to influence political movements, or institutions of government. He might make a temporary impression upon people by his own sacrifice through the fast. But for lasting change there could be no substitute for each and every one of the peoples of India making their own discovery: 'It is Swaraj when we learn to rule ourselves.'

If, then, Gandhi had survived one hundred of the one hundred and twenty-five years he once expected to live, he would (I think) have been saddened but not unduly surprised by India in 1969. India has attempted to go forward by means of centralised, *dirigiste* State Socialism. India has piled politicking on top of politics. India has discarded non-violence and strayed perilously near to violence. But Gandhi would have recognised that the present Indian leadership is only capable of operating at these levels. The Gandhian alternative remains, as the level which has been tested and tried only by the Mahatma, Vinoba Bhave, Jayaprakash Narayan, and a few others. It remains—India's great intellectual and moral resource—if India ever decides to draw upon it.

But (understandably, perhaps) India—and the World—adopts towards Gandhi an attitude which implicitly accepts what this essay has tried explicitly to argue: the conception of different levels of thought and action. The World says: 'Holiness is for holy men; for politicians there is politics'. Throughout 1969, the leaders of the World will extol the sayings and actions of the Mahatma: but none will venture to follow his dangerous experiment with truth.[12]

NOTES

[1] The 'official' biography, *Mahatma*, by D. G. Tendulkar, in eight volumes (Delhi), virtually bypasses the constitutional conflict which preceded independence, and Gandhi's part in the debate.

[2] See *Reorientations, Studies on Asia in Transition* (London, 1965), 'Magnificent Failure? The Gandhian Ideal in India', p. 147.

[3] B. S. Sharma, 'The Ideal and the Actual in Gandhi's Philosophy', in G. Ramachandran & T. K. Mahadevan (eds.), *Gandhi, His Relevance for Our Times* (Bombay, 1964), pp. 332-40. I find myself indebted to B. S. Sharma's analysis, though my application of his conception of 'levels' may not be exactly what he intends.

[4] Reproduced in C. H. Philips (ed.), *The Evolution of India and Pakistan, 1858-1947* (London, 1962), p. 223.

5 His plea secured JP's immediate release.

6 In his paraphrase of the meeting, V. P. Menon has Gandhi say: 'If he were not an *irrepressible* optimist. . . .' *The Transfer of Power in India* (Princeton, 1957), p. 240. But the transcript has *irresponsible*. Gandhi employed the expression 'irrepressible optimist' to describe himself on other occasions.

7 The record says 'no basis for argument': was this a Freudian slip? Or an example of Gandhi's rather special style?

8 Sudhir Ghosh, *Gandhi's Emissary* (London, 1967), p. 108.

9 V. P. Menon, *The Transfer of Power in India* (Princeton, 1957), p. 302.

10 In 1936 at a time of political crisis Gandhi had retired to Segaon, not to find a political solution but to find God; but perhaps the search was in both cases for the same goal. (See my essay 'Magnificent Failure? the Gandhian Ideal in India', *Reorientations*, esp. pp. 139-40.) In 1936, Gandhi was able to reconcile his different roles as seeker after truth, nationalist party leader, and lawyer in a correspondence between the search for God and service to humanity. In 1946-47 this reconciliation was beyond him.

11 See M. K. Gandhi, *My Experiments with Truth* (Ahmedabad, 1949), pp. 111-12.

12 In composing this essay I have benefited from discussion with my friend and colleague, Dennis Dalton, and from his paper 'The Theory of Anarchism in Modern India' (forthcoming).

GANDHI AND THE POLITICS OF DECENTRALISATION

Jayaprakash Narayan

Gandhi's political, economic and other ideas are parts of a whole, integrated philosophy of life. Yet Gandhi was not a philosopher in the accepted sense of the word, nor has he left behind him a systematic statement of his thought. He was essentially a man of action, and it was through the adventure of living, his 'experiments' with truth, that he came to formulate ideas that are strewn over thousands of pages of writings, speeches and correspondence. That meant, among other things, that he was ever learning and evolving, and, in the process, ever refining and restating his thoughts. Moreover, his greater experiments were yet to be made—in independent India, when he was to have the opportunity to translate his ideas into practice. But it was just at that moment, when he was perhaps at the threshold of his most creative period, that his life was abruptly cut short by an assassin's bullets. No one who knew him can doubt that in attempting, after independence, to give practical shape to his ideas, he would have modified, innovated and further developed them —keeping perhaps the essentials of his philosophy intact. All of which rather makes it difficult to discuss Gandhi's ideas, particularly those pertaining to politics and economics, because it was precisely in those spheres that his most creative 'experiments' were doubtless going to be made. The essentials of his philosophy, however, do offer a basis for discussion; and a dynamic understanding of them might even help one to relate them to contemporary society.

The essentials of Gandhi's philosophy as related to society and its institutions seem to be centred around his concept of (a) human happiness and development, and (b) the place of man in society and the relationship between the two. Though his *vaishnava* upbringing, reinforced by Jain associations, had inclined him as a boy to belief in non-killing, truthfulness and God, the two great foundations of his mature thought —Truth (or God) and Non-violence (or Love)—came to be developed slowly in the course of the pursuit of his human and social ends. It is all too commonly believed that Truth and Non-violence were Gandhi's *a priori* assumptions—arrived at through a sort of Kantian *a priori* cognition—on which he had built his entire edifice of thought and action. A close study of Gandhi's evolution would hardly support such a view. He had a keenly questioning mind, and hardly ever accepted anything without reason and experience (practice and experimentation). Even the beliefs that he had started with in early life he constantly put to the test of reason and experience and kept on refining and developing them. It was thus that in the course of his inner evolution beginning with a popular faith in God he came to a higher understanding of God being Truth, and finally, of Truth being God. This spiritual journey has led some scholars like D. P. Chattopadhyaya to go so far as to state 'that the ethical contents of Gandhi's thought could be defended without any theistic postulate'.[1]

It was the same with non-violence. It is well-known that in South Africa while he was engaged in his seminal experiments in non-violence, he organised and led a voluntary corps of stretcher-bearers to serve the British side in the Boer War; and on his final return to India he recruited soldiers for the British Indian Army during the last phases of World War I. Even when he had fully developed his philosophy of non-violence, he did not hesitate to emphasise that violence was preferable to cowardice.

Obviously, non-violence was a means and not an end. Man was the end—his material, mental and moral well-being and growth. 'The supreme consideration is man,'[2] he wrote, 'the end to be sought is human happiness combined with full mental and moral growth.'[3] The pursuit of Truth and steadfast adherence to it were not a priori values but were conceived as being essential for the fulfilment of 'the end' as defined above. Happiness and moral growth of the individual were not possible without freedom and equal opportunity for all. This was ideally possible only if both man and society were non-violent. Ideal non-violence may not be possible to reach, but to the extent man and society approach the idea, there will be human happiness and mental and moral development of men.

Having placed man at the centre of society, how did Gandhi conceive of their inter-relationship? This is a problem that neither the individualism of the West nor the collectivism of the East has yet been able to resolve. Gandhi tried to resolve it by introducing a moral solvent, that is to say, by assigning mutual moral responsibilities to both. While the well-being of the individual was a social aim, the well-being of society too was to be assured. In Gandhi's concept of society, both were inter-dependent. Neither was society to grow at the cost of the individual nor the individual at the cost of other members of society. 'Unrestricted individualism' he condemned as 'the law of the beast of the jungle.'[4] While the individual was entitled to complete freedom, he must learn to discipline himself so as not only not to infringe the freedom of others, but also to be of service and benefit to his fellowmen and the community at large. 'Willing submission to social restraint for the sake of the well-being of the whole society enriches both the individual and the society of which one is a member.'[5] Society, on the other hand, must work ceaselessly for the well-being of the individual, fully respecting his human rights and treating him as a human person. According to the collectivist philosophy, organized society has the right, in the professed interest of man, to treat the individual as it likes—murder him, suppress his freedoms, use him as a pawn or a mere animal. To Gandhi, that was an obnoxious and immoral doctrine. In a famous passage envisioning his picture of the future world society as made up of 'ever-widening, never-ascending circles' of communities, he wrote: 'it [the world society of men] will be an oceanic circle whose centre will be the individual, always ready to perish for the village, the latter ready to perish for the circle of villages, till at last the whole becomes one life composed of individuals never aggressive in their arrogance, but ever humble, sharing the majesty of the oceanic circle of which they are integral units.'[6] Aware that this concept might be brushed aside as utopian, he added: 'I may be taunted that . . . this is all utopian and therefore not worth a single thought. If Euclid's point, though incapable of being drawn by any human agency, has an imperishable value, my picture has its own for mankind. . . .'[7]

If Gandhi's moral solution of the problem of individual versus society is rejected as impractical, one wonders if there can be any other solution possible. Perhaps a complete solution will never be possible, but to the extent man and society develop morally, individual and social interest and well-being will coincide. The key to such coincidence lies in Gandhi's method of social change and reconstruction through truth and non-violence. But more of this later on.

Here then is the rationale of Gandhi's non-violence, of his political, economic and social ideas, the key to his attitude towards the question of power, the question of organisation of work, and the question of community. He believed that the human and social ends that he had set before himself could best be achieved in a non-violent society in which there is a thoroughgoing decentralisation of power and of production and control of wealth, and which is composed of comparatively small autonomous communities, willingly federated and co-operating together. He said, 'centralisation as a system is inconsistent with the non-violent structure of society',[8] because 'centralisation cannot be sustained and defended without adequate force'.[9] It is reasonable to suppose that had it been demonstrated to Gandhi that centralisation also, under a different system, could lead to the fulfilment of his objectives, he would have withdrawn his objection to it. Hitherto, no kind of centralised system can be found to have done that.

Gandhi was deeply suspicious of the State. 'The State represents violence in a concentrated and organised form. The individual has a soul but the State is a soulless machine, it can never be weaned away from violence to which it owes its very existence.'[10] Discussing his theory of trusteeship in relation to private property, he remarked: 'I look upon an increase in the power of the State with the greatest fear, because while apparently doing good by minimising exploitation, it does the greatest harm to mankind by destroying individuality, which lies at the root of all progress. We know of so many cases when men have adopted trusteeship, but none where the State has really lived for the poor.'[11]

Naturally, the ideal society according to Gandhi is a stateless democracy where social life is so developed as to have become self-regulated. He wrote: 'Political power means capacity to regulate national life through national representatives. If national life becomes so perfect as to become self-regulated, no representation is necessary.'[12] In such a society of what he called enlightened anarchy, 'everyone is his own ruler. *He rules himself* [emphasis added] in such a manner that he is never a hindrance to his neighbour. In the ideal state, therefore, there is no political power because there is no State.'[13] Elsewhere he expresses the same thought thus: 'Swaraj [self-government] of a people means the sum total of the swaraj of individuals.'[14]

Believing that means are ends, that every present step taken rightly will automatically lead to the distant goal, Gandhi refused to draw any blueprint of the future. He wrote in 1929: '. . . we do not know our distant goal. It will be determined not by our definitions but by our acts, voluntary and involuntary. If we are wise, we will take care of the present and the future will take care of itself.'[15] Again, 'I cannot say in advance what the Government based wholly on non-violence will be like.'[16]

However, Gandhi was realist enough to admit that the completely non-violent and stateless society might never be established because everyone in society might not reach the requisite level of moral development. Therefore he conceded that 'A government cannot succeed in becoming entirely non-violent because it represents all the people. I do not today conceive of such a golden age. But I do believe in the possibility of a predominantly non-violent society.'[17] While he thought it possible for non-violence to be so widely accepted and practised in a society that it can dispense with its army, it may not be able to do the same with its police. But he thought that in such a society the police would be of a 'wholly different pattern from the present-day police force. Its ranks will be composed of believers in non-violence. . . . The police force will have some kind of arms, but they will be rarely used if at all,' because there will be 'ever-decreasing disturbances' and policemen will be 'reformers' and 'servants' of the people who will give them 'instinctive' co-operation.[18]

Even this realism of Gandhi appears to be too idealistic. It would be rash, however, to dismiss him as a dreamer. Gandhi was nothing if not practical, and throughout his life he put into practice what he preached, and with as reasonable a success as perhaps was possible in an imperfect world. For more than a quarter of a century he dominated the Indian scene, drew the attention and respect of the world, converted many of his critics and detractors and silenced many others, not by virtue of his queer ideas, howsoever persistently put forth, but because he succeeded in putting those ideas into practice on a most impressive and effective scale. After independence, though most of his time and energy was taken up with healing the wounds of the partition of India, he wrote and said enough at that time to indicate that the broad outlines of his future plan of action were fairly clear in his mind.

Gandhi's ideas of decentralisation are usually brushed aside as being irrelevant to the modern technological society. Whether one considers Gandhi relevant or not depends very much on what one wants, what values one holds dear. If one has the same human concerns as Gandhi had, then instead of dismissing him one should seriously set about to enquire how in the context of modern technology and centralisation those concerns could be fulfilled. Technology is not a force of nature that man cannot control. Man can surely bend technology to his purpose. That is what Gandhi had meant when he said that he was not against the machine, but he did not want it to become the master of man (as, in fact, it has become in modern society). Surely, the advancement of the social and physical sciences has at last made it possible now for society to determine its destiny. Today most of mankind, particularly in the most developed countries, is at the mercy of a few feverishly competing national and international giant business concerns. Even the 'socialist' countries are not immune to this self-driven competition. Why should men remain helpless victims of this process?

While the motivations behind the recent abortive uprising of students and workers in France were rather complex, there is no doubt that a prominent one among them was a profound dissatisfaction with this process. One of the revolutionary leaders, Alain Geismar, a university teacher, when asked to define the aim of the revolution, described it as being 'workers' control and decentralisation. . . .'[19] Technologically, France is one of the most modern countries of the West, and if French intellectuals, without any Gandhian inspiration, consider decentralisation not only desirable but also practicable, these ideas cannot be brushed aside as the product of a backward society.

In a most valuable study of a pioneering effort towards a new industrial order, The Scott Bader Commonwealth of England, Dr Fred Blum, while pointing out that meaningful participation and human relations in industry were possible only in comparatively small units of production, says: 'At present size is not primarily the result of the desire to use the "best" methods of production. Most of the giants of industry consist of smaller production units which are combined for financial-power reasons. Technology, furthermore, can be used to make smaller production units viable and not only to make bigger production units bigger. . . . Once we have understood that technology is not the basic factor determining size we get a new basis for examining the relationships between meaningful participation and the size of an organization. . . . The truth is that the forces now determining our economy—including the forces making for increased concentration—are the reflection of a power and value structure which is incompatible with the true nature and destiny of man.'[20]

One of the most interesting pieces of Gandhi literature is Louis Fischer's *A Week With Gandhi*. That was just two months prior to what came to be known as the 'Quit India' movement, Gandhi's last peaceful campaign against British rule. Fischer was trying to get Gandhi to elucidate his picture of the new order. Fischer asked: '. . . will you help me to see the new order you speak of?' Gandhi replied: 'You see the centre of power now is in New Delhi, or in Calcutta and Bombay, in the big cities. I would have it distributed among the seven hundred thousand villages of India.'[21] But it is remarkable that when India became independent, largely due to his leadership, and a Constituent Assembly was convened to frame its Constitution, Gandhi hardly evinced any interest in its proceedings. When a correspondent drew his attention to the fact that his basic idea of village government had not been even mentioned in the Assembly, he wrote in his weekly journal just forty days before his death: 'I must confess that I have not been able to follow the proceedings of the Constituent Assembly . . . [the correspondent] says that there is no mention or direction about village panchayats and decentralisation in the foreshadowed Constitution. It is certainly an omission calling for immediate attention if our independence is to reflect the people's views. The greater the powers of the panchayats, the better for the people.'[22] After Gandhi's death, though there was a clause added to the 'Directive Principles' to the effect that the State should take steps to establish village *panchāyats* as 'units of self-government', the Constitution of India cannot be called Gandhian in any respect. Nor are the village *panchāyats*, established later, even a pale reflection of Gandhi's *grām-rāj* (village government). Gandhi's indifference to the Constituent Assembly might have been due to his feeling that the constitutional framework of a polity that was to be built up from below could more realistically be written by the people's deeds than in the words of constitutional lawyers.

As the village is so basic to Gandhi's polity, it is necessary to understand his meaning of it. The village to him was a 'manageable small group of people', constituting a 'unit of society'. Elsewhere he wrote, 'My imaginary village consists of 1000 souls'.[23] Vinoba Bhave, founder of the *bhoodān-grāmdān* movement, speaks of human society being 'organised on the basis of small village communities of, say, 2 to 3 thousand souls'.[24] Conceivably they could be much larger in a society of a higher technological level, providing better communication facilities. Characteristically, the Gandhian village is a primary community, large enough to offer a diversified life and small enough to generate and sustain a sense of community.

Two further points of clarification. As Gandhi's village was to be a self-governing autonomous community, he considered it necessary that it should be self-sufficient in the matter of its 'vital necessities'—food, clothing, shelter. (Self-sufficiency in these matters was necessary for another important reason too: economic decentralisation, conceived as a measure to prevent concentration of wealth and economic power). Secondly, Gandhi's village was not an exclusively agricultural community; there had to be a balance between agriculture and village industries. Had he been alive now, he might have called it an agro-industrial community. In an unrecorded conversation with one of his co-workers (now Governor of Andhra Pradesh), he spoke of 'urbanising' the villages and 'ruralising' the towns and cities.

With this concept of the village before us, we are ready to look at one of Gandhi's rare descriptions of village self-government:

> My idea of village swaraj (self-government) is that it is a complete republic, independent of its neighbours for its vital wants, and yet interdependent for many others in which dependence is a necessity. Thus every village's first concern will be to grow its own food crops and cotton for its cloth. It should have a reserve for its cattle,

recreation and playground for adults and children. Then if there is more land available, it will grow useful money crops. . . . It will have its own waterworks ensuring clean water supply. . . . As far as possible every activity will be conducted on a co-operative basis. There will be no castes such as we have today with their graded untouchability. Non-violence with its technique of Satyagraha (non-violent resistance) and non-co-operation will be the sanction of the village community. There will be a compulsory service of village guards, who will be selected by rotation from the register maintained by the village. The government of the village will be conducted by the *Panchayat* of five persons annually elected by the adult villagers, male and female, possessing minimum prescribed qualifications. These will have all the authority and jurisdiction required. Since there will be no system of punishments in the accepted sense, this *Panchayat* will be the legislature, judiciary and executive combined to operate for its year of office.[25]

There are a few things about this vision that strike one immediately. Those acquainted with the Indian scene will see at once what a far cry Gandhi's picture is from present realities even after twenty-two years of freedom and seventeen years of official community development programmes. But the most extraordinary thing about it is the large measure of political power, reinforced with the sanction of non-violent opposition, that Gandhi visualised for the village community. Even more interesting than the large measure of power is the fact that it was not conceived as something handed down from above. Gandhi believed that the people, who in *theory* are supposed to be sovereign, shall acquire power in *reality* by just being able to manage their affairs themselves—of course, within the limitation of their resources.

A remarkable fact of Indian socio-political history is that throughout the historical period the Indian village was able, in some measure or the other, to manage its affairs independently of the central authority. In fact, during certain periods, when the central authority over large areas had practically ceased on account of invasion or internal war, the only thing stable in Indian society was village self-government. This condition was drastically altered, by deliberate design of the British, so that by the time India won freedom, the villages had lost all traditions of corporate life and independence, and had become abjectly dependent upon the Government above.

Gandhi was alone among the national leaders of India at independence to realise this; and believing as he did in power at the ground-level, he not only showed almost complete indifference to power at the top, except perhaps to see that it was held by friendly hands, but also set about—despite his intense preoccupation with post-partition problems—the task of building India's polity from below. This is evident, first, from the manner in which he formulated his post-independent objectives. In his last piece of writing, described in his *Last Will and Testament* (drafted on the very eve of his martyrdom), he said that while India had won political independence, it still had to achieve 'social, moral and economic independence in terms of its seven hundred thousand villages'.[26] Another rather conclusive piece of evidence is the organisational proposal that he had set forth in that very document, namely, the transformation of the Indian National Congress from a political organisation into one devoted to the service of the people. The significance of this proposal can be properly understood only in the light of Gandhi's method of non-violent social revolution and reconstruction.

Until the success of Gandhi's non-violent national revolution in India, all revolutions in history had been brought about by violence. The methods of violent revolution are fairly well understood, but not so the non-violent method. The most important characteristic of this method is that its means must be in harmony with its ends. If the end is a non-violent society, the means also must be non-violent; if human freedom is the end, coercive means (except moral coercion) are ruled out; if man is an end in himself, he cannot be used as a means; if truth is to be the basis of the new life, untruthful means are inadmissable; if the end is dispersal of power, the means cannot be centralised power, etc., etc.

Among other elements of the method are (a) conversion by persuasion of individuals and groups to new ways of thought and action; (b) a programme of 'constructive work' designed to serve and help the people and to act as a medium through which to touch their hearts and minds; (c) non-violent non-co-operation and resistance when necessary; (d) raising a band of properly trained volunteers committed to non-violence and selfless service to the people, to act as the conscious cadres of the revolution. Just as a violent revolution changes society through the direct action of the people, so too the non-violent revolution. Regularisation by law, in both cases, *follows* after. The difference is that while in a violent revolution the old society is destroyed in one sweep and the new built slowly brick by brick, in a non-violent revolution change of the old and construction of the new both proceed side by side and step by step.

Gandhi did not live to launch his process of social revolution. After Gandhi his political followers, almost to a man, turned their backs upon his ideas and his vision of a new India. The reason seems to have been that they had accepted non-violence only as a political expedient, rather than as a philosophy of life. The result is that India, instead of contributing something fresh to modern civilisation, is floundering in a welter of pale imitations of western capitalism, socialism and communism. The only mitigating factor is Vinoba Bhave's *bhoodān-grāmdān* movement, about which space does not permit one to say much here. *Bhoodān* was not just redistribution of land but also introduction of some new values into society. *Grāmdān* is carrying the process forward. It is trying to establish the principle of community ownership of land, of regular sharing of labour and income in the community, and of decision-making by general consensus. Fulfilment of the *grāmdān* programme will lead, on the moral plane, to ever-growing coincidence between individual and social interests; on the political plane, to direct democracy in a self-governing community; on the economic plane, to community planning and endeavour.

Over a hundred thousand villages out of a total 556,000 in the country have already accepted *grāmdān*. Their acceptance, however, is only a declaration of intent; implementation is to follow. Such are the beginnings of a non-violent social revolution in India, including those of a new polity—the polity of dispersal of power, of power to the people. The strength of this polity is proportionate to the strength of non-violence in society.

The relevance of non-violence to what one may call the polity of the people becomes obvious when we take a look at the experience of violent revolutions. 'Power to the people' has been the slogan of so many of the modern revolutions of history. Yet, because they were all born in violence, it happened invariably that those who succeeded in taking hold of the means of organised violence usurped power for themselves, protesting no doubt that they were doing so in the name of the people and for the good of the people. Not that these revolutionary leaders were frauds and charlatans. They were only working out the logic of violence. It is nearly two centuries since the Great French Revolution. Yet the French revolutionaries of the present day are still crying for 'power at the level of the work-place . . . whether these workers be students, academics, industrial labourers or even peasants'.[27] Lenin marched to power on the crest of the slogan 'all power to the Soviets'. Soviet Russia is a super-power today, but the soviets of workers', peasants' and soldiers' deputies have no power, if they exist at all. In China the high-priest of ideology has himself ordained that power shall reside in the barrel of a gun; and it is not the people who hold the guns. 'Power to the People' is an empty and mocking slogan without non-violence and thoroughgoing decentralisation.

India's parliamentary democracy, despite its many faults, has proved to be a much greater success than was expected. It has shown far greater strength than the many democracies in the newly freed countries of Asia and Africa. This success becomes the more striking when one takes into account the vast population of the country, its mass illiteracy, its bewildering diversities of language, religion, caste and regional histories. Consider also the fact that it has been able to withstand the shock of Nehru's death and that of Shastri's soon after, as well as the shocks of two wars—withal shortlived—with China and Pakistan, and two severe droughts on top of rising prices, mass poverty and unemployment, and unconscionable economic disparities and social disabilities (as for the scheduled castes).

It may not be irrelevant to probe into the sources of the strength and stability of India's democracy. The major contributing factor, to my mind, was certainly the peaceful character of the mass movements for freedom led by Gandhi. There is no doubt that had there been a violent revolution, power would have passed into the hands of the army (the new revolutionary or people's army) or of those who had the army behind them. A sort of 'other side of the coin' of the peaceful campaigns was the emergence, again under Gandhi's active leadership, of a mass political organisation, with its roots running deep into the Indian soil, that was able to provide stability to the political system during the initial uncertain years. Another significant source of the strength of Indian democracy and its stability lies in the very nature of that democracy. Experience has shown that in spite of all drawbacks the Indian political system does provide a genuine and credible outlet for mass disaffection and desire for change. The reality and extent of the political and civic freedoms allowed by the Indian Constitution can be judged from the fact that a recently formed party of Indian Maoists, the Communist Party of India (Marxist-Leninist), is able openly to denounce parliamentary methods and preach armed insurrection! The demand for banning this party has been successfully resisted so far by the left parties (including the socialists and communists) on the ground that political opposition and vanquishment was a far better remedy than legal suppression.

Since the break-up of the Congress party's monopoly in the 1967 general election anxiety has been expressed about the future of the Indian system. The cause for anxiety is certainly real, but there is enough flexibility in the system and good sense in the country so that a political collapse is not likely to happen. The factors of regionalism, 'linguism', caste, etc. are prone to be exaggerated. They are certainly there, but mutual adjustments and reconciliation are taking place all the time. There also seems to be a reasonable possibility now of steady economic growth.

While in the respects discussed above Indian democracy is fairly satisfactory, examined from the Gandhian stand-point of power to the people, dispersal of power, participation, direct democracy, communitarian representation, etc., it is highly unsatisfactory. Moreover, the political climate today is far more unfavourable than, let us say, in Nehru's days. During that time a certain scheme of 'democratic decentralisation', known as *Panchāyati Rāj*, had been initiated, handing down certain developmental functions and privileges to elected bodies at the district, (community development) block and village *panchāyat* levels. But partly due to the highly centralised administrative system inherited from the British and still preserved, and partly due to the reluctance of political bosses (no matter of what party) at the State levels, the scheme, though established in form, has hardly got off the ground. Urban local government too, even in the great cities of Calcutta and Bombay, has only minimal powers, as compared to the municipalities of the West. Power still remains confined to New Delhi and the State capitals.

Except for the Gandhians, led by Vinoba Bhave, and a rather small but intellectually able and active group, known as 'radical humanists' (associates and followers of the late M. N. Roy—the famous international revolutionary and thinker and one-time collaborator of Lenin), hardly anyone in India is raising the fundamental questions about power and democracy that had been posed by Gandhi and by Roy.

Had not the hoary institution of village government that had survived until the beginning of British rule been destroyed in order to strengthen the roots of imperialism, the situation might have been very different today. But the situation being what it is, Gandhi's polity, which Vinoba has called the 'polity of the people' or *Lokniti*, will receive no more than polite mention. Nor would it be possible, in the absence of the foundation, to draw a realistic and convincing picture of the super-structure of this polity. Gandhi himself did not venture to do so. In fact, that would have been contrary to his whole way of thinking. Having a dynamic view of society, and believing that means determined ends, he was averse to drawing any blue-prints of the future.

Accordingly, there is little to go by as regards Gandhi's picture of Indian polity beyond village government. There is his picture of ever-widening, never ascending circles of communities; his statement that there will be 'voluntary co-operation' between the thousands of self-governing village units; there is a brief reference in his speech at the Round Table Conference to an indirectly elected structure. According to Gandhi, 'seven hundred thousand villages of India will be organised according to the will of their citizens, all of them voting. These villages, each having one vote, will elect their district administrators. The district administrations will elect provincial administrations, which in turn will elect a president who will be the national chief executive'.[28] It also appears that Gandhi wanted the representatives of the people to be removable at the will of the people; he was opposed to special representation of interests; he did not consider a majority decision to be sacrosanct and upheld the right of the minority—even the individual—to dissent; he thought a consensus of opinion in certain matters to be advisable.

That is about all that we have. It is reasonable to assume that he would have made many changes in this very sketchy and tentative system. One thing, however, seems to be certain: his political structure would have been based on organised communities rather than the amorphous mass of disparate individual voters. It also seems to be certain that in his decentralised and self-regulated order, there would have been no place for power-seeking political parties, though enough place for different schools of political thought. To Gandhi, party power and people's power could not but have appeared to be mutually contradictory.

Lest it should be overlooked, it is necessary once again to point out that Gandhi's political system is only a part of a whole, and cannot come into existence or survive without the rest. It requires the development of non-violence among the people; an economic order that is just and humane and, therefore, decentralised; a society that is made up largely of small communities. Without concurrent development along all these lines, Gandhi's polity would be an impossibility.

Reference has been made in a previous section to the *grāmdān* movement. So far, as was mentioned there, there are only declarations of intent. When, in the next stage of the movement, the intent begins to be carried out, the foundations of Gandhi's polity will begin to be laid down. Wherever the movement is reasonably well advanced, the contours of a new political system are already taking shape. There is talk, for instance, and some planning about *grām sabhās* (village assemblies) electing their delegates to constituency-wise councils, which shall set up candidates, conduct elections and act as links between the elected representatives on the one hand and the village assemblies on the other. It will be these councils of village delegates who will hear reports from the elected

249

representatives and give them guidance and keep them in touch with the opinions of the villages and their needs and problems. Taking the matter a step forward, there is already some discussion as to the functioning of the legislature and the government at the State level. It is too early yet to think of the Parliament and the Central government. Thus it is possible to hope that Gandhi's vision of democracy might yet rise from the soil.

NOTES

[1] From an unpublished seminar paper.

[2] *Young India*, 13 November 1924, p. 378.

[3] *Harijan*, 18 January 1942, p. 5. Happiness certainly included material well-being. Gandhi, though himself a 'half-naked fakir', did not idealise poverty, though he considered self-control and voluntary limitation of wants to be essential for human happiness and social justice. He said, 'Everyone must have a balanced diet, a decent house to live in, facilities for education for one's children and adequate medical relief'. (*Harijan*, 31 March 1946). These are objectives which have yet to be achieved—for *everyone*—even in the most prosperous societies.

[4] *Harijan*, 27 May 1939, p. 144.   [5] *Ibid*.

[6] *Harijan*, 28 July 1946, p. 236.   [7] *Ibid*.

[8] *Harijan*, 18 January 1942, p. 5.   [9] *Harijan*, 30 December 1939, p. 391.

[10] N. K. Bose, *Studies in Gandhism* (Calcutta, 1962), pp. 202-04.

[11] *Ibid.*, p. 204.   [12] *Young India*, 2 July 1931, p. 162.

[13] *Ibid*.   [14] *Harijan*, 25 March 1939.

[15] *Young India*, vol. 3, p. 547. 'They say means are after all means. I would say means are after all everything. As the means, so the end. There is no wall of separation between means and end. Indeed, the Creator has given us control (and that too very limited) over means, none over the end. Realisation of the goal is in exact proportion to that of the means. This is a proposition that admits of no exception.' N. K. Bose, *Selections from Gandhi*, (Ahmedabad, 1957), p. 37.

[16] *Harijan*, 11 February 1939, p. 8.   [17] *Harijan*, 9 March 1949, p. 31.

[18] Mahadev Desai, *The Diaries* (Ahmedabad, 1953), vol. I, p. 276.

[19] Alain Geismar of the National Union of Higher Education (*SNESup*) in Herne Bourges and B. R. Brester (eds.), *Student Revolt* (London, 1968).

[20] Fred H. Blum, *Work and Community* (London, 1968), p. 360.

[21] Louis Fischer, *A Week with Gandhi* (New York, 1942).

[22] *Harijan*, 21 December 1947.

[23] *Harijan*, 4 August 1946.

[24] *Bhoodan*, 8 September 1962.

[25] *Harijan*, 26 July 1942, p. 238.

[26] Pyarelal, *Mahatma Gandhi, the Last Phase* (New Delhi, 1966), vol. 2, Appendix B, p. 819.

[27] Bourges and Brester, *Student Revolt*, op. cit., pp. 54-55.

[28] G. N. Dhawan, *The Political Philosophy of Mahatma Gandhi* (Ahmedabad, 1967), p. 298.

ASPECTS OF GANDHIAN ECONOMIC THOUGHT

Amlan Datta

I have never made a fetish of consistency. . . . A careful eye would notice a gradual and imperceptible evolution. I have grown from truth to truth. — M. K. Gandhi.

Gandhian thought has been called utopian. But utopias, in correcting reality, are determined by what they attempt to correct. The significance of Gandhi's economic thought cannot be properly understood except in the context of the reality of which it was an inverted image.

I

In the development of capitalism, it is usual to make a distinction between two phases. In the earlier phase, sometimes called mercantile capitalism, production is still organized by and large on a household basis, but the producers work increasingly according to the orders of a growing merchant class and become dependent on that class. In the next phase, production takes place typically in factories and the era of large-scale production dawns. In India these two phases, which often overlap, developed in a special historical context and formed the background to Gandhian economic thought.

Let us recall a few salient features of a pre-industrial society. The village is the basis of such a society. Although agriculture is the main occupation of the people, there is a certain balance between agriculture and household or cottage industry, which is essential for the stability of the economic and social structure of the village. The products of cottage industry are partly sold on the city markets but largely consumed in the village itself. Even when they are produced for city people, the tastes they cater for are traditional and not subject to great fluctuations and the methods of production are also relatively fixed. The consumption needs of the village itself are limited. Finally, since production is carried out by family members largely for their own use and according to a long established pattern, there is very little of that sense of constraint and 'alienation' which arises when people have to submit to a will which is

251

not their own. There is a natural solidarity in the family and submission to its will is not felt as an abridgement of one's freedom.

Merchant capital tries to bend household production to the requirements of distant markets. The producers themselves are ignorant of the state of demand in these markets. In a period of industrial transition, market conditions continuously change and the basis of the traditional concept of 'just price' is knocked off. The merchant is goaded on by new opportunities of profit to bring the smaller producer increasingly under his subjection so as to secure from the latter what the former calculates to be most profitable. The small producer becomes dependent on the merchant for supply of credit, raw materials and instruments of production. The use of physical force is also not unknown. This whole drama was enacted with peculiar cruelty by the servants of the English East India Company in Bengal. This province had for long been known for the fine fabrics, cotton and silk, which its artisans produced and which found a market far beyond its borders. The Company brought to this trade a rapaciousness and freedom from the restraints of tradition such as was unknown before.[1] In order to ensure a regular supply of the desired commodities, merchants entered into forward contracts with Bengal weavers, forcing them, often on pain of flogging, to sign bonds and make deliveries of stipulated quantities of goods at unjust prices. The memory of this experience lingered long after the event.

In the Gandhian conception of *swarāj*, that is self-rule, the village occupies a central place and local self-sufficiency is regarded as essential. Beyond a point production for distant markets cannot develop further without exposing the village to the risk of being controlled by outsiders, that is, by people who are not bound by rules of good neighbourliness in relation to the village community. This is a situation which the Gandhian dreads and which he considers to be fatal to freedom, since freedom for him is but submission to the rules of good neighbourliness. But this is a matter to which we can come back later. In the meantime, let us pursue a little further our account of the economic background to Gandhian thought.

Till the Napoleonic wars India was chiefly an exporter of textiles. But already from the beginning of the eighteenth century British Parliament had adopted measures to discourage the use of Indian textiles in England. What the English East India Company sent out from India was often meant for re-export to other European countries. The cotton industry in England grew behind a tariff wall. Towards the end of the century the techniques of production in British textiles were revolutionised by a series of epoch-making inventions. In the nineteenth century the technological superiority of the British textile industry was unquestionable, and India became a net importer of cotton goods from Lancashire. The traditional cotton industry in India had already been disorganized by the extortionate methods of the servants of the East India Company, and before it could reorganize itself it was again crippled by the competition of cheaper goods from abroad. In the second half of the nineteenth century India set up a few cotton mills of her own and by the 1920's her mills were producing more cloth than her handlooms. Thus, a very important village industry declined upsetting the balance of India's rural economy.

There is a special point to note in this connection. In the fifty years from 1881 to 1931 a certain amount of industrialization along modern lines took place in India. The construction of railways was a notable event and the total railway mileage which was rather less than ten thousand in 1881 exceeded thirty thousand in 1913-14. This stimulated the growth of a number of other industries. The output of coal, for instance, increased from only about one million tons in 1880 to over twenty million tons in 1925. After a few abortive attempts, the foundations of a modern iron and steel industry were laid in India early in the present century. A reference has already been made above to the growth of the modern sector of the textile industry in India. But surprisingly the census figure for the number of workers employed in manufacture, mining and construction declined from 21.1 million in 1881 to 12.9 million in 1931. The lower figure for 1931 is not to be accounted for by the world-wide business depression of that date, since the Great Depression did not affect the Indian economy in the way it did the industrially developed countries. It is true that the census figures quoted above are not accurate. Indeed, they are possibly widely wrong, the data relating to the female component of the total working force being particularly unreliable and certain changes in the classification of occupations making a direct comparison of the figures of 1881 and 1931 hardly tenable. But allowing for a wide margin of error, it still seems safe to conclude that the proportion of the working force engaged in industry did not increase over the period noted above. Indeed, Indian nationalists spoke of a process of 'de-industrialization' during those decades; and so eminent an economist as Colin Clark observed that 'there was a really marked increase in the proportion engaged in agriculture between 1881 and 1911 and the proportion has been virtually stationary since that date'.[2] The main point here is that while the modern sector of industry expanded the traditional sector declined, and it seems possible that in terms of total employment the net effect of the adoption of modern technology was not very positive. In any case, the idea that modern technology creates unemployment has become an important component of Gandhian economic thought.

Gandhi wrote: 'I have no partiality for return to the primitive methods of grinding and husking for the sake of them. I suggest the return, because there is no other way of giving employment to the millions of villagers who are living in idleness.'[3] Again, replying to a question whether he was against all machines, he said: 'What I object to is the craze for machinery, not machinery as such. The craze is for what they call labour-saving machinery. Men go on "saving labour" till thousands are without work.'[4] It is in the same spirit that he recommended the use of the *charkhā* or the spinning wheel. In 1946, not long before his death, Gandhi said: 'Khadi [hand-spun cloth] will cease to have any value in my eyes if it does not usefully employ the millions.'[5]

One may feel tempted to criticise Gandhi on the ground that he generalised from a very special experience. The disintegration of cottage industry in India might have thrown labour out of employment faster than the factories could absorb. But does it not mean that what is needed is an even more massive programme of industrialization? In the West at any rate the gloomy prophecies of some nineteenth century critics of capitalism have not come true and the progress of industralization has not been accompanied by any longterm trend towards increased unemployment. In the Soviet Union since 1930 labour shortage has been more in evidence than mass unemployment.

Yet there is a core of truth in Gandhian thought that can stand up to this line of criticism. Western technology today has a labour-saving bias. In India and a number of other underdeveloped countries, the basic ratios between the available stock of capital and the existing supply of labour are far more unfavourable than they are or perhaps ever were in the industrially developed countries. The underdeveloped countries today must evolve methods of production suited to their own resource endowments.[6] Indiscriminate adoption of advanced Western technology in these countries will almost certainly produce more unemployment than is either safe or good for them. This is all the more true because the rate of growth of population in these countries is faster than it is among the richer nations of the world. While economists have often thought in terms of maximising production, Gandhi stressed the importance of providing the maximum number of people with productive work. Just as people must have bread so they need work; and even if it were possible to provide them with the one without the other, it would be unwise to do so. 'Our real malady,' Gandhi once said, 'is not destitution but laziness.' Nothing was more corroding than enforced idleness.

There is another aspect of India's experience of economic development which needs to be related to Gandhian thought. The cities which grew up as a result of the British impact on India conferred little positive benefit on the seven hundred thousand villages in the Indian sub-continent. The point is worth developing at some length. In England the towns and the country had developed through a kind of symbiotic relation. Eighteenth century political economists noted this carefully and, indeed, wrote about it at some length. Thus, Adam Smith had a whole chapter in the *Wealth of Nations* to which he gave the significant title 'How the Commerce of the Towns contributed to the Improvement of the Country.'[7] A similar proposition would hold true of other European countries, such as, Holland. But when the British and Dutch traders established commercial relations with countries in the East, the relation between the new centres of commerce and the country turned out to be notably different. A Dutch economist, J. H. Boeke, has recently described this phenomenon under the title of the Dual Society.[8] The Dual Economy consists of a modern sector, brought into existence by contact with foreign traders, and a traditional sector, which leads a life independent of or largely unaffected by the other sector. The modern sector has no pervasive modernizing effect on the economy as a whole.

Indeed, the actual situation is, in some respects, even worse. The city attracts to itself talent, capital and other resources from the rest of the country. By ruining old handicrafts, it upsets the natural balance between agriculture and village industry. People with qualities of enterprise and leadership move to the city and seldom go back to villages to improve the land. They become absentee landlords. Rural society is robbed of its potentially more progressive leaders; its economic life is disorganized; and social cohesion is steadily undermined. The city afflicts the country with a peculiar sickness.[9]

This is what Gandhi observed in India. On this basis he enunciated what may be called a theory of colonial exploitation which stands in contrast to the usual theory accepted by nationalists as well as Marxists. To the typical nationalist the British exploitation of India is at the basis of India's poverty. The British nation as a whole profited from the exploitation of the colonies. Even the British working class was enriched by the drain of wealth from the colonies to the mother country or the metropolis. Gandhi looked at the matter from a different angle. It is the city which exploits and the villages that are exploited. Wealth flows from the country to the city. This is at variance with the usual Marxist theory that the capitalist class exploits the proletariat. In the city the capitalists, people in the liberal professions and in the administration, and even the industrial working class live at a higher standard of living than the average for the rural masses, and it is the exploitation of the villages that makes this possible. To Gandhi the struggle to liberate colonies from imperialist domination appeared as part of a larger struggle to liberate villages from the oppression of those overgrown centres of power and wealth that are the cities.

Let us gather together the threads of the argument. Industrialization means large-scale production, competition and production for distant markets. It is accompanied by the 'de-industrialization' of rural areas and concentration of wealth and power in the cities. It leads inevitably to the exploitation of the village by the city. Gandhi was opposed to industrialization because and in so far as it has these consequences; and the same is true of his opposition to machines. As Gandhi himself explained in reply to a question by Maurice Frydman, 'Industrialization on a mass scale will necessarily lead to passive or active exploitation of the villages, as the problems of competition and marketing come in. Therefore, we have to concentrate on the village being self-contained, manufacturing mainly for use. Provided this character of the village industry is maintained, there would be no objection to villages using even modern machines and tools that they can make and can afford to use.'[10]

II

A sympathetic critique of Gandhi's economic thought can be developed along the lines indicated by Nehru. In 1945 Nehru wrote to Gandhi: 'It seems to me inevitable that modern means of transport as well as many other modern developments must continue and must be developed. There is no way out of it except to have them. If that is so, inevitably a measure of heavy industry exists. How far that will fit in with a purely village society! . . . The question of independence and protection from foreign aggression, both political and economic, has also to be considered in this context. I do not think it is possible for India to be really independent, unless she is a technically advanced country.'[11]

Others prefer to be more severe in their criticism. Nehru wanted India to be 'a technically advanced country'. But can India or any other country be technically advanced without discarding everything that Gandhi stood for? At a seminar on Gandhi organised by the Indian Institute of Advanced Study at Simla in October 1968, Dr Raj Krishna developed this line of criticism with relentless vigour. Modern technology has a logic of its own and the history of our times will be governed by that logic. It is futile to work against it. Modern technology both creates and is sustained by an insatiable desire for higher levels of consumption.

Mass consumption and large-scale production are ineradicable features of modern society. Equally unavoidable are urbanisation and concentration of power at a few centres. In all these respects, the Gandhian utopia stands contradicted by the laws of evolution of modern society.

The Gandhian would carry Raj Krishna's logic to its bitter conclusion as a prelude to rejecting it. Modern society, dissolving all idyllic relations, produces the atomised individual, who is armed with instruments of control over nature but is loveless and inwardly lonely. In an attempt to overcome this intolerable inner loneliness, the individual all too readily identifies himself with some campaign of hatred by which large numbers of people achieve a kind of transitory and destructive solidarity. Modern science increases manifold the destructive potentiality of such movements. Thus modern technology points towards a neurotic society bent on self-destruction. We must not allow our will to prevent an ultimate disaster to be paralysed by the pessimistic idea that a particular line of historical development is technologically pre-determined. The Gandhian utopia is, indeed, the very reverse of certain tendencies inherent in modern technology. But these tendencies cannot be allowed to develop unchecked without grave risk to humanity. The Gandhian utopia may never be completely realised, but social evolution is not pre-determined and we are free to choose to a certain extent. Gandhi wanted society to be based on those primary associations in which the relation of man to man is as of person to person. A humane society can only be based on felt good neighbourliness. Gandhi wanted machines to be introduced in society with the least possible disruption of this feeling of good neighbourliness. To the extent that technology permits of any choice, the Gandhian principle exhorts us to make the choice in a particular manner.

For Gandhi the really significant choice did not lie between capitalism and socialism, but between a centralised economic system and a decentralised economy. A centralised economic system could go under the name of capitalism or socialism; but in either case it would spell the oppression of primary human associations by those who held power in the cities. Sometimes he identified industrialization itself with a system centred on the cities and opposed it totally. Thus, he said in 1940 to an American journalist: 'Nehru wants industrialization because he thinks that if it is socialized it would be free from the evils of capitalism. My own view is that the evils are inherent in industrialism, and no amount of socialization can eradicate them.'[12] It is easy to get entangled in a sterile terminological controversy; but what Gandhi meant is reasonably clear.

It is not true that technology rules out choice or confines it within socially insignificant limits. Take for instance agriculture. Marx believed that the march of technology was bound to render small-scale farming uneconomic and obsolete. He looked forward to an era of large-scale, mechanised farming. The effective choice would lie then between capitalist farming, on the one hand, and collective or State farming, on the other. But this misrepresents the actual range of choice. It also misjudges the relevance of science to agricultural improvement. Mechanisation of a particular kind involving the use of labour-saving innovations may be particularly necessary in countries which are faced with labour shortage. Where this is not the case, chemistry and biology can still play a vital role in improving agriculture without requiring small-scale farming to be abandoned. Thus, family farming is compatible with modern science and has, in fact, provided the basis of an improved agriculture in a number of countries. It may be necessary to buttress family farming with service co-operatives, but neither science nor technology decrees that those who oppose capitalist concentration of ownership must be content to accept the bureaucratic alternative of collective or State farming. Agriculture, based on family farming, but with a conscious effort to strengthen the ties of community life in the village, as expressed through a variety of co-operative efforts ranging from village-level planning in certain matters to provision of social security or a minimum of education and livelihood to the poorest villager, will come closer to the Gandhian ideal than capitalist or State farming.

In industry, again, alternatives are not as completely closed as the technocrat would have us suppose. What we have to consider here is not simply the choice of techniques in a particular industry, but the alternative patterns of industrialization open to the developing countries today. An increasing number of economists are gradually coming to the conclusion that it just would not do for the underdeveloped countries to imitate the technology and pattern of industrialization of the developed nations. The following extract from Gunnar Myrdal, who has made a very careful study of the problems of the poorer countries, is illustrative of the new trend of thought. 'For various reasons,' writes Myrdal, 'the rich countries never faced during their development the need to absorb a large and growing labour surplus in agriculture . . . their research [is] directed toward greater production with less man-power. In the underdeveloped countries, this line cannot be followed.'[13] Myrdal further observes that 'in most underdeveloped countries industrialization [of the usual type] cannot possibly create much additional employment'. Where industrialization implies rationalization of earlier and more labour-intensive techniques, the net effect on demand for labour may be negative. Where the new investment is in heavy industries additional labour employment is relatively small. But society today is unlikely to tolerate for long a situation in which growing production goes hand in hand with growing unemployment. This line of thought has led to the search for a new technology, an 'intermediate technology' as it is sometimes called, which will be different from both traditional technology which corresponds to an earlier phase in the development of science and those capital-intensive methods of production which are common in the richer countries today.

The fact that disparities in economic development all over the world are so difficult to overcome has also made us conscious of another problem. In economic development as elsewhere success breeds success. A region which has once got a start over other regions tends continuously to widen its lead. It is true that there are also some competitive advantages of backwardness, such as lower wages, which sometimes help poorer regions to speed up their pace of growth. But lower wages give such advantage only when other things are approximately equal, and very often other things are not equal. Backward regions suffer from a variety of tangible (material) and intangible (cultural and educational) handicaps. The free market mechanism cannot be depended upon to remove these handicaps. A plan for dispersal of centres of growth seems to be called for. One effect of regionally balanced development would be to reduce the contrast between overgrown urban centres and impoverished villages. Agro-industry and 'intermediate technology' seem to indicate a new pattern of industrial growth.

Gandhi did not deny that some heavy industries will have to be accepted and he sometimes said he would favour nationalization of such industries. He wrote: 'I believe that some key industries are necessary. . . . Without having to enumerate key industries, I would have State ownership where a large number of people have to work together.'[14] But more typically he recommended a system of 'trusteeship'. The idea was that just as rights are correlated to duties so there can be no absolute right of ownership. A man should hold wealth in trust for the community as a whole and accept it as a bounden duty to manage such material resources as he has under his control with a view to the good of society. This idea has often been criticized as unrealistic. But in all progressive societies proprietary rights can only be exercised within a framework of laws and conventions of which a main purpose is to prevent gross misuse of these rights. Gandhi wanted the capitalist and the landlord to understand this inner tendency of modern society and adjust their conduct accordingly. He would appeal to their good sense as well as their enlightened self-interest. He would go even further and wage a non-violent struggle against them to make them accept their social duties. The alternative to peaceful conversion is violent revolution and the emergence of an oppressive State power. 'As for the present owners of wealth,' Gandhi wrote in 1946, 'they would have to make their choice between the class war and voluntarily converting themselves into trustees of their wealth.'[15]

Thus, Gandhi presented his utopia at many levels. He was not too anxious to preserve an appearance of consistency in all that he spoke and wrote. At one level he was a dreamer and he spoke of the Kingdom of Heaven on earth or expounded his conception of idyllic village life. At another level he was a pragmatist, a 'practical idealist'. It must be said to his credit that where he was utopian he was self-consciously so. As he himself once said: 'You must not imagine that I am envisaging our village life as it is today. The village of my dreams is still in my mind. After all, every man lives in the world of his dreams.'[16] But he tried so to dream that even his fancy would have some power to change reality in a particular direction.[17]

NOTES

[1] See N. K. Sinha, *The Economist History of Bengal* (Calcutta, 1956), vol. 1.

[2] Colin Clark, *The Conditions of Economic Progress* (London, 1957), p. 499.

[3] *Harijan*, 30 November 1934.

[4] M. K. Gandhi, *Hind Swaraj* (Ahmedabad, 1938), preface.

[5] D. G. Tendulkar, *Mahatma* (Delhi, 1962), vol. 7, p. 187.

[6] The matter has been discussed at length by Gunnar Myrdal in his recent book, *Asian Drama* (New York, 1968). See especially vol. 2, chap. 25.

[7] Book 3, chap. 4.

[8] J. H. Boeke, *Economics and Economic Policy of Dual Societies* (Leiden, 1953).

[9] See particularly E. F. Schumacher, *Roots of Economic Growth* (Gandhian Institute of Studies, Varanasi, India, 1962).

[10] *Harijan*, 29 August 1936.

[11] Tendulkar, op. cit., vol. 7, pp. 15-16.

[12] Tendulkar, op. cit., vol. 5, p. 336.

[13] 'Jobs, Food and People', *International Development Review* (June 1965).

[14] *Harijan*, 1 September 1946.

[15] Tendulkar, op. cit., vol. 7, p. 47.

[16] *Ibid.*, p. 15. Gandhi made this remark in the course of an exchange of letters with Nehru on the subject of industrialization. The extract from Nehru at the beginning of the second section of this essay belongs to the same correspondence.

[17] For a systematic exposition of Gandhian economic thought see Bharatan Kumarappa, *Capitalism, Socialism or Villagism?* (Madras, 1946).

GANDHIAN APPROACH TO SOCIAL CONFLICT AND WAR

Nirmal Kumar Bose

It is perhaps necessary to start with a brief statement about Gandhi's world-view; for whatever he tried to do in the social or political field was ultimately derived from his basic beliefs.

In essence, Gandhi was a man of religion; but the definition of religion to which he subscribed was very much his own. He held that the spiritual needs of every man were unique, and each had the right to order his life in accordance with his own world-view, provided he also guaranteed the same right to others. Every man could only see Truth in little fragments; but the more he progressed in his own way, the more he realized the ultimate unity of Truth, and also of the unity of the human family.

In the practice of this religious quest, one could not, therefore, impose one's view of Truth upon others by violence. But one was justified in opposing others by means of non-violence. According to Gandhi the non-violent way was the only decent way of opposing others, and of asserting the truth of one's own cause. For, in non-violence, the purpose is to convert, not coerce anybody into submission. Non-violence is thus the sole guarantee of a truly democratic life.

Secondly, Gandhi also held that in a genuine pursuit of religious life one could not break up life into separate compartments called economic, social, political and religious. A truly religious man would never put up with injustice anywhere. He would thus be involved in action against wrongs wherever human equality or brotherhood were denied.

Gandhi's views on religion were thus of an integrated kind. But in one respect he differed widely from Tolstoy, and in another, from Marx, whose writings he read only late in life, after he was more than 73 years of age.

Tolstoy held that it was not necessary for a man to oppose or try to reform the institutions through which men were oppressed. A true Christian was called upon to live in terms of the Commandments alone, and to refuse to co-operate with a government when his conscience demanded

261

this of him. He was not to 'resist evil'. If he lived the truly Christian life, the evil of all institutions would melt away as snow does when summer comes, and the sun shines brightly upon it.

Gandhi, however, believed differently. It is undoubtedly true that each man should try to live in accordance with the dictates of his conscience. But situated as he was in India, where we have a long tradition of ascetics retiring from confrontation with the everyday problems of life, he worked at the other, i.e., institutional, end. He took men in India as they were, and recommended *collective* action for them, if they felt that some institutions were wrong and had to be opposed. In this organization of non-violent resistance he showed great originality in devising progressive steps of non-co-operation.

In this endeavour, he asked the 'masses', as distinguished from the 'classes', to resist wrongs, while he also asked them to build up, by means of the Constructive Programme, the elements of a kind of life which he wanted them to establish in future. Gandhi knew that the masses would not immediately subscribe to his basic beliefs; but in a campaign of non-violent non-co-operation, or *satyāgraha* as he called it, he held that it would be enough if a hard core of *satyāgrahis* were firm in their belief, while the rest honestly followed the rules and discipline of non-violent opposition, and did not stray into the paths of violent resistance. He maintained that by progressive practice even common people would ultimately begin to subscribe inwardly to non-violence as a faith.

Gandhi thus differed from Tolstoy because he began at the institutional end and designed collective action against social wrongs. He did not minimize the importance of the individual or of individual action, but he held that reform should proceed at both ends: action at one end alone was insufficient to deal with the enormity of the complex problems of India.

Gandhi also differed from what might be designated as the communist approach to social change. Communists see in class war the key to social change in history. They are not particularly concerned about the individual. Members of the Communist party have undoubtedly to order their lives in accordance with a new code of morals. But this kind of moral endeavour is not recommended, to start with, for the masses in general. The proletariat would destroy the institutions which are based on the exploitation of human beings; and the Communist party would lead the working class in the violent overthrow of old institutions and their replacement by new ones. Those who oppose this revolutionary emancipation of the working classes would be weeded out automatically, or by deliberately planned measures. Others who fall in line with the interests of the working classes, as interpreted by the Communist party, would be saved.

Gandhi differed very much from this view. He held that no man had the right to claim that he had all the truth on his own side, and therefore the right to impose his view upon others *by means of violence*. The limitation was equally valid in the case of a class or a party.

Secondly, Gandhi also did not believe that the task of building up a new society free of exploitation should begin only after all opposition had been liquidated by means of the exercise of state power under the dictatorship of the proletariat. He held that the seeds of a new life could be sown even now, in a small way. And they must be watered by the suffering which the *satyāgrahi* would have to endure in the course of his organized, collective resistance against existing wrongs.

Thus although Gandhi came close to the communists in certain ways, he differed radically from them when it came to the means which he advocated for establishing an exploitation-free society, in which every man would have to earn his daily bread by the sweat of his brow, and 'the means of production of the elementary necessaries of life would be in the control of the masses'. His means were different; and for him the means were vital because if these were wrong the end was also likely to become perverted.

Gandhi was a believer in constitutional methods for bringing about social change, but he had also experienced its limitations. When a really critical issue arose, he had often found that both parties in a conflict tended to throw aside constitutional solutions and take recourse to direct action of one kind or another. As Gandhi described it an appeal to reason would often fail to work in a crisis, and it was when such a situation arose in South Africa that it suddenly dawned upon him that the Indian community ought to resist, and resist non-violently.

In 1931, Gandhi described in an article in *Young India* how this conviction had actually come to him.

> Up to the year 1906, I simply relied on appeal to reason. I was a very industrious reformer. I was a good draftsman, as I always had a close grip of facts which in its turn was the necessary result of my meticulous regard for truth. But I found that reason failed to produce an impression when the critical moment arrived in South Africa. My people were excited; even a worm will and does sometimes turn—and there was talk of wreaking vengeance. I had then to choose between allying myself to violence or finding out some other method of meeting the crisis and stopping the riot and it came

to me that we should refuse to obey legislation that was degrading and let them put us in jail if they liked. Thus came into being the moral equivalent of war. . . .

The conviction has been growing upon me that things of fundamental importance to the people are not secured by reason alone but have to be purchased with their suffering. Suffering is the law of human beings; war is the law of the jungle. But suffering is infinitely more powerful than the law of the jungle for converting the opponent and opening his ears, which are otherwise shut, to the voice of reason. Nobody has probably drawn up more petitions or espoused more forlorn causes than I and I have come to this fundamental conclusion that if you want something really important to be done you must not merely satisfy the reason, you must move the heart also. The appeal to reason is more to the head, but the penetration of the heart comes from suffering. It opens the inner understanding in man. Suffering is the badge of the human race, not the sword.[1]

In the course of a long life, Gandhi tried to apply the technique of *satyāgraha* to the solution of various kinds of problems. There were altogether three large-scale nation-wide movements for the assertion of political rights: the Non-co-operation Movement of 1921; the Salt *Satyāgraha* and Civil Disobedience Movements of 1930 and 1932; and the Quit-India Movement of 1942. Besides these there were perhaps forty small-scale movements for the assertion of civil, social, economic or religious rights all over India between the years 1921 and 1942. Some of these, like the Temple-entry *Satyāgraha* by 'untouchables' in Vykom (Kerala), or the Bardoli *Satyāgraha* in Gujarat against economic wrongs, were directly undertaken under his inspiration or guidance. Others, like one in Patuakhali (Bengal) for the assertion of civil rights, or the Gurdwara Movement in the Punjab for the establishment of public control over religious trusts, were inspired by the political campaigns of *satyāgraha,* but they were initiated by workers or organizations with which Gandhi was not directly connected.

One of the important tasks which remains to be done in India is the preparation of a critical study of all these *satyāgraha* movements for the purpose of finding out how they operated under Gandhi's guidance and how they fared without it; how he organized them and designed steps to curb violence when it arose; what the response of the *satyāgrahis* and of their opponents was when a religious or a social or an economic issue was involved, and so on. Such a study would indeed be of great value, for in India there were carried on for over a period of thirty years numerous experiments in the organization of non-violence, the results of which should be made available to the rest of the world.

We are however, at the moment, not involved in this particular study. Instead, after having so far described the basic ideas of Gandhi, especially those which lay at the root of his practice of *satyāgraha*, we now propose to indicate briefly what kind of a society he wanted to establish in India, and how he thought this was to be brought about.

The following conversation once took place (1947) between Gandhi and an interviewer.

Q. Is it possible to defend by non-violence anything which can only be gained by violence?

A. It followed from what he had said (above) that what was gained by violence could not only not be defended by non-violence, but the latter required the abandonment of ill-gotten gains.

Q. Is the accumulation of capital possible except through violence whether open or tacit?

A. Such accumulation by private persons was impossible except through violent means; but accumulation by the State in a non-violent society was not only possible, it was desirable and inevitable.

Q. Whether a man accumulates material or moral wealth, he does so only through the help or co-operation of other members of society. Has he then the moral right to use any of it mainly for personal advantage?

A. The answer was an emphatic no.[2]

We believe this forms the core of Gandhi's economic beliefs. If a community decides that it would use non-violence for the defence of its possessions, it must make sure that the prossessions have been gained by moral means, by the sweat of one's brow, and not by the exploitation of somebody else's labour. If a community is in possession of gains acquired by violence, its first duty is to get rid of such 'ill-gotten gains', as a preparation for non-violent defence.

According to the Gandhian theory, any man who lived by the toil of others was a thief. In this, he came close to Proudhon. In regard to the quest for moral life, he came close to Tolstoy in his recommendation that the duty of Bread-Labour be followed by every man. A poet or a scientist could perhaps be released from the obligation of bread-labour if other members of society so decided. But Gandhi held firmly to the belief that if a poet laboured for his daily bread, thus identifying himself

265

with labouring humanity, even the quality of his artistic creation would definitely improve.

But apart from that, Gandhi again and again exhorted his countrymen to spin in their leisure time, and produce the cloth which they wore. In 1925, he tried to define what kind of State he wanted for India. In an article he wrote:

> By Swaraj I mean the government of India by the consent of the people as ascertained by the largest number of the adult population, male or female, native born or domiciled, who have contributed by manual labour to the service of the State and who have taken the trouble of having their names registered as voters. I hope to demonstrate that real Swaraj will come not by the acquisition of authority by a few but by the acquisition of the capacity by all to resist authority when abused. In other words, Swaraj is to be attained by educating the masses to a sense of their capacity to regulate and control authority.[3]

With this end in view, requiring the preservation of the economic freedom of those who toiled in the fields and workshops, Gandhi held that the entire productive organization should be decentralized. He wanted peasants and artisans in India to produce for local consumption the basic necessities of life. This was not autarchy by means of lowered productive efficiency. Rather, Gandhi felt that once the basic requirements of life were thus in the control of the masses, such units could co-operate with one another *voluntarily* in order to raise the level of production, so long as it did not lead to subservience or domination.

In such a predominantly non-violent society, any industry which could not be owned or run by the small unit had to be nationalized. It had also to be run, not for profit, but to make available to every one concerned the benefits of reduced labour and increased consumption. In this connexion, he once wrote in 1924:

> What I object to is the *craze* for machinery, not machinery as such. The *craze* is for what they call labour-saving machinery. Men go on 'saving labour', till thousands are without work and thrown on the open street to die of starvation. I want to save time and labour, not for a fraction of mankind, but for all; I want the concentration of wealth, not in the hands of few, but in the hands of all. Today machinery merely helps a few to ride on the back of millions. The impetus behind it is not the philanthropy to save

266

labour, but greed. It is against this constitution of things that I am fighting with all my might.[4]

About one year before the second world war began Gandhi said that through *satyāgraha* he was trying to find a 'solution of world problems or rather the one supreme problem of war'. For, as he saw it, if an effective moral substitute for war could not be devised, mankind would become involved in a suicidal race for superiority in armaments. He felt that if he could develop and perfect in the small laboratory of India a non-violent resolution of social and international conflicts, and offer it as India's gift to the warring nations of the world, that would be the fruition of all his life's endeavour.

Even as early as 1925 Gandhi described in the course of a speech his own views of what he understood by nationalism. Gandhi said:

> We want freedom for our country, but not at the expense of exploitation of others, not so as to degrade other countries. I do not want the freedom of India if it means the extinction of England or the disappearance of Englishmen. I want the freedom of my country, so that the resources of my country might be utilized for the benefit of mankind. Just as the cult of patriotism teaches us today that the individual has to die for the family, the family has to die for the village, the village for the district, the district for the province, and province for the country, even so, a country has to be free in order that it may die, if necessary, for the benefit of the world. My love therefore of nationalism, or my idea of nationalism, is that my country may become free, that if need be, the whole country may die so that the human race may live. There is no room for race-hatred there. Let that be our nationalism.[5]

Gandhi was firmly of the opinion that not even the natural resources which lay within the boundaries of a State belonged to it exclusively. Collective national ownership was morally as indefensible as private ownership under his ideal scheme.

A Nation-State which thus started to place its possessions on a moral plane had to share them with any other member of the human family who was in need of it. In this connexion he wrote in 1924:

> Isolated independence is not the goal of the world States. It is voluntary interdependence. . . . There is no limit to extending our services to our neighbours across State-made frontiers. God never made those frontiers. [6]

A group of interviewers once asked him a pointed question: What should India do if, for instance, the neighbouring people of some State decided to march into the fertile plains of the Punjab for conquest. Gandhi's reply was that we should, all the while, try to build up an economy based on universal labour in our own country. But while doing so, we should not keep our eyes shut to the condition of our neighbours, whether in Afghanistan or in Tibet. Our experienced people should go into those countries in humility and help them, with superior technical knowledge, to develop their local resources to the utmost extent.

If that does not suffice, then we must invite them to come and share our resources, and live as we have been trying to do. If there is not enough to go round, we must all tighten our belts; but yet not exclude anybody who is really in want.

What is of great importance is that this attempt of one country to build up an exploitation-free economy, and share it with fellow men across so-called national boundaries, must be duly advertised. People everywhere must be made aware of what is being done by at least one community. Such an endeavour would give this particular community a moral prestige which would be of inestimable value later on.

Supposing that a 'nation' thus tries to build up a new economy and also a moral status, would that, of itself, prevent others from acting as aggressors against their land? When Gandhi was faced with this question his answer was that, taking human nature as it is, it is not unlikely that a political leader or a general may appear in one country, and begin aggression against the community described above for the purpose of enslaving them.

When this happens, the defenders should allow themselves to be mowed down by bullets, and yet not raise a finger in so-called 'self-defence'. They must refuse, even under the gravest provocation, to regard the aggressors as anything except their erring brothers, of the same human family to which they also belong.

It is possible that this would have no effect upon the oncoming aggressors. Gandhi's recommendation was that the *satyāgrahis* should still persist in offering non-violent resistance. If invading forces swarmed into their country, they would talk to them, tell them that they were wrong, and even be prepared to invite them to come and settle down among them and live like labourers as they did. If the aggressors refused, then they would have to face the complete non-co-operation of *satyāgrahis*.

One interviewer at this stage asked Gandhi, if he really hoped that the heart of the aggressor would be touched by the courage of the *satyāgrahis*. Gandhi's answer was that, as a practical man who had passed through many bitter experiences, he would admit that the heart of the General might not be touched by *satyāgraha*. But he said that the General could only act with the co-operation of the Army; and the Army was composed of men like everyone else. The common soldier's heart was yet open to the appeal of patience and of love; particularly if his life was not endangered by the *satyāgrahis*, who were never to indulge in reprisal. And once the *satyāgrahi* showed adequate courage—which would undoubtedly be one of a very high order—it would set the individuals among the aggressors thinking. And the moment this happened the General would become more and more isolated from his Army and would find it increasingly difficult to maintain his authority. This would be the maximum that can be achieved under non-violence, as he saw it in his time.

Whether the Gandhian ideal of defence in terms of non-violence is a practical proposal or not in a world which is now well into the atomic age still remains to be seen. At least, the threat of atomic destruction has changed the character of war itself. Positional warfare is giving place to guerilla tactics, while atomic weapons are being perfected and utilized, mainly for yielding political dividends. Instead of war being limited today to a short period of time, it is breaking out all over the world in a continuous series of small-scale conflicts which, in their totality, are no less a burden upon mankind than wars of the past.

Under these circumstances, and particularly when the formation of a World Court or of a World Government to which all nations would surrender a large part of their sovereign rights has apparently receded from immediate realization, it is time perhaps to examine the ideas and methods which Gandhi suggested in India, so that we could find a moral equivalent of war which would help us in solving problems of conflict in a more civilized manner than ever attempted before on a large scale anywhere in human history.

NOTES

[1] N. K. Bose (ed.), *Selections from Gandhi* (Ahmedabad, 1957), pp. 153-54.
[2] *Ibid.*, p. 39.
[3] *Ibid.*, p. 114.
[4] *Ibid.*, p. 66.
[5] *Ibid.*, p. 42.
[6] *Ibid.*, p. 42.

THE NON-UNIVERSALITY OF SATYAGRAHA

Stanley Maron

Satyāgraha is the key to Gandhi's thinking and action. He defined *satyāgraha* many times and in different ways. The difference does not arise from inconsistency or incoherency. Rather, it derives from the basic nature of the underlying culture, which involves a distinct way of looking at the world. *Satyāgraha* is not an *idea* in the Greek sense, and cannot be defined precisely in accordance with its place within some order of ideas or logical system. *Satyāgraha* stands in contrast to Greek thought in that it does not place Truth as an object of contemplation, but makes it an intimate part of the process of living. In order to grasp the meaning of *satyāgraha* one must approach it from within the primary context, which means approaching it from within the developing process of Indian life and culture.

An early attempt by Gandhi at a rather general definition states: 'Satyagraha is literally holding on to Truth and it means, therefore, Truth-force. Truth is soul or spirit. It is, therefore, known as soul-force. It excludes the use of violence because man is not capable of knowing the absolute truth and, therefore, not competent to punish.'[1]

From these words we may understand that *satyāgraha* assumes the existence of Truth as something very basic and having its own kind of force or influence. Man should hold on to it, or be guided by it, but may not presume to possess it. Above all, no man has the right to introduce physical force or violence into the realm of Truth. It is a moral transgression for any man to use violence in order to compel some one else to accept his notion of Truth. Only the force of Truth itself can be used to overcome the barriers of misunderstanding and differences of opinion, for only that force can reveal the underlying unity of Truth.

A cardinal feature of *satyāgraha* is self-restraint. One must overcome the impulse to use violence. Though violence may seem a natural impulse, actually it is a part of the material or physical world and its actualization means supremacy of the physical world over the spiritual. The demand of *satyāgraha* is to ensure at all times the supremacy of the spiritual. In his own words, Gandhi 'discovered in the earliest stages that pursuit of truth did not admit of violence being inflicted on one's opponent but that he must be weaned from error by patience and sympathy. For what appears to be truth to the one may appear to be error to the other. And patience means self-suffering. So the doctrine came to mean vindication of truth not by infliction of suffering on the opponent but on one's self'.[2]

Gandhi understood suffering to be neither negative nor a necessary evil. Rather, he understood it to be a positive force in its own right, and an even more powerful instrument than violence. In observing Boer women taken as prisoners during the war in South Africa, Gandhi noted: 'Real suffering bravely borne melts even a heart of stone. Such is the potency of suffering, or *tapas*. And there lies the key to Satyāgraha.'[3]

Violence is intended to achieve an end through the exploitation of fear. It strengthens the elements of passion and compulsion. Suffering appeals to man's moral nature. It brings out the elements of love and compassion. These two methods are incompatible, thereby compelling a choice between them. Those who wish for a moral life must forego violence and be prepared to endure suffering until love and compassion triumph.

Gandhi as a child came into contact with various Hindu sects, and also with Christianity. From these different influences came one dominant conviction, 'that morality is the basis of things, and that truth is the substance of all morality'.[4]

What this meant for Gandhi can be understood correctly only in the context of Indian sources. The term itself is derived from the core of traditional terminology. According to Gandhi's own explanation:

> The word *Satya* (Truth) is derived from *Sat*, which means 'being'. Nothing is or exists in reality except Truth. That is why *Sat* or Truth is perhaps the most important name of God. . . .
>
> Devotion to this Truth is the sole justification for our existence. All our activities should be centred in Truth. Truth should be the very breath of our life. When once this stage in the pilgrim's progress is reached, all other rules of correct living will come without effort, and obedience to them will be instinctive. But without Truth it would be impossible to observe any principles or rules of life.
>
> Where there is honest effort, it will be realized that what appear to be different truths are like the countless and apparently different leaves of the same tree. . . . There can be no place in it for even a trace of self-interest. In such selfless search for Truth nobody can lose his bearings for long. Directly he takes to the wrong path he stumbles, and is thus redirected to the right path.[5]

271

Satyāgraha means the holding on to Truth or that higher Being distinct from the physical world in which we live. Approach to Truth is our real purpose and toward that end we should be prepared to give up all else. Giving up one's attachment to the physical world is in reality an affirmation of one's holding on to Truth. Of decisive importance is the giving up of violence *(ahimsā)*, 'for without Ahimsa it is not possible to seek and find Truth. Ahimsa and Truth are so intertwined that it is practically impossible to disentangle and separate them'.[6]

There is a striking resemblance between this explanation of *satyāgraha* by Gandhi and certain central teachings of the Jains. Gandhi as a child lived in a region where Jaina influence was strong. Jaina *yoga* contains the three aspects of knowledge, faith and action. Action *(chāritra)* has a negative connotation and means cessation from doing evil. It contains five virtues of negative direction: *ahimsā* (non-injury), *sūnrita* (non-greed), *asteya* (non-stealing), *brahmacharya* (sexual abstinence) and *aparigraha* (non-attachment to possessions). In Jaina *yoga*, according to Das Gupta, 'the root of all these is ahimsā. The virtues of sūnrita, asteya and brahmacharya are made to follow directly as secondary corollaries of ahimsā. Ahimsā may thus be generalized as the fundamental ethical virtue of Jainism; judgment on all actions may be passed in accordance with the standard of ahimsā; sūnrita, asteya and brahmacharya are regarded as virtues as their transgression leads to himsā (injury to beings)'.[7]

Elsewhere, Das Gupta gives a slightly different list of virtues, including *satya* instead of *sūnrita*. Again referring to Jaina *yoga*, he states that 'before the mind can be fit for this lofty meditation, it is necessary that it should be purged of ordinary impurities. Thus the intending yogin should practice absolute non-injury to all living beings (ahimsā), absolute and strict truthfulness (satya), non-stealing (asteya), absolute sexual restraint (brahmacharya) and the acceptance of nothing but that which is absolutely necessary (aparigraha)'.[8]

Essentially the same account is given by Jadunath Sinha, who likewise lists *satya* instead of *sūnrita*. In the Jaina doctrine, he writes, 'perfection or self-realization is the highest good. But asceticism or passionlessness is the means to its attainment. Ahimsa is the fundamental and basic virtue. Truthfulness, non-stealing, sex-restraint, and non-covetousness are based upon ahimsa. The Jaina ethics is pre-eminently an ethics of ahimsa'.[9]

These very brief references to ancient Indian thinking could be expanded to show to what great extent Gandhi was a faithful exponent of certain aspects of traditional Indian teaching. From that point of view, Gandhi was a *yogin* employing asceticism as the path bringing him toward Truth. His approach is meaningful, in this sense, within the context of

Indian tradition; but there is no justification for asserting that it has more universal validity than does any other part of Indian tradition. There are basic differences which divide Indian thought from that of other cultures. There are assumptions which are specific to the Indian frame of reference and which are not shared by other cultures. Gandhi developed his position within the context of Indian tradition and he shared these limitations.

However, Gandhi did not live wholly within a world of tradition. His major concern was to cope with certain demands placed upon Indian society by virtue of historical developments (British rule) and the nature of modernism which threatened the very existence of India's traditional culture. His thinking was derived from a specific or non-universal tradition, but insofar as it was shaped by his encounter with modernism there are elements in it which have applicability wherever modernism is being confronted.

Gandhi struggled with the conflicting demands of tradition and modernism, and for the most part remained faithful to tradition. Instead of adapting himself and his thinking to the norms of modernism, he worked out an interpretation of modernism which he fitted into his traditional world-view. Thereby, he was able to act within the modern context according to his own criteria. This combination of traditional thinking interacting with modern problems produced a dramatic effect which brought Gandhi much publicity, but often little understanding of his real position.

One attempt to understand Gandhi in this light was made by Heinrich Zimmer, who could hardly be accused of superficial knowledge of India. Precisely for this reason, the example is instructive. According to Zimmer:

> The higher principle is Truth, as manifest in dharma, 'law: that which holds together, supports, upholds'. Government, 'law', based on 'untruth' is an anomaly—according to Mahātma Gandhi's archaic, pre-Persian, native Indo-Aryan point of view. Great Britain's perennial punitive aggressions to put down the 'lawlessness' of those who challenged the jurisdiction of her 'laws' based on lawlessness were to be countered, following Gandhi's programme, not in kind, but by the soul force that would automatically come into play as a result of a steadfast communal holding (āgraha) to truth (satya). The grip of the tyrant nation would disintegrate. The play of its own lawlessness throughout the world would be its own undoing; one had only to wait until it took itself apart. Meanwhile, in piety, decency, and the faultless practice—with faith (sraddhā)—of its own

ageless dharma, the land of India must remain with its passions of violence rightly curbed, firm in the power which is the mother of power, namely Truth.[10]

This interpretation by Zimmer is obviously exaggerated. Gandhi was not an advocate of quietism and definitely favoured an active response in order to gain Indian independence. What is important in this quotation is the way in which Zimmer has put his finger on Gandhi's mode of defining the problem in accordance with traditional views. Although Gandhi was himself an English-trained lawyer, he did not accept the British notion of legality. For him, *dharma* is the basis of lawfulness and not decisions by legal bodies. In this sense, Gandhi did not accept one of the central premises of modern society. He was not playing the political game according to the conventional rules. At no point was Gandhi interested only in a transfer of sovereignty. Although he called for Indian independence, he did not mean by it a demand for national freedom in the European sense. Rather, he was calling for liberation not only from the bonds of British rule but from the inroads of modern society as well. Gandhi's fuller objective was a return to the truth of Indian reality—its *dharma*—and a rejection of the corruptions introduced with European modernism.

There is no need to assume that Gandhi developed his view after profound study of the traditional literature. Actually, he had a relatively superficial knowledge of the classical texts. His understanding of tradition came through the medium by which the masses of India have been educated for thousands of years, through stories and plays. His mother frequently told him stories based on Indian mythology used to illustrate the essential features of Indian tradition. These stories, passed on from generation to generation, are the basis of Indian folk culture. Plays also form a very popular part of Indian folk culture and are a customary part of village life.

One play in particular had a singular and lasting influence. As a child, Gandhi saw a performance of the play giving the legendary account of Harishchandra, the king who symbolizes perfect truth. In the play Harishchandra goes through much suffering because he refuses even to pretend that he had not made a damaging promise. Instead, he endures all the consequences of the promise, including loss of his kingdom, exile, the death of his son and the sale of his wife into slavery, while he himself becomes the servant of an untouchable. In a certain sense, Harishchandra can be considered an Indian counterpart of Job. Throughout his trials, he remains steadfast in his allegiance to Truth, just as Job remained undeviating in his Faith. There is a similar happy ending which proves the wisdom

274

of perseverance in one's commitment. Gandhi was captivated by the play and returned to see it a number of times.

Truth as found in the story of Harishchandra tends to be a matter of moral principle, somewhat abstract and even formalistic. A preference for formal moral principle characterized Gandhi's approach, despite the Gandhi family ties to Vaishnavism. Gandhi was capable of going to extremes in holding fast to principle, even when there were damaging practical results. Since he held personal suffering to have positive value, he was not prepared to recognize that such results were damaging. He could even take pleasure in the causing of pain in the name of principle. One such incident Gandhi himself related proudly:

I had read and realized that the weak-bodied should avoid pulses. I was very fond of them. Now it happened that Kasturba,[11] who had a brief respite after (an) operation, had again begun getting hemorrhage and the malady seemed to be obstinate. Hydropathic treatment by itself did not answer. Kasturba had not much faith in my remedies though she did not resist them. She certainly did not ask for outside help. So when all my remedies had failed, I entreated her to give up salt and pulses. She would not agree, however much I pleaded with her, supporting myself with authorities. As last she challenged me saying that even I could not give up these articles if I was advised to do so. I was pained and equally delighted,—delighted in that I got an opportunity to shower my love on her. I said to her: 'You are mistaken. If I was ailing and the doctor advised me to give up these or any other articles I should unhesitatingly do so. But there! Without any medical advice, I give up salt and pulses for one year, whether you do so or not.'

She was rudely shocked and exclaimed in deep sorrow: 'Pray forgive me. Knowing you, I should not have provoked you. I promise to abstain from these things, but for heaven's sake take back your vow. This is too hard on me.'

'It is very good for you to give up these articles. I have not the slightest doubt that you will be all the better without them. As for me, I cannot retract a vow seriously taken. And it is sure to benefit me, for all restraint, whatever prompts it, is wholesome for man. You will therefore leave me alone. It will be a test for me, and a moral support to you in carrying out your resolve.'

So she gave me up. 'You are too obstinate. You will listen to none', she said, and sought relief in tears. I would like to count this

275

incident as an instance of Satyāgraha and as one of the sweetest recollections of my life.[12]

Various commentators have noted this tendency on Gandhi's part to impose his will on others through 'non-violent' coercion, and the pleasure that he derived from it. One of Gandhi's most persistent difficulties was to assure himself that his motivation in each case was 'pure' or based on truth. Although devotion to principle was fundamental in Gandhi's activities, certain inconsistencies gave rise to severe criticism and the feeling that Gandhi was not above using principle for political ends and even changing his principles where convenient.

There was a striking inconsistency in Gandhi's conduct with relation to war. Although he condemned absolutely the use of violence, he helped the British in the Boer War. Again, in both the First and Second World Wars he was prepared to help the British in return for political advantages. Further, Gandhi equivocated in his opposition to aggression. He urged some European nations to surrender to Hitler, and praised the Munich agreement as sound statesmanship. On the other hand, he called for the defence of India against possible Japanese invasion and commended the Chinese upon their determined resistance.

In 1938, Gandhi advised the Czechs against an armed resistance to invasion by the Germans. 'It is clear that the small nations must either come or be ready to come under the protection of the dictators or be a constant menace to the peace of Europe. In spite of all the goodwill in the world England and France cannot save them. Their intervention can only mean bloodshed and destruction such as has never been seen before. If I were a Czech, therefore, I would free these two nations from the obligation to defend my country. And yet I must live. I would not be a vassal to any nation or body. I must have absolute independence or perish. To seek to win in a clash of arms would be pure bravado. Not so, if in defying the might of one who would deprive me of my independence I refuse to obey his will and perish unarmed in the attempt. In so doing, though I lose the body, I save my soul, i.e., my honour'.[13]

In this call to the Czechs, Gandhi takes his stand within the non-attachment of traditional Hindu thought. The loss of the body is only of contingent importance. The soul goes on to another body and another cycle of existence. But can such an appeal have meaning to those who belong to a different culture and who do not accept those assumptions? Is honour really more important than life itself? Is honour an intrinsic value like truth, so that it is better to die in its defence than to live without it? Such would seem to be Gandhi's view, yet in a similar situation involving the

French, he took a different course. There he urged the giving up of liberty rather than life on the pragmatic grounds that liberty has no value anyway without life.

Gandhi praised the French surrender in 1940 as brave statesmanship. 'I think French statesmen have shown rare courage in bowing to the inevitable and refusing to be party to senseless mutual slaughter', he wrote. 'There can be no sense in France coming out victorious if the stake is in truth lost. The cause of liberty becomes a mockery, if the price to be paid is wholesale destruction of those who are to enjoy liberty. It then becomes an inglorious satiation of ambition. The bravery of the French soldier is world-known. But let the world know also the greater bravery of the French statesmen in suing for peace.'[14]

Two weeks later, Gandhi urged the embattled British to lay down their arms. 'I venture to present you with a nobler and braver way, worthy of the bravest soldier', he wrote. 'I want you to fight Nazism without arms, or, if I am to retain the military terminology, with non-violent arms. I would like you to lay down the arms you have as being useless for saving you or humanity. You will invite Herr Hitler and Signor Mussolini to take what they want of the countries you call your possessions. Let them take possession of your beautiful island, with your many beautiful buildings. You will give all these but neither your souls, nor your minds. If these gentlemen choose to occupy your homes, you will vacate them. If they do not give you free passage out, you will allow yourself man, woman and child, to be slaughtered, but you will refuse to owe allegiance to them.'[15]

There is something almost grotesque in the way in which Gandhi urged Europeans to die for the principle of non-violence. He spoke from the Himalayan heights of Hindu romanticism, urging upon them the example of Harishchandra. What he had to say belonged to a realm of mythical thinking and may be explained by the distance which separated him from the battlefields of Europe and the horrors of Nazi occupation. There may even have been a hidden wish to see the proud Europeans, and especially the rulers of India, humbled. Gandhi's attitude was markedly different when developments in Asia brought India under threat of invasion from Japan. With danger close at hand, Gandhi called for the defence of India by all means, including co-operation with the British forces and mobilization of Indian soldiers.

In a letter to Chiang Kai-shek during the dark days of 1942, Gandhi wrote: 'India must not submit to any aggressor or invader and must resist him. I would not be guilty of purchasing the freedom of my country at the cost of your country's freedom. That problem does not arise before

277

me as I am clear that India cannot gain her freedom in this way, and a Japanese domination of either India or China would be equally injurious to the other country and to world peace. That domination must therefore be prevented and I should like India to play her natural and rightful part in this.'[16]

Far from urging surrender to the Japanese, Gandhi indicated his personal willingness to participate in active and armed resistance. He added: 'To make it perfectly clear that we want to prevent in every way Japanese aggression, I would personally agree, that the Allied Powers might, under treaty with us, keep their armed forces in India and use the country as a base for operation against the threatened Japanese attack'.[17]

Gandhi concluded his letter to Chiang Kai-shek by praising China's refusal to surrender, even though he knew the bloodshed involved. These remarks are a far cry from the advice which he gave to the Czechs and the British. It would be too much to expect rigid logical consistency in the statements of any political leader, and Gandhi was that before all else. However, the differences reflected in these passages are too great to be dismissed as passing weakness or tactical necessity.

Advice to Europeans to allow themselves to be slaughtered rather than use violence to defend themselves, and praise for the determined resistance of the Chinese, is but one example of inconsistency in Gandhi's thinking. Others could be cited. They do not mean, though, that Gandhi had different standards for different situations or that he was insincere. Rather, they reflect Gandhi's continuing difficulty in coping with specifically modernistic conditions within the framework of traditional thinking. Despite his achievements, Gandhi did not succeed in forging a viable synthesis. Nor can this be attributed only to a personal failure. Although Gandhi struggled with the problem to his very last days, he did not reach a solution because the conditions of the problem do not permit one. The basic assumptions underlying the dominant version of Indian tradition and modernism are incompatible.

The foundation of Indian tradition is essentially spiritual, the determinative element of reality is consciousness. The key concept of *dharma* must be understood in this context. *Dharma* has a complex meaning approximating in an important sense virtue or right action. It is the ought to which man should adjust his conduct. In this sense, it can be equated with truth as ideal conduct. This conduct is not primarily behavioural but inner and having to do with one's spiritual pursuit of *moksha* or liberation. The external world is for the most part a hindrance in this pursuit, and in any event is not the primary arena.

The key concept for the understanding of modern society is institutionalization. Although it too, like *dharma*, bears a relation to an ideal structure, institutionalization has little to do with morality. While it too is concerned with right action, the purpose of such action is not a personal one. The end of institutionalization is efficiency, which may or may not be subordinated to human or moral values.

The tragedy of modernism is the helplessness of the individual against the 'system' which is invulnerable to moral pressure. *Satyāgraha* assumes a world in which men are dominant, and are subject to moral influence. In modern society institutions dominate, and they are non-moral. When irrational passions become institutionalized, the combination is invulnerable to such moral pressure as self-suffering. Indeed, self-suffering may only excite and increase the lust for power and domination. Modern totalitarian systems are founded on this combination of passion and institutionalization. They include as conscious policy the denial of that morality intended to curb passion. Where neither morality nor reason can prevail, violence may be the only recourse.

The Nazi régime and its persecution of the Jews is a paramount example of a totalitarian system based on passion and invulnerable to moral pressure. There were innumerable examples of self-suffering and of non-violent resistance, yet they had no noticeable effect other than to increase the cruelty and degradation of the slaughter. They are not instances which can be used in educating a young generation toward building a better world. However, the armed uprising of the Jews in the Warsaw Ghetto, as tragic and inadequate as it was, has become an educational influence of the first order—and not only for Jews.

Perhaps in no other instance was Gandhi so remote from the realities of modernism as in his approach to the persecution of the Jews. Nowhere did he allow himself more freely to advocate 'non-attachment' to life itself. In 1938, Gandhi advised the Jews to rely on *satyāgraha* as their response to Nazi persecution. His reasoning is that of a Himalayan sage: 'If one Jew or all the Jews were to accept the prescription here offered, he or they cannot be worse off than now. And suffering voluntarily undergone will bring them an inner strength and joy which no number of resolutions of sympathy passed in the world outside Germany can. . . . The calculated violence of Hitler may even result in a general massacre of the Jews. . . . But if the Jewish mind could be prepared for voluntary suffering, even the massacre I have imaged could be turned into a day of thanksgiving and joy that Jehovah had wrought deliverance of the race even at the hands of the tyrant. For to the God-fearing, death has no terror. It is a joyful sleep to be followed by a waking that would be all the more refreshing for the long sleep.'[18]

279

Gandhi's words have meaning within the context of Hindu tradition. They provide some understanding of the patience or passivity of the Indian peoples in the face of centuries of oppression and suffering. But those words could have little meaning for the Jews to whom they were addressed. According to Jewish tradition, any action leading to loss of life is bad, even if it arises out of the purest motives of love and compassion—and how much more so when the destruction of life arises out of hatred and lust. Central to Hindu thought is the expression *tat tvam asi* which blurs the difference between the murderer and the murdered. That lack of distinction can lead the Hindu to see the situation as a whole, and to regard his own role within it as an exercise in *dharma*. Jewish thought makes a clear distinction between the two, and calls for individual responsibility in moral action. The Hindu may regard deference to another as a virtue, and may prefer self-suffering rather than to inflict suffering on another. Jewish tradition is not life-negating and specifically holds that no one has the right to consider his own life as less important than that of another. This latter example, in particular, is an instructive instance of the non-universality of *satyāgraha*.

An important Jewish thinker writing under the name Ahad Haam referred to this question in an article published toward the beginning of this century. He selected as an illustration the case of two men journeying through the desert, only one of whom has a bottle of water. If both of them drink, they shall both die; but if one of them only drinks, he shall reach safety. Should the man carrying the water share it with his comrade, should he give him all of it, or should he drink it all himself? The view accepted in Jewish tradition holds: 'Where it is possible to save one of the two lives, it is a moral duty to overcome the feeling of compassion, and to save what can be saved. But to save whom? Justice answers: let him who has the power save himself. Every man's life is entrusted to his keeping, and to preserve your own charge is a nearer duty than to preserve your neighbour's.'[19]

In this example, Hebrew realism stands in marked contrast to Hindu romanticism. Hebrew thinking does not incline toward abstract altruism, nor is it life-denying. There is a basic and stabilizing practical touch which refuses the domination of sentimentality. This practical touch has kept Hebrew morality in contact with everyday life and away from ideals having little relation to action. Many cultures include in their moral code an admonition to protect the poor and the helpless. Hebrew morality is distinguished by forbidding prejudice in favour of either rich or poor. Awareness that the distinction between rich and poor can distort justice in either direction, is expressed in the Biblical words: 'Ye shall do no unrighteousness in judgment: thou shalt not respect the person of the poor, nor honour the person of the mighty: but in righteousness shalt thou judge thy neighbour'. (Lev. XIX, 15) The same idea is repeated in the phrase, 'Ye shall not respect persons in judgment; but ye shall hear the small as well as the great'. (Deut. I, 17)

If the Jews were the most rebellious people under Roman rule, the reason can be found in the importance given to self-respect. According to the Hebrew tradition, every man should consider himself as good as the next, or in the more fundamental sense, no man should think that another man's blood is redder than his own. The traditional explanation is that no man can be sure that another is more favoured in the sight of God than himself. In this sense, each man is charged with saving the life that is entrusted to him. He may not sacrifice his life non-violently, nor may he commit suicide. Within this context of Hebrew thought, *satyāgraha* is unacceptable.

Inconsistencies in Gandhi's position reflect the incompatibility of Hindu tradition with modernism. Hebrew tradition, because it is more realistic and closer to everyday life, has been more successful in meeting the demands of modernism. Hebrew thought accepts, for instance, the interrelatedness of moral ideals and human limitations. This 'natural' approach has been accurately captured by Buber, who spoke of the ongoing striving of man toward realization of the holy—a striving which cannot be pursued in a spirit of non-attachment. Such a pursuit requires the involvement of one's whole being. Man strives toward realization of the holy, but with an awareness of human limitations. These limitations may require the use of violence under certain circumstances, and at such times man should find the strength to do what is necessary.

In 1939, shortly after he left Germany to settle in Jerusalem, Buber addressed a letter to Gandhi in response to the article in which Gandhi had advised the Jews under Nazi domination to adopt *satyāgraha*. Buber wrote: 'In the five years which I myself spent under the present regime, I observed many instances of genuine *satyāgraha* among the Jews, instances showing a strength of spirit wherein there was no question of bartering their rights or of being bowed down, and where neither force nor cunning was used to escape the consequences of their behaviour. Such actions, however, exerted apparently not the slightest influence on their opponents. All honour indeed to those who displayed such strength of soul! But I cannot recognise herein a parole for the general behaviour of German Jews which might seem suited to exert an influence on the oppressed or on the world. An effective stand may be taken in the form of non-violence against unfeeling human beings in the hope of gradually bringing them thereby to their senses; but a diabolic universal steam-roller cannot thus be withstood. There is a certain situation in which from the "Satyāgraha" of the strength of the spirit no "Satyāgraha" of the power of truth can result.'[20]

In that same letter, Buber revealed a sympathetic understanding of Gandhi's dilemma in confronting the challenge of modernism. Because of his realism, Buber was able to appreciate the tension which existed between Gandhi's non-attached devotion to *satyāgraha* and his passionate desire for India's independence. Buber penetrated to the core of Gandhi's ambivalence, and did not consider it a fault. He quoted something that Gandhi had written in 1922 about preferring even violence to continued bondage for India, and he added: 'you asserted thereby that non-violence is for you a faith and not a political principle—and that the desire for the freedom of India is even *stronger* in you than your faith. And for this, I love you'.[21]

Buber then tried to explain to Gandhi the Hebrew position which denies an absolute commitment to non-violence: 'We have not pro-claimed, as did Jesus, the son of our people, and as you do, the teaching of non-violence, because we believe that a man must sometimes use force to save himself or even more his children. But from time immemorial we have proclaimed the teaching of justice and peace: we have taught and we have learnt that peace is the aim of all the world and that justice is the way to attain it. Thus we cannot *desire* to use force. . . . I would not deny however, that although I should not have been among the crucifiers of Jesus, I should also not have been among his supporters. For I cannot help withstanding evil when I see that it is about to destroy the good. I am forced to withstand the evil in the world just as the evil within myself. I can only strive not to have to do so by force. I do not want force. But if there is no other way of preventing the evil destroying the good, I trust I shall use force and give myself up into God's hands.'[22]

At the same time that Gandhi was calling upon the Jews to adopt *satyāgraha*, the noted sociologist, Kurt Lewin, took a very different stand. 'The Jew will have to realize, and he will have to realize it fast, that in fighting Nazis and their allies it does not pay to be polite,' he wrote. 'There is only one way to fight an enemy, and this is to return blow for blow, to strike back immediately, and if possible, harder. Jews can expect to get active help from others only if they themselves show that they have the courage and the determination to stand up for a fight of self-defense.'[23] This attitude conforms to the requirements of modernism. Nor was this attitude entirely foreign to Gandhi. Where Gandhi's own personal and passionate desire for Indian independence was concerned, he showed that he could part company with Hindu romanticism and grasp the realities of institutional power.

One of the most significant results of modern technology has been the rapid institutionalization of industrial society. Massive organization has come to overshadow the influence of personal leadership. Indeed, the very massiveness has come to be more of a hindrance than a help, more irrational than rational. Structures set up to facilitate the resolution of problems lose their rationality as the problems change, while the ability to take those structures apart and put them back together again in a more rational way diminishes. Existing needs are bent to the prevailing institutions, instead of the reverse. Gradually the institutions intended to serve men, become ends in themselves which men must serve. In such a 'system' human beings cease to be the controlling factor. They act out their appropriate role behaviour, measuring their success by their degree of adjustment to what they cannot change. They serve the system, but they do not control it.

On this point, Gandhi's vision was surprisingly clear. He recognized that the system is the root of social evil and not men. Men are influenced by the system in which they live. For this reason, Gandhi considered himself a more authentic socialist than those who officially carried the title. He was aware that in working for the independence of India, the primary attack must be made against the imperialist system, and not against individuals symbolizing the ruling power. In a debate with young communists in the year 1931, Gandhi stated: 'Non-co-operators never told the people that the British or General Dyer were bad, but that they were the victims of a system. So that the system must be destroyed and not the individual'.[24]

There is a two-fold question involved here: how the system can be destroyed, and what shall take its place. Gandhi felt that non-violent non-co-operation was the proper method to destroy the system since it paralyzed its functioning without injuring people. It is true that institutions are vulnerable in this sense, since they must keep functioning in order to survive. Complete non-violent non-co-operation should bring about the collapse of any institution. But the chaos arising out of the abrupt collapse of institutions in modern society could very well prove more damaging in the long run than the reasoned use of violence to compel changes in those institutions. If it is a matter of changing the institutional structure of the system, violence may well be the best means. If, however, the objective is to destroy the system as a whole, a choice of means requires first a decision on what should take its place. The alternatives would seem to be either chaos or some other social grouping.

283

Non-violent non-co-operation can very likely bring about chaos, but can it also bring about a different and better kind of society?

There is one fundamental point of clear difference between tradition and modernism. Hindu tradition, like Hebrew tradition, holds that the human element is the centre of reality. Modernism tends to stress institutions at the expense of the human element. Both Gandhi and Buber were exponents of tradition, seeking to meet the challenge of modernism through a defense of tradition. Each regarded himself a socialist, and yet each rejected the Marxist-Leninist notion that the answer lay in changing the institutional structure of society. Both shared the view that a proper social order must be a life of community. Each sought to work out a re-interpretation of his own tradition in order to facilitate the development of community life as the answer to the evils of modernism. Gandhi took as his model the *ashram*, while Buber looked to the Hasidic brotherhood and the *kibbutz*.

Modernization creates a radical social polarization. It produces a powerful trend toward the intensive institutionalization of social living to the exclusion of the personal element. But where the personal element is excluded, so too is the basis of morality. The absence of the personal element means that moral pressure can have little effect. What this means is that modernization pushes society toward the negation of morality. As such, modernism and *satyāgraha* are incompatible.

On the other hand, the very defects of modernism have stimulated a trend toward social living based on community as a reaction against the excesses of institutionalization. Within community, the personal element is dominant and therefore morality is the governing influence. *Satyāgraha* here can have full meaning.

Gandhi aspired to realize such a community throughout his life. The first attempts were made in South Africa at Phoenix Farm and Tolstoy Farm. More lasting attempts were made in India, at Sabarmati and Sevagram. Even in making these experiments, Gandhi was moving from modernism back to tradition. India has been for most of its history a land of relatively autonomous and self-governing village communities. These village communities were based on the kind of personal relation among its members which makes the concept of *dharma* meaningful. British rule disintegrated these village communities by subordinating them to a formal and centralized legal system. In doing so, the traditional foundation was demolished and along with it the inner cohesion which had kept the Indian village going for thousands of years.[25]

Gandhi often said that his idea of independence was not just changing the ruling class from white to brown. He wanted India as a whole to become independent and capable of working out its own destiny in the light of its own tradition. 'Independence must mean that of the people of India, not of those who are today ruling over them,' he said. 'Independence must begin at the bottom. Thus, every village will be a republic or Panchayat having full powers.'[26] Gandhi called this form of self-governing communities village *swarāj*, and he said: 'My idea of village Swaraj is that it is a complete republic, independent of its neighbours for its own vital wants, and yet interdependent for many others in which dependence is a necessity. Thus every village's first concern will be to grow its own food crops and cotton for its cloth. It should have a reserve for its cattle, recreation and playground for adults and children. Then if there is more land available, it will grow *useful* money crops. . . . The village will maintain a village theatre, school and public hall. It will have its own waterworks ensuring water supply. This can be done through controlled well and tanks. Education will be compulsory up to the final basic course. As far as possible every activity will be conducted on a co-operative basis. There will be no castes such as we have today with their graded untouchability. Non-violence with its technique of *satyāgraha* and non-co-operation will be the sanction of the village community.'[27]

This programme for a return to the traditional village community, elaborated by Gandhi over the years, is the social expression of *satyāgraha*. In effect, it calls for the actualization of *satyāgraha* by a return to that social *dharma* which is basic to Indian tradition, but which has been so badly neglected by the intellectually-orientated schools. It constitutes the Indian tradition's social and political alternative to modernism.

Village *swarāj* and centralized parliamentary (legal) government form the axis of social and political controversy in India today. Vinoba Bhave and Jayaprakash Narayan are the major exponents of the Gandhian position.[28] Through the *Bhoodan* Movement, they are attempting to create a national network of village republics capable of replacing the existing system of government through a non-violent revolution. Nehru and the majority of Congress leaders, however, remained loyal to the parliamentary system introduced by the British.[29] Neither the Congress Party itself nor the Indian government adheres to Gandhian principles or claims a policy aimed at achieving a social and political order based on *satyāgraha*. Tradition and modernism continue to be at loggerheads, thereby deepening the tragedy of contemporary India.

Gandhi undoubtedly was moving in the right direction in trying to work out a solution based on village communities. However, his inability

285

to increase the weight and importance of the elements of social and political realism within the tradition, while diminishing the influence of romantic idealism, left his position weak in the face of the enormous pressures for economic development that came in the wake of independence. Probably no major improvements can be expected in India until the necessary changes are made in the interpretation of tradition. When and if that comes about, India stands to become a leader among nations. Until then, India shall remain wracked by the pains of an unassimilable modernism.

NOTES

[1] *Young India*, 23 March 1921.

[2] *Young India*, 14 January 1920.

[3] M. K. Gandhi, *Satyagraha in South Africa* (Madras, 1928), p. 32.

[4] M. K. Gandhi, *An Autobiography* (Ahmedabad, 1948), p. 50.

[5] M. K. Gandhi, *Satyagraha* (Ahmedabad, 1951), pp. 38-39.

[6] M. K. Gandhi, *My Religion* (Ahmedabad, 1955), p. 103.

[7] S. N. Das Gupta, *History of Indian Philosophy* (Cambridge, 1957), vol. 1, p. 200.

[8] *Ibid.*, p. 270.

[9] Jadunath Sinha, *History of Indian Philosophy* (Calcutta, 1952), vol. 2, p. 264.

[10] Heinrich Zimmer, *Philosophies of India* (New York, 1956), p. 170.

[11] Gandhi's wife.

[12] M. K. Gandhi, *Satyagraha*, op. cit., pp. 4-5.

[13] *Harijan*, 15 October 1938.

[14] *Harijan*, 22 June 1940.

[15] *Harijan*, 6 July 1940.

[16] H. A. Jack (ed.), *The Gandhi Reader* (Bloomington, 1956), p. 353.

[17] *Ibid.*, p. 354.   [18] *Ibid.*, pp. 319-20.

[19] *Complete Works of Ahad Haam* (Tel Aviv: Dvir, 1961), p. 373. (Hebrew)

[20] *Two Letters to Gandhi from Martin Buber and J. L. Magnes* (Jerusalem, 1939).

[21] *Ibid.*   [22] *Ibid.*

[23] Kurt Lewin, *Resolving Social Conflicts* (New York, 1967), p. 167. The statement quoted was published originally in 1939.

[24] *Young India*, 26 November 1931.

[25] The reader will find a discussion of this subject in my article, 'Customary and Legal Democracy', *The Radical Humanist*, vol. 27, Nos. 3-5, Jan. 25, 1963, pp, 33-34, 36.

[26] *Harijan*, 28 July 1946.   [27] *Harijan*, 26 July 1942.

[28] Vinoba Bhave, *Swaraj Shastra* (Rajghat, 1958). Jayaprakash Narayan, *A Picture of Sarvodaya Social Order* (Tanjore, 1961); *Swaraj for the People* (Rajghat, 1961); *A Plea for Reconstruction of Indian Polity* (Rajghat, n.d.).

[29] Worthy of notice is the important attempt at synthesis made by M. N. Roy. Although an extreme adherent of modernism, Roy evolved a programme of village communities not unlike that which Gandhi envisaged, and which is today supported by Jayaprakash Narayan. However, Roy was personally too alienated from Indian tradition to undertake the difficult task of making substantive changes in it. The reader will find an account of Roy's views in my article, 'The Political Philosophy of M. N. Roy,' *Asian Studies* (Philippines), vol. 4, No. 3, December 1966, pp. 464-78.

CAN VIOLENCE LEAD TO NON-VIOLENCE? GANDHI'S POINT OF VIEW

Arne Naess

I

Gandhi called himself an experimenter. His experiment consisted in systematically developing and consistently following the voice of conscience—following it completely and relentlessly, and using no other guide-line, religious or otherwise. He spoke in these terms since it was the truth or truthfulness value of the voice of conscience that was important to him. The religious element enters with his identification of God with truth and justice. However, he substituted the formula 'truth is God' for the formula 'God is truth'. In doing so he kept his concept of truth but changed his concept of God.

As a *karma-yogin*, one who seeks the highest goals through action, it became inevitable for him to take sides in the most violent conflicts of his times. With the standard of truth as his master it was obvious that he had to fight deprivation, injustice, hypocrisy and untruth—and equally obvious that this would soon lead him to take part in political battles. The corollary of the identification of God with truth is that living a religious life is equivalent to pursuing truth. The worshipper of God will inevitably be involved in group conflicts.

> I could not be leading a religious life unless I identified myself with the whole of mankind, and that I could not do unless I took part in politics. The whole gamut of man's activities today constitutes an indivisible whole. You cannot divide social, economic, political, and purely religious work into watertight compartments.[1]
>
> To see the universal and all-pervading Spirit of Truth face to face one must be able to love the meanest of creatures as oneself. And a man who aspires after that cannot afford to keep out of any field of life. That is why my devotion to Truth has drawn me into the field of politics.[2]

287

One is justified in calling Gandhi a man of peace and good will, but one is also justified in calling him the greatest of agitators—he roused millions of Indians to battle. The peasants were indifferent and had resigned themselves to suppression. It did not occur to them to take part in any conflict until Gandhi called forth demands for justice, and, more fundamentally, demands for humane conditions of existence. He stimulated them to individual indignation at their condition and at the humiliations they were suffering.

The representatives of the Indian empire very clearly foresaw how the standard of unconditional truth, combined with the standard of action, had to create conflict. They were right in supposing that Gandhi's activity would create unrest, disorder and disobedience. The exchange between the Hunter Committee's Counsel and the accused Gandhi, prior to one of his many terms in prison, is famous:

> *Counsel*: However honestly a man may strive in his search for truth, his notions of truth may be different from the notions of others. Who then is to determine the truth?
> *Accused*: The individual himself would determine that.
> *Counsel*: Different individuals would have different views as to truth. Would that not lead to confusion?
> *Accused*: I do not think so.[3]

Of course truth leads to conflict; but it clarifies, it does not confuse. A crucial point, however, is the question of *how* the battle between groups is to be carried out, when both sides are relentlessly pursuing the voice of conscience.

It is commonly held that Gandhi regarded it as self-evident that the voice of conscience should dictate the non-violent form of battle as the only effective and the only justifiable one. But this is a fundamental mis-understanding. He fully realized that many will conclude that the use of violence is the only effective and the only right course of action after an honest and profound appraisal of themselves and the situation. In so far as the politicians in India held this opinion it was their duty, according to Gandhi, to arm. He criticized them for shrinking from openly accepting a programme of armament even though they obviously had no faith in the methods of non-violence. The politicians ought to have provided training in the use of arms if they lacked belief in non-violence.

Gandhi forced a decision on the Congress party politicians in 1934 when he proposed the replacement of their catch-phrase for action 'peacefully and legally' with 'truthfully and non-violently'. The proposal was not accepted and Gandhi left Indian party politics.

The methods of non-violence are rightly associated with the name of Gandhi. His originality in this field is unique, although some of his methods have been rediscovered independently of him. Martin Luther King is one of the outstanding names in this connection. But it is often forgotten that the standards of non-violent conduct and intention are for Gandhi subservient to another standard, the highest standard in his system. He wrote:

> If it is possible for the human tongue to give the fullest description of God, I have come to the conclusion that for myself, God is Truth. But two years ago I went a step further and said that Truth is God.[4]

Again, in a discussion with a friend he made this point:

> 'Nevertheless, your emphasis is always on *ahimsa*. You have made propagation of non-violence the mission of your life,' argued the friend, still unwilling to concede the point. 'There again you are wrong,' answered Gandhiji. '*Ahimsa* is not the goal. Truth is the goal. But we have no means of realizing truth in human relationships except through the practice of *ahimsa*. . . .'[5]

Consequently, the doctrine of non-violence cannot, according to Gandhi, be evolved in isolation from a higher goal, which is beyond the distinction between violence and non-violence.

The doctrine of non-violence rises from Gandhi's personal conviction of a fundamental equality in the destiny of all men, and of their equal right to self-expression. His personal identification with all men, however, equates injury to others with injury to oneself. In group conflicts one gains nothing by injuring others. No fully justifiable goal may be reached by means which include planned or accidental injury to others in such conflicts. Between one's own self-expression and the self-expression of others there is no sharp boundary.

Moreover the activist programme follows from this identification; it does not help to retire from existing battles in order to avoid committing violence oneself. Violence is an evil, whether it is one's own or that of another, and must be fought. Therefore one must seek the root of the conflict, must go to where violence is beginning or has begun.

Gandhi distinguishes between condemnation of an act and condemnation of the person who has carried out the act. Acts of violence are always wrong and evil. But this does not justify us in immediately condemning the person who acts violently. A person who in a good cause can see only the alternatives of cowardly reticence and violence does right in acting violently. That he should see only this alternative in spite of intensive analysis of himself and study of the situation discloses a lack of insight or experience or perhaps a lack of the opportunity of training himself in non-violence, due to having been brought up in an environment where it is thought good to be shielded from raw reality. Without taking part in agonizing conflicts the capacity for effective non-violence cannot, of course, be developed.

Gandhi understood what is now commonly called counter-violence, particularly when the opponent is physically utterly superior. In line with this he expressed understanding of Norway's war against Hitler's Germany. Germany's superiority in this case made violence something akin to a symbolic act—an unconditional no to injustice. To small powers that are attacked Gandhi did not say that they *ought* to offer non-violent resistance, but that they *may*. And further, that non-violence is in the long run the only thing that can reduce organized violence and suppression.[6]

When Gandhi left South Africa and started his work in India he soon realized that the Indian masses could not immediately be mobilized in a political struggle for freedom.

A starving man thinks first of satisfying his hunger before anything else. He will sell his liberty and all for the sake of getting a morsel of food. Such is the position of millions of the people of India. For them liberty, God and all such words are merely letters put together without the slightest meaning.[7]

Continuous hunger produces apathy. The apathy in India was so all-embracing that it hindered every constructive effort to improve the conditions of life. The situation seemed hopeless: apathy and passivity beget self-contempt, a feeling of being totally useless or superfluous, a feeling of infinite impotence, and hence a lack of personal identity.

It was impossible for Gandhi to make any substantial and immediate change in the food situation. Thus he had to increase the self-respect of each individual, to increase the belief that 'I am something worth caring for', despite the absence of such a change. One of his brilliant schemes to this end was the hand-spinning and hand-weaving programme, the *khādi* movement. Gandhi said of this:

If we want to give these people a sense of freedom we shall have to provide them with work which they can easily do in their desolate homes. This can only be done by the spinning wheel. And when they have become self-reliant and are able to support themselves we are in a position to talk to them about freedom, about [the] Congress [party], etc. Those, therefore, who bring them work and means of getting a crust of bread will be their deliverers and will be also the people who will make them hunger for liberty.[8]

Gandhi's plan was that every family in India's half a million villages should take part in the *khādi* movement by spinning or weaving. Most of the villagers were out of work for most of the year. During this time they were idle, without aim or purpose, and more often than not suffering from some disease. That Indians should henceforce be able to provide for some of their own basic needs became in itself a challenge to the government, and an act of self-assertion on the part of each Indian against his seemingly all-powerful rulers.

The *khādi* movement served also to knit the Indian nation closer together. Gandhi prevented the loom becoming a symbol of poverty by, among other things, passing a resolution that the membership dues of the Congress party should be 2000 yards of yarn spun by the member himself. Everyone was on the same footing, and this could only increase the self-respect of the poor in relation to the richer classes.

By means of the *khādi* movement and other brilliantly-conceived schemes Gandhi succeeded in bringing into being an elementary minimum of self-respect and feeling of worth and dignity in millions of Indians. This, more than anything else, was his ethical and political achievement. Gandhi then tried to utilize this minimum to get people to join constructive projects on a large scale. As a result of participation in such projects the emerging self-respect grew into a clear awareness of the right not only to survive but to live a worthy life, and thus of the duty to take part in the political freedom movement.

According to Gandhi the intimate connection between economy and personal identity necessitated the carrying out of extensive decentralization and the elimination of big cities. In his *Constructive Programme* Gandhi envisages that the 700,000 villages in India, instead of being exploited and destroyed by half a dozen cities in India and Great Britain, would be able largely to support themselves and serve voluntarily the cities of India, and even those of the outside world, so far as this was mutually beneficial. This, he said, would require a revolutionary change in the mentality of the masses. The non-violent way, although easy in many respects, was very difficult in others. It meant touching the life of each Indian, making him feel possessed of a force hidden within him, and making him proud of his identity with every other Indian.[9]

The essential point is this, that Gandhi acknowledged self-respect as an absolutely necessary pre-condition for non-violent action in group conflicts. When it becomes obvious that the self-respect is insufficient, the struggle for independence must change its emphasis to measures aiming at increased self-respect. Indignation and angry words are signs of insufficient self-respect, caused by powerlessness and a lack of belief in one's ability to convince the opponent.[10]

I give the following as an example of how Gandhi reacted when confronted with instances of abject anger.

In 1921 Gandhi organized the largest non-violent campaign ever carried through. According to the plan a constant escalation was to take place, month after month. The decisive phase was planned to begin on 1 February 1922 with collective law-breaking. But in Chauri Chaura the mob killed twenty-two policemen, cut them up, and burnt them, in desperate anger and counter-violence. Gandhi immediately called off the entire campaign, even though it now embraced more than one million men. Only the constructive programme was continued, that is, the hand-spinning, the religious tolerance movement and the help to the untouchables. Many politicians were intensely annoyed, and the multitudes despaired, over Gandhi's reaction.

But his motives were clear enough. What was important, to him, was that the conditions for extensive non-violence, involving mass participation, were not present. The requirements of self-respect and human dignity were not satisfied. Consequently, a retreat from the political to the more fundamental ethical and humanitarian level was necessary. This entailed intensifying the 'constructive' measures. The episode of Chauri Chaura illuminates the importance Gandhi attached to the preparations for non-violent action and how clear it was to him that if events disclosed decisive flaws in the preparations, the action had to be called off temporarily or else considerable de-escalation had to take place.

We can find the same pattern in his reaction to violence and counter-violence in Amritsar in 1919. Again he finds that self-respect gives way, and participants flee or use violence. Gandhi called off the action. He recognized his 'Himalayan mistake'. The masses had not been sufficiently mature for civil disobedience, a fact which he, as leader, ought to have understood. Collective excitement is a difficult factor to estimate, but it is primarily the sheer number of people involved in mass movements which makes consistent non-violence difficult. If even one in a thousand is actively destructive he may be followed by ten others in one violent act that spoils the entire campaign. Of course, encouraging events took place as well. In 1930 on several occasions the multitude stayed where they were when the armed police attacked them, with the result that the police refused to continue the attack.[11] This was exactly the kind of self-respect and self-restraint on the part of the demonstrators that, according to Gandhi, is necessary for the carrying out of an effective non-violent liberation struggle.

II

I will now try to show how Gandhi's ideas on self-respect, and the conviction of personal identity and worth, are relevant today.

The last ten years have seen a lack of belief in non-violent action within several liberation movements. Violence both in intention and action has become fashionable.[12] The recognition of violence today springs partly from the conviction that it is only a small minority who are able to remain non-violent in battle and that brutal opponents are impressed by nothing except violence and are not at all ashamed of assaulting the defenceless.

From close examination of the examples and teachings of famous violence-promoting negro leaders it seems clear to me that Martin Luther King and the other eminent advocates of non-violence in the 1950's did not quite succeed in formulating, much less in solving, the problem of self-respect. Critics of King's strict non-violence emphasize that a man who is without belief in himself can desist from counter-violence only by cowardice. His reflexes will require him to answer violence with violence. The only question for him is 'do I dare to?'

In explaining the lack of self-respect among the U.S.A.'s negroes several factors, social, mental and religious, must be considered.

The religious traditions in the Indian societies (including the Muslim) made it easier for Gandhi to appeal to religious and cultural standards than it has been for Martin Luther King, for example, to appeal to Christian standards in addressing the negro population of America's secularized industrial society. Furthermore, there has been no unifying, positive, concrete liberation program in the U.S.A., nor any constructive plan such as formed the basis of the *khādi* movement in India. This may partly account for the absence of a satisfactory solution to the problem of self-respect in America, and for the rare occurrence of conditions enabling the use of positive, aggressive non-violence on a large scale.

The difference between the situations in America and India is not, however, that the opponents in India were less brutal. Gandhi's main field was in the area of religious conflicts. When he lost control towards the end of the 1940's, more than a million people were killed in communal riots all over India. Hatred and white-hot anger were features of the situation where Gandhi and his helpers exercised their power, and it was not 'the kind Englishmen' who put his non-violence to the test.[13]

It is natural to interpret a considerable part of today's direct exhortations to counter-violence, that is, to meet violence with violence, as an attempt to give the apathetic, self-deprecating individual a chance to feel that he *is* something, is someone to whom the opponent must pay attention. It is probably this that Frantz Fanon has in mind (in his more sane moments) when he emphasizes 'the liberating effect of violence' upon the oppressed and underprivileged. He says:

> At the level of individuals violence is a cleansing force. it frees the native from his inferiority complex and from his despair and inaction; it makes him fearless and restores his self-respect.[14]

It is worth noting that he mentions the 'slave soul' in the same context. There are, in fact, reports from the U.S.A. which indicate that violence by negroes against the police has had an intensely stimulating effect upon the negro population. All have felt themselves a little bigger, a little more courageous. A more straightforward, natural mode of speech is being used in front of the whites. A new phenomenon on the university square of Berkeley (1968) is the sight of negroes cursing whites, who stand in a circle about them listening solemnly and obviously on the defensive. This helps, of course, but only in the short run: it solves no problems.

When the use of counter-violence is argued, the typical situation put forward is that of a coloured person assaulted by whites. The negro-leader Carmichael usually speaks of assaults by white mobs and nocturnal terrorists. In terms of the group conflict, however, these are relatively unimportant situations. It seems clear to Carmichael, and also to others who criticize Martin Luther King, that civil rights and a comprehensive participation in the process of decision cannot be obtained by fist-fighting or individual use of weapons. But it is equally clear that these cannot be attained by passivity in the face of assault. Of this, Carmichael and Hamilton say, in their book *Black Power*, that as leaders they increased the frustration of the Blacks boiling with anger at the lack of action taken after they had seen Martin Luther King take a rap, and small black girls killed by a bomb in a church, since the leaders had nothing concrete to offer them. Such frustration is understandable considering the feeling of paralysis and the lack of a constructive programme. These negroes had nothing to do except to go out in the street and be hit once more. The absence of a continuous non-violent struggle had its effects. To be struck down in a direct battle does not give rise to the frustration Carmichael describes.

From the point of view I have indicated it is misleading to say that in the U.S.A. non-violent methods have largely been given up in favour of violent methods. What has happened during the last few years may be interpreted rather as an attempt to create the necessary conditions for a future non-violent constructive campaign on a mass basis. In India, Gandhi succeeded in bringing about the conditions required for non-violent revolution; in other societies, it seems, these must be brought about partly by violent methods and incidents. But it is quite clear, even from the statements of extremists such as the Black Panther leader, Huey Newton, that counter-violence must not be regarded as a way of solving the major problems of liberation. Violence is only conceived of as a defensive and preliminary measure, a means of counteracting fear, panic, and the feeling of inferiority which is absolutely destructive in any effecting organization of campaigns toward liberation.

The latest reports from the U.S.A. indicate that the negroes are turning their backs on spontaneous riots and destruction, and are more and more carrying on the struggle with positive action. Co-operation, especially economic co-operation is popular. Riots and counter-violence may have had their importance, their regrettable function, in an environment where a kind of primitive self-respect and the use of violence are very close to each other. The use of violence may perhaps have contributed in preparing the ground for the use of more effective means.

The aggressive ideologists within the negro liberation movement today find that their situation is similar to that of the Indians in so far as in both cases it is a struggle against colonialism and in both cases it is a matter of revolution. Carmichael and Hamilton conclude their book *Black Power* with the pronouncement that there is a quickly growing group of blacks who are determined to 'T.C.B.' (take care of business) regardless of consequences, and who will not be stopped in their vigorous efforts to attain dignity, to grasp their share of power, and to exercise the right to shape their own destiny, here and now, no matter what means may be necessary.[15]

The point to which I am here trying to direct attention is that the violence which seems to be recommended or tolerated by the leaders of opinion is primarily a means of gaining self-respect and thence the foundation of dignity. 'T.C.B.' is of course not to be achieved by riots and violence. On the contrary the blacks were often the hardest hit, economically. Mastery of one's own destiny is only to be achieved by positive measures based on inner strength. Brute force can help only at the very outset. Gandhi envisaged, as the ultimate measure, forming institutions parallel to those of the oppressors, that is, being self-sufficient on the largest possible scale. But to form such institutions, for example one's own schools, courts and co-operative societies, positive, not negative means are necessary. Blind anger does not further this cause.

III

Gandhi's campaigns had a character other than what is today commonly called non-violent. Briefly, we can say that Gandhi's demonstrations were usually demonstrations *for* something rather than against: his agitation was *for* something, his strikes were in the same way constructive and even his boycotts and civil disobedience were *for*, not against. A campaign A was not an attempt to force the situation B; rather, the campaign itself consisted in bringing about the situation B. It follows that Gandhi's actions were usually directed towards something visible, something concrete and well-defined. At the same time specific aims were included as a small part of the large general aim, the inner and outer liberation.

But, many will say, since Gandhi had as opponents not primitive brutes but the kind and decent Englishmen, his methods cannot be carried over to the racial strife of our time, the wars in the colonies and student insurrection against police atrocities. The belief that Gandhi dealt primarily with the English stems from the fact that most of the world in the twenties and thirties was politically and economically interested in Britain and its empire.[16] There was little interest in the violent strife amongst India's cultural constituent societies—amongst Muslims, Hindus and Sikhs. Here a white-hot anger raged and, as I have already mentioned, when Gandhi let go the reins towards the end of the forties more than a million people died in the riots amongst the different communities. Gandhi and his supporters achieved their most shining successes in just those campaigns which were concerned with the elimination of inner strife. Gandhi had good reason to emphasize to Nehru and the more nationalistic political leaders that liberation *(swarāj)* had primarily to mean liberation from the conditions which led to oppression and violence on the inner front. He wished the politicians to concentrate on these aspects rather than on relations with England.

During campaigns one consequently anticipated and realized something of the future. One taught the opponent how one wanted the society of the future to be. Negative campaigns—those that occurred—were secondary, and usually in a comprehensible and obvious relationship to the

296

positive aims. They were frequently protests caused by the reactions of the authorities to the positive campaigns, or alternatives to discontinued or blocked positive actions. The fact that the main emphasis was placed on positive, concrete campaigns meant that when the non-violent freedom fighter met the enemy face to face the former was in the act of *doing* something, or carrying out or expressing something he felt to be indisputably justified. In such a case, the opponent, if he adopts countermeasures, violent or non-violent, must act so as to counter the positive aim of the non-violent freedom fighter. For example, the untouchables entered temples and prayed (1924-25 Vykom *satyāgraha*)[17] or the poor prepared salt from seawater at the coast. The untouchables did not demonstrate outside the priests' dwellings, nor did the poor march in processions carrying posters labelled 'down with the salt tax'.

The prevailing interpretation of the commandment to turn the other cheek illustrates the difference between positive and negative non-violence. It is not particularly difficult to train police to strike down peaceful but negative demonstrators. Passivity under attack makes it difficult for reasonably decent men to beat and abuse people, but if the police are recruited from the ignorant and the authoritarian, or are indoctrinated with the idea that the demonstrations are not advocating any good cause, the element of decency may be eliminated. Even in Norway and Sweden we have seen examples of this. Consequently, the good or just cause must show itself during the confrontation itself, whether this is with the police or with others sent to receive the non-violent freedom fighters with violence and suppression. One might say that the realization of the positive programme so to speak 'under the noses of the adversaries' entails the realization of the aims set by the campaigns.

> [The] Constructive Programme is the truthful and non-violent way of winning Poorna Swaraj [complete independence].[18]
>
> I have said and I repeat, that there is no swaraj for the masses except through Khadi and village-handicraft, for there is no non-violent disobedience without a continuous constructive effort. For a living, continuous mass contact is impossible without a constructive programme, that requires almost daliy contact between the (non-violent) workers and the masses.[19]

The constructive programme had to be concrete and well-defined so that the majority of the members of the society where the advocates of *satyāgraha* worked could realize that it was to the benefit of all.

The actions during the campaigns themselves were given a positive

297

form, so that the adversary who attacked, using violence, had to do so while the demonstrators were clearly showing what they wanted, for instance while they were entering the temples, or while they were extracting salt for their meals.

During extensive positive campaigns, for example the founding of one's own schools, universities, courts of law, etc., the attackers must destroy something that has an obvious purpose and clearly shows the intentions of the non-violent fighters. According to Gandhi this is impossible in a negative campaign where one only shows what one is against. What one is usually against is something well-established, something that most people regard as more or less unalterable. To recognize an alternative clearly requires imagination, and we cannot expect one's adversary to be in an imaginative mood if the emphasis is on annoying him.

Consequently, the decreasing adherence to so-called non-violent methods need not be attributed to disappointingly insubstantial results from positive non-violent actions based on a constructive programme. Wherever such actions have been carried through, the result seems to have been remarkably great in comparison to the effort expended. But the work of Martin Luther King and others, in the spirit of Gandhi, has revealed the importance of learning more about how the prerequisites for the participation of the masses in non-violent action may be gradually fulfilled.

To sum up, we may say that the reaction against so-called non-violence is a healthy reaction in so far as it is a reaction against *passive* resistance and *negative* campaigns. This reaction is likely to lead in the long run to increased acknowledgment and realization of Gandhi's ideas, which clearly point to the importance of the active and positive elements in campaigns. May the centenary celebration contribute to the strengthening of these ideas all over the world!

NOTES

[1] *Harijan*, 24 December 1938, in R. K. Prabhu and U. R. Rao, *The Mind of Mahatma Gandhi* (Oxford University Press, 1946), p. 81.

[2] M. K. Gandhi, *An Autobiography* (Ahmedabad, 1956), p. 504.

[3] D. G. Tendulkar, *Mahatma* (Bombay, 1952), vol. 1, p. 342.

[4] *Young India*, 31 December 1931, Prabhu and Rao, op. cit., p. 29.

[5] *Harijan*, 23 June 1946, in M. K. Gandhi, *Non-violence in Peace and War* (Ahmedabad, 1949), vol. 2, pp. 104-05.

[6] See Gandhi's article in *Harijan*, 9 December 1939.

[7 & 8] *Young India*, 18 March 1926, in Louis Fischer, *The Essential Gandhi* (New York, 1962), p. 223.

[9] See M. K. Gandhi, *Constructive Programme* (Ahmedabad, 1941).

[10] It is tempting to quote the Norwegian author Axel Sandemose's private quarrel with Gandhi in *Brev fra Kjorkelvik*, Arstidende No. 6, 1953: 'So-called restraint is useless, whether it is deliberate or forced. What you have constrained will sooner or later demand to be let out. You should not make believe that you can stop hitting people and abusing them before you have found something else to do.' Something else to do was exactly what Gandhi offered.

[11] See Joan V. Bondurant, *Conquest of Violence* (Princeton, 1958), p. 96.

[12] A Norwegian author is reputed to have gone so far as to identify hatred towards oppression with hatred towards the oppressors. This is an extremely un-Gandhian statement.

[13] Nevertheless, the British police in India were often brutal. Non-violent fighters with broken skulls and crushed genitalia were to be found in the hospitals. See Webb Miller's first-hand description of police brutality during the salt *satyagraha* in his book *I Found No Peace* (New York, 1936), quoted in Louis Fischer, *Gandhi. His Life and Message for the World* (Mentor Books, New York, 1962), pp. 100-01.

[14] Frantz Fanon, *The Wretched of the Earth* (Penguin, London, 1967), p. 35.

[15] Stanley Carmichael and C. V. Hamilton, *Black Power, the Politics of Liberation in America* (New York, 1967).

[16] Even Martin Luther King views Gandhi primarily in this light. Of his own struggle he said, in his Nobel Lecture in Oslo on 11 December 1964: 'This approach to the problem of racial injustice is not at all without successful precedent. It was used in a magnificent way by Mohandas K. Gandhi to challenge the might of the British Empire, and free his people from the political domination and economic exploitation inflicted upon them for centuries. He struggled only with the weapons of truth, soul-force, non-injury and courage.'

[17] For details see C. F. Andrews, *Mahatma Gandhi's Ideas* (London, 1930); and R. R. Diwakar, *Satyagraha: Its Technique and History* (Bombay, 1946).

[18] M. K. Gandhi, *Constructive Programme*, foreword to the 1945 ed., p. iii.

[19] *Harijan*, 23 March 1940.

SATYAGRAHA AND THE RACE PROBLEM IN AMERICA

Amiya Chakravarty

I

The race problem of America was born out of a turbulent and dynamic situation where cultural, ethnical and linguistic encounters took place on a large scale. 'The settling of the Western Hemisphere by peoples coming from Europe and Africa was an adventure on a grand scale, involving diverse peoples, varying cultures, millions of human beings, and hundreds of years.'[1] Although the migration of the African was a forced one, it was one of the world's largest. He came with the European as a slave, and he was black; 'the fact that the slave was a Negro merely added to the confusion; it did not create it'.[2] The Spaniards and the Portuguese had less problems than the English with the slave, for their culture had had a place for him for centuries, however unsatisfactory and marginal. The slave had a legal, moral, and religious sanction which put him at the bottom of the social scale, yet left room for him to rise above it. In Latin America therefore, 'not only was the Negro encouraged to secure his freedom, but once he was free, no obstacles were placed in his incorporation into the community, in so far as his skills and abilities made that possible'.[3]

'But this adventure of the Negro in the New World has been structured differently in the United States than in other parts of this hemisphere. In spite of his complete identification with the mores of the United States, he is excluded and denied. This barrier has never been completely effective, but it has served to debar him from the very things that are of greatest value among us—equality of opportunity for growth and development as a man among men.'[4] This situation arose here because the society lacked any experience with the institution of slavery.

The African was brought to America basically because of his economic value in clearing the land and working the plantations. Because he was bought and sold a new situation was created for the American settler. The closest social position to the slave was the indentured servant, who worked for a specific term of years and then received his freedom. Thus, not having a social classification, the place of the slave was disregarded and gradually evolved into the status of property. This took place slowly, but led to the exceedingly gross situation whereby the Negro was only seen as a financial investment. In such a circumstance, the attitude shown towards him became less and less human until brutality and horror became the everyday stuff of his life.

The institution of slavery set a barrier across the American society which cut off all hope of truth and decency. America grew cloudy under the sustained strain so necessary to maintain the system. Morality fell apart. Morality was deliberately denied of the Negro and the white lost his in his attitude towards the black man.

It took a long time for Americans to begin to set an attitude against slavery. In New England before the arrival of the black man the Indians had already experienced the superior attitude of the settlers. 'Indian slavery early arose in New England and grew out of the ordinary course of the Indian wars. The sanctioning of Indian slavery led to a ready sanction of negro slavery. The New England Calvinist considered himself God's elect and that to him God had given the heathen for an inheritance, and by enslaving the Indians and trading them for negroes he was doing nothing more than entering into his heritage.'[5] This attitude lasted in New England until just before the Revolutionary War. At this time a minister shocked the members of his church by his protest against slavery. They 'were surprised that they had not long before seen the evil of the system'.[6] Voices of Negro protest also began to be raised during the Revolutionary War: 'We were unjustly dragged by the cruel hand of power from our dearest friends and some of us stolen from the bosoms of our tender parents and from a populous pleasant and plentiful country and brought hither to be made slaves for life in a Christian land. Thus we are deprived of every thing that hath a tendency to make life even tolerable, the endearing ties of husband and wife we are strangers to for we are no longer man and wife to our masters and mistresses. . . .'[7]

The protest continued into the nineteenth century. About 1830 there was a shift in emphasis of the protest. Up to then it primarily took the form of discussion. But when the horrors of slavery were fully revealed there came a demand for action. The American Anti-Slavery Society founded by William Lloyd Garrison in 1833 had a quarter of a million members in five years. Garrison asked for 'immediate and unconditioned emancipation which was indeed a revolutionary doctrine for its time and represented a threat to what many believed to be the foundation of the existing social and economic order'.[8]

On its positive side one of the articles of the American Anti-Slavery Society stated: 'This Society shall aim to elevate the character and condition of the people of colour, by encouraging their intellectual, moral and religious improvement, and by removing public prejudice, thus that they may, according to their intellectual and moral worth, share an equality with the white, of civil and religious privileges.'[9]

Slavery now became the main issue in the churches across America. In 1833 in Utica, New York, a group of clergymen broke away from the hesitant stand maintained by those who repressed the issue of slavery in the attempt to keep the churches of America united. During the next ten years all of the churches divided on the issue.

In 1859, John Brown, who had done much previously to help the cause of freedom, came to Harpers Ferry, Virginia, with both black and white men to instigate an insurrection. Although he always wanted a minimum of violence, his last words were: 'I, John Brown, am not quite certain that the crimes of this guilty land will ever be purged away but with blood. I had, as I now think vainly, flattered myself that without very much bloodshed it might be done.'[10]

But the protests were unsuccessful for the nation. The North did succeed in giving enough freedom to the Negro to allow him a limited degree of opportunity. But the South made every effort to maintain a static society. In the 1860's the Civil War broke out. 'The abolition of slavery in the United States was cataclysmic and violent just because it seemed so eternal, so faultless, because the gap between the Negro and the white man had been made so impassable and so absolute that it could not be bridged by any means of transition, by any natural growth and adaption. It was broken by violence and war and social catastrophe because it could not be moulded by other means.'[11]

The Emancipation Proclamation of 1 January 1863 freed the Negro. Frederick Douglas, an ex-slave who travelled around the country witnessing against slavery, wrote: 'Unquestionably, for weal or for woe, the First of January is to be the most memorable day in American Annals.'[12] But it left the Negro in a difficult position. 'When freedom came, my mama said Old Master called all of 'em to his house, and he said, "You all free, we ain't got nothing to do with you no more. Go on away. We don't whup you no more. Go on your way".'[13]

It took five years before some sort of order could be established and land was found for farming. The Reconstruction lasted for twelve years during which time the government co-operated with the Negroes in the attempt to reconstruct a society of decency. During the remainder of the nineteenth century much was accomplished. But not enough.

The limitations which were imposed upon the slave on the plantation were severe, causing him to have a stunted personality within a narrow, moulded world. His character developed in submission to his master and in communion solely with his fellow slaves. Yet out of these restricting confinements the Negro reached out into a marvellous spirituality—to a world away from the fleeting and rigid attitudes he found here. He sung hymns sounding a religious depth not often witnessed by Americans. But at the same time the spirituality grew onesided—to reach heaven where all things stolen from him were returned:

> Oh Freedom! Oh Freedom!
> Oh Freedom, I love thee!
> And before I'll be a slave,
> I'll be buried in my grave,
> And go home to my Lord and be free.[14]

> I got a robe, you got a robe,
> All God's children got robes.
> When we get to heaven
> We're going to put on our robes,
> We're going to shout all over God's heaven.[15]

The slave had a small world here, he had to build his earthly dreams in the heavenly domain. Though the anguish created some great lyrics and songs the earthly battle against wrongs, waged with the irresistible power of moral organization and a creative cohesion, had yet to come.

The Civil War and the Reconstruction only brought to the Negro some extension of physical freedom from slavery. In the minds of Southern white society and even in his own estimation he was barely a person. At the turn of the twentieth century segregation became law and W. E. B. DuBois declared that 'the problem of the twentieth century is the colour line'.[16] It appeared that Southern Society had regressed. But it 'was due not so much to a conversion as it was to a relaxation of the opposition'.[17]

The outright institution of slavery was removed, and in its place came the Jim Crow laws and segregation. The legality of the Jim Crow laws of 'separate but equal' institutions was challenged in the Supreme Court in 1896. But the Negro lost and second-class citizenship became a fact. Mr Justice Harlin, upon dissenting over this issue wrote: 'There is no caste here. Our Constitution is colour-blind, and neither knows nor tolerates classes among citizens. In respect of civil rights, all citizens are equal

303

before the law. The humblest is the peer of the most powerful. The law regards man as man, and takes no account of his colour, or of his surroundings when his civil rights as guaranteed by the supreme law of the land are involved. It is therefore to be regretted that this high tribunal, the final expositor of the fundamental law of the land, has reached the conclusion that it is competent for a state to regulate the enjoyment by citizens of their civil rights solely upon the basis of race.'[18]

Booker T. Washington set a voice for the Negro at this time emphasizing his pride in being a Negro. 'From any point of view, I had rather be what I am, a member of the Negro race, than be able to claim membership with the most favoured other race.'[19] Washington was a successful Negro who asked that the races be brought together in friendship and co-operation. In so doing he emphasized that each Negro should start working towards improvement from where he found himself. He said: 'Cast down your bucket where you are', for 'it is at the bottom of life we must begin, and not at the top'.[20] This was in 1895, and in response to his plea W. E. B. DuBois took another position. He saw Washington as too concerned with work and money and as not reaching far enough. In *The Souls of Black Folk,* DuBois asks for political power, civil rights, and higher education for Negro youth. DuBois spent his long life in ceaseless agitation for the cause of Negro rights. Because of this he was not respected by the white community as Washington had been. At the end of his life he was forced by the government to leave America. Upon his death in Ghana he had this read: 'And one thing alone I command you. As you live believe in life. Always human beings will live and progress to greater, broader and fuller life. The only possible death is to lose belief in this truth simply because the great end comes slowly, because time is long.'[21]

During the twentieth century many organizations have sprung up to render assistance to the cause of freedom in America. In 1909 the Niagara movement of DuBois merged with a new organization to become the National Association for the Advancement of Coloured People (NAACP). This became the legal arm of the civil rights movement culminating in 1954 with the Supreme Court decision that separate but equal schools were inherently unequal. During this time great advances were also made in the area of gaining legal rights in the local courts. Efforts were also made to curb the still frequent lynchings in the South. The New York office of the NAACP would witness this atrocity by putting out a flag with the words, 'A man has died today' each time a Negro was lynched.

The National Urban League also had its beginning about this time. Its concern was for the Negroes coming from the rural South to the indus-

trial North. Its aim was to offer education, housing, and ac
opportunity for the Negro. Its ultimate aim was 'to work i
job'.[22] In 1942 CORE came into existence—the Congre
Equality. The 1950's saw the Montgomery Improvement
become the Southern Christian Leadership Conference. In 19
people began the Student Co-ordinating Committee. All of
combination of black and white efforts to work construc
moral and sensitive society. Yet there were also the other i
emphasizing the extreme views on both sides.

This was the situation when the ideas of Gandhi began
the American struggle for racial equality and justice.

II

Frank Tannenbaum, in his book *Slave and Citizen: The N
Americas*, has brought forth an argument that human d
naturally become a part of our world. 'The import of all this
he concludes, 'is merely to point out the fact that the in
slavery was inevitably mobile, that it had a logic of its own b
any system of law, or custom, tradition, or belief. . . . Socie
tially dynamic, and while the mills of God grind slow, they gr
ingly sure. Time—the long time—will draw a veil over the
black in this hemisphere, and future generations will look bac
record of strife as it stands revealed in the history of the peo
New World of ours with wonder and incredulity. For the
understand the issues that the quarrel was about.'[23] Throughou
we find no mention of the persons who took a strong stand c
for Tannenbaum it is a race problem transcending the individ

Martin Luther King, in the *Letter from Birmingham Cit*
written: 'We must come to see that human progress never r
wheels of inevitability. It comes through the tireless efforts and
work of men willing to be co-workers with God, and without
work time itself becomes an ally of the forces of social stagn
must use time creatively, and forever realize that the time is al
to do right.'[24] Dr King goes on, 'We know through painful e
that freedom is never voluntarily given by the oppressor; it
demanded by the oppressed. . . . For years now I've heard
"Wait!" . . . This "wait" has almost always meant "never".
have come to see with the distinguished jurist of yesterday that
too long delayed is justice denied". We have waited for ov
hundred and forty years for our constitutional and God-given

Mr Tannenbaum has asked nothing of humanity. He only tal

it. Dr King asks that we take a stand in life, that we strive with all our being to make the world a better place to live in. This is *satyāgraha*, to take a stand in Truth, and to work from that stand for the weal of the world—truth force. *Satyāgraha* is constructive action, 'insistence on the creative power of the soul and its life-giving quality at a time when the destructive forces seem to be ascendant'.[26]

Here we have the influence which Mahatma Gandhi offered, and which was accepted in America's racial struggle. Truth gives the insightful power from which righteous action will come forth. When Gandhi was asked if the pursuit of truth would perhaps be different in each case, he answered, 'That is why non-violence is a necessary corollary. Without that there would be confusion and worse'.[27]

The pursuit of truth was not new to the world. Neither was righteous action, nor civil disobedience. What was new was the blending of these on a national basis, where group encountered group. King has said: 'Gandhi was probably the first person in history to lift the love ethic of Jesus above mere interaction between individuals to a powerful and effective social force on a large scale.'[28]

By the pursuit of truth and righteousness on a national scale Gandhi 'has stirred the people from their lethargy, given them a new self-confidence and responsibility and united them in their resolve to win freedom'.[29] Dr King has expressed a similar notion: 'Recognizing this vital urge that has engulfed the Negro community, one should readily understand public demonstrations. The Negro has many pent-up resentments and latent frustrations. He has to get them out. So let him march sometime; let him have his prayer pilgrimages to the city hall; understand why he must have sit-ins and freedom rides. If his repressed emotions do not come out in these non-violent ways, they will come out in ominous expressions of violence. This is not a threat; it is a fact of history. So I have not said to my people, "Get rid of your discontent". But I have tried to say that this normal and healthy discontent can be channeled through the creative outlet of non-violent direct action.'[30]

Satyāgraha is the realisation of the need to bring problems into the light for the greater witnessing; it is to make the greater society aware of the old problems which are preventing the discriminated groups from growing and reaching towards greater effectiveness and responsible freedom. By vivid demonstration in the midst of inhuman circumstances, man's outraged and yet undefeatable humanity can be challenged and affirmed; opposed sides could be brought to a new level of confrontation which promises direct negotiation and possible adjustment. The adjustive process can often be more revolutionary than blind revolutionism. This con-

crete, direct action to expose stagnating evils through greater witnessing aims at purging the social evil by sharing the suffering and by yoking the victim and the tyrant to a new and dangerous enterprise of collective responsibility. Voluntary suffering for a righteous cause forces individuals and social groups to see the evil as it actually is.

Satyāgraha, even if it fails or seems to fail in a particular situation, makes us aware of the primacy and persistence of the right cause; it leaves us with no place to hide; we find it difficult to steal away into some hidden corner hoping to sidestep the full flow of things. *Satyāgraha* stands against cowardice whether it takes the form of quiescence or of vindictiveness. It admits of strength; the strength to conquer violence, to maintain one's position and to move toward greater strength in spite of the menacing surge of brutality. Truth will set us free: this is the language both of Christianity and of *satyāgraha* as practised by Gandhi. Dr Martin Luther King was an heir to a dual inheritance of truth; he was born to the dynamics of Jesus and his witness, also he caught the flame of Gandhi in the modern revolutionary setting.

In South Africa and India, Gandhi had experimented with and developed *satyāgraha* as an effective force in encountering social problems. In South Africa the Indian community had both a minority and an inferior social status, and in consequence suffered oppression. Here *satyāgraha* was born. Co-operation was shown towards the government until conscience compelled counter-action. Great hardships were encountered and Indian volunteers had to be trained to suffer and to resist evil. 'People who voluntarily undergo a course of suffering raise themselves and the whole of humanity.' Here strength was gained for conducting long and strenuous campaigns for righteousness. Training and discipline were essential for a truth-worker; *satyāgraha* as a principle and practice was more demanding, as Gandhi put it, than the command of an army.

In India Gandhi took up the twofold task of gaining political freedom and uplifting the Indian society. These two problems became inseparable. 'It was his ambition to rid the country of its divisions and discords, to discipline the masses to self-dependence, raise women to a plane of political, economic, and social equality with men, end the religious hatreds which divided the nation, and cleanse Hinduism of its social abomination and untouchability.'[31]

Here *satyāgraha* became the means of neutralizing those factors which led to limitations and discords, as well as offering constructive action to overcome these and build a strong and united nation. The frustrations and small-minded attitudes of the so-called 'educated' classes had to be changed by closer contact between all communities and social levels; the rural and urban population had to accept a common national purpose which was morally sound and universally applicable. The difficulties encountered were constant and tremendous, but 'unceasing is the toil of those who are labouring to build a world where the poorest have a right to sufficient food, to light, air and sunshine in their houses, to hope, dignity and beauty in their lives'.[32]

This was the inspiration the Negroes visiting India and Gandhi brought back to America. But although Gandhian ideas were beginning to spread, the movement of the Negroes lacked the dynamic personality needed to give clarity and to voice the emotions fermenting for the wanted change. Many persons had striven to channel the unrest of the American Negro into constructive civil disobedience, yet not successfully on the huge scale demanded.

A. Philip Randolph had, for decades, dramatized the civil rights movement. He had brought out many marches and much protest. It was Randolph who suggested the unique March on Washington in the summer of 1963, uniting all the civil rights movements in the largest march to date.

Yet it was in the person of Dr Martin Luther King that the movement gained its greatest clarity. Through his life he was able to bring together, again and again, the different strands of protest and unite them into a single direction, to mould the many fires into a blaze aimed directly at injustice.

Dr King's first encounter with the life and ideas of Gandhi occurred while he was a student at the Crozer Theological Seminary. In nearby Philadelphia, Dr Mordecai Johnson was giving a lecture on Gandhi and his ideas. Dr Johnson, the president of Howard University, had travelled to India and was greatly impressed by what he encountered there. He gave many lectures throughout the nation when he returned. King was greatly stirred by the lecture, and wrote a few years later:

> His message was so profound and electrifying that I left the meeting and bought half a dozen books on Gandhi's life and works. . . . As I read I became fascinated by his campaigns of non-violent resistance. . . . The whole concept of 'Satyagraha' . . . was profoundly significant to me. As I delved deeper into the philosophy of Gandhi my scepticism concerning the power of love gradually diminished, and I came to see for the first time its potency in the area of social reform. Prior to reading Gandhi, I had about concluded that the ethics of Jesus were only effective in individual relationships. . . . It was in this Gandhian emphasis on love and

308

non-violence that I discovered the method for social reform that I had been seeking for so many months.[33]

Martin Luther King came close to Gandhi's teachings at Boston University where he studied Christian ethics and theology. Gandhi's non-violent revolution, initiated in South Africa and in India, made King aware of the immediate context of world revolution. He was unsure of his own strength in conducting a revolution in America, in the Negro as well as the white community, but he was sure that the time had arrived, that he had to act, to test himself and his fellowmen. It was in the midst of his first crisis that his absolute faith in Truth came forth. In his *Stride Toward Freedom* he gives us a vivid account of this profound moment:

> In this state of exhaustion, when my courage had all but gone, I decided to take my problem to God. With my head in my hands, I bowed over the kitchen table and prayed aloud. The words I spoke to God that midnight are still vivid in my memory. 'I am here taking a stand on what I believe is right. But now I am afraid. The people are looking to me for leadership, and if I stand before them without strength and courage, they too will falter. I am at the end of my powers. I have nothing left. I've come to the point where I can't face it alone.'
>
> At that moment I experienced the presence of the Divine as I have never experienced Him before. It seemed as though I could hear the quiet assurance of an inner voice saying: 'Stand up for righteousness, stand up for truth; and God will be at your side forever.' Almost at once my fears began to go. My uncertainty disappeared. I was ready to face anything.[34]

This incident occurred during the Montgomery boycott of 1956 in Montgomery, Alabama, where King had recently begun his first ministry at the Dexter Avenue Baptist Church. It began on 1 December 1955, when Mrs Rosa Parks refused to give up her seat on the city bus to a white passenger who had just boarded it. Mrs Parks was arrested and fined for committing a crime. The following day the Negro community of Montgomery boycotted the city buses. That day stretched into a year.

The indignation of the Negro community had reached its bursting point. The direct action taken united the community in defiance of the injustice and set them on the path of non-violent opposition. It was on the occasion of the bombing of his house that King became the dominant spokesman, asking his community not to retaliate.

The fresh outlook he offered to the Negroes who were groping in racial segregation and internal squabblings, helped them to bring their dis-satisfaction into a clear channel of expression. The other leaders of the community were able to put aside personal strife and rise to a new level of brotherhood by turning towards greater and greater participation in the community.

The greatest achievement of the Montgomery boycott was that it reached throughout the entire Negro community. It asked each and every person there not to travel the city buses. It gave to each a place, allowing all to rise in defiance to injustice. The community was welded, and their righteousness now confronted the stubbornness of the white community.

Yet the conscience of Montgomery and the United States was such that before a change could come forth the incident had to be tried in the courts. It was not until the Supreme Court granted that the decision of the Federal Court was binding that the boycott was ended.

To place civil law before morality is a peculiar situation. Law is the child of morality, but in America the regard for law has been placed higher than the regard for morality. In fact, the only room left for morality is on a marginal individual basis. In such a case the society loses its sensitivity to other groups, expecting all to obey the 'just' laws which it holds to be sacred. And humanity is actually expected to flow from this situation. This is one of the tragedies of white America, as well as one of its blind spots. Parallels can be found in the caste and class systems of India and Europe. It is forgotten that social laws ultimately stem from the concept of a greater humanity and from the sensitivity that such an attitude brings out.

Human morality, the love of one's neighbour, and ultimately the love for one's enemy (while hating the evil in him) is born from an absolute concept of love. Civil law is rooted in concern for one's neighbour. Therefore, for Truth to purge civil law there must first be love for one's neighbour. We cannot hold that from civil law itself we shall gain that sense of transcending truth which must support our civic conscience. American society holds some of the greatest systems of civil law the world has yet witnessed. But it is respected above humanity. It is believed on too many sides that this system of law as such shall give the 'perfect' society.

But the evidence of American history has shown that this is not so. Many Americans walk the streets in legal freedom and social bondage. What this has vividly shown is that civil law alone cannot and will not give social justice. There is the need to love one's neighbour which transcends legality and supports the righteous system. And for this we need to be rooted in that Truth which Gandhi equated with the divine.

The concept of morality, of ultimate principles must support our social conscience.

The glory of Dr King is that he offered this light to America. He united the scattered protest of the Negro in the fire of a divine Truth and brought it into the streets of the nation, as Gandhi had done in Africa and India. It was the demand that all men shall be brothers, 'black and white together', in the sight of Truth.

It seems odd that in a democracy in 1956 a group of citizens could not even sit equally on a bus. But there were many more types of segregation to battle. Negroes could not eat at the same counters where the whites ate. Nor could they use the same restrooms. Nor could the races vote together, although voting is considered so sacred to Americans. It was necessary for the Supreme Court to pass the Voting Rights Act in 1965 to give the Negroes the right to vote.

Segregation was exposed in its subtle and crude forms through the challenge of the new Negro opposition. A non-violent war was declared by the Negro upon the hardened and decaying bastions of racial prejudice. Segregation was revealed in the glare of publicity in department stores, on the streets, in libraries, in hotels, throughout the hundreds of thousands of American institutions clinging to rights of perversion and limiting walls.

The challenge of Truth burned in Negro hearts. In 1960 a group of four Negro youths sat down at an all white lunch counter in a department store in Greensboro, North Carolina. Lerone Bennett, in his fine biography of Dr King, has suggested that the bus boycott established King as a symbol of manhood towards which Negro youth looked and aspired, thus touching off the civil disturbances of the early 1960's. Here was *satyāgraha* in its dynamic side thrusting into righteousness. In Greensboro the character of fearlessness, another inseparable aspect of Truth force, became a firm part of the civil rights movement.

The sit-ins took place across the South resulting in a change in the Southern society. Although much was gained against some of the grosser forms of segregation, the freedom attained was still far from the heart of the matter. There was needed a still farther and deeper meeting of the races where a full integration could be worked out. Its ultimate aim is to cure the economic and social inequalities, to give dignity and justice to all men and women. 'During the lunch-counter sit-ins in Greensboro, North Carolina, a night-club comic observed that, had the demonstrators been served, some of them could not have paid for the meal. Of what advantage is it to the Negro to establish that he can be served, in integrated restaurants, be accommodated in integrated hotels, if he is bound to the kind of financial servitude which will not allow him to take a vacation or even to take his wife out to dine?'[35] King has emphasized that a spiritualism that does not take into consideration materialism is worthless and need not be given much thought.

It is in the light of the still unachieved greater encounter that King began to appreciate more deeply the need for planned operations against corruption. Instead of waiting for scattered situations to develop, he began to understand the necessity to bring about deliberate and many-sided confrontations with racism on a vast scale. Montgomery had been a spontaneous happening. Now King saw the need for greater non-violent militancy to deliberately force the issue on the conscience of the nation. Here was the method which Gandhi had used so successfully against the British in India.

In Albany, Georgia, in 1962, Dr King, with the Southern Christian Leadership Council, an organization which grew out of Montgomery, set out on the first self-conscious confrontation with racism. It failed, but King drew his lessons from the encounter.

The following year, 1963, saw the march on Birmingham. King had to face Bull Connor, a rabid segregationist. Birmingham was the capital of the Old South. The defences were high-water hoses, police dogs, billy clubs, blockades, and huge amounts of security forces. The Negro community was hesitant and watched from the distance during the early days. King's aim was to change the entire city. America sat and waited.

King chose Birmingham for two reasons. The first was that Fred Shuttlesworth, a leader of an affiliated of the SCLC in Birmingham, asked him to come. Shuttlesworth had been fighting an uphill battle since 1957 for Negro rights. He had set the foundation upon which the cause could grow.

The second reason was that Birmingham was 'probably the most segregated city in the United States. Its ugly record of police brutality is known in every section of this country. Its unjust treatment of Negroes in the courts is a notorious reality. There have been more unsolved bombings of Negro homes and churches in Birmingham than any city in this nation. These are the hard, brutal, and unbelievable facts. On the basis of these conditions Negro leaders sought to negotiate with the city fathers. But the political leaders consistently refused to engage in good faith negotiations'.[36]

King aimed at cracking Birmingham—to lead the demonstration until 'Pharaoh lets God's people go'. King specifically wanted to establish fair hiring practices, a bi-racial committee, and desegregation of the downtown stores. In the 'Birmingham Manifesto' he wrote:

312

The patience of an oppressed people cannot endure for ever. . . . Birmingham is a part of the United States and we are bona fide citizens. . . . We have always been a peaceful people, bearing our oppressions with a super-human effort. Yet we have been the victims of repeated violence. . . . Our memories are seared with painful experience of Mother's Day 1961 during the Freedom Ride. For years, while our homes and churches were bombed we heard nothing but the rantings and ravings of racist officials. The Negro protest for equality and justice has been a voice crying in the wilderness. . . . We believe in the American Dream of Democracy. . . .'[37]

King received little sympathy from any side. Still he pushed forward against the sharp criticism from eminent lawyers, from religious leaders like Billy Graham, and even from the Negro community in Birmingham. During the slow build-up King talked down internal resistance. The external resistance was so high that it culminated in the court order making it illegal to demonstrate in any way in the streets of Birmingham. But King continued to push forward and landed in jail. Here he wrote the 'Letter from Birmingham Jail', which Bennett has called 'by far the most incisive and eloquent statement of his racial philosophy'. In this letter he answered eight white clergymen who denounced him. He wrote: 'I am in Birmingham because injustice is here. . . . I am cognizant of the interrelatedness of all communities and states. I cannot sit idly by in Atlanta and not be concerned about what happens in Birmingham. Injustice anywhere is a threat to justice everywhere. . . . Anyone who lives inside the United States can never be considered an outsider anywhere in this country'.[38]

Gandhi has said: 'So long as the superstition that men should obey unjust laws exists, so long will their slavery exist.' King wrote: 'Any law that uplifts human personality is just. Any law that degrades human personality is unjust. All segregation statutes are unjust because segregation distorts the soul and damages the personality.'[39]

In the second month of the campaign as the confrontation was increasing, King decided to bring Negro children to the front lines. The children had been anxious to take a frontal position, but King and others had at first been reluctant. On 2 May, one thousand children went through the police lines and reached city hall. The following day more children came, emptying the schools. Bull Connor let loose all the power he had on the children,—hoses, dogs, and billy clubs. Now the Negro community united and pressed harder. King had no intention to relax the pressure.

313

'We are ready to negotiate. But we intend to negotiate from strength.'[40]

Two thousand demonstrators were in jail and the city of Montgomery was reaching total social disorder. King had his crisis. The conscience of the city was at last stirred. Although a riot had broken out against police brutality, it was quickly calmed by King, and integration became a part of Birmingham.

The voice of Birmingham reached across America. 1963 was the year of revolt on a mass scale. The Negro ghettos in a thousand cities across the land broke forth in indignation.

King travelled across America, as he had been doing for years, giving lectures and continually speaking to all manner of people to create the awareness of the racist problem. He had learned that truth had a heavy demand; it continually required him to come forth and speak up in its behalf. In the summer of 1963, came the March on Washington and 'I have a Dream'.

> I have a dream that my four children will one day live in a nation where they will not be judged by the colour of their skin but by the content of their character.
> I have a dream today.
> I have a dream that one day the state of Alabama whose governor's lips are presently dripping with the words of interposition and nullification, will be transformed into a situation where little black boys and black girls will be able to join hands with little white boys and white girls and walk together as sisters and brothers.
> I have a dream today.
> I have a dream that one day every valley shall be exalted, every hill and mountain shall be made low, the rough places plain and the crooked places will be made straight, and the glory of the Lord shall be revealed, and all flesh shall see it together.
> This is our hope. This is the faith with which I return to the South. With this faith we will be able to hew out of the mountain of despair a stone of hope. With this faith we will be able to transform the jangling discords of our nation into a beautiful symphony of brotherhood. With this faith we will be able to work together, to pray together, to struggle together, to go to jail together, knowing that we will be free one day.[41]

Through non-violent direct action 'Black men have slammed the door shut on a past of deadening passivity'.[42] 'Without this magnificent ferment among Negroes, the old evasions and procrastination would have continued indefinitely.'[43] Yet this ferment had led to many limited objectives by certain Negro leaders.

The greatest of these is the appeal for separateness. Because there has been only token integration there is still frustration. And for some it is unbearable. The few lunch counters, buses, rest rooms and libraries won have not cured the evil of segregation. The appeal, therefore, to completely cut oneself away from such a society readily gains its place here. The long suffering is seen as too much to continue enduring. Quick solutions are wanted. The appeal for a divided attitude, where the Negroes would be given a state in Africa, or the Americas, is as old as the racial problem. Both blacks and whites have turned to this appeal throughout American history. But the difference today is that the only means of separation is a violent one. The militancy gained through non-violent action against separation is seen by separatist leaders as needing to be channeled towards a great blood bath. Malcolm X has voiced this appeal. In his criticism of non-violent means, his appeal is to allow violence.

> I, for one, believe that if you give people a thorough understanding of what it is that confronts them, and the basic causes that produce it, they'll create their own programme; and when the people create a programme, you get action. The only time you see them is when the people are exploding. Then the leaders are shot into the situation and told to control things. You can't show me a leader that has set off an explosion. No, they come and contain the explosion. They say, 'Don't get rough, you know, do the smart thing'. This is their role—they're just there to restrain you and me, to restrain the struggle, to keep it in a certain groove, and not let it get out of control. Whereas you and I don't want anybody to keep us from getting out of control. We want to get out of control. We want to smash anything that gets in our way that doesn't belong there. . . .[44]

Commenting on this King has said: 'I guess I should not have been surprised. I should have known that in an atmosphere where false promises are daily realities, where deferred dreams are nightly facts, where acts of unpunished violence towards Negroes are a way of life, non-violence would eventually be seriously questioned. I should have been reminded that disappointment produces despair and despair produces bitterness, and that the one thing certain about bitterness is its blindness. Bitterness has not the capacity to make the disinction between some and *all*.'[45] Elsewhere King continues: 'Millions of people have fought thousands of battles to enlarge my freedom; restricted as it still is, progress has been made. This is why I remain an optimist, though I am still a realist, about the barriers before us.'[46] Speaking further of those who in despair advocate violence, King writes: 'They fail . . . to perceive the sense of affirmation generated by the challenge of embracing struggle and surmounting obstacles. They have no comprehension of the strength that comes from faith in God and man.'[47]

As the struggle to win freedom in India had forced Gandhi to reach out into the community problems of the masses and seek to lift the whole society, so King had to embrace the wider world as he became more involved in human rights. Because King fought for non-violent action, to be consistent with himself, he had to stand against the brutal violence the American government was perpetuating in Vietnam. Similarly, he took a stand against poverty for all people of America, not just the Negro poor.

In this reaching for the greater world he lost much of the appeal he held as a civil rights worker. Many of his friends and associates asked him to remain with them in their limited struggle. White protest also mounted, condemning King for entering realms where they felt he should not be. Commenting on America in 1968 King wrote: 'It is not easy to describe a crisis so profound that it has caused the most powerful nation in the world to stagger in confusion and bewilderment. Today's problems are so acute because the tragic evasions and defaults of several centuries have accumulated to disaster proportions. The luxury of a leisurely approach to urgent problems . . . was forfeited by ignoring the issues for too long. The nation waited until the black man was explosive with fury before stirring itself even to partial concern. Confronted now with the interrelated problems of war, inflation, urban decay, white backlash and a climate of violence, it is now *forced* to address itself to race relations and poverty, and it is tragically unprepared. What might have been a series of separate problems now merge into a social crisis of almost stupefying complexity.' 'The problem is so tenacious because, despite its virtues and attributes, America is deeply racist and its democracy is flawed both economically and socially.'[48]

In his 'A Testament of Hope' Dr King, speaking of America's attitude in international relations and world peace, affirms that there will be no 'world peace until America has an "integrated" foreign policy. Our disastrous experiences in Vietnam and the Dominican Republic have been in one sense, a result of racist decision making. Men of the white West, whether or not they like it, have grown up in a racist culture, and their thinking is coloured by that fact. They have grown on a false mythology and tradition that blinds them to the aspirations and talents of other men. They don't really respect anyone who is not white. But we simply cannot have peace in the world without mutual respect.'[49]

To build the greater world the old limitations must give way to the new idea continually developing in man's consciousness. As the idea grows stronger, reaching ever more of mankind in an increasingly integral, global community, work needs to be done to bring about an international or a supernational federation of States. This would broaden and deepen the genuine patriotism, not negate it. Genuine traditions, unique cultures and spiritual inheritances would shine in a new atmosphere of world-wide fellowship. Martyrs like Gandhi and King shall not have lived and died in vain.

NOTES

[1] Frank Tannenbaum, *Slave and Citizen: The Negro in the Americas* (New York, 1946), p. 3.

[2] *Ibid.*, p. 101.

[3] *Ibid.*, p. 91.

[4] *Ibid.*, p. 42.

[5] William Warren Sweet, *The Story of Religion in America* (New York, 1939), p. 412.

[6] *Ibid.*, p. 415.

[7] Joanne Grant (ed.), *Black Protest: History, Documents and Analysis: 1619 to the Present* (New York, 1968), p. 30.

[8] Louis Ruchames, *The Abolitionists* (New York, 1963), in Joanne Grant, *ibid.*

[9] Grant, *ibid.*, p. 70.

[10] *Ibid.*, p. 83.

[11] Tannenbaum, op. cit., p. 109.

[12] Martin Luther King, Jr., *Where Do We Go From Here: Chaos or Community?* (New York, 1968), p. 92.

[13] Langston Hughes and Milton Meltzer, *A Pictorial History of the American Negro* (New York, 1957), p. 186.

[14] H. Thurman, *The Negro Spiritual Speaks of Life and Death* (New York, 1947), p. 15.

[15] *Ibid.*, p. 50.

[16] W. E. Burghardt DuBois, *The Souls of Black Folk* (New York, 1961), p. 23.

[17] C. Vann Woodward, *The Strange Career of Jim Crow* (New York, 1966) in John Hope Franklin and Isidore Starr (ed.), *The Negro in Twentieth Century America: A Reader on the Struggle for Civil Rights* (New York, 1967), p. 61.

[18] Franklin and Starr, *ibid.*, p. 77.

[19] Booker T. Washington, *Up From Slavery* (New York, 1965), in Franklin and Starr, *ibid.*, p. 18.

[20] *Ibid.*, p. 86.

[21] Herbert Aptheker, *Soul of the Republic: The Negro Today* (New York, 1964).

[22] 'Freedom to the Free, A Report to the President by the United States Commission on Civil Rights', in Franklin and Starr, op. cit., p. 108.

[23] Tannenbaum, op. cit., pp. 126-28.

[24] Martin Luther King, Jr., 'Letter from Birmingham City Jail', in Franklin and Starr, op. cit., p. 161.

[25] *Ibid.*, p. 157.

[26] S. Radhakrishnan, *Great Indians* (Bombay, 1949), p. 19.

[27] M. K. Gandhi, *Non-Violent Resistance (Satyagraha)* (New York, 1961), p. 29.

[28] Martin Luther King, Jr., *Stride Toward Freedom: The Montgomery Story* (New York, 1964), pp. 78-79.

[29] Radhakrishnan, op. cit., p. 35.

[30] King, 'Letter from Birmingham City Jail', op. cit., pp. 162-63.

[31] Radhakrishnan, op. cit., p. 29.

[32] *Ibid.*, pp. 27-29.

[33] King, *Stride Toward Freedom*, op. cit., pp. 78-79T.

[34] *Ibid.*, pp. 114-15.

[35] Martin Luther King, *Why We Can't Wait* (New York, 1964), pp. 135-36.

[36] King, 'Letter from Birmingham City Jail', op. cit., p. 155.

[37] Lerone Bennett, Jr., *What Manner of Man: A Biography of Martin Luther King, Jr.* (New York, 1968), pp. 104-05.

[38] King, 'Letter from Birmingham City Jail', op. cit., p. 154.

[39] *Ibid.*, p. 158.

[40] Bennett, op. cit., p. 117.

[41] *Ibid.*, p. 122.

[42] Martin Luther King, Jr., 'A Testament of Hope', in *Playboy*, XVI, 10 (January 1969), p. 175.

[43] *Ibid.*, p. 175.

[44] Malcolm X, *Malcolm X Speaks* (New York, 1965), in Grant, op. cit., p. 449.

[45] Martin Luther King, Jr., *Where Do We Go From Here*, op. cit., pp. 30-31.

[46] King, 'A Testament of Hope', p. 175.

[47] *Ibid.*, p. 175.

[48] *Ibid.*, pp. 175 and 194.

[49] *Ibid.*, p. 231.

THE POWER OF VIOLENCE AND THE POWER OF NON-VIOLENCE

Maurice Friedman

Each new day sees still more killings, maimings, and burnings in Vietnam, exchanges of bombs and gunfire in the Middle East, continued starvation in Biafra, murders, rapes, and muggings on our city streets, gang wars, routine police beatings in Negro ghettoes, endless misery of the Brazilian peasant, and brutal manhandling of protesting students and of workers for peace and civil rights. Racism, poverty and war are already violence by their nature and by their origin. The history of racism is a history of overt and covert violence, the killing of millions of blacks in Africa, the killing, maiming, subduing, dehumanizing through centuries of violence of slavery in America, and another century of violence after liberation from slavery. Poverty always means violence: holding down the poor through intimidation, through the threat of coercion, through reliance on actual coercion. War is violence by definition though we have tried to forget this by defining war as 'containment' or 'liberation' or 'defence of the peace' or 'defending the free world'.

It was the violence of the Second World War that led me to the agonizing moral decision to become a conscientious objector. In making this decision, I read Richard Gregg's famous book, *The Power of Non-violence*.[1] Then the idea of non-violence was only known to a few. Since then the whole world has been impressed by the power of non-violence through the success of Gandhi's *satyāgraha*, his non-violent campaign and the final liberation of India, through Martin Luther King and the civil rights movement, which began as a non-violence movement, through many peace protests which also have been non-violent. A great many people have adopted non-violence as a technique of political and economic resistance in a spirit kindred to Herbert Marcuse's statement, 'Non-violence is not a virtue; it is a necessity'.[2]

Today, however, we are absorbed by the power of violence which flowers around us in ever more grotesque and omnivorous forms. What is more, those who have awakened to the imperative necessity for social change are less and less looking to non-violence as the change agent and more and more to dynamic violence as the response to the congealed and static violence of the *status quo*. Our understanding of the power of non-violence must be deepened and toughened, therefore, through a new look at the power of violence.

Two of the great social theorists of all time, Thomas Hobbes and Jean-Jacques Rousseau, had completely opposite understandings of violence. To Hobbes violence was the natural state of man and only a strong central compulsive government could do anything about it since in this state of nature man's life was nasty, raw, brutish, and short, a war of all against all. Jean-Jacques Rousseau, in contrast, imagined man in the state of nature as a good, spontaneous, loving creature. Only the chains of civilization turned him into the predatory animal that he now is. The English poet Alexander Pope was able to accept all evil in terms of the 'great chain of being', and to tell us that whatever is, is right: 'We are but parts of one tremendous whole, whose body nature is, and God the soul'. *(An Essay on Man.)* William Blake, also an eighteenth-century English-man, had exactly the opposite view of violence: 'A Robin Redbreast in a cage/ Puts all Heaven in a rage'. Confinement, imprisonment, destruction, mutilation is already violence and will produce more violence. 'The Harlot's cry from street to street/ Shall weave Old England's winding sheet.' *(Auguries of Innocence.)* As Blake walks down the chartered streets of London and sees the mind-forged manacles of woe, he under-stands that the tigers of wrath are wiser than the horses of instruction, and he cries out against 'the human abstract', the deceit, mystery and humility, and pseudo-charity, where 'mutual fear brings peace, till the selfish loves increase', cries out against the violence done to the chimney sweep, who says in Blake's poem, 'And because I am happy, & dance & sing,/ They think they have done me no injury:/ And are gone to praise God & his Priest & King,/ Who make up a heaven of our misery'.[3]

From Karl Marx to Herbert Marcuse, violence has been explained in terms of the economic system. The humanistic ideals of liberty, equality, fraternity, say Marx, Lenin, Marcuse, cannot be transformed into reality under a capitalist system the very nature of which is the exploitation of those below by those who control the means of production. Since the state in the capitalist system is there for the express purpose of keeping the control of these means of production in the hands of the capitalists, the entrepreneurs, and the managers, there can be no hope of gradual social change. One of the terrible ironies of this theory is that Marx believed that a socialist state would make unnecessary a police force and an army, that socialism would be followed by an automatic withering away of the state. The one thing that has not happened is that. The capitalists and the communists can claim equal honours in violence!

There really is a double standard, as Herber Marcuse says, when you count only the violence that it takes to produce or perhaps even to carry along or conduct social change, but you do not count the far greater daily violence that is used to preserve and maintain the *status quo*. Violence is the monopoly of the *status quo*. Lao-tzu put it very beautifully a long time ago: 'However a man with a kind heart proceed,/ He forgets what it may profit him;/ However a man with a just mind proceed,/ He remembers what it may profit him;/ However a man of conventional conduct proceed, if he be not complied with,/ Out goes his fist to enforce compliance.'[4] Our genteel society has that fist hidden just beneath the surface to enforce compliance. In Emile Zola's novel *Germinal* in this French town where the people lived in great poverty, the grocery storekeeper would take out the credit that people owed him by sleeping with the men's wives. When finally rebellion came, this static violence produced the counter-reaction of actual violence. Not only was the grocery man killed, but the organ with which he had collected his credit was displayed on high.

The task of interpreting violence has been largely taken over in our day by the psychoanalysts. Sigmund Freud, impressed by shellshock in the First World War and the phenomena of repetition, went beyond seeing violence as merely the frustration of a basic libidinal impulse. He saw it finally as a separate death instinct which was just as natural to man as the instinct of life. If the other person has power over me, he said in *Civilization and Its Discontents*, he will destroy, seduce, exploit, and kill me without even getting any advantage out of it, or even any pleasure, and he will do it so much the more surely the more he has power over me and the more I am helpless. The sad bit of truth is that man is a wolf to man. 'Who has the courage to dispute it in the face of all the evidence in his own life and in history?' Freud wrote those words in 1931.[5] Could he have lived for another ten or twenty years, he would have seen as much new evidence as all past recorded history together for the truth of his statement. Although a theory of natural instincts that takes man out of the context of history is untenable, the amount of evidence of how man acts in history is overwhelming. We cannot go back to Rousseau and look at man as a simple, lovable creature.

Erich Fromm is also aware of this violence and destruction. In one of his latest books he calls it 'necrophilia', love of death.[6] In contrast to Freud, Fromm holds that violence is the product of social character, of authoritarian domination and repression. But this reaches the point where

some people's whole biological, psychological, personal, and social structure is based upon destruction and negation. Carl Jung, who delved
deeply into what he called the collective unconscious and the archetype,
spoke of violence as a projection of the 'shadow', that is the projection of
those dark parts that we have repressed into the unconscious. When they
are repressed, they turn malignant and evil, and then we project them
onto the other, the 'enemy', whoever he may be. We imagine that he is
going to vent on us our own unconscious hostility of which we are not
aware.[7] Rollo May, similarly, thinks that America is the most violent
nation in the world today as a result of the repression of the 'daemonic'.
The 'daemonic' is not evil. It is a force that we must use and that we
repress at our peril. Once repressed, we project it on others.[8]

Violence is the product of frustration, rage, shame, envy, the product
of all those things that Rainer Maria Rilke called 'unlived life'.[9] A man
noted for his asceticism came to see a Hasidic rabbi and the rabbi said to
him, 'Yudel, you are wearing a hairshirt against your flesh. If you were
not given to sudden anger, you would not need it. And since you are
given to sudden anger, it will not help you!' Another Hasidic rabbi said,
'Anger injures and makes impure all the members of one's household as
well as oneself'. But he also said, 'Since I have tamed my anger, I keep it
in my pocket, and when I need it, I take it out'.[10] We must not identify
anger and violence. Violence is often the result of repressed anger,
repressed rage, what breaks out of you unexpectedly, suddenly, like the
conflagration that comes when everything is dry and it takes one spark
to set it off. William Blake's famous poem, 'The Poison Tree', originally
bore the ironic subtitle, 'Christian Forbearance'.

> I was angry with my friend:
> I told my wrath, my wrath did end.
> I was angry with my foe:
> I told it not, my wrath did grow.
>
> And I watered it in fears,
> Night and morning with my tears;
> And I sunned it with smiles
> And with soft deceitful wiles.
>
> And it grew both day and night,
> Till it bore an apple bright;
> And my foe beheld it shine,
> And he knew that it was mine.

> And into my garden stole,
> When the night had veil'd the pole:
> In the morning glad I see
> My foe outstretch'd beneath the tree.'[11]

'Christian forbearance' is one of the things which, along with slavery, the white man gave to the black man in the United States. He gave him a religion which promised him 'pie in the sky by and by', but demanded of him here Christian forbearance. When Martin Luther stood before the German princes he said, 'Here I stand. I can do no other.' But when there was a peasant revolt, Luther was horrified. To the peasants, he said, 'As Jesus has written, you must turn the other cheek and obey your masters'. But he said to the princes, 'As Paul has written, the government is ordained by God, so you must crush the peasants without mercy'.[12] This sort of double standard is also what America has applied to the Blacks, the American Indians, and the Mexican Americans.

Unlived life itself is something more than the failure to express yourself or to dominate others, though that is what the Nietzschean and the romantic often think. It is the failure to give our passions direction by bringing them into the dialogue with the other human beings with whom we live—in our family, in the community, in the neighbourhood, in the city, and in the country. The failure to give our passions direction has to do with the fact that we do not take our stand, that we do not make our objection when we must, that we allow a pseudo-harmony to continue to exist. Often we cannot do otherwise; for we do not even consciously know that we have another point of view from that of the dominant group. Or if we do know it, we know the consequences of not staying 'in our place'. This goes right through our society—not just the poor and underprivileged, but the worlds of business, commerce, and government. It is this that leads many young rebels not only to 'drop out' but to adopt every way possible of not conforming and of showing 'disrespect for their elders'.

Genuine dialogue has to do with becoming yourself in going out to meet the situation which demands you, the situation which calls you. This is true for a people or a group or a community or a family, as well as for an individual. Simone Weil defined violence as reducing a person to a thing, the ultimate of which is killing, i.e., reducing a person to a corpse.[13] If that is so, then violence can no more be avoided in our culture or any culture than we can avoid what Martin Buber calls the 'I-It relation',[14] that is, the relation in which we use, and know, classify and categorize one another; for this is an enormous part of our culture and

323

becomes more so every day. It is these very categories, indeed, which lead us in the first place to prejudice, racism, and violence. But if violence means converting the human Thou into an It, then violence is no more inevitable than the domination of the It. We live in an age, God knows, in which the machine, the corporation, and the technocrat dominate to an incredible degree. Yet a real possibility remains, through fighting and standing one's ground, of bringing these back into human dialogue. It remains with us and cannot be removed by the fist of any number of economic, psychological, social, military, or political realists who say, 'This is the way it is'. But, if we are going to take this possibility seriously, then in each concrete situation we have to discover the hard way what are the resources for dialogue, what are the resources for creating something human and bringing the passion which explodes into violence into a real interchange.

It has taken us a quarter of a century, says Robert Lifton, really to begin to feel the impact of Auschwitz and Hiroshima. It has taken us a quarter of a century to begin to realize that there are no limits to man's readiness to destroy himself and all other men.[15] The eighteenth century could believe in the universally human, in a limit to inhumanity; this we cannot believe. When men are turned into cakes of soap, you cannot believe any longer that there is any limit to turning a person into a thing. It was done with the utmost scientific efficiency as was the transplantation and freezing of genitals, and it was done with the practicality of modern business as when the skins of victims were made into lampshades and the hair of countless women into rugs. We cannot hold, as Thomas Jefferson did, 'these truths to be self-evident, that all men are created equal'. The Nazis made them *not* self-evident, and the burden of proof remains on us. An SDS manifesto of 1962 reads, 'Our work is guided by the sense that we may be the last generation to experiment with history'.[16] All of us, whether we know it or not, have lived in the shadow of the cold war and the atomic bomb. The real possibility of the extinction of the human race may account in part for the eruption of violence and assassinations, of small wars here and there all over the globe, as well as for revolt and revolution as a symbol of transcending death in the way that our old institutions and establishments in society do not seem able to do.

This underlying anxiety is only one factor in the youth rebellion, of course. The fathers in our day can no longer confront the youth with an image of man, an image of meaningful personal existence. The young people are revolting against a revolting absence of meaning, against the belief in continual progress, against the scurrying for security that seems to their parents the only thing worth while. So we have had our hippies, and then their political counterpart, the yippies. We have our SDS-ers and the 'Crazies' who are so desperate that they go in and break up SDS meetings.

The black revolution begins with the fact of racism, both conscious and unconscious. It begins with the Negro ghettoes, with living on welfare with an enormously greater rate of sickness, death, unemployment, poverty, overcrowding, illiteracy, delinquency, mental illness—a daily life of daily violence beyond our capacity to imagine. This has led to a civil rights movement and a movement for integration which then has been superseded by the Black Muslims and Malcolm X, by demonstrations and riots, by Black Power and black militancy, and by separation—the claim for the right to identity and pride and a separate power base. America has seen the assassinations of black and white alike, but always of those who are concerned with social change. Four days before the assassination of Martin Luther King one woman from the radio station, the Kansas City Christian Voice, who had come to interview me spoke up in a seminar in Kansas City and said, 'By his very *presence* in Memphis, Martin Luther King is inciting violence'! Thus a man who believes in non-violence and stands his ground and acts is blamed when some violence accrues out of the reaction of both sides. That means that violence equals change in the *status quo*, whereas, non-violence by her definition means keeping the *status quo* unchanged even by use of violence, like the police in Memphis.

What has concerned me most deeply in our time is the polarization of our situation, and this is why the old formulas of non-violence no longer mean anything. Polarization is necessary to destroy pseudo-harmony, but it always goes beyond that. The real categories in which we live lead to polarization, but so do the pseudo-categories. The beginning of racism is in part just this distinction: this man is black and this man is white, or red, or yellow. No prejudice need be there; just the distinction itself is already the beginning.

Mutual mistrust is what we encounter most often if we try to go to where the problems are and where the people are dealing with one another. Mutual distrust both is caused by and leads to the failure to hear. And finally we have the *politization* of polarization: the polarization which is already implicit in the fact of poverty and racism becomes political; it becomes slogans, catchwords. Sometimes this is deliberate and tactical, done because people believe this is the only way, whether from the right or from the left. More often it is semi-deliberate and programmatic or expressive, a symbol, such as the students telling their faculty to go die, a symbol of throwing off something oppressive. Then you get an antagonistic interaction of the two sides combined with *wilful* misunderstanding. There is always misunderstanding, but there is a step beyond this in which people refuse to see the position of the others from within. Those who are content with their practical analyses become programmed in such a way that anything they hear is fitted into one of the either-ors that they expect to hear—those who are with them and those who are against them.

Our choice today is not between conformity and rebellion, but between two types of rebellion. The first I have called the 'Modern Promethean', the rebel with a simple either/or; the other person or group is the enemy; he must be destroyed or we must die in the attempt to destroy him. The other type of rebel to whom I point, and to whom Albert Camus, A. J. Muste, and many others have pointed, I call the 'Modern Job'. The Modern Job can stand his ground and contend, he can trust and in that trusting fight and honour his opponent by opposing him.[17] This is the link to which Martin Buber pointed between genuine dialogue and the possibilities of peace.[18]

Peace is not just the fact of civil disobedience, it is not just the fact of non-violent action. Non-violence may be congealed violence, perfectionist rage, apocalyptic intolerance, especially when used by people who see it merely as a technique. One of the sad facts of our time is that the movements both of civil rights and peace have turned away from non-violence toward violence. Even the 'peace movement' today becomes for the 'New Politics' the 'support of wars of liberation everywhere'—the politization of polarization of the Modern Promethean.

It is because Thoreau spoke as a man standing his ground in a situation that his civil disobedience has something important to say to us that we cannot afford to miss. We stand in a world where our leaders will not see and will not heed what happens in the mutual building up of the armaments that are leading us, as Martin Buber puts it, to a chaos beyond which we cannot even think. Gandhi with his *satyāgraha*, as V. V. Ramana Murti suggested, was establishing dialogue with the British in Buber's sense of the term because he was confronting them with respect as an equal and bringing India stage by stage to the place where there could be a real dialogue.

> The way of violence works as a monologue, but the nature of non-violence is a dialogue. . . . The technique of Gandhi's *satyagraha* is capable of creating the conditions that are necessary for the fulfilment of Buber's concept of dialogue. The history of non-violent resistance as it was practised by the Indian National Congress under Gandhi's leadership eminently proved this. . . . If Gandhi was able

to carry on *dialogue* with England, it was only because of *satya-graha*. . . . The old relationship between master and slave was changed thereby into a new partnership between equals in a 'dialogue'. . . . Gandhi was able to win by his non-violent technique a progressive response from the British government that led to the development of a 'dialogue'. Each of the major campaigns of non-violent resistance evoked the necessary recognition of India's emerging nationalism by Great Britain at successive stages of the struggle. . . . There has not been a greater example of a genuine *dialogue* between two nations in recent times than that between India and Great Britain through Gandhi's *satyagraha*.[19]

Buber would not have agreed that invariably '*Satyagraha* is the answer to the basic question that is inherent in the *Dialogue*', as Murti states, or that 'The methods of *satyagraha* such as non-violent non-co-operation, genuine self-sacrifice, and voluntary suffering' invariably 'fulfil the great end of the *dialogue*'. On the contrary, in his famous 'Letter to Gandhi' Buber rejected Gandhi's suggestion that the Jews in Germany could use *satyagraha* effectively against the Nazis since death in the concentration camps was anonymous martyrdom, not political witness.[20]. But he did see non-violent civil disobedience as something that was more and more likely to be the demand of the particular situation upon those contemporary men who are concerned not only for justice but for man as man.[21] He also knew the meaning of tragedy where 'each is as he is' and oppositeness crystallizes into unbridgable opposition. This is a tragedy that Gandhi and Martin Luther King knew too—long before each was assassinated.

Martin Luther King in his civil rights campaign was also using non-violent resistance in the spirit of genuine dialogue. Gandhi was King's great hero, of course, but he also quoted Martin Buber. In King too the Modern Job was present, the man who held his ground and did not let himself be pushed over into a position of simple reaction. There are tragic limitations of non-violence, situations such as South Africa where the polarization has gone too far. Perhaps, it has gone too far already in America—and even more ominously so in the Middle East. Much of what is happening today cannot be called either violence or non-violence, and certainly it cannot be called dialogue—whether it is a climbing of the Polaris submarine or the occupation of the Pentagon, or spilling blood on or burning draft files. It is very hard, moreover, for any man in our time to make a personal or social witness that cannot be immediately corrupted and distorted by television and by the press.

Genuine dialogue, whether between persons, groups, or nations, means

327

holding your ground, but also, in opposing the other, confirming his right to stand where he is. This approach is more fruitful than the one of violence versus non-violence. Non-violence often is not dialogue at all, but just monologue—an attempt to use a technique to impose something on someone else, underneath which there is often real hatred and congealed violence. Violence, on the other hand, is not always monologue. It usually is; for, as Camus says, it silences the other man:[22] it reduces him to the place where he has to submit, where he cannot stand his ground. But there are situations in which—not so much as a planned but as a tragic thing—violence too expresses a caring not just about yourself but about the relationship, about our society, about America, about the world. The danger today, though, is that violence too is so politicized that people set out to use it as merely a technique.

It is important to contrast dialogue with a word that has become very popular in our time, 'confrontation'. The notion of confrontation as being anything real when the other is a caricature and you are a caricature and there is mutual mistrust—this is the thing we have to fight. Confrontation will come when people will not listen in any other way. But to turn confrontation into a slogan and a political technique, to say, as many who never understood the meaning of 'dialogue' in the first place say, that the time for 'dialogue' is over, the time for 'confrontation' is here, means to politicize real polarity into a false either/or.

What we need for our time is an openness, a flexibility, a willingness to resist and withstand the concrete situation. If dialogue means the recognition of real limits and real tragedy, it also means hope because it does not assume that what was true this moment will necessarily be true the moment after—hope, not as an idealism, therefore, but as a readiness to assess the new moment in its concreteness. This also means, of course, the readiness to know the needs of the other, like the first peasant who said to the second one, 'Do you love me,' and the second one said, 'Yes, I love you, I love you like a brother,' but the first one replied, 'You don't love me, you don't know what I lack, you don't know what I need.' That is what the black man properly says to the white man: how can you say you are for brotherhood, peace, integration, progress, when you don't even hear me, when you don't live here in the ghetto, when you don't know what it means to be black. Dialogue, therefore, has to include not just hope of something happening but hope that will enable you to enter again into the concrete situation to witness, to risk yourself, to involve yourself, to stand there and to discover in that situation what the resources are.

I believe that dialogue in this sense is a hope in the black/white confrontation. Neither integration as we have tried it in the past, nor separatism in the Black Muslim sense of giving to the Blacks a few states, is ultimately going to work. Certainly the black man has to find the ground from which he enters into the dialogue. It is not the affluent white new class that will determine about the black man; it is the black man who will determine about himself. Then the white man will discover how he can and may and must respond. For Vietnam too I believe that dialogue is a possibility. The United States has at last reached the point where no reputable politician will say this is a good war that we want to continue. The mutual distrust is still there, the 'let-him-make-the-first-move', but there is also the possibility of acquiring enough trust in dialogue to ask ourselves, 'Why can't we be more concrete? Why do we have to use this just for home consumption? Why can't we discover the real situation?'

The conflict in the Middle East is likely any time to become as bad as Vietnam or worse. For many years I was chairman of the American Friends of Ichud, a group for Israeli-Arab rapprochement. I believed then, and I believe now, that Israel cannot live indefinitely in a sea of hostile Arab neighbours. I believed then and I believe now that there can be no reconciliation to violence which acts as if there is only one side that is 'right' whether it is that of the Arabs or of the Israelis. Whatever the opinions of either side, it is a basic fact that people exist face to face. You cannot properly reduce any conflict to one point of view, whether it is from above or from one side or the other. Each day leads to greater polarization, greater mistrust, and greater whipping up of hate in the Middle East. Yet if there were to be a change in the cold war, if there were to be a beginning on each side to find their ground, there would be the beginning of movement in the only direction in which this conflict can move, short of plunging the whole world into war. That is in the direction of genuine dialogue, of people talking with each other, of cultivating the resources together, of recognizing, as the United States has not yet done with Red China, the actual existence of the other, of confirming the otherness of the other even in opposing him.

We have been deluded by the notion that political power is the only power. Of course, political power is great power, and usually behind it is economic power and military power. Yet a large part of what we call politics is only the façade—a façade of catchwords, slogans, pretenses, nuances, innuendoes, and downright lies. The real movements go on behind the façade. If there comes a time when all the students of a university really want to walk out, that university will shut down. If there comes a time when the black people in the ghettoes really organize themselves, things will change. I believe with Martin Buber that the reality is in fact more basically social, even though the political always tries to get more power and domination than it needs. In 1954 the Supreme Court struck down the 'separate but equal' clause of the Interstate Commerce Act. We have learned to our great cost that this decision was necessary but not sufficient, that it has to become a social reality in every neighbourhood, and it is not just law enforcement alone that is going to do that. At the time of the Northern Student Movement and SNCC and the freedom rides, young people were beginning to take part in real social action and not just political demonstrations. There is a danger today that even these young people are being politicized, but I believe that they will not lose sight entirely of the fact that concrete reality is found first of all in actual social living. This reality of our actual human and social life takes a while to manifest itself. But it is there beneath the surface, awaiting the day when social suffering will transform itself into unmistakable social movement. In contrast to the few young people like myself who were conscientious objectors in the Second World War, today, wherever young people are socially aware, they are also opposed in one way or another to the war in Vietnam. That is not just politics. When Martin Luther King said that the problem of civil rights and the problem of peace are one problem, he was attacked by many of his co-workers as tactically wrong. Yet King was right and not the tacticians, because it is not just politics that causes a disproportionate number of Negro youths to be drafted, sent to the front lines, and killed. It is our whole social, economic, and educational situation.

If you lose sight of the concrete and everything becomes tactics, then you also lose sight of the actual goal you are working toward. Every structure has to be used in one way or another, whether it is a university or a legislature. But if you hold to the 'lived concrete', you will be fighting in the direction of really getting to what are the actual needs of peoples. Some day in the Middle East that massive political block that stands in the way might be overcome to the extent where there can be a certain amount of interchange, perhaps first of all through mediators and then later more directly. When Reinhold Niebuhr and I sent around secret petitions to twenty people around the world to support Dag Hammarskjold's nomination of Martin Buber for the Nobel prize in literature, the one person who I thought would not answer was Charles Malik, who had been the United Nations ambassador from Lebanon. Martin Buber had told me in 1960 how Malik had wandered by mistake into the Israeli pavilion in the World's Fair at Brussels, had signed the register, and the press had picked it up. From then on he was out of any public position. Yet Malik not only signed the petition; he also wrote a letter to the Nobel Prize Committee saying that if the Arabs and the Israelis would meet in the spirit of Martin Buber, there would be a possibility of achieving peace.

Whether it is a labour union confronting management or the troops confronting the young people at the Pentagon, you never entirely remove the human factor. The dangerous consequence of equating politics *tout court* with reality is the depersonalization which turns that situation over to the smoothest and best politician. If you say that politics has nothing to do with persons, people, social reality, and community, then you have indeed made it into what it usually is—the Frankenstein's monster that marches to doom of its own accord. Then the politically most 'realistic' people become the people who, like the Gadarene swine, are heading over the cliff to destruction—domestic, social, and international.

This recognition of the human factor in the confrontations of our age can lead us to a new and deepened appreciation of Gandhi's *satyāgraha*. This 'soul-force', or 'truth-force', should not be understood as a universal metaphysical, political, or ethical theory but as *an image of man*, an image of the relations between man and man and between men and society. The effectiveness of *satyāgraha* did not lie primarily in Gandhi's theories but in his embodiment of it and in his leadership of others, including his insistence that *satyāgraha* practised without the proper spirit is really *durāgraha,* or the force of evil. The truest understanding of Gandhi's non-violence can only be attained, therefore, through pointing to Gandhi himself as an image of man.

Gandhi was very clear in his teachings that *satyāgraha* is not a technique to be applied in miscellaneous acts but a way of life that has to arise out of the deepest human attitudes. Gandhi saw *ahimsā* not only as non-killing but also as boundless love that 'crosses all boundaries and frontiers' and envelops the whole world. 'A little true non-violence acts in a silent, subtle, unseen way and leavens the whole society.' He knew too that the taking of life is sometimes benevolent compared to slow torture, starvation, exploitation, wanton humiliation and oppression, and the killing of the self-respect of the weak and the poor. *Ahimsā* demands bravery and fearlessness. If the only choice is between violence and cowardice, then violence is preferable. If we do not know how to defend ourselves by the force of non-violence, we must do so by fighting. But the force of non-violence is no method that can be taught, like judo or karate. It is the quality of the life that takes place between man and man: 'The very first step in non-violence is that we cultivate in our daily life, as between ourselves, truthfulness, humility, tolerance, loving-kindness.' 'One who

331

hooks his fortunes to *ahimsā*, the law of love, daily lessens the circle of destruction and to that extent promotes life and love.'[23]

Gandhi's *satyāgraha* cannot be applied to all situations regardless of who is applying it. It is a direction of movement within the interhuman, the social, and the political which brings men away from the vicious circle of violence and toward co-operation and mutual respect. *Satyā-graha* is not possible, said Gandhi, unless others have assurance of safety. The only way to conduct campaigns of non-co-operation, Gandhi asserted, is if the crowds behave like disciplined soldiers so that the opponents might feel as safe as in their own home 'by reason of our living creed of non-violence'. 'Civil disobedience is sometimes a peremptory demand of love,' said Gandhi, but he denied that it was any more dangerous than the encircling violence from the soul-destroying heat of which it was the only escape. 'The danger lies only . . . in the outbreak of violence side by side with Civil Disobedience.'[24]

The nature and extent of the power of violence in the world today is such that we cannot assure the safety of those whom we resist or guarantee that violence will not break out side by side with civil dis-obedience. We cannot conclude from this that Martin Luther King should have given up his non-violent civil disobedience because of the violence on the part of both blacks and police. But we can conclude that non-violence must be wed to a situational ethic as a direction of move-ment in so far as the resources of those involved and the situation itself make possible. For this reason we cannot agree with Ramana Murti's unqualified assertion that Gandhi's *satyāgraha* is the only way of carrying out Buber's genuine dialogue.[25] Only insofar as *satyāgraha* is permeated by the life of dialogue and concretely embodied in the meeting between man and man will it be able to fulfil the claims that Gandhi made for it. In the midst of so many tragic situations of conflict, non-violence points to a way of reconciliation—a way upon which we must set foot again and again and walk as far as we can.

NOTES

[1] Richard Gregg, *The Power of Non-violence* (Philadelphia, 1934).

[2] From a speech given by Herbert Marcuse at the Symposium on 'Marxism, Religion, and the Liberal Tradition', Temple University, Philadelphia, 17 April 1969.

[3] The paraphrases and quotations from Blake are from *The Marriage of Heaven and Hell*, 'Proverbs of Hell', and from *The Songs of Experience*, 'The Human Abstract' and 'The Chimney Sweeper', respectively.

4 *The Way of Life according to Lao-tzu*, tr. by Witter Bynner (New York, 1962), p. 49.

5 Sigmund Freud, *Civilization and Its Discontents*, tr. by Joan Riviere (New York, 1958), pp. 59-61.

6 Erich Fromm, *The Heart of Man, Its Genius for Good and Evil*, Vol. 12 of *Religious Perspectives*, ed. by Ruth Nanda Anshen (New York, 1964).

7 C. G. Jung, *The Undiscovered Self*, tr. by R. F. C. Hull (Boston, 1958).

8 Rollo May, 'The Daemonic', unpublished paper read at the Conference on 'The New Apocalyptic: Forms of Rebellion', sponsored by the Association for Existential Psychology and Psychiatry, New York City, 12-13 April 1969.

9 Rainer Maria Rilke, *Letters to a Young Poet*, tr. by M. D. Herter Norton (New York, 1954), Letter 8.

10 Martin Buber, *Tales of the Hasidim: The Early Masters*, tr. by Olga Marx (New York, 1961), pp. 153 and 128 respectively.

11 William Blake, *Songs of Innocence and of Experience*, with an introduction and commentary by Sir Geoffery Keynes (New York, 1967).

12 Martin Luther, 'On the Thieving, Robbing, Plundering Horde of Peasants' (tract).

13 Simone Weil, *The Iliad: The Poem of Force* (Pendle Hill Pamphlets, Wallingford, Pennsylvania).

14 Martin Buber, *I and Thou*, tr. by R. G. Smith (New York, 1960).

15 Robert Lifton, 'Youth and Age', unpublished paper read at the Conference on 'The New Apocalyptic: Forms of Rebellion', New York City, April 1969.

16 Statement from the 'Student for Democratic Society Port Huron Manifesto', quoted in Robert Lifton, op. cit.

17 Maurice Friedman, *Problematic Rebel: Melville, Dostoievsky, Kafka, Camus* (2nd reorganized ed., Chicago, 1970).

18 Martin Buber, *A Believing Humanism. My Testament, 1902-1965*, tr. with an Introduction and explanatory comments by Maurice Friedman (New York, 1967), pp. 195-202.

19 V. V. Ramana Murti, 'Buber's Dialogue and Gandhi's Satyagraha', *The Journal of the History of Ideas*, vol. 29, no. 4 (October-December 1968), pp. 608-12.

20 Martin Buber's open letter to Gandhi was printed in full in Martin Buber and Judah Magnes, *Two Letters to Gandhi* (Jerusalem: Reuben Mass, 1939). It was reprinted in part under the title, 'The Land and Its Possessors' in Martin Buber, *Israel and the World* (New York, 1963), pp. 227-33, and in greater fullness under the title, 'A Letter to Gandhi', in Martin Buber, *Pointing the Way*, ed. and tr. with an introduction by Maurice Friedman (New York, 1963), pp. 139-47. Buber's earlier essay, 'Gandhi, Politics and Us' (1930) also appears in *Pointing the Way*, pp. 126-38.

21 Buber, *A Believing Humanism*, op. cit., pp. 191-93.

22 Albert Camus, *The Rebel*, tr. by Anthony Bower (New York, 1956), p. 283.

23 *The Gandhi Sutras: The Basic Teachings of Mahatma Gandhi*, arranged by D. S. Sarma (New York, 1949), pp. 31, 36, 54, 58-60, 63, 66, 68.

24 *Ibid.*, pp. 132, 161.

25 V. V. Ramana Murti, op. cit., pp. 611-12.

INDEX

335

A!